Bringing the War Home

The publisher gratefully acknowledges the generous contribution to this book provided by the General Endowment Fund of the University of California Press Associates.

Bringing the War Home

The Weather Underground,
the Red Army Faction,
and Revolutionary Violence
in the Sixties and Seventies

Jeremy Varon

UNIVERSITY OF CALIFORNIA PRESS
Berkeley · Los Angeles · London

University of California Press
Berkeley and Los Angeles, California

University of California Press, Ltd.
London, England

© 2004 by
The Regents of the University of California

Library of Congress Cataloging-in-Publication Data

Varon, Jeremy, 1969–.
    Bringing the war home : the Weather Underground, the Red Army
  Faction, and the revolutionary violence of the sixties and seventies / Jeremy
  Varon.
        p.   cm.
    Includes bibliographical references and index.
    ISBN 0–520–23032–9 (cloth : alk. paper).—ISBN 0–520–24119–3
  (pbk. : alk. paper)
    1. Weather Underground Organization.   2. Weatherman (Organiza-
  tion).   3. Baader-Meinhof gang.   4. Radicalism—United States—
  History—20th century.   5. Radicalism—Germany (West)—History—
  20th century.   6. New Left—United States—History—20th century.
  7. New Left—Germany (West)—History—20th century.   8. Political
  violence—United States—History—20th century.   9. Political violence—
  Germany (West)—History—20th century.   I. Title.

HN90.R3 V37   2004
322.4'2'0943—dc22   2003019002

Manufactured in the United States of America

13 12 11 10 09 08 07 06 05
11 10 9 8 7 6 5 4 3 2

The paper used in this publication meets the minimum requirements
of ANSI/NISO Z39.48–1992 (R 1997) (Permanence of Paper).♾

To the loving memory of my mother,
Barbara Frass Varon

In Hell they say Heaven is a great lie.
Daniel Berrigan

Contents

Plates follow p. 195

Acknowledgments

The "spirit of the sixties" has always seemed to me to involve at its core individuals with shared passions working together in pursuit of common goals. Scholarly work, while not entailing quite that kind of cooperation, is far from an isolating endeavor. Indeed, my project has been shaped by many scholars, friends, and others, through whom the rewards of cooperation and something of the spirit of the era I have tried so hard to understand has brightly shone.

Professor Dominick LaCapra of Cornell University played the central role in the conception and execution of this book. He has set a standard for intellectual intensity and professionalism I shall always take as my guide. At Cornell, he headed a team of professors who coached and challenged me: David Bathrick, Laurence Moore, and Michael Steinberg. My friends and colleagues in graduate school are owed equal thanks: Ajay Agrawal, Paul Apostilidas, Michael Doyle, Jeannie Moorefield, Libbie Rifkin, Douglas Usher, and Greg Wawro. Juliet Williams's intellect and character deeply inform all aspects of the project.

Outside of Cornell, numerous scholars have enriched my work: Omer Bartov, Frank Beiss, Bella Brodzki, Michael Burleigh, Belinda Davis, Gary Darden, Ron Grele, Jeffrey Herf, Dagmar Herzog, Matt Matsuda, Elizabeth Pfeiffer, and Michael Schmidtke. Several institutions also provided invaluable support. I am grateful for that offered by the Rutgers Center for Historical Analysis, by the German Historical Institute, and by the staffs at the Columbia Oral History Research Office, the Freie Universität in Berlin, the Hoover Institution, and the research libraries at Cornell University, Stanford University, and the University of California at Berkeley. My colleagues at Drew University have made the transition into professional life a happy one, while supporting me in completing this project.

Monica McCormick of the University of California Press has been an ideal editor, grasping right away the "essence" of my project and guiding it to completion with unwavering care. Her staff at the press has been impeccable. Peter Dreyer is owed special thanks for his stellar job in refining the text. Sam Green, a filmmaker working on similar themes, provided assistance and encouragement; it was always a comfort to match impressions and to see our projects as complementing each other. I extend thanks also to Lynne Okin, Alan Trist, and Meegan Lee Ochs for granting me permission to quote the song lyrics of Bob Dylan, the Grateful Dead, and Phil Ochs, respectively. The music of the 1960s was woven into the events of the era—even when it did not provide direct political and social commentary—and served as a constant companion as I studied, thought, and wrote.

This project, by its nature, has drawn me far beyond academia into the worlds of political activism, both past and present. I am immensely grateful to the women and men formerly of the Weather Underground who spoke to me with great honesty and insight about their experiences. I hope to have honored the trust they placed in me by dealing responsibly and fairly with their histories.

Contemporary activists—Brooke, David, Stuart, Tyler in New York, all those in the Philly house, and my dear friends Jordan Ash and Jonathan Rosen—have reminded me that "making history," or simply "making a difference," as the sixties generation did, is the far greater challenge than studying the past. Habib Gharib has uniquely embodied for me the ideal of the scholar-activist, demonstrating that good acts start with sound thinking.

I have the privilege of counting as colleagues, friends, companions, and family people of great caring and intellect, who shared generously their ideas, advice, and editorial talents. John McMillian, inspired by the same intellectual callings, has my enduring loyalty and respect. Knowing Anne Kornhauser has been a recent blessing, for the text and in my life. My sister Elizabeth Varon and her husband William Hitchcock, both history professors, blazed the trail I now walk. Barbara and Ben Varon, my parents, provided more than familial love, engaging the substance of the project and the intellectual and political dramas it spawned.

Key Acronyms

APO	Ausserparlamentarische Opposition
CDU	Christlich Demokratische Union Deutschlands
DDR	Deutsche Demokratische Republik ("East Germany")
J2M	June 2 Movement (2. Juni Bewegung)
KPD	Kommunistische Partei Deutschlands
LNS	Liberation News Service
NLF	National Liberation Front (Vietnam)
NYT	*New York Times*
PFOCs	Prairie Fire Organizing Committees
PL	Progressive Labor [Party]
PLO	Palestine Liberation Organization
RAF	Rote Armee Fraktion [Red Army Faction]
RYM	Revolutionary Youth Movement
SDS	Sozialistischer Deutscher Studentenbund
SDS	Students for a Democratic Society
SLA	Symbionese Liberation Army
SPD	Sozialdemokratische Partei Deutschland
UCB	University of California at Berkeley
WP	*Washington Post*
WUO	Weather Underground Organization

Introduction

All over the world during the 1960s, movements led by the young radically challenged existing forms of political and cultural authority. With great optimism and energy, they attacked governments, militaries, institutions, ideologies, and common ways of thinking, feeling, and acting. The year 1968—that potent symbol of the 1960s as a whole—can be evoked by reciting the places where left-wing rebellion erupted with special force and drama: Paris, Prague, New York, Tokyo, Berlin, Saigon, Mexico City.[1]

New Leftists were not only implicitly united across national boundaries by their shared opposition to oppression, their commitment to democratic participation, and their use of militant direct action as a means of protest; they were also *consciously* internationalist. In what amounted to a global crusade, students and youths throughout the world protested the Vietnam War. They assimilated dimensions of Black Power and Third World revolutionary ideologies, in which they saw near-universal appeal and relevance. They created an international protest culture organized around master texts, chiefly those of Karl Marx, Mao Tse-tung, and Herbert Marcuse, and "revolutionary" icons like Che Guevara and Ho Chi Minh. And, in instances, they responded directly to the triumphs and failures experienced by their foreign New Left comrades. In their wildest dreams, they saw themselves waging a revolution that would overthrow both the U.S.-led imperialism of the West and the ossified, bureaucratic communism of the East.

1

Despite the global nature of 1960s rebellion, little has been done to probe the New Left's internationalism—the common aspirations of radicals in different settings and the synchronic quality of New Left activism generally. Instead, each country touched by New Left protest has produced a literature on the meaning and legacy of its "own" 1960s. As a result, neither scholarship nor popular commentary on the 1960s has helped us much to move beyond the imprecise sense that New Leftists forged an international zeitgeist of radical rebellion, or the simple observation that in a number of countries, similar things seemed to have happened at roughly the same time.[2]

This book explores the international character of New Left rebellion by focusing on complementary experiences in two countries: the "armed struggles" of American and West German radicals. Violence against the state is not supposed to happen—not in formally democratic societies that boast institutional channels for addressing the grievances of dissident minorities. Not in prosperous, technologically developed societies that provide most of their citizens with the opportunity to earn a decent living. And not, certainly, at the hands of well-educated youths of the middle or upper classes who have seemingly everything to lose and little to gain from attacking societies that have endowed them with great privilege and promise. Political violence, rather, is expected to be the last resort of the disenfranchised and dispossessed, fighting oppression in societies that permit them no other choice.

And yet in the 1960s and 1970s, middle-class white youths in the United States and West Germany took up arms in hopes of overthrowing their governments. Chief among the "armed struggle" groups in the two countries were America's Weatherman (later renamed the Weather Underground) and Germany's Rote Armee Fraktion (Red Army Faction), or RAF.[3] In 1969–70, both groups began to wage guerrilla campaigns modeled on those in Latin America. Although their attacks on military, corporate, and political targets were meant to be the catalyst for larger armed revolts, neither group was able to attract more than several dozen members into its highest ranks, and their violence was a dramatic failure from a tactical standpoint. Yet Weatherman and the RAF provoked reactions vastly disproportionate to the violence they unleashed. They each became a potent symbol of both the extremes to which New Left rebellion had gone and the profound social and political divisions their societies experienced in the 1960s and 1970s. As both a cause and a symptom of broad-based crises of legitimacy, their violence constituted an important episode in the histories of their nations, of the developed West as a whole, and of global conflict.

Even so, their violence may appear far removed from the mainstream of the New Left. "Armed struggle" emerged in the United States and West Germany only at the tail end of the 1960s, and shortly before the New Left's decline in both countries. Most activists rejected violence as a political strategy, and many accused its advocates of corrupting the New Left's core values. Weatherman and the RAF were denounced by leftists in their own countries as everything from self-indulgent fools living out Bonnie-and-Clyde fantasies to "left-wing adventurists" hopelessly cut off from "the masses." Yet armed struggle was an extreme expression of ideologies, attitudes, and sensibilities deeply embedded in both the American and West German New Left movements. As early as 1967, New Leftists in both countries discussed the possibility of taking up arms. (America's Black Panther Party, formed in 1966, both preached and practiced from its inception the armed self-defense of African-American communities.) Though such discussions often remained at the level of speculation or fantasy, many activists took the prospect of violence very seriously. Some promoted violence as a means of self-defense against police assaults at demonstrations, but others advocated waging an actual guerrilla war. And in both countries, state repression, coupled with activists' declining faith in the value of peaceful protest, caused those skeptical about violence to seriously contemplate it and those persuaded of the need for violence to take the radical leap into action.

Weatherman and the RAF were only the best-known New Left groups to make this leap. In the United States, dozens if not hundreds of collectives—most often small circles of friends and fellow activists whose identities were never publicly revealed—committed bombings, arson, and other destruction of state, corporate, and university property in the late 1960s and early 1970s. Though no fully reliable figures exist, one estimate counts as many as 2,800 such attacks between January 1969 and April 1970 alone.[4] Such protest violence, combined with eruptions of civil unrest, prompted urgent studies on the causes and scope of political violence and the widespread sense that America was experiencing one of the most violent periods in its history.[5] The RAF was joined in combat by the West Berlin anarchists of the "June 2 Movement"; by the Socialist Patients Collective, a group of psychiatric patients who formed armed cells; by the semi-underground Red Cells, formed in 1973; and by a slew of small, ad hoc "urban guerrilla" groups. However fresh the memories of the Nazi era and the turmoil that had preceded it, violence was once again part of the German political landscape.

Given the extent of political violence in the United States and West Germany, it would be a mistake to view armed struggle as an aberration or as simply a fringe phenomenon. Although this view dominates commentary on the New Left, it minimizes the broader revolutionary impetus of the late 1960s and threatens to make scapegoats of those who acted on the prevalent rhetoric among radicals encouraging violence. More deeply, it serves in the present day to subdue or even repress potentially painful memories of how contentious the late 1960s and early 1970s were in the United Sates and West Germany. Focus on the margins of the New Left may therefore disclose something about its center—the principles, passions, ideals, desires, fantasies, and fears that defined young activists' consciousness and conduct.

Beyond what they tell us about 1960s radicalism, Weatherman and the RAF raise questions of enduring importance in the United States, Germany, and elsewhere. One set of questions concerns the origins, purpose, and effects of political violence: How and why does violence develop from within social movements? Under what conditions may violence not sanctioned by the state be considered legitimate? What, if anything, can it accomplish, and what are its special hazards as a form of political action? What can states do—and what may they legitimately do—to protect themselves from the threat of violence? In addition, the examples of Weatherman and the RAF pose questions for the contemporary Western left, however distant the issues and imperatives of the 1960s and 1970s may now seem: How can political and moral outrage be turned toward constructive ends? What are the possibilities of, and barriers to, solidarity across economic, racial, and national boundaries? What limits must social justice movements observe, such that one's actions remain consistent with one's values? As a student of social theory who finds societies most interesting when they experience crisis—when the legitimacy of established institutions and ideologies is widely questioned—I am keenly interested in the first line of inquiry. As someone committed to social change, my attention never strays far from the latter.

The recent World Trade Center tragedy has added urgency to a final set of concerns. For Americans, 9/11 illustrated the capacity of terrorism truly to terrorize. It also prompted the controversial restriction of civil freedoms, the further militarization of American culture, the killing of innocents by the United States and its allies in the name of fighting "terror," new wars, and the articulation of a new set of reductive frames for understanding the world and America's place within it—frames that may poorly serve the goals of security and peace. Troubled by all this, I seek from the past some insight into how to address profound conflicts of ideology and interest constructively and nonviolently, so as to strengthen the possibility of creating a meaningful and lasting peace, the foundation of which is justice.

New Left violence in the United States and West Germany has nowhere been systematically compared.[6] Historians and others typically attribute the violence in the United States to qualities they present as specific to America: despair over the inability of peaceful protest to end the war in Vietnam; the impulse of middle-class whites, plagued by race and class guilt, to emulate "authentic" revolutionaries like the Black Panthers; a characteristically American preference for action over critical reflection; and the desire for instant gratification rooted in the ideology of the consumer culture.[7] Weatherman, it is said over and over again, was a quintessentially *American* phenomenon, an *American* story. Conversely, scholars of the German 1960s and 1970s typically cite Germany's historic illiberalism, principally its tendencies to political extremism and tradition of authoritarian rule, to account for the emergence of violence and the severe reaction it provoked.[8]

In studies of "left-wing terrorism," most often conducted by those who find it deplorable and seek to understand it in order to eliminate it, comparisons of violence in different countries have not been uncommon. However, the mistaken assumption prevails that New Left violence developed significant force only in the former Axis powers, Germany, Italy, and Japan, and not in the former Allied powers.[9] The inference follows that the absence of established liberal-democratic traditions accounts for the emergence of violence in those countries, and that the United States, with its "mature" democracy, was spared such strife. This interpretive bias distorts the sense of the causes and scope of New Left violence, obscuring the similarities between the American and West German cases. It also implicitly reinforces two deeply ideological, inverted modes of historical analysis: American exceptionalism, which holds that the United States, as the West's great democratic frontier, has largely escaped the tensions and traumas that have afflicted Europe; and the notion that German history has followed a "special path" *(Sonderweg)*, dominated by a resistance to democratic values that has doomed the country to cycles of destructive violence. Neither view adequately captures the American and German 1960s and the internationalism of the New Left. Whatever its history and reputation, American democracy was not functioning exceptionally well in the decade, given the violation of the basic civil rights of African Americans and other racial minorities, fierce opposition to a war fought on the basis of government lies, and the widespread belief among the young that American democracy was a sham. Nor were the circumstances precipitating the RAF's violence unique to Germany or shared only by societies with fascist pasts.

Focus on national experiences and narrow comparisons also inhibit an understanding of how the dynamic *interplay* of global and national contexts served simultaneously to unite and separate individual New Left movements. On the one hand, global opposition to U.S. power, mediated through Third World revolutionary discourse, gave ballast to the New Left's professed internationalism. On the other hand, the American and West German armed struggles—particularly as they diverged in the mid 1970s—reveal the importance of national experiences in shaping individual New Left movements. In their inability to transcend their own cultures more fully and create political links across national boundaries, Weatherman and the RAF expose the limits to the New Left's internationalism.

Much recommends the comparison of radicalism in the United States and West Germany. Following World War II, the two countries were both leading industrial democracies and among the world's staunchest opponents of communism. The United States had tried to create the Federal Republic of Germany—West Germany—largely in its own image, and West Germany saw its alliance with the United States as key to both its survival and its redemption; adopting American values was to enter the modern family of nations and achieve the long-elusive "normality" so desperately sought after the catastrophe of National Socialism. America and "Americanism" were also focal points for criticisms of the Federal Republic. For West German leftists, to attack the United States was to condemn their own society. Conversely, Germany played a role in the minds of American activists, who often invoked Nazism to denounce their own government, whether for its "genocide" in Indochina or its "fascist" response to protest. Activists also made reference to Nazism to frame their rebellion. Just before a violent protest, a Weatherleader exclaimed, "We refuse to be 'good Germans!'" (by failing to take a stand of militant opposition as their society grew more destructive).[10] American and German activists alike described the postwar United States as the world's arch-oppressor, as if it had taken over that role from the defeated Nazi regime. The narratives of Weatherman and the RAF, as they dovetail and then diverge, convey a larger story of America and Germany's close alliance, shared destinies, interwoven cultures, and enduring differences.

. . .

With the barest hindsight, the notion of 1960s radicals waging successful armed revolutions in the United States and West Germany appears utterly fantastical. But for at least some activists in both countries, armed struggle had a compelling political basis. American and West German radicals were united, above all, by their mutual commitment to "revolutionary anti-imperialism," whose main premise was that the prosperity of advanced industrial societies depended on the economic exploitation of developing countries, evident in the intensity with which the United States battled left-wing insurgencies in the Third World. Relatedly, an anti-imperialist analysis saw the decolonization movements in Asia, Africa, and Latin America as clear signs of a crisis of global capitalism.

New Leftists derived a mandate for revolution from Third World movements. Che Guevara's global call to "create two, three, many Vietnams" succinctly conveyed that the greatest contribution First World radicals could make to Third World struggles would be to bring the war for socialism home to their own countries. Anti-imperialism also provided a way for the New Left to account for the absence of the conditions considered from a traditional Marxist viewpoint to be prerequisites for revolutionary change. Within an anti-imperialist framework, the working classes in wealthy societies could be seen as benefiting from the exploitation of foreign labor and resources. By extension, the initial or even primary impetus for radical change would have to come from new groups, among them students and intellectuals, who were not fully integrated into the benefits of the capitalist economy and absorbed by its ideology. However counterintuitively, anti-imperialism allowed for an indigenous revolutionary critique of *affluent* societies that had satisfied many of the traditional material demands of socialism.

Armed struggle was only one, highly controversial approach to political change. America's Students for a Democratic Society (SDS)—for years the New Left's most important organization—split in the summer of 1969 over strategies for broadening the appeal and increasing the power of the student movement. One wing asserted the importance of organizing the industrial working class by conventional means. The "Weatherman" faction, hoping initially that violence would awaken working-class youths to revolution, advocated armed struggle. In Germany, the student movement dissolved in 1969 along similar lines, giving rise to a host of small, Marxist-Leninist parties and an armed struggle wing, led by the RAF.

The bifurcation of the leadership of the American and West German New Left has been widely recorded as the moment of the New Left's self-destruction in each country.[11] The intense factionalism precipitating the split left many New Leftists dispirited and unwilling to identify with any of the organized alternatives. My understanding of the split calls for appreciating the gravity of the dilemma faced by the New Left at the decade's end. Some New Leftists in each country had become so convinced of their societies' corruption that they saw revolution as the only answer. But the New Left in the United States and West Germany remained small. Politically isolated and facing overwhelming state power, New Leftists had both a political and a broadly psychological need to secure at least a body of theory or a set of narrative resources—a model or paradigm for change—ensuring that revolution was indeed possible.

Rejecting the antiquated Marxism of the sectarian left, proponents of violence appealed to Third World examples such as Cuba, where a small band of guerrillas had incited "the masses" to a near-spontaneous revolt. Weatherman and the RAF concluded that the assertion of revolutionary will could create a revolutionary situation where its "objective" determinants were lacking. Though this vision of their struggle was clearly errant, it did not result simply from naïveté or hubris. It also reflected the dizzying sense of possibility of the late 1960s—inspired, above all, by the implausible success of the Vietnamese resistance to the U.S. military—that tempted radicals to think the unthinkable, in defiance of established models of how social change happens.

Armed struggle was more than an approach to the daunting task of making revolution. It was also a vivid expression of the importance of militancy for New Leftists. At a political level, militancy sought to correct for the apparent ineffectiveness of conventional forms of protest. In an ethical register, it responded to conditions of moral emergency caused most forcefully by the destruction in Vietnam and the state's often violent response to domestic protest. In existential terms, militancy provided a way of expressing outrage and living the substance of one's values. Weatherman and the RAF also exemplified the hazards of militancy. Both groups, for a time, declared all opposition to armed struggle to be counterrevolutionary and embraced danger as a way of showing the depth of their sacrifice. Taken to extremes, militancy turned into a kind of militarism that divided the left into a crude hierarchy of virtue based on one's readiness to "pick up the gun."

In addition, armed struggle was to function as the chief medium for forging new, revolutionary subjects who transcended their prior socialization and dedicated themselves *totally* to political struggle. In service of this ambition, Weatherman and the RAF engaged in radical experiments in self–re-creation. Their belief in the capacity of violence to transform its agent gave rise to a conspicuous tension that went to the heart of contradictions within the New Left. On the one hand, they saw violence as an act of extreme transgression or defiance. Objectively, it challenged the state's power. Subjectively, it promised to free them from internal psychic restraints and provide an experience of politics in its most vital form. The guerrilla, within the mythology of each group, was an anti-authoritarian icon who embodied the mystique of the outlaw. On the other hand, Weatherman and the RAF aspired to overcome the individualism and decadence they saw as integral to consumer capitalism. In their views, the New Left itself reproduced these qualities in its libertine spirit and at times narrow concern with personal freedom. As an antidote, they sought to cultivate an appreciation of the collective enterprise and of the kinds of discipline required for their dangerous political work.

Their efforts, however, proved far from liberating. Weatherman initially used psychologically brutal rituals to suppress the individuality of its members in hopes of turning them into "tools of the revolution."[12] The RAF, declaring that "the guerrilla is the group," saw the revolutionary as a fully collectivized subject who had transcended the self in his or her complete submission to the demands of guerrilla warfare.[13] The RAF toggled between an oppressive group-think and vindictive infighting. Both groups, at their worst, were rigidly hierarchical. Along with their rebel images, then, they projected a hyperdiscipline and severity jarring to many in the New Left. At root, Weatherman and the RAF embodied the peculiar unity of transgression and submission, self-expression and self-renunciation. But here the groups were only an extreme expression of competing desires in the New Left as a whole—the desire for radical autonomy, enacted through resistance to the norms of their societies, and the desire to dedicate oneself to a higher, *collective* purpose that demanded rigorous loyalty.

The American and West German armed struggles failed for essentially the same reasons. Like their Marxist-Leninist rivals, Weatherman and the RAF horribly misread their domestic scenes. The United States and

West Germany lacked the seething mass discontent and the near-total denial of democratic rights—both prerequisites for armed struggle according to its Third World theorists—that made revolutionary violence in some Third World countries transparently legitimate to so many of their citizens. Both groups fell victim to equally flawed, contradictory assumptions, between which they oscillated. In one emphasis, defined by an exaggerated pessimism, they saw imperialism as a monolith. Its power to absorb, delude, and dispirit its subjects was so great that no sustained internal resistance was possible. Effective rebellion could come only externally from Third World struggles, or, internally, from American blacks. Within this understanding, the New Left's armed struggle was an ethical stand that answered a moral imperative of resistance and solidarity, and whose integrity *did not depend on its political success or failure.* Weatherman and the RAF thus removed political efficacy as a criterion for evaluating their efforts. The guerrillas' "victory" lay simply in existing.

In a second emphasis, driven by an exaggerated optimism, the Weathermen and the RAF saw imperialism as on the brink of collapse. Resistance was everywhere—in the Third World certainly, but also in the institutional fabric of their own societies: in the schools, the military, the factories, the bureaucracies, halfway houses, ghettos, and working- and middle-class homes. Their violence, in this model, needed only to light the spark to ignite mass discontent into revolutionary conflagration. Both views, despite their apparent polarity, had the same effect: to discourage the difficult work of addressing, through redoubled efforts to educate and organize ambivalent populations, possibilities that lay somewhere in between.

.   .   .

If the armed struggles in the United States and West Germany had similar origins, their courses quickly diverged. In the United States, violence crested in the spring of 1970 in the wake of the killing of student demonstrators at Kent State and Jackson State universities, but then steeply dropped. The Weathermen, shaken by the deaths in March 1970 of several members making bombs in a New York City townhouse, abandoned plans for assaults on military personnel and police. Though the Weather Underground survived into the mid 1970s, it was not able to reestablish momentum on the left for violence. Never "broken" by the FBI, it disbanded voluntarily in 1976.

In West Germany, the armed struggle began in earnest with the for- *West Germany* mation in 1970 of the RAF, which along with other groups committed bombings, kidnappings, and assassinations. In response, the state waged a comprehensive war on domestic terrorism that entailed the killing of fugitives in shoot-outs, harsh treatment of RAF prisoners, and controversial measures to destroy what it saw as the intellectual and cultural roots of left-wing violence. The fall of 1977 was the high point of the conflict. The Deutscher Herbst ("German Autumn"), as it is often called, culminated in the hijacking of a German plane by Palestinian guerrillas demanding the release of RAF prisoners, the storming of the plane by German commandos, the apparent suicide in prison of several of the RAF's founders, and the RAF's murder of a leading economic official, whom it had kidnapped six weeks earlier. For much of the 1970s, the group was at the center of a grueling, high-stakes public drama in which West Germans played out their ambivalent relationship to democracy and authority. Only in 1992, following the collapse of the Soviet Union and German reunification, did the RAF announce its cessation of violence.[14] The group finally disbanded in the spring of 1998, declaring in a public statement what had for years been obvious: that it had long outlived its political relevance.[15]

New Left violence in West Germany was, in sum, more deadly, more divisive, and longer-lasting than that in the United States. The very different trajectories of Weatherman and the RAF reveal how each group was shaped by and responded to its national context. When the New Left faded as a global phenomenon in the early 1970s, those contexts became all the more important in defining the destinies of individual New Left movements.

The Weathermen turned to violence largely in opposition to the Viet- *Weatherman's restraint* nam War and out of their desire to help militant blacks like the Black Panthers. These commitments lent an immediacy to their violence, irrespective of the group's larger revolutionary ambitions. With its bombings of military and police targets, Weatherman was able to provide at least moral and political censure of the war in Vietnam and the state's assaults on people of color in the United States. The group, in short, could moderate its approach to, and eventually withdraw from, violence with some sense of accomplishment. Former members typically concede that violence failed miserably as a revolutionary tactic but defend its integrity and limited utility as a response to the Vietnam War and to institutional racism.

Issues of identity contributed to the group's restraint in another sense.

Weatherman's desire to match the sacrifices of blacks and Vietnamese fueled the group's initial belief in the singular value of violence. Weatherman's violence, in this aspect, was a volatile and often vexed effort of members of the white middle class to confront and somehow renounce their structural privilege. In the mid 1970s, the Weathermen broadened their conception of revolutionary politics and reassessed what kind of practice would be most beneficial, given their backgrounds. Chiefly, they recognized the need to organize other whites, for which nonlethal violence and the distribution of conventional propaganda was a more promising approach than a literal guerrilla war. By the time the group asserted the need to build a mass movement, it was far too small and too isolated to play a leading role on the left. Nonetheless, by revising their sense of mission, the Weathermen avoided mistaking *themselves* for the causes they meant to serve.

West Germany, by contrast, was only very indirectly involved in prosecuting the Vietnam War and lacked a highly visible and vocal oppressed racial minority. Though German New Leftists bitterly opposed the war, they never felt as intense a sense of identification with the Vietnamese or responsibility for their fate as did American activists. As the number of immigrant workers increased in the Federal Republic in the 1970s, the RAF did little to make growing German resentment of foreigners an object of its protest. The RAF's armed struggle therefore always had a more abstract and protean quality than that of its American counterparts. Frustrated in its ambition of violent, communist revolution in western Europe, the RAF had few ways of claiming any real successes. Lacking a national subject of emancipation, the RAF also lacked a structure of accountability. This circumstance contributed to the group's strikingly self-referential quality, wherein the RAF saw itself as the sole wager of meaningful political struggle in West Germany. With the emergence in the mid 1970s of the "free-the-guerrilla guerrilla," whose chief aim was to extort the release of jailed comrades, the RAF's campaign degenerated into what one critic called a "private war" with the state security apparatus.[16]

Weatherman and the RAF differed also in their ways of negotiating a tension between excess and limits. The Weathermen, on the verge of attacking human targets, instituted a prohibition on lethal actions. The Germans repeatedly crossed the threshold of lethal violence. Far more than a tactical difference, Weatherman's and the RAF's approaches to political murder constitute profound differences—perhaps the most important differences—between the two groups. Their comparison elicits a basic question of political morality: when and under what conditions may one assume dominion over life and death and kill another human being on behalf of a political ideal or goal?

The Weathermen claimed to represent the promise of a society that would be more just and humane than the one they sought to destroy. At times, however, their rhetoric and actions belied this claim. In their early days, the Weathermen spun grisly fantasies of limitless destruction and planned attacks that would almost certainly harm "civilians." Behind Weatherman's recklessness lay a fascination with transgression and a desire to shock. Within a logic of excess, political murder could be seen as the ultimate transgressive act. But by contemplating or engaging in acts of brutality, the Weathermen reproduced qualities they attributed to their enemy and that they ostensibly opposed. The group's challenge, then, was to develop an internally constrained practice. The Weathermen responded to the 1970 townhouse explosion by imposing limits on their violence. In short, they made the conscious decision not to be killers.

The RAF's brutality, most pronounced in the mid 1970s and early 1980s, has been the object of intensive, if often highly speculative, analyses. Explanations range from the psychopathologies of the individual members, to the internal dynamics of the group, to the specter of Hitler returned in the RAF as his depraved children.[17] The most promising interpretive framework highlights the influence of the fascist past on the political conflict of the West German 1960s and 1970s.

The RAF sought to punish Germany both for the sins of that past and for what it saw as their repetition in the present through such things as police repression and German support for American "genocide" in Vietnam. Here the RAF practiced a logic of vilification, in which it equated the political and judicial custodians of the Federal Republic with Nazi perpetrators. It thus felt an imperative to use any means available, including the murder of state agents, to bury finally the archenemy of political modernity. The RAF also employed, however unselfconsciously, a logic of vindication, in which armed rebellion now would compensate for the virtual absence of violent resistance in Germany to the Nazi regime. In this capacity, lethal violence promised to liberate RAF members from the psychological and political burdens of the past and break the chain of German guilt.

By practicing terror themselves, RAF members compounded their political failure with moral failure, while deepening their connection to the damage of the past from which they sought an escape. The RAF's extreme violence also crystallizes the differences between the American and West German armed struggles. Weatherman's violence was equally ineffective in bringing about the kind of social change it imagined. But by observing limits, Weatherman contained the cost of its choices. In one of the few statements of comparison between the two movements, Hans-Joachim Klein of Germany's Red Cells lamented in 1978 that "the members of the guerrilla [movement] are no longer capable of acting like the Weathermen in the States. Of saying now we stop."[18]

The American and West German armed struggles differed, finally, in the reactions they elicited from their governments and societies. In the 1960s and early 1970s, U.S. security agencies employed invasive, illegal, and violent means in combating domestic dissidents, particularly the Black Panthers. The FBI aggressively pursued the Weathermen and other New Left fugitives. Yet its campaign against them was nothing in scale and intensity like the West German state's assault on left-wing violence. Partially, this was a consequence of Weatherman's restraint. Avoiding injury to persons, Weatherman never inspired the diffuse public fear that would doubtless have prompted even greater governmental wrath. In part, the Weathermen were granted a kind of preferential treatment relative to black radicals, who remained objects of fierce pursuit. But the Weathermen also benefited from a broad shift in the national climate in the mid 1970s. In the wake of the strife of the late 1960s, the Vietnam War, and Watergate, attention turned to the reestablishment of public trust in government and to reconciliation. Congress exposed abuses of power by the FBI in its pursuit of dissidents and acted to constrain its activities. Under this scrutiny, security agencies curtailed their campaign against the Weather Underground and generally let the group—now considered more a nuisance than a threat—fade into obscurity. Only a few underground Weathermen were ever captured, and those who surfaced voluntarily in the late 1970s and early 1980s served little or no time in prison.[19]

The RAF and other violent German groups were objects of relentless vilification and police action. As in the RAF's excesses, the fascist past figured heavily in the state's response. The government and its supporters insisted that the terrorists were the authentic heirs of fascism, who, like the Nazi SA during the Weimar Republic, threatened a fragile democracy. Fear of communist subversion enhanced the imperative the state felt to use extreme measures to preserve what it saw as the integrity of Germany's postwar democratic experiment. The means the state chose had mixed results. Though effective in capturing the RAF's early leaders, antiterrorist measures only deepened the RAF's view of the West German state as fascist and its determination to attack it by violent means.

state reactions

 haunted by Nazi past

Students, intellectuals, and others extended sympathy to the RAF as victims of repression, fearing that antiterrorism threatened to turn West Germany into a police state, where the mantle of constitutionalism was used to mask an unreconstructed authoritarianism. In short, West German terrorism was a tortured form of *Vergangenheitsbewältigung*—a symptom of Germany's difficulty in confronting and working through its Nazi past. Rather than shedding light on the conflict, the antifascist rhetoric of the RAF and the government contributed to excesses on both sides, demanding a new process of reconciliation.

· · ·

A final index of the different impacts of Weatherman and the RAF on their respective societies is the degree and kind of commentary devoted to each group. Neither Weatherman nor the violence of the American New Left more broadly has generated a distinct historiography. Scholars most often discuss such violence as a small part of larger contexts and movements: antiwar protest, SDS, and the New Left as a whole. The dominant attitude toward Weatherman has been a highly critical or even dismissive one, reflecting both widespread antipathy to the group, then and now, and its limited resonance in American politics and culture. Many Americans who lived through the 1960s have few particular memories of the Weathermen, whose actions can easily fade into general recollections of turmoil.[20] For small groups of mostly young rebels, the Weathermen have exerted an enduring fascination over the past two decades, though the group's activities have typically been appreciated more as lore than as political history. Only with the recent release of the documentary *The Weather Underground* has the group emerged from the shadows of history into the light of public memory and popular culture.[21]

The RAF, in contrast, has been the object of persistent reflection in Germany. Works on German violence include a 1985 bestseller, several biographies, and other popular histories, memoirs by former members, voluminous studies by government agencies and security experts, and all manner of scholarly treatments from the disciplines of political science, history, sociology, and psychology. The RAF has also made a strong mark on popular culture, inspiring movies, plays, paintings, museum exhibits, musical compositions, photo-essays, and countless TV and print retrospectives on the anniversaries of key events in its history. For much of the RAF's early existence, the group's leaders were household names in West Germany, where their fate approached a national obsession. Every ·

West German who lived through the peak years of the terrorist drama seems to have some vivid "RAF memory," whether seeing a wanted poster in a public place, hearing rumors that a fugitive was nearby, being stopped at a security checkpoint, or following harrowing moments in the conflict in the media.

The very different standing of Weatherman and the RAF in their nations' consciousnesses demands different approaches to their presentation. I provide separate sections on them that complement, rather than mirror, each other. In the case of the Weathermen, I furnish a textured account of the group's experience, drawing extensively on interviews with former members. In these, I have sought less a record of "the facts" of Weatherman's history than the reflections of former members on the political meaning of their experiences, as well as what they thought and how they felt when they entered, engaged in, and withdrew from the armed struggle. I appeal to oral history, then, for representations of the past generated through the subjective work of memory—with its exclusions, contingent connections, and spontaneous eloquence—and not for the "objective" reconstruction of the past. Given Weatherman's efforts to define itself through action, my analysis consists mostly of the close reading of events—of actions themselves as complex texts. I concentrate on the late 1960s and early 1970s, when Weatherman's importance was at its peak.

In the case of the RAF, I provide condensed narratives of key episodes in the group's existence until 1977, when the first era in its history came to an end. I am unable to use the methods of oral history with the RAF, many of whose members died in the 1970s; nonetheless, they achieved great notoriety, and ample material exists for conveying their experiences.

I favor juxtaposition over direct comparison of the two groups. Chapter 1, which explores the similarities in their origins, moves between discussions of the American and German settings. Thereafter, I treat Weatherman and the RAF more or less separately. This permits flexibility in stressing those issues and experiences most important to each group. All historical comparisons seek to have each "case" illuminate the other, and I hope to guide, but not rigidly control, that process of mutual illumination.

Some continuities of approach exist throughout. One is my effort to present both Weatherman and the RAF in competing and even contradictory ways. Analysts have commonly portrayed the groups in essentially pathological terms by describing their members as zealots, whose activism, beyond a certain point, had little to do with politics as such.

The groups' "ideology," within this framework, amounted to a delusional belief system built on an irrational contempt for their societies and the sense of themselves as a revolutionary elect, "chosen" to fulfill a world-historical mission. An observer of the American New Left who saw Weatherman as a "passionate aberration" concluded, "in a burst of almost religious enthusiasm, the Weathermen plunged beyond politics, which measures things in the here and now, to a higher realm where the student movement could not survive."[22] German analysts have similarly charged that the RAF suffered from an acute *Realitätsverlust*, or "loss of reality," that doomed it to its destructive illusions.[23] Understanding political violence then becomes largely an exercise in deconstructing superstitions and interpreting the behavior of what amount to cults.

A more layered perspective, developed largely by social scientists, sees violence like that of Weatherman and the RAF as an exotic form of political action that emerges at the far margins of legitimate politics and at very specific moments in the evolution of social movements. The agents of violence, in this view, retain a limited rationality, but their behavior remains on the whole pathological, driven by such structural factors as their isolation and the policing strategies deployed by the state. Issues of politics and morality generally recede in the effort to understand their actions.

I seek to restore a stronger measure of rationality and moral purpose to Weatherman and the RAF in order better to understand both their political histories and the complex nature of political violence more generally. Far from being simple zealots with more or less totally warped worldviews, members of both groups were driven by political conviction and a commitment to serve their ideals with radical action. In reconstructing their beliefs and the political cultures of which they were a part, I therefore do not confine myself to pointing out their flawed premises. I also stress the coherence of their beliefs within the context of their times, as well as the pathos of their core longing for a radically different and better world.

At the same time, both Weatherman and the RAF did have a driven and even crazed quality, which makes their histories at once so fascinating, disturbing, and difficult to fully comprehend. At times, the views of both groups seem to have been far removed from political realities, and their behavior to have exceeded the rational pursuit of distinctly political goals. Their members strayed far beyond the realm of "normal" politics into the rarefied world of the underground—a world of extraordinary danger, determination, fear, arrogance, trust, triumph, togetherness, suspicion, exhilaration, and despair. At their worst, both groups violated their stated morality and, whether in word or deed, showed streaks of cruelty. Doing justice to their histories—as well to the experiences of those whom they offended, attacked, injured, and killed—means also understanding the radical nature of their practice and their many errors in political and moral judgment. Gaining this understanding is not primarily a matter of deciding where politics ends and religion begins, where the rational and irrational or good and evil separate, or how conviction can be clouded by delusion. Rather, it requires appreciating how seemingly religious longings—for a transcendent future, for societal perfection, and for a sense of ultimate purpose—may infuse politics and culture; how the rational and the irrational may coexist with political conflicts; and how desires, dreams, and delusions may feed and confound one another.[24]

With both Weatherman and the RAF, my strongest accent is on the mutually informative relationship between research and theory. Though I draw on the insights of social movement theory—which provides elaborate models of how social movements and certain forms of protest emerge, evolve, and decline—I do not speak its distinctly sociological causal language. I work instead with other forms of theory, principally varieties of critical theory, ethics, and psychoanalysis. With these, I develop political, psychological, moral, and existential perspectives on forms of political behavior that may ultimately resist even the most carefully wrought explanations. Psychoanalysis is commonly used to interpret the psychology and behavior of individuals, and it could be fruitfully applied in this way to Weatherman and the RAF. I use it, in a somewhat different fashion, to explore the often hidden logic of *collective* political and cultural processes.

The German-born Jewish Marxist philosopher Herbert Marcuse, who fled to America during the years of Nazi rule, holds special value for my study. In the 1960s, Marcuse became the great intellectual patron of New Left movements the world over. Addressing audiences in the United States and West Germany, he embodied the New Left's internationalism and serves as a bridge between the two national experiences I consider. Marcuse, in addition, provided powerful insights into the structure of postwar societies, the promise and failings of the New Left, and ethical questions raised by its militancy, always informed by his analytical rigor and uncommon commitment to hope. I therefore both treat Marcuse as a historical actor and draw on his ideas to think through the tensions and conflicts of the era.

The fiercely controversial nature of New Left violence introduces a final challenge—one enhanced by the shocks of our own era. Political violence, especially when committed by agents other than established states, summons strong passions and invites blunt assessments. Much of the commentary on Weatherman and the RAF has been organized around extreme binaries that suggest that the groups were necessarily one thing or the other, with the negative view clearly dominating most historical commentary. This divide is evident in basic choices of terminology and possibilities of judgment: Were the Weathermen and RAF members "terrorists" or "urban guerrillas"? Villains or heroes? Crazed or courageous? Was their violence, in the last instance, wholly unjust or in any sense justified? Yet these stark polarities, rather than providing sound options for judgment, obscure the complex and even paradoxical nature of the meaning and legacy of both groups. The events of September 11, 2001, by deepening the antipathy of Americans to all violence labeled "terroristic," have likely made the impulse to categorically condemn the antigovernment violence of the 1960s and 1970s swifter and more severe. But all forms of violence are not equal in their origins, intent, and effects; and labels, whatever their promise of moral clarity, can distort what they seek to describe. Going beneath surface passions, while retaining a connection to the deep passion for justice animating the movements of the 1960s, yields a different set of questions and answers.

CHAPTER I

"Agents of Necessity"

Weatherman, the Red Army Faction, and the Turn to Violence

To describe how one became a Weatherman, Bernardine Dohrn is reported to have said: "One day you'll wake up and look out your window. And there, on your front lawn will be a great flaming W and you will know the time has come for you to be a WEATHERMAN!"[1] The initiation, in this account, was a moment of near-holy illumination. One did not so much choose to be a Weatherman as one was chosen by Weatherman.

In May 1970, Ulrike Meinhof helped free Andreas Baader, imprisoned for an act of political arson, from a research institute in West Berlin. Following a firefight, Baader and Meinhof jumped from the second story of the building and fled. Within days, Meinhof, Baader, and their accomplices announced the formation of the Rote Armee Fraktion. The leap was patently metaphorical: Baader plunged into a precarious freedom. Meinhof, a gifted journalist and outspoken critic of West German society, leapt into an entirely new life of danger and notoriety, in which bombs replaced words as her main weapons. More than anything else, they both took a leap of faith; trusting in their cause, each other, and their comrades forming the RAF, they somehow imagined victory in a literal war against the government of the Federal Republic.

But if those forming Weathermen and the RAF had the sensation of being seized in an instant by a calling, the roads that brought them to that point were long and winding ones—through the passionate beginnings of the student movement in each country; through years of questioning, organizing, demonstrating, and, as the 1960s ground on, angrily confronting the authorities; and through the urgent discussions toward the end of the decade about the possibility of making revolution by means of violence. The early path of the members of Weatherman and the RAF was, then, little different than that traveled by tens thousands of young Americans and West Germans in the 1960s. To understand the choice for armed struggle is therefore to understand something of the New Left's origins and evolution—and how the idea of violence became so captivating by the decade's end.

(handwritten margin note: looking at choice for armed struggle)

If many were called to serious, sustained violent insurrection, few were ultimately chosen. Shortly after forming, Weatherman declared the need "to be a movement that fights, not just talks about fighting."[2] The RAF, in its first manifesto, announced, "We will not talk about armed propaganda, we will do it."[3] In making good on their pledge to match action to words, the Weathermen and members of the RAF distinguished themselves within their movements, where talk of violence always greatly exceeded violence itself. To understand the two groups is also to understand the extraordinary nature of the leap they took.

(handwritten margin note: more talk of violence than getting to it)

.   .   .

Trails of trouble,
Roads of battles,
Paths of victory,
We shall walk.
            Bob Dylan,
    "Paths of Victory"

In the United States in the early 1960s, young, gifted thinkers, confessing a profound unease with the world they had inherited and calling themselves a New Left, judged their society by measuring it against its promise. America, in their view, had failed to live up to its democratic and egalitarian ideals. As the southern civil rights movement brought to national attention, racism barred a segment of the population from participating fully in American civic life, while poverty riddled the "affluent society" with pockets of misery. Hatred of a foreign, communist enemy provided a rationale for a policy of nuclear brinkmanship that threatened the globe with annihilation. Mainstream politics, in the eyes of New Leftists, were dominated by elites who preferred a docile public to an engaged one. And the middle-class culture in which young dissidents were socialized appeared politically and spiritually de-

(handwritten margin note: origins of American New Left)

bilitating, because it encouraged unquestioning obedience to authority, the narrow pursuit of self-interest, and superficial comfort through ever-expanding consumption.

The New Left set out to change all that. Drawing on a blend of American pragmatism, existential humanism, and ideas about participatory democracy derived largely from the civil rights movement, young leftists combated the widely pronounced "end of ideology" as itself an ideology that denied disturbing realities in declaring liberal, capitalist democracy the unequivocal moral victor in the global clash of political systems.[4] At the same time, they rejected as inflexible the "strong" ideologies of the socialist groups that made up the "Old Left" of the 1930s and 1940s. They especially criticized the "labor metaphysic" that dogmatically considered the working class to be the necessary agent of radical change. Wary of ideology in general, New Leftists held that knowledge derived primarily from hands-on experience and favored practical efforts to change society over abstract theorizing.

In the early 1960s, northern students returned from trips to the South filled with a passion for organizing. SDS, as it rapidly spread across campuses, bristled with optimism born of a belief in the transformative possibilities of civic initiative, critical thought, and the democratic process that it vigilantly practiced. In governing itself by means of participatory democracy, SDS sought to model the new, vigorously democratic society it desired. Immersion in activist culture offered individuals a potent sense of identity. For the future Weatherman Jeff Jones, who first encountered SDS at Ohio's Antioch College in 1965, the attraction was immediate. To him, the SDSers seemed "very smart, sophisticated, courageous, . . . people I wanted to be with, and work with, and be like."[5] SDS soon became "the only thing that was really important" to him, as it did for the burgeoning ranks of the SDS faithful. The New Left's initial radicalization—its belief in its capacity to dramatically change American society—reflected enthusiasm over its accumulating size and strength.

Heightened expectations also led activists to see the limitations of their efforts. The civil rights movement met barriers even as its success peaked. The eradication of legal segregation did not, in itself, address the relationship between racism and poverty, as the 1965 riots in Los Angeles's Watts neighborhood painfully dramatized. Nor did the movement's nonviolence speak to the experience and anger of many urban blacks. In 1966, the Black Panther Party formed in Oakland, California, to provide a militant response to poverty and police brutality. Panther chapters, which asserted the right of armed self-defense against the white power structure, quickly spread throughout America. Some black activists, challenging the integrationist dream, questioned the motives and doubted the contribution of whites working in alliance with them.[6]

The New Left experienced frustrations in its own organizing. New Leftists recognized that activism on campuses, where they were most successful, had only limited impact and appeal beyond the university, but the Education and Research Action Project (ERAP), in which SDSers lived and worked in poor urban communities to combat economic inequality, largely failed to generate concrete, lasting results. They discovered that little progress could be made without a large, well-organized movement of the poor, and they had difficulty transcending the class barriers separating them from those they sought to help. Finally, the New Left faced a new challenge in the mid 1960s: thousands of miles away, U.S. military involvement in Vietnam was escalating into a full-blown war.

From their experiences, New Leftists developed a sense that all the injustices they protested were connected and could not be eliminated if fought in isolation. Analyzing their connection, activists sought to correct for what now appeared to some to be an ideological deficit, whereby broad commitments to equality and democracy substituted for an integrated critique of power and a broad-based strategy for social change. "It is time to stop fearing ideology and lay the basis for a new one, more suitable to the times," one SDSer insisted in the mid 1960s.[7]

In April 1965, SDS's president, Paul Potter, addressed the first national demonstration, organized by SDS in Washington, D.C., against the Vietnam War. Potter's speech, widely recorded as a threshold in the history of the New Left, provided the broad outlines of such an ideology, as well as the ingredients that some would soon weave into a "revolutionary" consciousness. After intimating the existence of a system of oppression, Potter proclaimed:

> We must name it, describe it, analyze it, understand it and change it. For it is only when that system is changed . . . that there can be any hope for stopping the forces that create a war in Vietnam today or a murder in the South tomorrow or all the incalculable, innumerable more subtle atrocities that are worked on people all over. . . . [T]he people in Vietnam and the people in this demonstration are united in much more than a common concern that the war be ended. In both countries there are people struggling to build a movement that has the power to change their condition. The system that frustrates these movements is the same. All our lives, our destinies, our very hopes to live, depend on our ability to overcome that system.[8]

Potter posited a unified structure of domination responsible for discrete forms of oppression, whose elimination required changing *the whole*. Consistent with this premise, New Leftists increasingly used "the system" as a label for the complex entity they opposed and focused their protest on the structures that elites served. Potter's successor as SDS president, Carl Oglesby, explained that the Vietnam War was perpetrated not by evil men but by decent, even "honorable" men serving an evil corporate system.[9]

Though Potter did not himself name the system, capitalism was clearly the object of his polemic. To describe the system, New Leftists first used the language of "corporate liberalism," which stressed the alliance between business and governmental elites, but they soon graduated to a more overtly Marxist vocabulary. To the system, they counterposed "the movement," a capacious term that referred to everyone from student and antiwar activists to black militants and politically engaged hippies. It captured, in a word, activists' sense of "us"—of being an extended community distinct from a common adversary. With these contrasting terms, New Leftists cast political conflict as a battle of two fundamentally incompatible forces that could be resolved in their favor only through some radical, even revolutionary, transformation.

By linking American activists and Vietnamese rebels, Potter spoke to the New Left's internationalism. The system, conceived most expansively, was a *global* capitalist order that above all served U.S. interests. Fighting their country's power, American activists assumed a place in an international movement. Likening domestic racism to U.S. aggression in Vietnam, Potter also conveyed the centrality of race in the New Left's worldview. Through the black struggle, whites learned about the worst abuses of American society and the connection between racism domestically and abroad. Some blacks described black America as an "internal colony," rendering the black movement one of "national liberation," akin to struggles in the Third World. Finally, Potter spoke with a sense of romantic desperation. He declared a condition of moral emergency whose ultimate stakes were life and death and that demanded that leftists actively fight the system in order to "overcome" it. Echoing Potter's spirit, the future Weatherman Scott Braley described how the frustration of making modest demands in the mid 1960s fed the more ambitious rebellion of the late 1960s: "There were very few wins in the sense that you got anything you wanted. . . . We might have fixed some smaller issues, but we didn't want to fix smaller issues. We wanted to fix issues that would change the world. It was clear to many people that something much more radical was needed."[10]

But what? How did one go about fighting the system once one had begun to "name" and "analyze" it? One approach was to block the system's destructive operations; another was to attack the centers of its power. October 1967 featured both. As part of "Stop the Draft Week," thousands of demonstrators in Oakland tussled with police and temporarily shut down a military induction center. A few days later, protestors laid siege to the Pentagon, condemning the five-sided building as a demonic symbol of American militarism. Above all, the demonstrators brought a new energy: deep into the night they fought with police, argued with soldiers with fixed bayonets about war and duty, and danced around bonfires in scenes of almost pagan abandon. A final way to challenge "the System" was to attack the bigger issues by attacking the smaller ones—to address the whole by first confronting its parts. This is what the students did at Columbia University in 1968 and what made their rebellion so significant. The Columbia protests, as they escalated into the takeover of the university, also became one the primal scenes of New Left radicalism, from which the idea and then the reality of "armed struggle" emerged. A striking number of Weathermen participated in the rebellion, whether as students or as agitators from the outside.

Columbia had a strong SDS chapter, which in 1966–67 protested the presence of CIA and military recruiters on campus. The SDSers initially pursued institutional channels for changing university policies but soon came under the leadership of an "action faction" that favored polarizing confrontations. In 1968, two issues dominated SDS's attention: the proposed building of a university gym in Harlem and Columbia's involvement with the Institute for Defense Analysis (IDA), which coordinated academic research used by the military in Vietnam. Critics charged that the proposed gym, which would encroach on neighboring Harlem but bring no benefit to its largely poor, black population, epitomized Columbia's racism, and that the relationship with IDA revealed Columbia's complicity with U.S. militarism. As the university ignored student demands and punished student leaders, "student power" became another potent issue.

After black students occupied a campus building in late April, whites seized four others. Together, they shut down the university, forming a makeshift government that "ruled" by means of participatory democracy. National activists, including Tom Hayden, a co-founder of SDS, rushed to the campus to join the rebels. Radicals, in a conscious play on Che Guevara's call to "create two, three, many Vietnams," proliferated the slogan "create two, three, many Columbias." (The slogan seemed to have real agency when, in May, French students—conscious of events at

Columbia—occupied universities and then other institutions, precipitating a crisis that almost toppled the French state.) As national and international media descended upon the campus, student protest in the United States achieved unprecedented visibility. The initial uprising ended after a week when university officials called in over 1,000 police to clear the students from the buildings. Police made over 700 arrests, injuring dozens of students in the process.[11]

The Columbia protest was significant for the links the students made among the issues of racism, militarism, economic injustice, and student power. One protester explained that "the uprising was begun . . . not to achieve student power alone, but to advance the struggle for liberation outside the university itself."[12] The protest was also important for its militancy, which enhanced the students' sense of connection to that larger "struggle." Shutting down a major university in America's premier city, the students felt a taste of power that encouraged them to think in the exalted language of revolution. They called the occupied buildings "liberated zones" and experienced the exhilaration of participating in what Jeff Jones described as a "culture of total resistance."[13] The use of police violence against the students was another hallmark of Columbia. It fed an uncompromising rhetoric of condemnation and compelled the protesters to see political conflict in overtly confrontational terms. In variously heartfelt and grandiose language, a flyer asserted that the students now "know personally the brutality and inhumanity of a System which kills its young men without remorse and allows the poor to starve. . . . We will free Columbia of the Company men and profiteers and cake-eaters who control its future and direct its participation in the death industries. Our weapon is our solidarity."[14] Another flyer encouraged new battles to be fought with more than the figurative arms of the spirit: "We must prepare ourselves to deal with the enemy. Our weapons: political education and tactical organization for students and workers: rocks, clubs, fire bombs, plastique, guns—but most of all—commitment and courage."[15]

The New Left would soon cross another threshold in its evolving politics of confrontation. In response to a call from the Yippies—a flamboyant, largely mythical group headed by New York's Abbie Hoffman and Berkeley's Jerry Rubin—five thousand young radicals massed in Chicago to protest the convention of the Democratic Party in August of 1968. The Democrats were set to nominate Lyndon Johnson's vice president, Hubert Humphrey, who had pledged to continue Johnson's Vietnam policy. With the assassination of the progressive Democrat Robert Kennedy and the certain defeat of the antiwar candidate Eugene Mc-

Carthy, radicals lost any hope of working within the electoral system. Partly as a show of force and partly as a playful provocation, the Yippies warned that Chicago would be a scene of fantastic disruptions.[16] Rubin even seemed to welcome a violent police response, urging the group to "force a confrontation in which the establishment hits hard, thereby placing large numbers of people in a state of crisis and tension."[17] Though the Yippies rejected this suggestion, their sense of looming danger proved prophetic. When protesters failed to leave a park near the Convention Hall, police attacked them with brutal force. The bloody mêlée, shown live on national TV, provided spectacular images of a city, a political system, and a society out of control.

How and why young activists would turn so aggressively on "liberal" institutions like Columbia University and the Democratic Party may now seem hard to fathom. Yet liberalism was the target of relentless attacks by the left from the mid 1960s on. Partly, enmity toward liberalism grew out of activists' sense that so much of what was wrong with America had been perpetrated or was presided over by liberals. The Vietnam War, its critics repeatedly said, was a "liberal's war," insofar as it had been conceived and then expanded by the Democratic administrations of Kennedy and Johnson. More broadly, the Pax Americana of the postwar years—with its assertion of American military supremacy, vigorous anticommunism, and aggressive promotion of U.S. interests—was fully as much a part of the foreign policy agenda of liberals as it was of conservatives (though some liberals were outspoken in opposition to U.S. involvement in Vietnam).[18] For leftists, President Johnson, Secretary of Defense Robert McNamara, and Secretary of State Dean Rusk—liberals all—became the archvillains of the era.[19]

Liberals were less vulnerable on issues of race and poverty, but there, too, they attracted the suspicion and eventual condemnation of young rebels. The federal government had supported the effort to end legal segregation with legislation and even troops, and Johnson's "Great Society" programs addressed poverty with an intensity not seen since the New Deal. Yet the extension of formal political rights addressed neither the connection between racial and economic oppression nor, as blacks argued with growing insistence, the institutional foundations of racism. Federal antipoverty programs went only so far in expanding the opportunities for the poorest Americans. As white activists became alert to the message of figures like Malcolm X and groups like the Black Panthers—who harangued the liberal establishment for its alleged condescension and half-measures—their criticisms of liberal attitudes grew more probing. The essential charge was that white liberals supported the equality of people of color only up to a point; by the mid 1960s, "liberal" had become a dirty word among young activists, used to denounce a worldview that subscribed to tepid versions of all the right things, while recoiling from the kinds of change that would fundamentally challenge the supremacy of whites.

Disenchantment with liberalism was a virtual right of passage for those becoming Weathermen. In the Columbia experience, the process by which some became radicalized and peeled themselves away from the preordained script of their lives comes into focus. Robert Roth, the gifted and studious son of a middle-class family in Queens, entered Columbia in 1966 at the age of sixteen; by 1969 he had left and joined Weatherman. Roth credits his early interest in social justice to the "progressive Jewish tradition" of which his parents were a part. Growing up, he "compulsively" followed the civil rights movement in the South, which offered images of the brutality of American racism but also of the "courage and spirit" of those resisting it. Participating in civil rights rallies in New York, he came to see racism as a northern problem as well. Columbia represented, in his words, "the chosen path" for someone of his background; its message, as he encountered it, was "there's room for everyone here . . . this is the place where you can finally make your contribution . . . you've reached the pinnacle, so don't blow it." Yet Roth came to feel that the truth of "success" at Columbia was better expressed in the SDS slogan "Work, Study, Get Ahead, Kill," insofar as the endpoint was an elite position in a social system predicated on inequality and violence. Roth discerned in his fellow activists, beyond the competitiveness nurtured by an all-male institution, an admirable willingness to take a "risk in life and blow it" by rejecting the rewards of Columbia. For Roth, the issues of the gym and IDA did not contradict but rather exemplified Columbia's liberalism.[20]

David Gilbert, also a future Weatherman, had graduated from Columbia in 1966 but, still living in New York, joined the 1968 rebellion. Raised like Roth in a liberal Jewish household, he recalls first being sensitized to injustice through education about the Holocaust. He locates the roots of his eventual radicalism in his sincere wish as a teenager that America "live up to the rhetoric of democracy." The politically precocious Gilbert became active in his Boston-area high school in protests against racism and U.S. foreign policy, which often seemed to violate his country's freedom-loving creed. Columbia, with its highly traditional curriculum and imposing neoclassical architecture, represented to him the "pretense of humanism." Despite its great wealth, the university paid its largely black and Hispanic workforce poorly. At orientation, the deans had warned the students not to stray into Harlem (and certainly not wearing Columbia sweatshirts); curious and defiant, Gilbert promptly toured Harlem, and he later tutored a child there. He described his experiences in Harlem and working with the campus chapter of CORE (the Congress on Racial Equality) as far "more educational" than what he felt was the "mindless regurgitation" practiced at Columbia.[21] When student protest heated up in the spring of 1968, Gilbert eagerly reimmersed himself in the activism on the campus.

Columbia was hardly unique among American universities for its involvement with the military-industrial complex, its questionable practices as a landlord and employer, or its exclusion of students from university governance. What was striking was the students' response: not to see these qualities as mere taints that compromised an otherwise sound institution, but to declare them morally unacceptable expressions of Columbia's true identity. As the inadequacy of the "official" channels for redressing their grievances was quickly exposed, the rebels adopted the uncompromising stance of "no business as usual." Since the university also proved unyielding, a complex conflict became for some on each side an all-or-nothing struggle to be settled, at last, by force. A journalist who covered the events at Columbia and then the rise of Weatherman reflected: "The more I witnessed, the more I felt that what was happening in the country had been prefigured at Columbia [where] SDS politics centered on collision. . . . When all the arguments about issues had been made, the only certain thing was violence."[22]

Columbia stood out, finally, in how the protests pushed the protesters—in ways both political and deeply personal—beyond the confines of the university. In the spring of 1968, Gilbert was called before the faculty to discuss a possible student strike. He recalls the faculty asking:

> "Do you say you stand for democracy?" We said, "Yes, we do." They said, "Would you stand by a referendum, of the students and faculty, everybody at the University?" . . . And I was really torn between what I considered fundamental issues and the commitment to democracy, participatory democracy, and I sort of hesitated and said, "Well we would stand by a referendum, as long as the people in Harlem, and people in Vietnam, who are the ones most affected by this, can vote, because that's really participatory democracy."[23]

According to Roth, it was Columbia's black students who, above all, honored this robust sense of democracy in choosing to "side with their community [in Harlem] on the issue of the gym" by initiating the building takeovers.

Columbia soon became less and less relevant to its radical students. Roth, who was elected a leader of Columbia SDS for the new academic year, recalls that by 1969, "the powerful stuff was happening at other places," led largely by people of color fighting for basic access to life opportunities. At the City University of New York, the battle over open admissions erupted into a major class and race conflict, in which Roth and other Columbia activists participated. Even so, Roth helped lead more building occupations at his own university, for which he was arrested and served a thirty-day prison sentence. The experience proved a "stepping stone to withdrawing . . . to see my life differently [and realize,] 'No, I wasn't going to finish Columbia.'"[24] He was going to join the revolution instead.

This dynamic of a "local" protest escalating into a major confrontation was repeated in countless settings—if most often beyond the glare of instant celebrity shone on Columbia's comparatively privileged radicals in America's leading city. At San Francisco State College, the movement for black and ethnic studies programs was part of a larger struggle against racism. The combination of the university's intransigence and the students' militancy led to the continuous occupation of the campus in the fall and winter of 1968–69 by police and soldiers; by the year's end, there had been more than 700 arrests, 80 injuries to students and 32 to police, and several attempted bombings.[25] At Cornell University in the same year, students used the demand for a black studies program as a vehicle for advocating Black Power more generally; the photograph of black students brandishing rifles outside a campus building is an enduring symbol of the profound racial and social divisions of the era. In each case, radicals confronted a local injustice as an instance of a much broader system of oppression, which served as the ultimate target of their protest.

.   .   .

Protest is when I say this or that doesn't suit me.
Resistance is when I ensure that what doesn't suit
me no longer occurs.

> Ulrike Meinhof, "Vom Protest zum Widerstand"
> ("From Protest to Resistance")

The West German New Left, like its American counterpart, initially sought to unsettle the politics of consensus that prevailed in the 1950s and early 1960s. Emerging from the ruins of war and the American-Soviet conflict, the Federal Republic of Germany (FRG) based its identity on three main foundations: its striking prosperity, achieved through its *Wirt-schaftswunder* ("economic miracle"); its staunch opposition to communism; and its adoption of Western-style democracy, typified by the drafting of a constitution and creation of parliamentary institutions. Much of the public seemed content to have the new nation pursue an agenda restricted to promoting economic growth and political stability. *"Kein Experiment"*—the great slogan of the republic's first chancellor, Konrad Adenauer—served as the motto for this cautious course.

The left, meanwhile, was weak. With little public reaction, the Constitutional Court banned the Communist Party (Kommunistischen Partei Deutschlands, or KPD) in 1956 for allegedly threatening the principles of the constitution. In its 1959 Godesberger Program, the Social Democratic Party (Sozialdemokratische Partei Deutschland, or SPD) essentially renounced its founding commitment to socialism and assumed a voice of only mild and occasional dissent. When, in 1966, the SPD joined the Christian Democrats (Christlich Demokratische Union, or CDU) and the Christian Socialist Union (Christlich-Sozialen Union, or CSU) in forming the "Great Coalition" government, the SPD's abandonment of its radical roots was total.

In the early 1960s, perceiving a lack of meaningful alternatives within the political establishment, leftists formed an "extraparliamentary opposition" (Ausserparlamentarische Opposition, or APO), which operated outside of party politics and the electoral process. Student organizations played an important role in the coalition of groups comprising APO.[26] Chief among the student groups was the Sozialistischer Deutscher Studentenbund (SDS), the youth wing of the SPD, which had been expelled in 1959 for remaining too strongly committed to socialism. Early on, APO opposed West German rearmament, the basing of nuclear weapons in West Germany, and the proposed "Emergency Laws" (*Notstandge-setzte*), which would permit the curtailment of democratic rights in times of crisis. To their supporters, these measures were vital to both West Germany's security and the establishment of its full sovereignty. To APO, they violated the constitution's stated commitments to peace and democracy. The dissenters additionally questioned whether, in light of the Nazi past, the Federal Republic deserved or could be trusted with greater power.

Germany's fascist legacy affected the New Left in profound ways. Young leftists condemned their parents' generation both for its complicity with Nazism and its conspicuous silence about the Nazi period. The accusation of the *near-total* suppression or evasion of the past, common in the recollections of the postwar generation, likely represents in many cases the selective application of memory. The postwar society had in fact periodically confronted the Nazi past through high-level discussions of reparations for the Nazis' victims; various war crimes trials, which received extensive media coverage in West Germany (the most notorious were those of Adolf Eichmann in 1961 and the "Auschwitz Trials" of 1963–65); the development of educational materials detailing German crimes during the Nazi period; and the introduction of books, plays, and television programs about the war and the Holocaust (Anne Frank's *Diary* was a best seller in Germany in the late 1950s, and millions saw theatrical versions of it either live or on television).[27] Yet however intense and seemingly pervasive, such encounters were only intermittent, and the reaction of officialdom and the public alike was often self-justificatory and tinged with resentment at the extraordinary burden of guilt that focus on the past entailed. Crucially, such moments of public reflection did not necessarily translate into sustained, *private* discussions in German households about the Nazi era, in which parents shared with their children the truth about their connection to the Nazi movement. As a result, members of the New Left generation felt uninformed or even lied to about events of the past that defined their parents' generation and, ultimately, the identity of all Germans.

The recollections of Margrit Schiller, who grew up in the new capital of Bonn and later joined the RAF, powerfully convey the reign of silence that many among her generation endured. Schiller's education about German history ended with World War I.[28] Her father, though not a member of the Nazi Party, had fought in World War II. When she asked her parents about the Nazi period, the constant refrain was, "We could not possibly have supported what Hitler did." About the worst of Germany's crimes, they "knew nothing."[29] Yet when Margrit was fourteen, her father confessed in a moment of drunken candor that he had tortured a captured Russian soldier to death.[30] An additional trauma came when she discovered that songs she was learning on the piano had been written or adapted by the Nazis to promote their cause.[31] Thereafter, she disdained all German songs.

For young West Germans, the Nazi past was not only a source of confusion and anger but an impetus to activism. Determined not to repeat their elders' failings, they reacted strongly to contemporary forms of injustice. In the late 1950s, left-wing journals such as *Das Argument* developed an understanding of fascism as an extreme response of capitalism to economic crises. The transition in the postwar years to democratic capitalism, by extension, did not *in itself* represent a decisive break with fascism. More than that, young intellectuals saw fascism—following the lead of the Frankfurt School and the iconoclastic psychologist Wilhelm Reich—as a cognitive structure and a cultural condition, manifest in subjects who were at once extraordinarily pliant and dictatorial, submissive and aggressive. In keeping with this view, West German New Leftists condemned the attitudes and behavior of the adult generation—from the defense of order to disdain for nonconformity—as signs of the persistence of the "authoritarian personality" integral to fascism.

More tangibly, students and youth pointed to the considerable linkages in personnel between the Nazi regime and the new German state as evidence of "fascist continuity." As of 1965, fully 60 percent of West German military officers had fought for the Nazis, and at least two-thirds of judges had served the Third Reich.[32] Students clamored to know the pasts of their professors and conducted research revealing that many of them had been affiliated with the Nazis. Initially, their findings were presented in more or less civil ways, often with the cooperation of the institutions whose faculty they investigated. By 1967, however, students began angrily confronting their professors during lectures. In addition, some high-ranking officials in the Federal Republic had been Nazis. Most notorious was the CDU's Kurt Kiesinger, who years before becoming federal chancellor in 1966 had held an important position in the Nazi propaganda ministry. At a public gathering in 1968, the twenty-nine-year-old Beate Klarsfeld slapped Kiesinger; Klarsfeld, who then made it her life's work to hunt down Nazi war criminals, described her audacious act as "the children of the Nazi generation slapping the Nazi face."[33]

The fascist past also helped to shape the opposition of young Germans to the Vietnam War. As for American New Leftists, the war was the primary issue around which West German students mobilized. German activists, relative to their American counterparts, were generally well versed in Marxist principles; the SDS and the "Republican Clubs" found in major German cities generated a dizzying array of "working groups" that meticulously applied Marxism in analyzing contemporary political phenomena. Far from being a conceptual revelation, then, the view of capitalism as an international system of oppression was something many German leftists took as axiomatic. Early on, they saw the Vietnam War in anti-imperialist terms and adopted the militant position of support for the Viet Cong. In 1965, German activists organized a "Vietnam Summer," during which they both learned and educated the broader populace about the conflict in Southeast Asia (American activists would do

the same only two summers later).[34] At a May 1966 antiwar conference
in Frankfurt—fully a year before American activists expressed such views
in great numbers—more than 2,000 participants ratified a statement describing the armed "national and social liberation struggle of the South
Vietnamese people" as an act of "political necessity," as well as a model
for other anticapitalist movements in the Third World.[35]

Some activists even claimed a direct affinity with the South Vietnamese
rebels (the Viet Cong) based on what they saw as the close parallels between West Germany and South Vietnam: both countries had occupying
U.S. armies and "puppet" governments whose true purpose—behind the
rhetoric of defending democracy against foreign communists—was to
contain indigenous revolts. The poet Erich Fried starkly asserted this
connection: "Vietnam is Germany / its fate is our fate / The bombs for
its freedom / are bombs for our freedom / Our Chancellor Erhard / is Mar-
shall Ky / General Nguyen Van Thieu / is President Lübke / The Americans / are also there the Americans."[36] For its less radical critics, the Vietnam War called into question West Germany's identity. Seeing the United
States engage in mass violence against a poor country struggling for self-
determination—as leftists commonly saw the conflict—potentially undermined Germans' already fragile sense of their own society's legitimacy,
which was derived in part from its effort to emulate the Americans. The
United States, one commentator concluded, "forfeited its status as a role
model as the result of the Vietnam war."[37]

West German anger at the Vietnam War was also stoked by the Nazi
past. With deliberate provocativeness, young activists denounced the war
as an act of "genocide" (Völkermord), which they, as Germans, had a
special duty to oppose. The German-born Daniel Cohn-Bendit, who became a leader of the French student movement, explained: "Our parents'
generation had supported the Nazis, whether actively or passively. We did
not want to be complicit in the genocide in Indochina."[38] By extension,
German leftists regarded the support for the war by the government and
much of the public as evidence of how little German values had changed
since the Nazi era. The Vietnam War, then, was subject to the double-coding
that defined young Germans' perceptions. The violence in Vietnam was
repellent to them both in its own right *and* insofar as it recalled Nazi violence; the apparent indifference of Germans to the suffering in Vietnam
was infuriating in its own right *and* as it recalled the public's tacit support for the Nazis' terror. Opposition to the war, in short, did not depend
upon the drawing of historic parallels. Consciousness of the German past,
however, made the war all the more disturbing.

New Left references to fascism entailed a thicket of often contradictory judgments and associations. At times, leftists drew comparisons between the past and present with blunt and even reckless force. In 1966, banners were secretly placed on the memorial site entrance at the Dachau concentration camp proclaiming, "Vietnam is the Auschwitz of America" and "American leathernecks are inhuman murderers like the SS."[39] By virtue of this elision, to oppose the war was to implicitly denounce the horrors of the German past, if not also to diminish German guilt by relativizing its crimes. Whatever the implications of these comparisons, German leftists' relationship to their country's past and present, their stance toward the United States, and their understanding of their protest were mediated through one another. In this complex way, national memory and notions of collective identity played themselves out on a global stage.

· · ·

If you plant ice, you're gonna' harvest wind.
   The Grateful Dead, "Franklin's Tower"
      (lyrics by Robert Hunter)

As the protests in New York City, Chicago, San Francisco, and elsewhere erupted in violence, establishment voices increasingly denounced students and youths as hooligans and malcontents with no respect for law and order. Yet such violence and the anxiety it elicited were only a small part of a larger climate of crisis driven by violence in various forms; for New Leftists to gravitate toward violence—whether as a means of self-defense, an expression of outrage, or a broad assault on their society—was to cross a threshold commonly transgressed.

   Above all, there was the violence in Vietnam. By the end of 1968, over 30,000 American servicemen had died there, with the television news reporting the daily losses.[40] In this manner, violence entered American families and communities, steeping everyday life in bitter and often confusing loss. Through the draft, millions of American men confronted the possibility of killing or being killed in a war whose purpose many questioned. There were also the assassinations of Martin Luther King Jr. in April 1968 and Robert Kennedy in early June, which produced a widespread sense of devastation and foreboding. To many blacks, King's assassination was the ultimate affirmation of the virulence of American racism, which claimed the life even of a man of peace. For some, it was an incitement to violence. On the night of King's murder, the Black Panther Leader Eldridge Cleaver insisted in a radio broadcast that by 1968, King was hated both by racist whites and by black people "who wanted to be rid of the self-deceiving doctrine of non-violence." Declaring a "requiem for non-violence," he warned that "the death of Dr. King signals the end of an era and the beginning of a bloody chapter that may remain unwritten, because there may be no scribe left to capture on paper the holocaust to come."[41]

Blacks responded to King's death by rioting in cities throughout America. These riots repeated the massive "civil disorders" in Detroit, Newark, and elsewhere of a year earlier, when police violence triggered the eruption of poor black neighborhoods. The Kerner Commission, appointed by President Lyndon B. Johnson to investigate the causes of the 1967 riots, declared in its 1968 report that "two societies, one black, one white— separate and unequal" had emerged in the United States.[42] Cautioning that "[d]isruption and disorder nourish repression, not justice," the report warned of more unrest if racial and economic inequality were not addressed by all levels of government.[43] What the commission intimated by calling for an end to violence "in the streets of the ghetto and in the lives of people," radicals boldly asserted: that poverty, lack of opportunity, and racism *were themselves forms of violence* whose consequences were despair and, inevitably, violent rage.[44]

The police themselves, as they dealt with demonstrators, set a course of collision. The future Weatherman Jim Mellen vividly described another event from 1968 that provided a chilling sense of things to come. Born in the mid 1930s, Mellen was older than the others who would make up Weatherman. After earning his Ph.D. at the University of Iowa and being forced out of a teaching job in New Jersey for his opposition to the Vietnam War, he went in the spring of 1966 to teach in Dar-es-Salaam, Tanzania. He returned in April 1968, two days after Dr. King had been shot, to what seemed a different student movement in a different America. A week or so later, he attended a demonstration near New York City's Rockefeller Center protesting the role of a conservative West German newspaper chain (which had offices there) in fomenting violence against Germany's young rebels. At the protest, which took place before a throng of tourists, a brash anarchist collective from New York's Lower East Side called the "Up Against the Wall Motherfuckers" burned a German flag, after which Mellen observed:

> Immediately, from out of the crowd, came these thugs . . . great big guys with work clothes on, and they began beating the people, not arresting them, but beating the people who had burned the flag. And it turned out

that they [the "thugs"] were policemen. . . . There I was, pushed up against this granite wall, with all these people in their pastel, nylon Easter outfits, screaming and running in all directions. . . . I was petrified. I had no idea that anything like this was going to happen. And then my friend told me, "This is the way it's going now and you are going to have to learn that any time we step into the street now, they beat the shit out of us. We are either going to get off the street or learn how to withstand [it.]"[45]

Within this climate of crisis and violence, the idea of revolution came to define activists' sense of themselves. Assessing what made the Panthers so challenging to the white power structure, the Chicago Black Panther leader Fred Hampton explained: "I am a revolutionary."[46] One chronicler of the student movement remarked: "In 1964 or 1965 someone in SDS declared himself [or herself] a revolutionary; by 1969 it was impossible for any SDS member to admit that he [or she] was *not a* revolutionary."[47] Such self-descriptions were hardly confined to radical blacks or to militants at select campuses. A 1970 poll estimated that more than one million young Americans considered themselves "revolutionaries."[48] In 1971, fully 25 percent of students polled at the University of California at Santa Barbara—hardly thought of as a bastion of radicalism—believed that change would take place by means of "revolution." A student there, describing the calling she and her radical cohort felt, declared, "For us there was no future. Revolution was the future."[49] The historian Kirkpatrick Sale concluded that revolution was "the pattern woven by all the threads of the sixties."[50]

A description of the New Left as "revolutionary" may well seem an exaggeration or idealization. Historians have recently argued that methodological biases and unchecked instincts have contributed to the overestimation of the revolutionary nature of the New Left. These include the narrow study of movement "elites" in major cities; focus on leaders, who were often more radical than rank-and-file activists; and susceptibility to the seductive power of violence to dominate attention. As a result, historians have called for greater study of the New Left's grass roots, where one presumably finds the more sober and, so the prevailing view goes, more inspiring reality of sustained commitment to nonviolent protest and to institutional reform.[51]

But these correctives yield their own distortion—one that conceals the extent to which a diverse and overtly revolutionary culture (at least in aspiration and self-perception) had taken shape by the end of the 1960s. That culture had its theorists, chiefly Marx and Marcuse. The Black Panthers were the vanguard, with the Panther leader Huey Newton and Che

Guevara heading the pantheon of New Left heroes. Eldridge Cleaver, who blasted American racism and foretold doom for its defenders, served as its prophetic voice. The Yippies played the part of tricksters; San Francisco's Diggers, who blended art, life, and service to their community, were among the visionaries. The Jefferson Airplane, Country Joe and the Fish, and other "political" musicians were the minstrels. The San Francisco Mime Troupe served as bards. The "revolution" had also its cinema, such as Gillo Pontecorvo's 1965 film *The Battle of Algiers,* which offered a rousing portrait of anticolonial rebellion. Young rebels had their own storied battles, like the Pentagon, Columbia, and Chicago, as well as their strongholds—Berkeley, Madison, and New York's East Village, certainly, but also the countless enclaves where young people pursued alternative lifestyles and, by means both political and cultural, struck out at "the system." The New Left even had its own media, the "underground press." Most American cities boasted at least one grassroots newspaper in which young leftists debated ideology, announced demonstrations, denounced the police, reviewed albums, concerts, books, and plays, and, most broadly, shared their vision of themselves and the world. Combining all of these was a mythology, in which the New Left imagined itself a liberating agent of history. The Weathermen, as they emerged from this culture, declared themselves the revolution's warrior leaders and shock troops.

.   .   .

So long as capitalism exists,
violence will not disappear.
                   Rudi Dutschke et al.,
                   "Gewalt" ("Violence")

Even more so than their American counterparts, West German New Leftists were radicalized by specific moments of conflict with their state and society.[52] Anticommunism, historically strong in Germany, was intensified by Germany's partition. It was especially virulent in West Berlin, where Cold War tensions were the highest and the student movement was the strongest. Much of the West German public and the media viewed the New Left as a red menace that did the bidding of the Eastern Bloc. This was especially true of Axel Springer's conservative tabloids, among them *Bild, BZ,* and *Berliner Morgenpost;* all told, Springer publications accounted for more than 70 percent of the West Berlin press and more than 30 percent of the national daily newspaper market.[53] As the press fed a climate of antistudent hysteria, the reaction of the media to the New Left itself became a major object of protest.

Tensions exploded on June 2, 1967, when an undercover policeman shot and killed a twenty-six-year-old protester, Benno Ohnesorg, at a demonstration against a visit to West Berlin by the shah of Iran. Ohnesorg had been attending his first major demonstration and was survived by his pregnant wife. West German students, and those sympathetic to their plight as the scapegoats of the Springer media, found the shooting traumatic. The novelist Günter Grass described it as "the first political murder in the Federal Republic."[54] At an emotional meeting on the night of June 2 of the German SDS (Sozialistische Deutsche Studentenbund), the future RAF founder Gudrun Ensslin exclaimed ominously: "This fascist state means to kill us all. . . . Violence is the only way to answer violence. This is the Auschwitz generation, and there's no arguing with them."[55] Following the killing of Ohnesorg, which the police falsely claimed was an act of self-defense, denunciations of the students as threats to law, order, and democracy—themselves reminiscent of the fascists of the past—only intensified. The CDU's chief Berlin official commented on June 3: "It is high time to remove from the universities the student ringleaders, who study at the cost of the public."[56] The Springer papers falsely reported that Ohnesorg had been shot to ward off a mob of rioters wielding knives.[57] Springer's *Berliner Zeitung* remarked: "What happened yesterday in Berlin had nothing to do with politics. . . . It was criminal in the most sickening way."[58] *Bild* announced: "Up until now there has been terror only east of the wall. Yesterday, malicious and misguided people tried for the first time to bring terror into the free part of the city. . . . Creating a racket no longer suffices. They must see blood. They wave the red flag and believe the red flag. Here the fun ends . . . and democratic tolerance. We have something against SA methods."[59]

By February of the following year, students had organized a "Springer Tribunal" at the Technische Universität Berlin, in which intellectuals and activists analyzed Springer's monopoly, documented the defamation of protesters, and issued a "verdict" condemning the Springer press as dangerously reactionary and itself a purveyor of violence. During the presentation, a short film entitled *Herstellung eines Molotow-Cocktails (The Making of a Molotov Cocktail)* was screened, which plainly showed how to fashion petrol bombs. Its closing imagery suggested that buildings of the Springer press would be ideal targets. That evening, demonstrators

smashed the windows of Springer offices. The film's author was Holger
Meins, a twenty-seven-year-old film student and future RAF member.[60]

The near-fatal wounding of the New Left leader Rudi Dutschke on
April 4, 1968, by a mentally disturbed right-wing fanatic and avid *Bild*
reader was a second tragedy that instantaneously escalated the conflict
between the New Left and West German society. As with Ohnesorg's
shooting, students attributed the attack to the "pogrom journalism" of
the Springer press. "Springer shot too!" became a common slogan
among enraged protesters.[61] Here again, New Leftists saw a connection
to the fascist past. The Berlin Evangelical Student Union warned: "Since
the Third Reich, the object of attack has been switched: the hooked Jewish nose in [the infamous Nazi weekly] *Der Stürmer* has been replaced
in the cartoons in *Bild* and *BZ* by the beard of the student, considered
subhuman like a gorilla. The demand 'Jews Out' prepared the way for
the gas chamber."[62] The student movement, in this questionable comparison, was Germany's new victim.

The students were not alone in blaming the media for Dutschke's
shooting. Important intellectuals, among them Heinrich Böll, Theodor
Adorno, and Alexander Mitscherlich, drafted a statement asserting:

> Fear and an inability to engage the arguments of the student opposition
> seriously have created a climate in which the intentional defamation of a
> minority provokes acts of violence against it. This climate has been system-
> atically created by a press that presents itself as a guardian of the constitu-
> tion and claims to speak in the name of the majority and of order, but that
> means by order nothing more than its domination of an immature populace
> and the way to a new, authoritarian nationalism.[63]

Students reacted to the shooting of Dutschke—a beloved figure on the
left, prized for both his staggering intellect and personal humility—with
large, aggressive demonstrations over the Easter weekend. The working-
class anarchist Michael "Bommi" Baumann, who revered Dutschke, recalls sensing after the attack that "the bullet was just as much against
you [i.e., oneself]; for the first time they were really shooting at you."
Baumann responded by throwing Molotov cocktails at Springer trucks.[64]
In some of the demonstrations, the students were joined by workers
protesting the imminent passage of the Emergency Laws. With the battle cry "Expropriate Springer!" they physically attacked Springer facilities, halted the distribution of newspapers, and destroyed Springer publications. Two people died in the Easter turmoil. The shooting of Dutschke

was also the cause of outrage worldwide, spawning protests at Springer offices or West German embassies in Washington, New York, London, Amsterdam, Paris, Milan, Tel Aviv, Vienna, and Prague.[65]

The Easter demonstrations represented a qualitative shift in the goals, tactics, and sensibility of the New Left, captured by the journalist Ulrike Meinhof. Born in 1934, Meinhof was older than most New Leftists. Her father had died when she was just six, and her mother when she was fifteen, leaving her in the care of Renate Riemeck (who had survived the war, with Ulrike's mother, as a silent critic of Hitler). After the war, Riemeck became a well-respected scholar, and she exposed Ulrike to philosophy, literature, and the progressive causes of the German 1950s, such as disarmament. Intelligent and free thinking, Ulrike quickly found a place in the budding circle of young left-wing intellectuals who would help to shape the values and politics of the student movement of the 1960s. In 1960, she began writing for the Hamburg-based magazine *konkret,* which blended left-wing political commentary with provocative, if often shallow and brazenly sexist, celebrations of the libertine attitudes sweeping Germany. Part pundit, part polemicist, and part moralist, Meinhof addressed everything from relations with the communist East to the arms race, the West's support for dictators like Iran's shah, and U.S. aggression in Vietnam. By 1967, her columns were eagerly read by young radicals seeking inspiration, insight, and a language in which to frame their rebellion.

To Meinhof, the Easter protests marked the passage of the German movement from "protest to resistance." Paraphrasing an unnamed African-American radical, she explained: "Protest is when I say this or that doesn't suit me. Resistance is when I ensure that what doesn't suit me no longer occurs."[66] Meinhof conceded that the demonstrators fell far short of eliminating the injustices they had targeted. But she lauded the new militancy as an expression of the New Left's refusal to be any longer "a powerless opposition that disturbs nothing and no one."[67] Another act drew Meinhof's praise. On April 2, just days before the shooting of Dutschke, Gudrun Ensslin, the charismatic ruffian Andreas Baader, and two others started small fires in Frankfurt department stores as an act of protest. (The fires were quickly put out, causing no injuries and minimal property damage.) The arsonists were captured a few days later. Meinhof, though judging the action politically misguided, asserted: "The progressive moment in the burning of a department store doesn't lie in the destruction of commodities but in the criminality of the act, its breaking of the law."[68]

The arson was significant in other senses. At their high-profile trial in
October 1968, the defendants described it as an effort to "light a torch
for Vietnam" in "protest against indifference toward the war" and "monopoly capitalism."[69] Conceived in these terms, it sought to illuminate
the connection between First World consumption and the exploitation of
the Third World. As a political act, the arson was also fantastically reductive, at once pathetic and quixotic. Critics of advanced industrial society such as the theorists of the Frankfurt School argued with great sophistication that consumer capitalism was responsible, not only for
economic exploitation, but also for the near-total degradation of subjectivity, culture, and critical reason. Young leftists, in keeping with this view,
saw "the system" as a repressive totality, rooted in a commodity fetishism
that exerted a pervasive *"Consumterror"* ("terror of consumption"). But
how, some puzzled, did one strike out at this totality, whose power was
at once overwhelming and diffuse? The arsonists appeared to answer this
question with stunning literal-mindedness: destroy goods in a department
store!

The arson also signaled a new level of militancy, whose justification
demanded a new vocabulary. At the trial, Baader defended the act by invoking the "natural right of resistance" described by Marcuse in his 1965
essay "Repressive Tolerance,"[70] which argued that the ideal of tolerance
had been perverted in advanced industrial societies such as the United
States and West Germany. Its original purpose had been to enable the
discovery of ethical truths by promoting open discussion and the expression of dissident views. However, in societies predicated on the "in-
stitutionalization of inequality," tolerance is extended overwhelmingly
to "policies, conditions and modes of behavior which should not be tolerated because they are impeding, if not destroying the chances of creating an existence without fear and misery."[71] This tolerance "towards
that which is radically evil" reflected, according to Marcuse, the stranglehold on public consciousness by political and corporate forces intent
on preserving their domination.[72]

As a remedy, Marcuse advocated active *intolerance*—including
censorship—toward views and behavior that serve the oppressive status
quo. In addition, Marcuse identified a "'natural right' of resistance for
repressed and overpowered minorities to use extralegal means if the legal
ones prove to be inadequate" to compel social change.[73] Such resistance
could even *legitimately* take a violent form. Lamenting that "nonviolence is normally not only preached to, but extracted from the weak,"
he insisted that "to refrain from violence in the face of vastly superior

force is one thing, to renounce a priori violence against violence, on ethical or psychological grounds (because it may antagonize sympathizers) is another."[74] By the late 1960s, student movements throughout the developed world claimed the right of extreme resistance, evident in Baader's appeal.

Marcuse's ideas had special resonance among Germans. Not only was he a German Jew, an impassioned opponent of Nazism, and, after the war, an ardent critic of both Western capitalism and Soviet-style communism, but his sketch of contemporary repression, which he elaborated in celebrated lectures in Frankfurt and West Berlin in 1967, closely matched the perceptions of young Germans. Toward the decade's end, the West German New Left saw itself precisely as a "repressed and overpowered minority" fighting a system of "absolute evil" within an impoverished public sphere. The protests against the Springer papers tapped powerfully into Marcusean themes. In their defamations and willful misrepresentation of events, the papers were a clear barrier to rational debate and a source of physical danger to the student movement. The destruction of actual newspapers as an act of protest—something virtually unthinkable in the United States, however great the anger of radicals, by virtue of the near-sacred status of "free speech" in America—seemed an expression of the kind of intolerance Marcuse sanctioned.

The spring of 1968 represented, in sum, a decisive transformation in the West German New Left's relationship to violence—one that closely paralleled the evolution of the American New Left. In a June 1968 essay in *konkret* titled simply "Gewalt" ("Violence"), a group of intellectuals that included Dutschke and his closest collaborators spelled out that relationship. Reflecting on the Easter demonstrations, they insisted:

> Only since we have begun, however cautiously, to speak the language of the system have we made ourselves understandable to workers and a danger to Springer. That language is violence. The system speaks it, because the system is constituted by violence. . . . It is not accidental that the attack on Rudi Dutschke was the spark. Dutschke is distinguished among us for maintaining from the outset that it is not a purely moral-intellectual choice that compels us to fight our system; rather, our physical and spiritual existence is threatened by this system, which we cannot reform but must destroy. . . . [One must distinguish] between *mediated* (latent) and *unmediated* (manifest) violence. The idiotic sentence that suppresses this difference runs: "We are against all forms of violence in political life." . . . But our oft-praised free and democratic system . . . is itself a gigantic act of violence[, which] manifests itself only reluctantly and in exceptional situations with batons and guns. In its daily and normal occurrence, it flourishes in "independent"

newspapers, in value-free science, in "humane" culture, in "friendly" work-place environments, in church, fashion, and sports. . . . Violence is integral to capitalism, just as the police are integral to private property, and so long as capitalism exists, violence will not disappear.[75]

The statement is striking for how thoroughly violence dominates the authors' understanding of their society and the task of changing it. The goal, unequivocally, is revolution, waged against a system itself grounded in violence. The "latent" violence that shapes consciousness is no less real or important than forms of "manifest" violence (though the authors concede that they suffer primarily from alienation—not exploitation or deprivation—rendering their "oppression" far less severe than that experienced by the poor and by racial minorities like American blacks).[76] The system, they explain, "chooses" between the two forms of violence based on how severely its power is threatened.[77] The purpose of protest violence, then, is to make the latent violence of the system apparent either by provoking state repression or, at least, by inspiring public reflection on the complex nature of violence. Protest violence therefore aims "to enlighten" (*aufklären*). A dimension of that enlightenment is internal: "When we employ violence, we change not only our objective world, but also our subjective world . . . we break the stranglehold of the norms we have internalized."[78]

.   .   .

The line it is drawn
The curse it is cast
Bob Dylan, "The Times
   They Are A-Changin'"

Conscious of the barriers they faced, activists serious about revolution turned with great urgency in the late 1960s to the questions of what constituted revolutionary agency, what class or other group might be the "revolutionary subject," and how it could best be activated or supported. It is from this field of questions that Weatherman and the RAF emerged. Each group offered what it felt was a way for the New Left to transcend its limits and build, in Weatherman's phrase, a "strategy to win" in the face of imposing odds.

However confidently American and German activists may have identified themselves as revolutionaries, they made up only small segments of their societies and had little apparent means of actually threatening state or corporate power. More fundamentally, societies like the United States and West Germany seemed to preclude in their very structures the possibility of revolution—a condition Marcuse spelled out in his 1964 book *One-Dimensional Man*. Marcuse observed that gross exploitation no longer defined advanced industrial societies, and that they therefore lacked the foundational "contradiction" between capital and wage labor that had served as the "objective" basis for revolutionary socialist politics. On the contrary, the relatively low levels of social antagonism the two countries experienced in the 1950s and early 1960s reflected in part their "objective" achievements, chiefly their "increased standard of living" and "overwhelming efficiency" from a technological and organizational standpoint.[79] In the face of these achievements, Marcuse lamented, "the very idea of qualitative change recedes."[80] With few exceptions, citizens extended their loyalty to "the whole," to the entire system they credited for their prosperity, security, and comfort.

Given the affluence of postwar society, any widespread revolt would have to be largely a moral and aesthetic response to the various conditions that served the interests of "domination." Chief among them were the perpetuation of unnecessary forms of alienated labor; the persistence of poverty amid immense wealth; racial inequality (in the United States); the maintenance of peace with the Soviet Union by constant preparation for war; the degradation of the environment; and the restriction of autonomy by administration and "one-dimensional" forms of thought and culture. To the extent that he had hope, Marcuse vested it in the possibility that some would engage in a "Great Refusal" of the entire system. Such a refusal, as the source of hope for those "without hope," was most likely to come from the "outcasts and outsiders, the exploited and persecuted of other races and colors" who were largely excluded from the benefits of advanced industrial society.[81] The rebellion of blacks and other people of color in the mid 1960s showed Marcuse's prescience and affirmed his hope. By the late 1960s, Marcuse also saw a hint of genuine revolutionary promise in the New Left, whose activism derived largely from ethical and existential bases.[82] Yet student and youth activism had failed to break the identification of millions with capitalist systems that, despite growing tensions, continued to deliver very real rewards. Unable to win the allegiance of the masses, the New Left appeared to have reached the structural limit of its revolt.

For the New Left to transcend this limit, new approaches were required. In America, ideological and strategic debates were carried out most strenuously within SDS, where Marxism had become the common coin of political discussion. Some SDSers took to Marxism with striking zeal, as if they had discovered a previously hidden language that promised to make transparent the deep structure of their society. Yet in the rush to tap its analytical power, activists often applied Marxism with little sophistication or willingness to revise assumptions that squared poorly with contemporary realities. This was conspicuously true of those who, like the Progressive Labor Party (commonly called PL), clung to the idea that the industrial working class was the exclusive agent of revolutionary change.

PL, which had started as a small Maoist group in the mid 1960s, vied by the end of the decade for control over national SDS. With its members' tactical skill and talent for Marxist exegesis, PL gained a foothold in important campus chapters, among them Harvard SDS, and considerable influence in the organization as a whole. PL argued that the duty of students was to enhance workers' struggles. As its main initiative, it tried to build "worker-student alliances" on campuses, while condemning militancy—and violence especially—as dangerous expressions of "left-wing adventurism" divorced from "mass struggle." Yet PL largely failed to create lasting alliances between students and workers, underscoring both the weaknesses of its political vision and the New Left's isolation.

In its dogmatism and dour affect, PL elicited considerable criticism and even ridicule within the New Left. The future Weatherman Russell Neufeld had graduated in 1968 from Vermont's Goddard College and then entered graduate school at Harvard. He recalls the Harvard PL chapter arguing that "there's no such thing as black culture and white culture [but] only working-class culture and bourgeois culture." "It occurred to me," he joked years later, "that you could only say that in Harvard Yard."[83] The radical journalist Andrew Kopkind was unsparing in his derision, concluding in 1969: "PL peoples a Tolkein middle-earth of Marxist-Leninist hobbits and orcs, and speaks in a runic tongue intelligible only to such creatures. It is all consistent and utterly logical within its own confines. But that land at last is fantasy. The real world begins where PL ends."[84]

PL's chief national rival in SDS, the Revolutionary Youth Movement (RYM, pronounced "rim"), emerged in late 1968, beginning less as a formal faction than as a group of activists and friends with a similar political outlook and a shared dislike of PL. Those forming RYM coalesced in the Michigan-Ohio region of SDS, home to a new breed of SDS militant. Jim Mellen, immersing himself in the student organization upon his return from Africa, joined ranks with Bill Ayers, Diana Oughton, and

Terry Robbins. Ayers, the son of a Chicago energy executive, had graduated from East Lansing's Michigan State, where he engaged in early anti-draft activities. He then used his enthusiasm, initiative, and famous charm to become a leader in the Ann Arbor chapter of SDS at the University of Michigan. Oughton, the daughter of a wealthy Illinois businessman, had become radicalized while working in Guatemala and now ran, with Ayers, an experimental school for young children. Robbins, from Ohio's Kent State University, rounded out the inseparable foursome.

Excited by the militancy at August's Democratic Convention and the recent spike in interest in SDS everywhere, they set out to transform SDS's identity in their region. As part of the so-called Jesse James Gang they took over the leadership of the Ann Arbor SDS, foreshadowing the conflict between PL and the Weathermen. Equally important, they used confrontational action, an in-your-face politics, and their boisterous, even anarchic, spirit to help build large SDS chapters at colleges and universities in such places as Ypsilanti and Kalamazoo, Michigan—never before strongholds of student activism. Mellen, contrasting their appeal with the failure of their rivals, explained, "We wanted all kinds of people to rebel. Also, our dynamism, our ability to manipulate symbols, our charismatic leadership and ability to move crowds proved frightening to some of these staid Stalinist intellectuals, who were frightened by crowds, frightened by new ideas, frightened by the massive, impetuous, spontaneous development of people's feelings. Hence, they hated us with a passion."[85]

At a national level, their activities culminated in the presentation of a proposal, called "Toward a Revolutionary Youth Movement" and conceived chiefly by Mellen, at a National Council meeting of SDS in December 1968. Asserting that SDS's "most crucial ideological decision" was to determine "its direction with regards to the working class," the proposal urged that SDS organize white working-class youths as a way of reaching workers as a whole.[86] Working-class youths, RYM reasoned, were open to a radical message by virtue of their limited stake in a system that subjected them to the draft, few economic opportunities, and harassment by authorities. The New Left, to play a revolutionary role, would have to transform itself from a middle-class student movement, hamstrung by its commitment to "student power" (this, RYM explained, was a form of "economism" rooted in students' "petite-bourgeois" class interest) and strongest still at "elite campuses," into a trans-class youth movement that penetrated into the junior colleges, the high schools, and even the military.[87] Militancy, RYM conceded, might alienate older workers, but would be impressive to youth and was therefore an important tool in their radicalization. RYM also insisted on the vanguard status of black radicals, and the Black Panthers especially, in the movement as a whole. Radicalizing working-class white youth therefore meant educating them about racism and the need to accept black leadership.

The infusion of revolutionary "ideology" into SDS caused a dramatic shift in the organization's discourse and culture. Marxist theory, though giving the New Left a language with which to talk about class and to understand global struggles, largely served to tangle SDS in factional, jargon-laden debates reminiscent of the sectarianism of the Old Left. (The RYM proposal had been followed by a torrent of critiques and rebuttals, each of which invoked the letter of Marx, Lenin, and Mao to accuse the other of deviation from the "correct" analysis paving the proper revolutionary path.)[88] This new climate disillusioned many SDS veterans and repelled newcomers, many of whom had little comprehension of the often esoteric arguments between the organized factions. Bernardine Dohrn was one of SDS's later adherents. She had grown up in a Republican family in Wisconsin, attended law school at the University of Chicago, and then, after Martin Luther King Jr. brought his "Poor People's Campaign" north, immersed herself in the contentious politics of race and class of Chicago. Schooled in organizing by activists from the southern civil rights movement, her main work was assisting tenants associations as they battled Chicago's slum lords. Dohrn became active in SDS in 1968, rising within a year to a position of national leadership within the male-dominated organization. SDS, when she joined, was "famous for being anti-leadership and decentralized and grassroots and anarchistic." By 1969, however, "the ideological debates," in which Dohrn reluctantly, if skillfully, participated, had "reduced everybody to nitwits" and left SDS "talking in slogans."[89]

As an expression of SDS's emerging class politics, some sharply repudiated their identity as students. A column in the SDS newspaper in the fall of 1968, co-authored by the future Weatherwoman Cathy Wilkerson, had stated bluntly: "The university is a place DEDICATED to the perpetuation of class exploitation" and urged SDSers to "de-studentize" their lives.[90] RYM insisted that activists' acceptance of their "student classification" had been responsible for the "reactionary tendencies in SDS."[91] Others denigrated the cultural expressions of New Left rebellion. At one extreme, PL members rejected long hair and drug use as signs of "bourgeois" self-absorption and styled themselves as disciplined, short-haired proletarians, clad in work shirts. To have a place in the revolu-

tion, many seemed to believe, one had to renounce one's prior socialization and affiliate strongly with some properly revolutionary group.

In the spring and early summer of 1969, eleven SDS members affiliated with RYM drafted a 15,000-word statement titled "You Don't Need
a Weatherman to Know Which Way the Wind Blows" after a lyric from
Bob Dylan's "Subterranean Homesick Blues." (The title, Mellen recalls,
was slapped on at the last minute with little deliberation. The tract was
nearly named "The Vandal Statement," both to quote the line "the pump
don't work cause the vandals took the handles" from the same Dylan song
and to capture the group's ambition to "disarm the United States.")[92] The
statement's principal author was J. J. (John Jacobs), a charismatic but notoriously domineering Columbia graduate who had defected from PL and
now used his considerable knowledge of Marxist theory on behalf of a
new revolutionary model. With the statement, the RYM members sought
to limit PL's power in SDS by responding to what they felt were PL's here-
sies: its single-minded focus on the industrial working class; its refusal to
fully support the Black Panthers and Vietnam's National Liberation
Front (PL opposed "all nationalisms" as antithetical to "proletarian internationalism"); and its opposition to SDS's youth politics. The statement appeared in a special issue of *New Left Notes* printed for SDS's National Convention in Chicago in late June, where PL and RYM were
primed for a showdown.

True to predictions, the convention was notable for vitriol among the
dominant factions. One reporter describing the mood in the vast, dank
auditorium, observed: "SDS isn't the free and open, free form group it
once was. . . . Increasingly it is bedeviled by the incomprehensible, Marxist sectarianism which wrecked the old left, as people calling themselves
Maoist and Leninist tussle over abstruse, revolutionary metaphysics in
a social atmosphere that is depressingly Stalinoid and paranoid."[93] In
the proceedings, RYM adherents and others rallying around the "Weatherman" statement successfully portrayed PL as anathema to SDS. With
shrewd determination and great drama, they expelled PL by means of
plebiscite. (Duplicity may have been involved as well. The Weatherman
Johnny Lerner recently alleged that he and two other SDSers threw out
pro-PL ballots; if true, the group, with "democratic" in its name, rigged
perhaps its most pivotal election.)[94] From the rubble of the convention,
in which SDS crumbled into several warring parts, Weatherman was born.

The meeting concluded with the election of a number of "Weatherman" advocates as SDS's national officers. Among these were Bernardine
Dohrn; Mark Rudd, the former head of Columbia SDS, who became a

nationally known figure during the 1968 protests; and the veteran organizers Bill Ayers and Jeff Jones. This group and their supporters, known
collectively as the Weathermen, now controlled SDS's national office in
Chicago and the SDS newspaper *New Left Notes*. Though PL, based in
Boston, insisted that it was the true SDS, most New Leftists recognized
the Weathermen as the organization's leadership. But many rank-and-
file SDSers did not identify with either Weatherman, PL, or any of the
smaller factions. As they withheld their support, SDS functionally dissolved as a national organization.

Weatherman represented much more than an answer to PL. The statement offered what the Weathermen felt was a bold new direction for SDS
(or what was left of it) and a way for the New Left to make itself into a
genuinely revolutionary movement. Though not all Weatherman followers were necessarily versed in the detail of the cumbersome statement,
it nonetheless articulated the key components of the group's politics to
which all Weathermen at least implicitly adhered.

The essence of Weatherman's ideology was contained in the statement's opening declaration that "the main struggle going on in the world
today is between US imperialism and the national liberation struggles
against it." Weatherman gave this conflict the status of the world's "principal contradiction" and announced that the task of the revolutionary
was "to solve this principal contradiction" on the side of "the oppressed."
The goal was "a classless world."[95]

Targeting imperialism, the Weathermen took aim at their society's apparent crowning achievement: its vast wealth. "We are within the heart-
land of a world-wide monster," they proclaimed. "The US empire . . .
channels wealth, based upon the labor and resources of the rest of the
world, into the United States. . . . [A]ll of the Holiday Inns, all of Hertz's
automobiles, your television set, car and wardrobe already belong, to a
large degree, to the people of the rest of the world."[96] Weatherman also
rejected the approach to socialism of much of the American left. To
Weatherman, the comparative privilege of the American working class
made any effort to organize domestic workers without addressing the
exploitation of foreign labor an expression of "national chauvinism."
Furthermore, the "white skin privilege" of white workers virtually precluded the possibility of their alliance with blacks, who had a lesser stake
in supporting a system in which they would always be subordinate to
whites, irrespective of their economic status.[97]

Weatherman concluded that the impulse to revolution in the United
States—at least initially—could not possibly come from the adult white

working class. Instead, it would come from three main sources: libera- [*need revi'n from below* — handwritten] tion movements in the Third World, the struggle of American blacks, and the activism of white working-class youths supporting the first two. To the Weathermen, Third World movements were chiefly responsible for the current "crisis of American imperialism," manifest not only in America's futile intervention in Vietnam but also in conflicts at home spawned or exacerbated by the war, from widespread protest to rampant anti-authoritarianism and even, Weatherman insisted, the breakdown of the family.[98] Beyond declaring the Black Panthers to be the leaders of the American movement, Weatherman held that blacks could overthrow imperialism "alone if necessary."[99] Weatherman hoped, however, that blacks would be joined in doing so by white working-class youths. The immediate task of SDS was therefore to take the message of militant anti-imperialism to working-class youths in their own communities and build a "mass revolutionary movement" that, like the Chinese "Red Guards," would "participate in violent and illegal struggle."[100]

Though late-1960s radicals often invoked the notion of imperialism, [*notion of "imperialism"* — handwritten] they rarely defined it with any specificity and thereby avoided confronting its problems as an analytical frame. Principally, they were hard pressed to demonstrate a strongly economic—and hence narrowly imperialist—motive for American intervention in Vietnam and other parts of the Third World. Neither the natural resources, nor labor, nor markets of poor countries like Vietnam were vital to the U.S. economy, in which exports and foreign investments played only secondary roles. In this light, the charge that the Vietnam War was fought essentially for the sake of corporate profits appears grossly exaggerated. Less credible still was Weatherman's claim that *every* commodity in the United States was somehow the result of imperialist plunder.

The notion of imperialism fared far better, however, as a general description of U.S. power internationally. The United States, according to both the proponents and critics of its policies, sought to retain or expand its "spheres of influence." Though individual countries like Cuba or Vietnam might fall to communism without any great impact on the domestic economy, the United States could scarcely afford to lose whole *regions* like Latin America or Southeast Asia. The economist Harry Magdoff defended the use of the term "imperialism" along precisely these lines:

> [A]ttempts to explain isolated actions in "bookkeeping" terms make no sense. Small Latin American countries that produce relatively little profit are important in United States policy-making because control over all of Latin America is important. . . . [T]he killing and destruction in Vietnam

and the expenditure of vast sums of money are not balanced in the eyes
of U.S. policy makers against profitable business opportunities in Vietnam;
rather they are weighed according to the judgment of military and political
leaders on what is necessary to control and influence Asia.[101]

The other side of this image of American power was the sense that many
Third World populations rising in concert *could* effectively erode the American empire. Russell Neufeld, reflecting on the optimism he felt in the late
1960s, pointed to just this sense. Raised in a progressive Jewish household in Long Island, he became an activist at a very early age (he was
twelve at the time of his first march). A regional director of "Vietnam Summer" in 1967, Neufeld found himself attracted by 1969 to Weatherman's
internationalism and militant approach to protesting the war. As the American war effort faltered and left-wing movements worldwide gained
strength, he came to think "that the Vietnamese revolution would be decisive" in a process of global revolution—a position akin to "believing in
the domino theory, but thinking it was good."[102] Weatherman's task was
to help topple the last (and first) great domino: the United States itself.

Fighting imperialism, American activists were able to transcend their
national identities and affiliate with a movement of world-historical importance and great moral force. In implying the possibility of *global* emancipation, anti-imperialism spoke powerfully to the utopian longings at
the heart of the New Left. Believing that the world's liberation required
not only revolt in the Third World but also militant and even violent rebellion in the centers of imperialist power, the Weathermen made themselves bearers of the possibility of perfect, global justice. Jim Mellen,
speaking in the radical parlance of the times, explained, "We [the Weath-
ermen] figured ourselves a small leadership group of a mass movement
which could have a critical role in the development of the history of imperialism: That is very heavy stuff."[103]

American activists' connection to anti-imperialism was often rooted
in experience. Neufeld had visited Cuba in December 1968 on the tenth
anniversary of the Cuban revolution and marveled at the "unbelievable
gains" Cuban society had made with America "sitting on top of it."[104]
Other American activists, among them a great many Weathermen, had
similar experiences traveling with the "Venceremos Brigades"—the
teams of young people who, starting in 1969, made trips to Cuba to cut
sugarcane and learn about Cuba and the world. Face-to-face encounters
with Vietnamese proved equally inspiring. In 1967, Dohrn had traveled
with an SDS delegation to Bratislava, Yugoslavia, where she met North

Vietnamese and NLF representatives. The Vietnamese utterly "captivated," "dazzled," and, ultimately, "sobered" the Americans. Many of the Vietnamese had traveled for weeks on foot through jungles and battle zones just to attend the meeting; their pathos made an overwhelming impression on Dohrn, who described the American delegation as "serious," but also "exuberant and into having fun." The Vietnamese urged the young activists to adopt a "big picture strategy" in their opposition to the war and kept asking, to their great annoyance, what their *parents* thought about the conflict. The Vietnamese also patiently explained why, given their resolve and military approach, an American victory was impossible. As a result, Dohrn boasted, "we were able to predict the subsequent failure of every U.S. military and political strategy." Dohrn then went to Prague and Frankfurt, where she met activists from across the world. The whole experience was "a big dose of internationalism" that gave her and the other Americans "a mission, a purpose . . . and a sense of what our role was" in the global movement.[105]

Anti-imperialism, finally, offered an antidote to a central frustration of New Left radicals, namely, the indifference or hostility of workers to the message of revolution. To some avowed anti-imperialists, the problem remained one of "false consciousness," wherein the meager privileges and ideological conditioning of American workers blinded them to their exploitation. To Weatherman, which insisted that the benefit of imperialism to American workers was great, the problem was largely one of *true* consciousness. Weatherman tried to confront a possibility it felt the New Left was unwilling to face: that a more equal distribution of global wealth required that citizens of the First World, workers included, give something up materially; to preach otherwise, Weathermen believed, was to sell out the Third World and mislead Americans.[106] To Scott Braley, who "didn't know a political tendency from a fog" when he joined the group, this aspect of Weatherman's message made intuitive sense. "We were up front about that," he explained. "A lot of left groups at that point said, 'Oh no, we just want to end the war and it's not going to mean anything to you.' Well it is going to mean something to you. You're not going to have two cars [and] gasoline that costs a quarter of what it does for everybody else in the world. . . . Sorry, but you're not." More and more, Braley found discussions about the war that did not mention "the 'I' word" "tortured."[107]

However much rooted in experience or the desire for a better world, Weatherman's statement was plagued with profound difficulties that haunted the group throughout its life. One was Weatherman's basic mode of conceptualization. The group transposed onto a global stage obsolete Marxist understandings of class struggle within a single capitalist economy. Instead of the explosive contradiction between capitalists and proletariat, Weatherman posited a near-mythic conflict between imperialist oppressors and Third World oppressed. It thus substituted a new reductive dualism for an older one and collapsed the complexities of radical politics into a single choice for or against the world's (would-be) liberators. In truth, neither the "imperialist powers" nor those resisting them were as unified as their vision implied. Failing to see this, Weatherman fell prey to the seductive optimism of global voices like Che Guevara and Mao Tse-tung, who insisted, in ways both romantic and severe, that revolution was the direction of world history, making victory near certain. The group also risked idealizing movements whose actions often belied their emancipatory rhetoric. Years later, Neufeld conceded that he and other American radicals had "greatly underestimated" the "difficulty of Third World countries in building genuinely democratic revolutions."[108]

When discussing the means of revolution in the United States—and especially the role of blacks in it—the Weatherman again translated potentially constructive judgments into contradictory and untenable theses. Roth, like others in the group, had grown up with an abiding interest in race. From an early age, he recalls, "My sense of justice . . . and the person I wanted to be were inextricably linked to what happened with African Americans."[109] As he became involved in antiracist struggles, a consistent message to white activists emerged from blacks, whether students at Columbia or national figures like Malcolm X. It held, in essence: "There are all these racists out there, they're white. We're not going to organize them. You have to organize them. . . . [D]on't worry about organizing black people and being our saviors in that way—we can lead our own movement."[110] For Roth, part of the attraction of Weatherman was precisely its understanding of how deeply this kind of condescension ran. But it was one thing, as Roth urged, to respect the autonomy of blacks and work to overcome racism in one's community; it was another to assert on the basis of a false assumption about blacks' "centrality to the economy," as the Weatherman statement had done, that blacks could somehow defeat American imperialism *by themselves*. With this position, the Weathermen plainly idealized blacks, imputing to them capacities they could not possibly possess.

This view of revolution forced Weatherman into wild reversals on the crucial question of agency. In one voice, Weatherman suggested that whites could at best play only an auxiliary role in a struggle in which

they were ultimately unnecessary. In another, it anointed young working-
class whites and their militant leaders—the Weathermen themselves—
important players in the revolutionary crusade. In a similar vein, Weatherman suggested that white American workers were irreversibly on the side
of imperialism, only to stipulate that once imperialism was on the verge
of toppling, they would discover that their "long-term interests" had actually favored its defeat.[111] Finally, Weatherman's belief that in a just
world, working-class whites would have to cede some measure of their
wealth may have had a certain logic; but it was a poor basis for actually
organizing them.

Weatherman's cynicism about the working class drew sharp attacks
from the left. One indignant critic concluded that Weatherman's message "is not that workers are robbed by the capitalist class of the sur-
plus value they create . . . [but] that the workers themselves are rob-   *critics*
bers."[112] Some of Weatherman's initial allies objected so strongly to this
position that immediately following SDS's June convention, they formed
the Revolutionary Youth Movement II (RYM II).[113] Holding that "the
leading force" of the revolution "must eventually be the proletariat,"
RYM II called for the creation of a Leninist vanguard party.[114] Less dogmatic critics speculated that Weatherman had abandoned the hope of organizing a mass movement and, hence, the democratic values of the New
Left.[115] Still others accused Weatherman of being unable to rationally
assess the movement's actual capabilities. "We are not now free to fight
the revolution except in fantasy," Carl Oglesby, a former president of
SDS, declared.[116]

The problems with Weatherman's statement went beyond its assumptions and conclusions. It was so steeped in sectarian concerns that
it largely failed to resonate within the movement, let alone outside. The
New Left "appears to have utterly and decisively freaked out," the New
Leftist Paul Breines lamented. "Normal and intense factional debate
has . . . been replaced by a blaring carnival of fetishized and mind clog-
ging rhetoric. . . . It is as if there were a self-propelling mechanism which
brings everyone into the general reduction of the *entire terrain* of debate
and consciousness to the level of retail sanity within wholesale madness."[117] A combination of insecurity and exaggerated self-importance,
Breines thought, had led to the New Left's "self-alienation" and "self-
mystification."[118]

Yet the precarious position of the New Left at the end of the 1960s
was itself a potent source of its destructive in-fighting. Marxism, as a
"science" of social change, has always been reluctant to view historical

processes as subjective or contingent, positing instead structural "laws" and the clash of "objective" class interests as the primary motors of social transformation. The challenge of the revolutionary, then, is to "seize destiny" and help realize historical possibilities that have a momentum not reducible to human will. The New Left had good reason to adopt this perspective. If revolution were *only* the function of moral choice or political will, then the New Left's revolutionary endeavor would be disconcertingly subjective. Given the massive imbalance of power between the movement and "the system," that prospect could be frightening. "We went from being young kids with a moral vision, to realizing we were up against the heaviest power structure in the world," David Gilbert recalled. "There was [a] sense [that] . . . either we get a power base or retreat. And so people looked for almost what I considered magical solutions, because it was scary."[119]

New Leftists generated a number of such "solutions"—from the Vietnamese to American blacks, industrial workers, and working-class youths—over which they sharply divided. They imputed to each not only implausible powers but also "objective" reasons as to why its revolutionary potential was so great. In this way, New Leftists tried to compensate for their political weakness. At times, Weatherman presented revolution as a process that already had inexorable momentum. In late September 1969, a reporter asked Mark Rudd, who had just declared that the "primary purpose" of the Weathermen was to fight, how exactly the tiny group planned to defeat capitalism. "It doesn't make any difference what you or I say or what I want to see," Rudd replied. "The only significant thing that bears on this question of revolution is that it has already started. The Vietnamese have made the revolution against the U.S. . . . . [Y]ou and I don't have a choice."[120]

Weatherman's statement paved the way for the group's next task: molding itself into a "white fighting force" that would open up the United States as a "second front" in the worldwide struggle against imperialism. What was needed was militant leadership that would demonstrate to American youth the need for violent insurrection. Weatherman was to provide that leadership.

Drawing on the theory of Régis Debray, a young, well-educated member of the French elite who had become deeply involved through journalism in revolutionary movements in Latin America, the Weathermen held that the experiences of Third World guerrillas had special relevance for the United States. In the mid 1960s, in consultation with Fidel Castro, Debray wrote *Revolution in the Revolution?* to communicate the lessons of the Cuban revolution. Though addressed specifically to Latin Americans, the book was read by leftists all over the world. Debray stressed that the Cuban revolution had not been made by a mass movement led by a communist party but by a small band of guerrillas using light weapons to attack military and political targets. Rooted in the aspirations of the Cuban people, the guerrillas' violence soon instigated a mass revolt; Cuba had thus "skipped" the protracted phase of mass mobilization that many Latin American revolutionaries had thought necessary.[121] In Debrayism, Weatherman found an alternative to the "base-building" approach of much of the American left, as well as a rationale for engaging immediately in violence. According to Jeff Jones, the Weathermen concluded from Debray that "a small group of very politically advanced, ideologically committed militant people can carry out revolutionary actions that will serve as an inspiration for other people."[122] Debrayist violence, in short, was *exemplary* violence and did not have to produce tactical victories to be successful. The Weathermen need not, therefore, be deterred by their tiny numbers and "military" inexperience.

[margin note: exemplary violence]

The Weathermen spent the summer of 1969 preparing to turn their Debrayist vision into reality. Part of their effort was to transform themselves into disciplined cadres capable of committing "exemplary" violence. Here Weatherman drew on Che Guevara's *foco* theory, which called for the building of small, semi-autonomous cells guided by a central leadership. Weatherman set up collectives of one to several dozen members in a number of cities, among them New York, Philadelphia, Buffalo, Boston, Seattle, Cincinnati, Detroit, and Chicago (some of these had been established by RYM at the beginning of the summer, prior to the formal creation of Weatherman in June). Weatherman's leadership, calling itself the "Weatherbureau" and based at the SDS National Office in Chicago, guided the five hundred or so people belonging to the group.

[margin note: training]

Weatherman sought, above all, to destroy any vestiges of "bourgeois individualism" that would dilute members' commitment to the group and its goal of revolution. To this end, the collectives instituted a strict set of rules, rites, and rituals. All personal property was either shared or renounced outright. To sustain themselves and fund their political activities, the members stole food from grocery stores and begged or borrowed money from friends and family (though some held jobs, turning their income over to the group). Even so, the Weathermen were nearly broke and lived in Spartan dwellings on a diet of noodles and other simple foods. Nais Raulet had entered the University of Michigan in 1968 at seventeen and within a year plunged into the world of Weatherman. While in

[margin note: collective rules, rigidity]

a Detroit collective, she worked full-time, donating her modest income to the collective, which was already purchasing firearms. "Guns," she lamented, "took priority over food."[123] In the collectives, conventional comforts—from conversations with old friends to afternoons devoted to idle pleasures—were forbidden as well. Entranced by the Leninist notion of "democratic centralism," Weatherman exalted their leaders, granting them immense power to control—and, as former "cadre" members would later charge—to manipulate those below them. In some collectives, nearly all personal decisions in the collectives, as basic as where one went at any given time, were subject to the approval of the leadership.[124]

As part of its infamous "smash monogamy" campaign, Weatherman mandated the splitting apart of couples, whose affection was deemed impermissibly "possessive" or even "selfish"; the forced rotation of sex partners, determined largely by the leadership for reasons both political and, it is alleged, crudely "personal" (the charge is that some male leaders essentially shuttled particular women between collectives in order to sleep with them);[125] and even eruptions of group sex in which taboos broke down in variously uncomfortable and exhilarating scenes of libidinal confusion. On occasion, collectives deemed the "most advanced" in "smashing monogamy" were called in to discipline others, savaging their members for their "counterrevolutionary" attachments and purging those deemed incorrigible.[126] To sharpen their skills at fighting, the collectives held karate practice; to spread their message, they spray-painted "revolutionary" slogans in subway stations and on building walls. All this was done on virtually no sleep and frequently on drugs—large amounts of speed initially, but also pot and LSD.[127] (Phoebe Hirsch, a Weatherwoman based in Chicago, confessed to having become "hooked on speed" just to keep up with the group's "frantic" pace; fearful of a breakdown, she left the collective and went to New York, where she "collapsed on [her] sister's doorstep," before being drawn back to the group by a friend.)[128] Finally, Weatherman used "criticism-self-criticism" sessions to keep members unflinchingly wed to the "correct line."

By all accounts, the "criticism-self-criticism" sessions—also called "CSC" or "Weatherfries"—were the most harrowing aspect of life in the collectives. Loosely derived from techniques used by Maoist revolutionaries in China, CSC ostensibly sought to encourage political and emotional honesty and group bonding (criticism came first so as to prevent members from using "self-criticism" to preempt the scrutiny of others). More deeply, the Weathermen used the practice to confront and root out

[margin annotation: smashing monogamy]

[margin annotation: CSC sessions]

their racist, individualist, and chauvinist tendencies. In tone and substance, the sessions were part political trial, part hazing, part shock therapy, part exorcism, and, in a word used by more than one former member, part "brainwashing."[129] At their most intense, collectives singled out individuals for "criticism" and then berated them—five, seven, a dozen hours or more without break—about their flaws. Though they were designed to break down barriers among members, the effect of the sessions was to enhance suspicions and rivalries within the group and to suppress fears and doubts.[130] Ayers recalls being denounced as a "liberal creep" after confessing to a friend his affection for the poem "To Posterity" by Bertolt Brecht, which pleaded that future generations "judge not too harshly" the necessarily harsh actions of revolutionaries.[131] Hirsch explained that the group would batter you until you admitted, in a moment of exhausted "catharsis," to being "deep down a white supremacist."[132] Wilkerson complained that the Weathermen set the stakes unbearably high as they judged one another, such that some "error" of political understanding was declared "a mortal sin that will stain history forever."[133] Raulet described CSC as a "vicious tool to disgrace people into accepting collective discipline."[134] Dohrn wondered years later: "I don't know if there's a good Maoism somewhere, but the Maoism that we adopted was stupid and lethal."[135]

Life in the collectives could be especially difficult for the women, who made up nearly half of Weatherman. On the one hand, their strong presence in the group was evidence of how deeply outrage at the Vietnam War and racism cut across gender lines; women and men joined Weatherman for essentially the same reasons. On the other hand, the Weatherwomen had significantly different experiences from their male counterparts, as a growing awareness of sexism was part of their political awakening. Hirsch, in a scene familiar to women activists, recalled her aggravation "sitting silent" in the mid 1960s in the University of Wisconsin's "Socialist Club" while the men, rapt in theoretical discussion, "were being 'profound.'" Later, while in an apartment of the "Up Against the Wall Motherfuckers," she observed the men debating and the women "cooking, cleaning, and changing diapers," leading her to ask "So what's different here?"[136] Future Weatherwomen, similarly frustrated, at times openly challenged the male domination of New Left organizations, worked to have them address issues of gender oppression, and participated in all-women organizations and initiatives. Yet in Weatherman, the women were confined mostly to the "second-tier leadership," had to mute or disavow certain of their feminist beliefs, and, no matter

their activist credentials, had to prove their commitment once again by
showing their ability to engage in "independent" actions as part of
"women's cadres."[137] Raulet explained: "The male Weather line was,
'Our women can fight as well as anyone. Our women can kick ass. Our
women are tough.' [So] we all spat nails and wore combat boots."[138] Yet
for Raulet, the actions of the women's cadres were driven by a coerced
machismo and encouraged neither true autonomy nor solidarity among
the women. Finally, while the group's sexual politics provided a space
for women to assert desire and explore relationships with one another,
they also invited the sexual exploitation of female members.

As word of the group's behavior seeped out, the "Weathermyth"
steadily grew, and rumors quickly spread. One collective, it was alleged,
had skinned and eaten an alley cat.[139] The Weathermen themselves, while
acknowledging excesses, remember the collectives as being far more serious and purposeful than such sensational and surely apocryphal stories suggested. Part of their energy was devoted to the sober study of "revolutionary" texts. Deep friendships *did* develop within the group, beyond
the contrivances of the "revolutionary bond." In moments declared "off
the record," members could speak more frankly about their anxieties.
And some of the collectives were certainly more restrictive than others.
The collectives nonetheless remained chaotic and often dismal places,
driven by a strange combination of excess and asceticism, self-indulgence
and self-renunciation. Psychologically harsh environments, they re-
warded assertive and even aggressive personalities, while chewing up
those less confident or able to defend themselves. Reflecting on what he
described as the group's "cultish" qualities, Neufeld confessed: "I think
all that stuff was really horrible" and caused "real harm to a lot of
people."[140] One Weatherwoman in the Cleveland collective, where ten
people slept in two bedrooms on two ratty mattresses, recalled: "Our
lifestyle was in so many ways so hideous back then." Observing the de-
pressing scene, she doubted whether the group represented "a path that
we should go in. . . . Before I joined Weatherman I had . . . a sense of the
counterculture and radical political movements leading to something positive, but I think once I was in Weatherman . . . I knew there was something fundamentally wrong."[141] Raulet had similar reservations, which
drove her from the group within a matter of months. Weatherman, she
recalled, felt "that because we were in [an] army . . . we, ourselves, were
not going to be able to live in any way suitable for human beings. We
were well aware we weren't living like human beings. We weren't even

acting like human beings. We would have been unfit for any society we wanted to see by the time [the revolution] was over."[142]

The main work of the Weatherman collectives in the summer of 1969 was to build enthusiasm for demonstrations in Chicago on October 8–11 in which the group would showcase its strategy of leading working-class youths in revolt. The June SDS meeting had ratified a call for a "National Action," conceived of as a series of conventional protests against the war, racism, and domestic repression. Weatherman, now the leadership of SDS, rebaptized the demonstrations the "Days of Rage" and gave them a new purpose: "to establish another front against imperialism right here in America—to 'bring the war home.'"[143] The choice of Chicago was significant. National SDS, put off by the Yippies and fearful of police violence, had not supported the demonstrations at the Democratic convention in 1968 (although individual SDSers, including several future Weathermen, participated in the demonstrations). The Weathermen would redeem SDS's failure. They left the scenario for Chicago vague but spoke of their intention to "tear up pig city" and "kick ass" when fighting the police. Violence was the incessant theme of Weathermen promoting the action to student activists around the country, and rumors quickly spread that they intended to bring guns to Chicago. RYM II, fearful of the Weathermen, planned to hold its own, nonviolent demonstrations in Chicago the same weekend.

To attract working-class youths to the demonstration, the Weathermen leafleted at high schools, talked to teenagers at popular hangouts, and engaged in calculated displays of toughness. These included skirmishes with police and "jailbreaks" in which Weathermen invaded high school classrooms to deliver lectures about the evils of imperialism, talk up the Days of Rage, and invite the students to "escape."[144] Student reactions ranged from shock, to anger, to delight, at least at the prospect of fleeing class.[145] In one "jailbreak" at a community college in suburban Detroit, nine Weatherwomen barricaded the doors of the classroom they entered, briefly held the class hostage, and allegedly assaulted a professor, for which they were arrested and served time in jail. Though they had worn conventional clothes during the action, Weatherman later dressed them in its unofficial uniform of boots, jeans, and jean jackets, put a photo of them in a mock bust in the SDS newspaper, and dubbed the group the "Motor City Nine" (a reference to the "revolutionary" rock band "MC5" from a working-class Detroit neighborhood). In another action, Weathermen ran with Viet Cong flags on a Detroit lakeside beach where working-class kids gathered. The latter apparently took offense at the flags and promptly got into fistfights with the Weathermen, their would-be allies. Unfazed by the chilly response, the Weathermen confidently predicted that tens of thousands of youths would flock to Chicago and give birth to a "white army."

More dramatically, the Weathermen engaged prior to the Days of Rage in what Hirsch called, half seriously, "low-level molestation of the police." The purpose seemed, more than anything else, to break down internal barriers by shattering the aura of the police. Hirsch explained that at one point she had "socked [a] cop to prove to myself that I wasn't intimidated." Her audacious act, as a small-framed woman, left her feeling, "If I can do that I can do anything, because that uniform is so scary."[146]

. . .

The organization of armed resistance groups in
West Germany and West Berlin is correct, possible,
and justified.

RAF, "Das Konzept Stadtguerilla"
("The Concept of the Urban Guerrilla")

The birth of the Red Army Faction in May 1970 was both slow and sudden. In October 1968, Andreas Baader, Gudrun Ensslin, Horst Söhnlein, and Thorward Proll had been convicted of the Frankfurt arsons and sentenced to three years in prison. In June 1969, the four were released while their conviction was being appealed. Baader and Proll began working with troubled teens in two youth centers in Frankfurt. With the backing of the centers' administrators and money from SDS and private donors, they established an "apprenticeship" program with the youths. Baader and Proll led them mostly in rebellion: against the regulations of their residence halls, against the maze of institutions—from courts, to social agencies, to churches—that had tried to "reform" them; and against "the system" as a whole, presented as a main source of their difficulties with authority and troubles in life. Ensslin soon took similar initiative with young women in Frankfurt halfway houses. Without quite trying to build a "revolutionary youth movement," as Weatherman had explicitly done, Baader, Proll, and Ensslin seemed intent on shaping the disaffection of those young and disadvantaged into a source of sustained political rebellion.

In November 1969, the appeal was rejected, and Baader, Ensslin,

Proll, and Söhnlein were ordered to return to prison. Söhnlein did so, but the others chose to flee. With the help of Proll's sister Astrid and a loose network of sympathizers, they made their way to Paris, where they stayed in the vacant apartment of Régis Debray (imprisoned at the time in Bolivia for political activities). Lacking focus and direction in France, Ensslin, Baader, and Astrid Proll soon reentered the Federal Republic, leaving behind Thorward, whose commitment to the fugitive life they questioned.[147]

Buoyed by their success in hiding, Baader and Ensslin went to West Berlin in search of comrades willing to join them in some form of clandestine struggle. Among those they sought out was Horst Mahler, a radical attorney who represented young protesters and had served as Baader's lawyer in the arson trial. Ulrike Meinhof was another. Meinhof had come to know Baader and Ensslin while they worked with the Frankfurt teenagers, and she herself studied the world of Frankfurt's troubled youth. She wrote a screenplay dramatizing the struggles of the young people she met, and in December, production began on the made-for-television movie.[148]

Baader had been just the kind of adolescent in whom Meinhof now took interest. Born in Munich in 1943, he was an incorrigibly rebellious youth with a seemingly innate contempt for authority. As a teenager, he stole cars, got into fights, and created trouble in school. As a young adult living in Frankfurt and West Berlin, he shunned "bourgeois" manners, work habits, and sexual norms. With his Brandoesque swagger, streetwise demeanor, and lack of inhibitions, he became a charismatic figure among some German leftists, who were drawn to his anti-authoritarian persona (though others thought him rather ridiculous). Baader also had dark good looks, quite unlike the archetypal blond German. His appearance, it would seem, enhanced his appeal as a quasi-outsider among Germans who represented an uncommon form of (non-"Aryan") physical vitality. In political circles, and later in the RAF, Baader had little patience with theory; he preferred instead to act, providing a counterforce to what RAF members feared was their own potentially debilitating intellectualism.

Gudrun Ensslin, born in 1940 in southern Germany, embodied another kind of passion. During the early years of Nazi rule, her father, Helmut Ensslin, had been a member of the Wandervögeln, a nature-oriented youth group that offered an alternative to the highly nationalist forms of youth culture the Nazis sponsored.[149] After the war, he became a pastor in a successor organization of the Confessional Church, which had formed in the mid 1930s to resist Nazi control of German Protestantism. Its legacy was one of conscientious opposition to authoritarian conformity; Helmut, true to tradition, became a critic of the Federal Republic, especially its plans to rearm. Gudrun aspired to an even purer form of her family's principles. Attending university in Tübingen and then West Berlin, she became active in the student movement, where she emerged as a voice of great moral intensity. Günter Grass, who came to know her in Berlin, recalled that "she was idealistic, with an inborn loathing of any compromise. She had a yearning for the Absolute, the perfect solution."[150] That yearning soon provided the ethical impetus that led the RAF to take a position of "no compromise" with the powers it opposed.

A couple since 1967, Baader and Ensslin adopted "Hans" and "Grete" as nicknames during their underground travels in Europe.[151] The names, drawn from the brother and sister in the famous Grimm fairy tale, conveyed an innocence that belied their lives together as fugitives. Yet reference to the fairy tale was also eerily fitting, because it evoked the vulnerability, fatalism, and anxiety—approaching narcissistic paranoia—felt by some among Germany's postwar generation. In the macabre tale, Hans and Grete are left to die in the forest by their hateful stepmother and pliant father. Later, they are lured into a gingerbread house by a wicked old woman who intends to eat them. In a scenario plainly summoning up, to the postwar ear, the imagery of the Holocaust, the old woman plans to force Grete to assist in her brother's murder, and she is to be roasted alive in an oven. Identifying with Hans and Grete (who are saved in the story by their cunning), Baader and Ensslin seemed to fear their society as willing to abandon and devour its young.

When back in West Germany, Baader and Ensslin sought weapons, whether simply to engage in robberies to fund their lives on the run or to begin some form of armed struggle. Meinhof helped house the fugitives; Mahler, part of a circle of Berlin radicals poised for clandestine action, promised the guns. In the early morning hours of April 3, 1970, Peter Urbach, a factory worker and friend of Mahler's, led Baader, Mahler, and several others to a cemetery near the Berlin Wall, where he insisted weapons were buried. Hours of digging proved fruitless, so they returned the next night, again coming up empty. While driving away from the cemetery, Baader and the passengers in his car were pulled over by police and arrested; a second car carrying Mahler and Urbach—in fact a police informant—drove away.

No sooner was Baader back in jail than his comrades conspired to get him out. In the weeks following, Meinhof visited Baader in prison, as did Ensslin, who wore a disguise to conceal her identity. Mahler worked, successfully this time, to obtain firearms. Swayed by Ensslin's pleading, Meinhof agreed to be the linchpin of the plot to free Baader. She arranged to meet him on May 14 at the "Institute for Social Issues" in a Berlin suburb, allegedly to discuss writing a book about German youth. While Baader and Meinhof were in the library watched by a guard, two female accomplices wearing wigs helped Ensslin, masked and armed, and an armed male enter the building. They quickly freed Baader, in the process shooting the security guard and an Institute staff member, George Linke, who almost died from his wounds. The conspirators immediately went underground, and in late May, they published a communiqué in the Berlin anarchist weekly *833* announcing the formation of the Rote Armee Fraktion (Red Army Faction), or RAF.[152] The name itself was doubly provocative: RAF was, of course, the acronym for Britain's Royal Air Force, which had bombed Germany during World War II, and the "Red Army" was the Soviet military, Germany's great nemesis. Wanted posters went up throughout West Germany for Baader and Meinhof, now sought for attempted murder. Meinhof's movie was promptly withdrawn from state-run TV, and the media quickly dubbed the group the "Baader-Meinhof Gang" ("Baader-Meinhof-Bande").

The RAF did not issue its first ideological statement until eleven months later. By that point, RAF members had traveled to Jordan to train in a Palestine Liberation Organization (PLO) guerrilla camp, established safe houses throughout West Germany, built a stockpile of arms, robbed banks of tens of thousands of marks, and had several of its two dozen or so members arrested, among them Mahler. Thereafter, the RAF rarely attempted systematically to articulate its ideology; from the start, its writings were fragmentary, sloganistic, and, on important points, contradictory. Analysts have concluded from the jumble of the RAF's "theoretical" statements that its "ideology" amounted to little more than ex post facto justifications for actions not guided by a properly political agenda. Some have even doubted whether Meinhof, Ensslin, and Mahler had intended to form a clandestine fighting force when they conspired to free Baader; the shootings added greatly to their criminal status, virtually requiring that they become an underground "army."[153] Others have concluded that action *as such* was the core of the RAF's ideology, resulting in its pronounced *Theoriefeindlichkeit* (antipathy to theory), despite the many pages it wrote in defense of "guerrilla war."[154] Yet the RAF, as much as Weatherman, grew out of a political context and sought to legitimate its violence in political terms.

The fate of the West German New Left mirrored that of its American counterpart. As its revolutionary ambition increased and its conflict with the state intensified, unity broke down. Reeling from the passage of the Emergency Laws in late 1968, APO dissolved in the months following. Germany's SDS splintered into numerous factions and formally disbanded in March 1970, hopelessly divided over how to become a properly "revolutionary" group. A period of "dogmatization and resignation" set in among the stalwarts of the student movement, while new forms of political expression and experimentation—from alternative schools, to communal homes, to feminist collectives—gained momentum.[155]

The shift in climate had been severe. For several years, anti-imperialism was the dominant ideological current of the West German New Left, providing young radicals with a robust sense of mission. Rudi Dutschke, the New Left's leading theorist, promoted this new global vision. SDS's Jürgen Horlemann summarized Dutschke's position:

> Imperialism, not the proletariat, constitutes the totality of the world; the counterrevolution, not the side of revolution, currently dictates the unity of world history. How can revolutionary forces assert themselves in this totality? The answer was: the subject of the worldwide revolutionary process is the poor, the oppressed, rendering the world's principal contradiction that between imperialism and the Third World. In the metropoles, enlightened persons—and that meant above all the intelligentsia—must unite with the suffering masses of the Third World, support Third World liberation struggles, and themselves employ illegal, direct action against the state apparatus to weaken the imperialist powers.[156]

This worldview drove the 1968 "International Vietnam Congress" held in Berlin. Hosted by the German SDS and led by Dutschke (just prior to his being shot), it was the high point of the West German antiwar movement. Conference participants from throughout Europe and North America expressed their sense of the strength of anti-imperialist movements worldwide and the urgent need for militant protest. Peter Weiss proclaimed: "When we begin to destabilize the established political oligarchy . . . we are no longer spectators, but participants in the liberation struggle. The NLF . . . has given us the task to organize resistance in the metropoles. . . . Our actions must . . . include sabotage, wherever this is possible. This demands personal decisions. This demands changes in our private, individual lives."[157] Dutschke framed the challenge facing young activists with even greater drama. Warning that a U.S. victory in Vietnam might usher in a "new period of authoritarian world domination from Washington to Vladivostok," he implored: "Comrades, we don't have much time. . . . How this period of history ends depends primarily on our will."[158] The conference concluded with a march through West Berlin, during which "international solidarity" seemed at last a reality.

The reign of Dutschke's brand of anti-imperialism proved short-lived. Perhaps its mandate was too broad; perhaps it lacked a strategy for appealing to "the masses"; perhaps it paid insufficient attention to the concerns of emerging social movements like feminism and environmentalism; perhaps it presented history as too dependent on political will. Whatever the objections, Marxism-Leninism returned with a vengeance. Distressed by their isolation and increasingly convinced that real revolutionary politics were necessarily class politics, young leftists flocked in droves between 1969 and 1973 into the rapidly proliferating Marxist-Leninist groups. Several were founded by students and encouraged their members to become proletarians by going to work in factories, where they organized cells to educate workers about class struggle. Meanwhile, on the streets, they relentlessly distributed party propaganda in fierce struggles for workers' allegiances. Building on Germany's tradition of militant socialist organizations, repressed since the early 1930s, the so-called "K-groups" *(kommunistische Gruppen)* had reasonably large memberships and some influence in local and regional politics, including at the electoral level. There were in 1971 some one hundred and thirty orthodox communist organizations, twenty Maoist groups, and five Trotskyite parties, with a combined membership of 80,000.[159] (By contrast, America's student-led sectarian groups such as the PLP had tiny memberships and negligible influence outside the universities.) Yet the K-groups' impact was conspicuously weak where it mattered most: among West German workers, who took little interest in their radical message. Frustrated in their organizing, the groups devoted much of their energy to arguing with one another over such issues as the role of the vanguard party in class struggle and the relative merits of the Chinese, Soviet, and East German "models." Their popularity among young radicals in the early 1970s represented the retreat of the New Left into history (or its construction of history), where it hoped to find answers to contemporary challenges.[160]

Although also convinced of the limits of the student movement, the RAF advanced a very different understanding of revolution from that of the K-groups—one that reached back to the anti-imperialism of the Vietnam Congress, while transforming the imperative of militancy into a call to arms. As with Weatherman's, the RAF's ideology can be discerned both negatively, in the ways it criticized the mainstream Marxists of its day, and positively, as it articulated its own vision of revolution.

The RAF had no single position on class struggle. In one guise, it described itself as a communist organization and declared the working class to be a vital part of its revolutionary program. More often, however, it doubted the potential for revolutionary initiative among West German workers. In "The Concept of the Urban Guerrilla," Meinhof wrote cynically that the system "has pushed the masses so deeply into its dreck that they seem to have lost a sense of being exploited and oppressed." In exchange for cars and houses, she said, they gladly "excuse[d] the crimes of the system."[161] Attempts to organize workers based on "material" interests amounted, in the RAF's view, to "trade union economism," which strengthened workers' loyalty to the system.

Against the emphasis of the K-groups on building socialism in West Germany, the RAF advocated "proletarian internationalism" and "struggle in the metropoles," whose main task was to challenge the imperial power of the United States. The RAF charged that the fact "that the working class in West Germany and West Berlin can only think and act on a national level does not remove the fact that Capital thinks and acts on an international level."[162] The RAF denounced imperialism with unalloyed contempt, proclaiming: "Vietnam is the horrifying message to the people of the Third World that imperialism is determined to wage genocide against them when there is nothing more to extract from them as markets, military bases, natural resources, and cheap labor."[163] Though the United States was the focal point of its outrage, the RAF also targeted West Germany by virtue of its alliance with America. "By participating in development and military aid for the wars of aggression of the USA, West Germany profits from the exploitation of the Third World, but without having to take responsibility for these wars," it insisted. "No less aggressive than the USA, West Germany is less vulnerable to attack."[164]

Striking in such rhetoric is the RAF's hyperbole and seeming inability to make qualitative distinctions. As if describing the Nazis' nihilistic murders, which ultimately defied any instrumental purpose, the RAF asserted that modern imperialism systematically sought to kill those it could no longer exploit. The RAF thus translated its anger at U.S. conduct in Vietnam and elsewhere in the Third World into an untenable thesis about the nature of American power. Furthermore, the RAF extrapolated bizarrely that the West German state was *as dangerous* as the United States because its imperial designs and destructive powers were less obvious. The "new fascism, consumerism, and media domination" were "most developed" in the two countries, the RAF explained. Ensslin apparently wanted to visit the United States to meet with the Weathermen, whose "outlook and praxis" she felt were "identical" to those of the RAF.[165]

The RAF's militant support of the Palestinian cause was another expression of its anti-imperialism. The student left in Germany, like the Federal Republic as a whole, had for much of the 1960s consistently supported Israel, reflecting both its view of Middle Eastern politics and the sense that Germans had a moral obligation to support Israel's Jews. The left's attitude changed dramatically with the Six-Day War of 1967, during which Israel defeated Arab armies and occupied additional Palestinian territory. Exposed to media images of the Palestinians as underdogs and the Israelis as the chief aggressors, young German leftists became increasingly sympathetic to the Palestinian struggle. The PLO, founded in 1964, soon emerged as the leading force for the "national liberation" of Palestinians; like the Viet Cong, it fought what it described as an imperialist oppressor and had as its official goal the creation of a (secular) socialist state. For leftists worldwide, Arab nationalism was a vanguard force in the global anti-imperialist struggle.[166] This was certainly true of the German left; according to one historian, by 1968, "Radical anti-Zionism and solidarity with the Palestinian liberation struggle became in the eyes of SDS a revolutionary duty, equally as much as support for the Viet Cong."[167]

Even so, the affinity of young German leftists for the Palestinian cause was conspicuously strong. Geography in part explains the bond. The United States, not the nations of Europe, fought the Vietnam War, and Latin America, another great arena of anti-imperialist rebellion, was an ocean away. The Middle East was comparatively close to Europe, where the PLO had established a strong political presence and worked to build an active following. There was another, largely existential source of affinity between young Germans and the Palestinian cause. West German New Leftists, one may speculate, felt politically and spiritually homeless in their own country, causing them to empathize with the Palestinians' literal homelessness; the "stateless Palestinian," in short, emerged as an icon through which Germans expressed their alienation. The Nazi past, finally, drove the more extreme—and often disturbing—attitudes of German radicals toward the conflict in the Middle East. At times, their rhetoric seemed an echo of the anti-Semitism of the past. In 1970, the Frankfurt SDS chapter protested the visit to Germany of Israel's foreign minister, declaring its opposition in a flyer to "the Zionist, economically and politically par-

asitic state of Israel."[168] Interpreting such virulence, commentators have
pointed to a range of possible impulses in the New Left: a thinly veiled
anti-Semitism, essentially inherited from the Nazi generation; a largely unconscious desire to paint Israel as an arch-oppressor, and thus diminish
the guilt of Germany for its historic mistreatment of Jews; and the self-
serving sense that they, as the post-Nazi generation, were utterly free of
anti-Semitism and therefore had license to condemn Israel without
qualification or apology.[169]

German support for the Palestinians did not immediately spawn a
working alliance between German and Palestinian militants. RAF members who went to Jordan were promptly kicked out of the guerrilla
camp—their hosts found their commitment to armed struggle superficial,
and their libertine ways were anathema to Arab mores. Yet within a few
years, by which time the RAF had demonstrated its skill and staying
power, German and Palestinian guerrillas collaborated in building their
networks and engaging in joint actions.

When addressing the question of just who would make the revolution in West Germany, the RAF again provided shifting answers. In one
view, the "revolutionary subject" was decidedly *not* the proletariat, but
rather "anyone who locates his political identity in the liberation struggles of the peoples of the Third World."[170] Mahler, in another of the
RAF's manifestoes, asserted that "the revolutionary portion of the student movement . . . is today the bearer of revolutionary consciousness."[171] Elsewhere, the RAF claimed that "anyone who starts to fight"
was by definition a revolutionary.[172] The RAF condemned the K-groups
most strongly for their indulgent theorizing and caution in warning
against "adventurist" violence. "If you want to know what communists
think look at their hands and not at their mouths," it chided.[173] Believing that "when the conditions are right for armed struggle, it will be too
late to prepare for it," the RAF insisted:

> It is correct, possible, and justified to wage urban guerrilla warfare here
> and now. . . . If it is correct that American imperialism is a paper tiger,
> which means it can be defeated . . . because struggles against it have risen
> up all over the world . . . there is no reason to exclude any country or any
> region from the anti-imperialist struggle on the grounds that either the
> forces are too weak or the forces of reaction are too strong.[174]

Consistent with this assessment, the RAF declared "decisiveness" and
the "will to act" to be the essential qualities of the guerrilla.[175]

Like Weatherman, the RAF upset conventional Marxist assumptions by asserting that one's social class no longer dictated one's political role. In light of the RAF's priorities and ethos, it is fitting that Baader was considered both within and outside the group to be its natural leader, even though he was no great student of the ideas from which the RAF drew inspiration.[176] Baader assumed chief responsibility for the practical and highly risky aspects of clandestine struggle, such as stealing cars and procuring weapons. (He also seemed something of a roguish dandy, preferring to steal BMWs, which some in the press dubbed "Baader-Meinhof Wagens" [cars]).[177] Within the broader culture, as the RAF's exploits multiplied, Baader and the others attained a kind of celebrity as renegade antiheroes, dangerous and likely doomed, but determined.

Rounding out the RAF's early leadership was Mahler, who vied with Meinhof for the role of ideological leader in the early 1970s. Bald, bespeckled, and over thirty, Mahler was the quintessential egghead radical. Having defended young militants in court, his great challenge now was to convert his dissident beliefs into militant action. With the coaxing of Baader, he made that transition. In the RAF, he fancied himself something of a modern-day Lenin, authoring punishingly long treatises on the task for the left as he saw it. His key text was "Über den bewaffneten Kampf in Westeuropa" ("On Armed Struggle in Western Europe"), an openly seditious seventy-page tract that he drafted in prison in 1971 on behalf of the RAF, which originally appeared under the deceptive title "The Old Traffic Regulations." It promised to "determine correctly . . . whether a 'peaceful transition to socialism' . . . is possible under current concrete social conditions."[178] It was not, Mahler answered confidently, declaring that the notion that violence had to be deferred until the capitalist state was weakened by political means was "the perspective of endless errors and bloody defeats."[179] "[I]t is not the certain expectation of failure, but rather the vision of victory," such as the RAF offered, he said, "that stirs the masses to revolutionary consciousness."[180] Mahler concluded by calling for the building of "commando groups" to broaden the insurrection that the RAF had begun.[181]

As a model for its armed struggle, the RAF adopted the strategy spelled out by Brazil's Carlos Marighela in his *Minimanual do guerrilheiro urbano* (Minimanual of the Urban Guerrilla), which was meant to instruct Latin American guerrillas like Uruguay's Tupamaros in methods of clandestine warfare.[182] Avidly read in translation by the RAF, the Weathermen, and other First World radicals, the *Minimanual* recommended assaults on military, police, and corporate targets as a way to undermine confidence in the state's authority. It also offered a romantic conception of the urban guerrilla as a master of alertness and self-discipline. True to Marighela's prescriptions, the RAF established small cells in cities throughout West Germany and even performed the rituals of conditioning the *Minimanual* recommended. Early on, part of the RAF's regimen consisted of swimming together every week in reservoirs. Beate Sturm, a founding member who soon left, described the tight-knit group as "so spontaneous and naïve and romantic, unbelievably romantic."[183]

For some joining the RAF, the group's illegal status and conspiratorial air were part of the attraction. Margrit Schiller attended the University of Heidelberg, where she became increasingly drawn to the Socialist Patients Collective (Sozialistisches Patientenkollektiv, or SPK)—a group of psychiatric patients whose charismatic leader, Dr. Wolfgang Huber, had encouraged them to see society as the source of their illness and to "turn their illness into a weapon" by building armed cells.[184] In February 1971, with the police hunt for the RAF raging, a friend of Schiller's asked her if she would take in some people experiencing "trouble with the law." Schiller quickly became aware of her guests' true identity but confessed: "My fear was far smaller than my interest in getting to know these people, who had lived their lives far differently than anyone I had known, and learn about their fight."[185] In the weeks following, she joined the group, and she describes a "typical" RAF safe house circa 1971 as a scene of alluring danger. All of the RAF's principals—Meinhof, Ensslin, Baader, Holger Meins, Irmgard Möller—gathered there, arguing about politics, laughing, and resting, surrounded by the tools of their hazardous trade: one radio for listening to the news, another for listening to police frequencies, pistols—which they put down beside them, for everyone to see, after they came in—and explosives.[186]

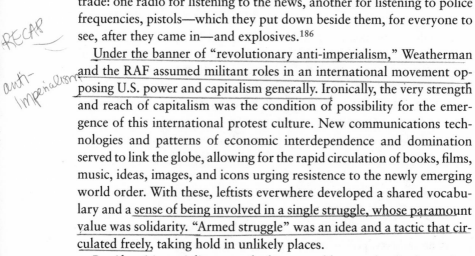

Under the banner of "revolutionary anti-imperialism," Weatherman and the RAF assumed militant roles in an international movement opposing U.S. power and capitalism generally. Ironically, the very strength and reach of capitalism was the condition of possibility for the emergence of this international protest culture. New communications technologies and patterns of economic interdependence and domination served to link the globe, allowing for the rapid circulation of books, films, music, ideas, images, and icons urging resistence to the newly emerging world order. With these, leftists everywhere developed a shared vocabulary and a sense of being involved in a single struggle, whose paramount value was solidarity. "Armed struggle" was an idea and a tactic that circulated freely, taking hold in unlikely places.

But if anti-imperialism sent the hearts and hopes of radicals soaring, it could also be dizzying and even distorting, especially as it blurred distinctions between disparate contexts and challenges. Jürgen Habermas, the leading voice of the Frankfurt School's new generation, had warned the West German New Left in 1967 of the possible emergence of a "left fascism."[187] In a conference the day of Benno Ohnesorg's burial, Habermas declared the apparent efforts of demonstrators to elicit state violence to be "masochistic" and criticized Dutschke for espousing a "voluntarist ideology" reminiscent of the "utopian socialists" of 1848 and the German reactionaries of the 1930s.[188] The following year, Habermas issued an equally urgent, if less hyperbolic and vituperative, warning:

> To be sure, moral outrage at the barbarity—in the name of freedom—of the Americans in Vietnam . . . is warranted. But the emotional identification with the role of the Viet Cong, the blacks in urban slums, the Brazilian guerrillas, the Chinese cultural revolutionaries, or the heroes of the Cuban revolution has no political basis. The situations here and there are as incomparable as the problems that each poses and the tactics each demands.[189]

Heedless of such pleas, the RAF and Weatherman insisted that the ethic of solidarity demanded sacrifice equal to that of the Vietnamese and the need for a single struggle, to be fought everywhere by the same means.

The Importance of Being Militant

The Days of Rage and Their Critics

Until the Days of Rage, Weatherman existed primarily as an analysis, an impulse, a promise, and a threat. The group proclaimed action to be the great catalyst—the agony of the New Left and the riddle of imperialism solved. Violent confrontation in Chicago would overcome demoralization within the movement, greatly expand its base of support, and, most ambitiously, spark a second American revolution. With this exhortation to militancy, conveyed with a mix of heartfelt conviction and thuggish righteousness, Weatherman had aroused the curiosity, suspicion, and fear of the left and of those few within the mainstream conscious of its voice. The group had provided little basis, though, for judging the substance of its gospel of action.

The prediction of movement skeptics that the Weathermen would lead vulnerable youths into massacre did not come to pass; nor did the Days of Rage remotely satisfy Weatherman's hope of devastating a major American city. Only a few hundred demonstrators, nearly all of them Weathermen, came to Chicago. They used chains and pipes to destroy property and battle police. Denounced by much of the left, ignored by working-class youths, and opposed by thousands of police and soldiers, the Weathermen were routed in Chicago. Weatherman had nonetheless honored its commitment. It had acted. Yet during and after the Days of Rage, there was little understanding of what the action meant, either for Weatherman, the movement, or the nation as a whole; in their lack of precedent and with their crazed energy, the Days of Rage challenged basic efforts to render the protest comprehensible, raising a problem of reading or representation.

However enigmatic, the Days of Rage revealed the importance of militancy for the New Left. Much more than a tactical orientation or style of protest, militancy was a defining ethos of the movement. Young radicals invested militant action with special power to enlighten, inspire, and mobilize. It provided a way for them to establish the authenticity of their commitments, to assert their dissident or "revolutionary" identities, and to live what they considered meaningful and engaged lives. The Weathermen drew on each of these attributes in promoting violence as the highest expression of militancy.

The Days of Rage also exemplified the hazards of this action ethos. Militancy, as the Weathermen both illustrated and discovered, could encourage fatally reductive analyses, alienate potential supporters, and turn activism into a contest of personal dedication tending toward self-destruction. In extreme form, it violated outright the ends it meant to serve. Militancy was also intimately bound up with the efforts of New Leftists to define and connect with "reality." Their concern with "reality" stemmed from two main desires: to understand the true nature of the forces that shaped their existence, and to separate themselves from an "inauthentic" or "unreal" world that discouraged political and moral engagement. The New Left's politics of reality had its own ironies, however, in that it distanced militants like the Weathermen from credible apprehension of a reality they so desperately sought to change, even as it drove them to confront realities America tried so hard to deny.

· · ·

Hope you have got your things together
Hope you are quite prepared to die
Looks like we're in for nasty weather
One eye is taken for an eye
        Creedence Clearwater Revival,
          "Bad Moon Rising"

The Weatherbureau, Weatherman's leaders, anticipated arrests and injuries at the Days of Rage. A leaflet it issued from the SDS National Office in Chicago urged that cadres bring bail money and be familiar with basic first aid.[1] The leadership felt, however, that a wholesale massacre was highly unlikely, reasoning that from the standpoint of the "ruling class" the killing of large numbers of white demonstrators would be "impermissible." Not wanting to instigate lethal violence, it ordered that firearms, which some collectives had already begun stockpiling, not be brought to the protest.[2]

Even so, the Weathermen conceded the possibility of serious injuries and even deaths in Chicago. The prospect seemed both to terrify and to intrigue them. Shin'ya Ono, a New York Weatherman, admitted to being afraid but explained that the killing of whites would have a devastating impact on Weatherman's opponents. In addition, by suffering what "were by Third World standards relatively light casualties, when the probable political gains were so clear," the Weathermen would decisively renounce their "white-skin privilege" and demonstrate their solidarity with other revolutionaries.[3] In her richly descriptive memoir, the Seattle Weatherwoman Susan Stern evokes the desperate pride and almost manic determination she felt as the Days of Rage approached:

> We weren't just a bunch of superviolent kids out to destroy Chicago because we enjoyed vandalism. . . . We were serious revolutionaries, who felt the necessity of doing something so earth-shattering in America that the American masses would finally take notice. Mr. and Mrs. America would . . . see our bodies being blasted by shotguns, our terrified faces as we marched trembling but proud, to attack the armed might of the Nazi state of ours. Running blood, young, white human blood spilling and splattering all over the streets of Chicago for NBC and CBS to pick up in gory gory Technicolor. . . . But in order to make America really look and see, we had to do something so unholy, so strong and so deadly, that they would have no other recourse. And that is what we're about.[4]

For Stern, the prospect of martyrdom—in all its spectacular gruesomeness—defined the Days of Rage and the very spirit of Weatherman.

As the Weathermen made their way from cities across America to Chicago on October 6, 1969, they had good reason to be afraid. The spirits of the travelers were temporarily raised by news that Chicago Weathermen—in fact, Bill Ayers and Terry Robbins—had blown up the landmark statue commemorating the deaths of policemen in the 1886 Haymarket riots (after which labor leaders clearly innocent of any crimes had been cruelly executed).[5] But this small triumph did little to assuage the creeping sense of the catastrophe to come. The promised flood of SDS militants and working-class youths into Chicago turned out to be a trickle. The New York collective, which had anticipated bringing a

thousand people, managed to attract only thirty recruits. At the bus station, police had taunted the departing Weathermen about their meager
numbers.[6] By Weatherman's estimation, only one out of every seven
people who had pledged to come to the Days of Rage actually made the
trip. Hundreds of police would be waiting for them.

Developments behind the scenes were scarcely more encouraging. The
night before the action, the Illinois Black Panther leader Fred Hampton
met with several Weatherleaders, with Dave Dellinger, one of the defendants in the trial of the so-called Chicago 8 for conspiring to cause the
1968 Democratic National Convention riots, and with the attorney
William Kunstler mediating between the two sides. Earlier in the day, when
Mark Rudd had answered Hampton's criticisms of the protest by questioning Hampton's political dedication, Hampton knocked Rudd flat with
a punch. In the evening session, Hampton reiterated his view that the Days
of Rage would likely result in useless arrests and injuries and invite greater
repression of both white and black activists. After assurances by the Weathermen that they would show restraint, Hampton agreed not to denounce
the group publicly but stopped short of pledging the Panthers' support
for the action.[7]

Despite weeks of intense organizing—speeches at campuses, outreach
to other movement groups, daily trips to high schools, and "exemplary"
acts of militancy—the Weathermen brought almost no one new to Chicago. There was some sense to Weatherman's goal of organizing a "revolutionary youth movement." White working-class youths seemed to
have much to gain and, relative to middle- and upper-class youths, little
to lose in opposing a system that held few economic opportunities for
them and shipped them off to war by the hundreds of thousands. But
Weatherman's belief that its anti-imperialist raps and scattered displays
of toughness could transform the youths' anxiety about the future and
dislike of authority into enthusiasm for combat proved entirely misguided.
One Weatherwoman said of her attempts to recruit high school students:

> [T]hey agreed that there were a lot of things wrong. But the plans for them
> was to get them to fight the police . . . and get them to attack the schools
> and whatever, go to Chicago. . . . These kids weren't going to do it. I mean
> they lived in the neighborhood, they wanted to stay out of trouble and
> they wanted to make a living . . . [We were] telling them to throw away
> any chance they got and fight, and fight even though they were going to
> lose. . . . [M]aybe you'll get killed, but the movement will grow . . . that's
> a helluva thing to go and tell a kid, I mean a kid who grows up on the
> street—he's gonna say you're crazy.[8]

As if in search of Weatherman's mythical youth army, Jeff Shero, the editor of New York's *RAT: Subterranean News,* toured working-class towns in Arizona and talked to teenagers there just before the Days of Rage. He concluded that their basic aspirations—for romance, stable jobs, and perhaps a taste of the adventure the counterculture offered—hardly squared with Weatherman's designs for them.[9] Assessing the Days of Rage years later, Phoebe Hirsch bluntly described the group's failure: "The goal was to bring a lot of people . . . but we were creating the kind of action that was designed to not have anybody come."[10] Russell Neufeld lamented that Weatherman's message boiled down to, "'The streets belong to the people, off the pig, dig it, do it,' and it left out why [we] were doing these things."[11]

Weatherman's insistence that teenagers were ready to fight sprang in part from the group's sense of how the political climate had changed since even the early and mid 1960s, when most of the Weathermen became politicized. Widespread opposition to the war, the growing generation gap, and the crisis atmosphere that characterized the late 1960s, they erroneously reasoned, made becoming a revolutionary a near-instantaneous process. The Weathermen thus imposed expectations on others that greatly diverged from their own experiences. Their radicalization had typically entailed years of political education, membership in left-wing organizations, interaction with black activists, participation in demonstrations, and skirmishes with police. Working-class youths were somehow to skip this process and discover revolutionary identities virtually ex nihilo. At root, Weatherman held a romanticized view of the working classes, believing that their beleaguered social position and presumed familiarity with violence at the level of everyday life gave them an instinctive rebelliousness and disposition to revolution. Years later, Cathy Wilkerson described the Weathermen's militant posturing as "intellectuals playing at being toughs." Even worse, by celebrating the anti-intellectualism, sexism, and violence of working-class culture as political virtues, the Weathermen appealed to the "most reactionary macho instinct[s]" of the youths they tried to recruit.[12] Tellingly, the FBI informant who most successfully penetrated the group, Larry Grathwohl, was a working-class Vietnam veteran from the Midwest. The Weathermen seemed so enamored with his "authenticity" that they looked past clues to his actual identity.[13]

On the night of the October 7, the Weathermen checked into designated "movement centers" at area churches and seminaries, where they would stay during the demonstrations. The following evening a small crowd officially began the Days of Rage with a commemoration in Lincoln Park of Che Guevara's death one year earlier. Describing the scene, Kirkpatrick Sale voiced what any observer would wonder: "What must it have felt like . . . standing in the darkness on a light rise at the south end of Lincoln Park, gathered around a small bonfire to ward off the chill of a Chicago fall, waiting for the thousands of revolutionaries to appear, and finding yourself in the midst of a tatterdemalion band of no more than two hundred people?"[14] Ono gave a glimpse of the sensation. He reported being so numb with dread and disbelief that he could hardly concentrate on the speeches.[15] A Chicago-area teenage girl suffering from epilepsy had a grand mal seizure on the spot. Stern thought to herself,

> This is all there is, there are no more coming, no train from Michigan, no band of ten thousand whooping Indians from everywhere, just us, us only. . . . Tears formed in my eyes and slid down my cheeks. Beverly muttered, in a voice choked from between clenched teeth, "All that work, and our lives almost destroyed and nothing." . . . I really didn't mind dying, but only if I had to. But this really was suicide.[16]

Stern did not ultimately know why she stayed to do battle and what her possible martyrdom might be worth. She speculated: "Maybe I actually believed that I was part of the real revolutionary vanguard. I don't really think so, but I have no other answer."[17] According to Larry Weiss, doubts and fears by that point "didn't make a difference. We were revolutionary; you had to do it."[18]

Naomi Jaffe seems the exception in confessing no great fear. The daughter of communist farmers in upstate New York, she had been "born with the sense that mainstream American culture . . . did not work for a lot of people." Her father had taught her that a key lesson of the Cuban revolution was that the oppressed "had a right to seize their rights by armed struggle"; at her high school valedictory address in 1961, she had denounced the House Committee on Un-American Activities. As protest grew in the 1960s, her feeling was that "something really important was happening" that "I had longed for all my life and I didn't want to miss." In order to be part of what she saw as a growing revolution, she joined Weatherman, and took a hard-nosed approach to being a revolutionary. As for the Days of Rage, she explained: a "willingness to take risks . . . didn't come hard for me. . . . People said they were terrified. I wasn't. [They] thought they were going to die in October. I just didn't."[19]

Members of the Weatherbureau arrived at Lincoln Park an hour late. They alone knew the destination of the march. Undeterred by the small numbers, they made speeches praising Guevara and the courage of the Weathermen prepared to follow his example. SDS co-founder and Chicago 8 defendant Tom Hayden briefly addressed the crowd. The Weathermen, in their battle dress of football and motorcycle helmets, heavy jackets and clubs, looked to him "like a primitive, neophyte army." Despite his misgivings about the Weathermen, Hayden told them not to believe media reports that the Chicago 8 defendants disapproved of the action. Co-defendants Abbie Hoffman and John Froines had also come to the park, but they chose not to make speeches and quickly left.[20]

The Weatherleader Jeff Jones, announcing himself with the code phrase "I am Marion Delgado," then revealed the target of the action. (Marion Delgado was a Chicano boy who had derailed a train by placing a concrete block on the tracks in 1947; the Weathermen and other radicals took him up as a rebel folk hero and, on occasion, used his name as an alias.) The group, by now 350 or so strong, was to tear through Chicago's fashionable Gold Coast and pounce on the home at the Drake Hotel of Judge Julius Hoffman, who was presiding over the Chicago 8 conspiracy trial. Jones shouted, "Marion Delgado don't like [Judge Hoffman], and the Weathermen don't like him, . . . so . . . let's go get him!"[21] The Weathermen then trotted in orderly columns to the Gold Coast while, in a surreal scene, hundreds of plainclothes police kept pace alongside them.[22] On cue, the Weathermen erupted. With bricks and pipes, they smashed the windows of automobiles, restaurants, stores, and hotels. The destruction appeared to be both targeted and indiscriminate. They attacked not only a Rolls Royce, police cars, and the façades of "upperclass" establishments, but also ordinary cars, a barber shop, and, on side streets, the windows of lower-middle-class homes. Twice the Weathermen charged police blockades. The police opened fire, wounding an attacking Weatherman in the neck and another, who posed no immediate threat, in the shoulder. Those captured were pummeled by the police. The Chicago photographer Duane Hall reported: "[The police] had a couple of guys in the street and they were beating them real bad. . . . And there were [women] in this too. They were bleeding all over. And one guy was laying there knocked out and I was shooting a picture of three policemen beating the guy. They were just beating and kicking him."[23] The fighting subsided after an hour. Hobbled Weathermen returned to the movement centers, while activists sympathetic to the group made sweeps in vans to pull the wounded off the streets and take them to hospitals far from the center of Chicago, where they might avoid the police.

Sixty-eight had been arrested, twenty-eight police had been injured (though none seriously), and at least six Weathermen had been shot.

Early the following morning, Phoebe Hirsch vividly recalled, the Weathermen were paid an unexpected visit by members of the Mafia, who candidly introduced themselves, pointed out that Mafia-owned property in downtown Chicago had been damaged during the march, and warned that the Weathermen "would hear from them" if it happened again.[24]

The morning's main activity was to be a raid on a Draft Board office by the "Women's Militia." Some seventy Weatherwomen gathered at Grant Park, where Bernardine Dohrn gave a speech praising their valor. As they attempted to leave the park, however, they were easily overpowered by the police, who were clearly livid from the day before. Hirsch says that a policeman tried to break her arm as "added punishment" for the mayhem. The police were not the only ones upset at the Weathermen. Hirsch's uncle, in order that she "learn a lesson," refused to bail her out of Cook County Jail, where she remained for a week.[25] Dohrn later confessed to the contradictory feelings she had during the Days of Rage: "This can't be done. I'm doing it." Elaborating on her resolve, she joked that the protest was like "showing up at the wedding knowing this is a terrible mistake, but going through with it anyhow."[26]

Later in the day, Illinois Governor Richard Ogilvie announced that more than 2,500 National Guardsmen had been called in to protect the city. The Weathermen wisely canceled scheduled "jailbreaks" at area high schools and an evening rally, advertised as a "Wargasm." Instead, they would join the demonstration organized by RYM II to protest the Chicago 8 conspiracy trial at the Federal Building, claiming that they were attending under the leadership of the Black Panthers.[27] But at the rally, Fred Hampton denounced the Weathermen, who had broken their promise of restraint. "We do not support people who are anarchistic, opportunistic, adventuristic, and Custeristic [i.e., suicidal]," he said.[28]

The last of the Days of Rage featured the most intense fighting. The night before, there had been a chilling prelude when the group discovered a police informant in its midst—a young Hispanic man whom a Weatherman had recently seen in a police station while being processed for an arrest. A Weatherman severely beat the informant before releasing him. Wanted posters immediately went up, accusing the assailant of felony assault. The Weatherman in question soon fled Chicago and changed his identity, making him the first among the group officially to go underground.

The day's violence began when police charged a noon rally at Haymarket Square, picking five Weatherleaders out of the crowd and beating them with clubs. Later, at Chicago's downtown Loop, the Weathermen and police again engaged in combat. During the battle, Assistant Corporation Counsel Richard Elrod, the mastermind of the Chicago 8 conspiracy indictments and a close friend of Mayor Richard Daley, tried to tackle Weatherman Brian Flanagan. In the process, Elrod hit his neck against a concrete wall and became paralyzed. Insisting spuriously that Flanagan had beaten Elrod, the police charged the young Weatherman with attempted murder. Duane Hall observed with stunned awe the scene of near-mortal carnage: "You'd see the police chasing [Weathermen] into alleys . . . ; you'd hear them screaming and then you'd see them laying on the ground, and you knew they'd be dead. By some miracle, they just weren't dead."[29] By midafternoon, the fighting had ceased, one hundred more Weathermen had been arrested, and the Days of Rage were finally over.

Perhaps 600 people altogether participated in the four-day action. A total of 287 were arrested (some more than once), mostly on charges of "disorderly conduct" and "mob action." At least twelve demonstrators were charged with assault or aggravated battery. Of those arrested, roughly two-thirds were male. Most were between the ages of nineteen and twenty-two, but one was only eleven, and two were as old as fifty-one. Their combined bail exceeded $2 million. More than 800 automobile and 600 residential or store windows had been smashed.[30] As prosecutors prepared their cases, the FBI's Chicago office drafted a lengthy report, sent to all FBI field offices with significant SDS activity, that chronicled Weatherman's activities in the early fall and, as best it could, described the tumultuous protest.

.   .   .

Because something is happening here
But you don't know what it is
Do you, Mister Jones?

> Bob Dylan,
> "Ballad of a Thin Man"

The city of Chicago, although conditioned by the 1968 Democratic Convention to being in the eye of a political storm, reacted to the Days of Rage with bewilderment and disgust. Mayor Daley denounced the "riots" as an "outrage."[31] Clergy who had let the Weathermen use their churches also condemned the violence, claiming that they had been misled by the group about the nature of the protest. (The Weathermen had even taken wooden poles from coat racks in one of the churches to use as clubs, naïvely planning to put them back once the protests were over.)[32] Using headlines like "Radicals Go On Rampage" and "Cops, Troops Guard City," the *Chicago Tribune* portrayed a community under siege.[33] Following the last of the Days of Rage, the paper triumphantly declared "105 Seized in Loop Battle" and lavished praise on law enforcement.[34] By adopting a kind of battle reportage, the *Tribune* oddly affirmed Weatherman's intention to "bring the war home." But if the city was certain it was locked in battle, it strained to understand just what and whom it was fighting.

Daley set the tone for expressions of confoundment by announcing, "This senseless and vicious behavior is not dissent. . . . We witnessed planned attacks on persons and violent destruction of property with no provocation or justification."[35] Even sharper condemnation came from the mother of Brian Flanagan, whose son was held responsible for the paralyzing injury to Elrod. She declared, "I don't blame the Chicago police. They should have knocked the heads off every one of them. . . . I don't understand these kids at all. The world I knew is much different from the one they inhabit now. I just don't understand."[36] Describing the Weathermen's actions as a "carnival of mindless terror" and "insane efforts to organize a putsch," the *Tribune* called for an uncompromising crackdown against the "New Barbarians."[37]

Denunciations of New Leftists for pushing beyond the limits of "responsible" dissent had been a stock reaction of the media and public officials for years. Shocked parents incredulous at the behavior of their activist children were virtually a cliché in the strained relations between the generations, but Weatherman's leap from self-defensive violence and petty "trashing" of property to planned offensive assaults caused a total breakdown in the dialogue between the establishment and the radical left. Weatherman's aggression could neither be sanctioned by any civic principle nor even explained within any familiar political frame of reference. Neither could it be easily forgiven, in light of the admonitions of the clergy and Mrs. Flanagan, by Christian or parental love. While the demonstrations at the Democratic Convention had been repellent and confusing to many Americans, they were the object of a widely publicized trial in which the politics of the antiwar movement and the counterculture could to some degree be displayed and debated. The Days of Rage would be subject to no such public evaluation. Many of the Weath-

going underground

Lofts rxn

ermen would go underground before the most serious indictments aris-
ing out of the Days of Rage were handed down. In a pretrial hearing
shortly after the action, a group of Weathermen marched into the courthouse wearing street-fighting clothes and chanting revolutionary slogans,
to which a stunned judge declared, "I feel like I'm in a mob action right
now."[38] In the Days of Rage, Weatherman revealed itself to the mainstream as monstrous; incapable of being comprehended, the monster had
only to be stopped.

Much of the left nearly concurred. Movement critics found the Days
of Rage not so much inscrutable—they were familiar with Weatherman's
rationale for the action—as politically senseless. Hampton complained
to reporters that the Days of Rage were "not revolutionary even. . . .
[G]oing out on the streets and getting people shot, killed and maimed is
insanity."[39] Others saw the action as evidence of Weatherman's "adventurism," which made a fetish of violence and turned against, rather
than to, "the people" in its efforts to build a socialist future. New York's
Guardian, an independent socialist weekly widely read on the left, commented derisively that "the most significant aspect of the surrealistic con-
tretemps created by the Weatherman microfaction of SDS last week was
that the rest of the movement had the revolutionary sense to stay away."
To the claim of the Weathermen that their willingness to die in street battles signified their singular commitment, the *Guardian* answered: "If
American radicals must die it shall be in genuine struggle for the people,
not for a bit part in a penny dreadful Keystone Kops melodrama."[40]

The Liberation News Service, whose syndicated stories appeared in
dozens of underground papers, complained that Weatherman had failed
to "define and isolate the enemy" or educate "the masses" on how capitalism oppressed them.[41] It noted that Weatherman clubs had hit both
Volkswagens and Cadillacs, barbershops as well as banks. RYM II supporters contrasted glowing accounts of solidarity among students, blacks,
Hispanics, and workers at their events with the familiar criticism that
the Weathermen pursued revolutionary struggle without popular support.[42] The Progressive Labor Party, with characteristic vindictiveness,
described the Days of Rage as "the work of police agents and hate-the-
people lunatics," whose true goal was to discredit the "real SDS," namely,
itself.[43] Chicago's main underground newspaper, *The Seed,* feared that
the Days of Rage would legitimize the repression of activists of every sort
in the eyes of an anxious public. According to much of the left, in its first,
great moment of truth, Weatherman had demonstrated only the futility

of middle-class radicals using anti-imperialist diatribe and acts of machismo to organize white working-class youths into a suicidal Red Army.
The monstrous Weatherman, judging by the Days of Rage, would soon
stop itself.

A minority of commentators who were witness to the protests offered
something other than unalloyed contempt. The *Berkeley Tribe* reporter
Steve Haines was a veteran of the tumultuous struggles in 1969 over Berkeley's "People's Park." (After activists seized an empty plot of land owned
by the University of California and turned it into a community garden, a
battle ensued for control of the park. In one confrontation, police opened
fire, wounding more than fifty of the park's unsuccessful defenders and
killing an unarmed protester, James Rector.) Haines, seeing the Weathermen march in tight formations, erupt in a torrent of destruction, fight police in hand-to-hand combat, and then "disappear into the night," described the first evening of the Days of Rage as "the most incredible thing
[he] had ever experienced." The Weathermen, he concluded, "confronted
the gut issue of personal courage in a way few of us who consider ourselves revolutionary ever have. They confronted it and they won."[44] David
Schanoes of the *Ann Arbor Argus* saw the Days of Rage as evidence of
Weatherman's complete detachment from the working class and poor. In
his telling, a member of the Young Lords—a radical Puerto Rican group
based in Chicago's poor neighborhoods—provided the most "coherent
criticism of the action" with the comment, "Who ever heard of breaking
windows and not taking anything?" Schanoes nonetheless praised Dohrn
for saying in a speech to the battle-ready group: "'We are not going to be
good Germans in a Fascist State.'" "That's it on the line, and forget the
rest," he exclaimed. "Right on Bernardine!"[45] The radical journalist Andrew Kopkind wound up in jail with the Weathermen and reported: "We
all thought in the cell block that night that simply not to fear fighting is
a kind of winning. . . . Almost everyone . . . now thinks the spirit of the
Sixties has found its end. But at night in the cell block, we believed that
it had found a new beginning."[46]

In the immediate wake of the protests, journalists from several underground papers held a roundtable discussion about the Days of Rage,
titled with honest wonder "What Was Chicago?" Their conversation was
a mosaic of ambivalence, in which optimism and skepticism, excitement
and dread combined in efforts to solve Weatherman's enigma without
resort to dogmatic dismissal. One sympathetic reporter gave an achingly
conflicted appraisal of the action: "It was a tremendous loss, but it was

a victory because we've been talking for years about armed struggle, in a context that has always been completely abstract. Nobody ever knew what it meant. It still isn't what we mean . . . but the thing is that much less abstract."

The Yippie Stew Albert used a dramatic, if questionable, analogy in defending the moral impulse of the protest, regardless of its political consequences:

> What if you picked up a history book and read that in 1938 a thousand University of Berlin students ran through the streets on behalf of the Jews in the concentration camps, breaking car windows, knocking over fat, old German ladies, and beating up members of the Gestapo? . . . These guys, no matter what came out of their actions in a tactical sense—they might have even speeded up repression, Nixon may have become even more paranoid, you might have speeded up the flow of Jews into the concentration camps and some of the Jews might have hated "The Vethermen"—but they would still be the moral heroes of the 20th century. The Pope would bless them, Mao would write an essay on them, Nehru probably would have liked them, trees would be planted in Israel for them, even Nixon would have dug them. On a moral level, they're perfect.[47]

Finally, the roundtable participants granted a certain credibility to Weatherman's contention that behind the reluctance of whites to risk injury or death lay the assumption that their lives were somehow worth more than those of Vietnamese and blacks, although one objected, "You can't organize whites around dying."

· · ·

Paradise, sacrifice, mortality, reality.
But the magician is quicker and his game
Is much thicker than blood and blacker than ink
And there's no time to think.

        Bob Dylan, "No Time to Think"

The Days of Rage and the debates surrounding them reveal the importance of militancy not only for Weatherman, but for the New Left as a whole. By giving substance to the notion of a white army, Weatherman represented a transition from abstraction to reality for a movement feverishly trying to develop "a strategy to win." But Weatherman's combat was impressive to some observers for having accessed "reality" in deeper senses.

Stressing the existential roots of 1960s protest, Doug Rossinow asserts that "the search for authenticity lay at the heart of the new left."[48] In that search, young people reacted against what they saw as a dominant culture of "death and artificiality," "fronts and disguises," and sought through the politics and culture of protest experiences defined by conviction, cooperation, and "a sense of vital life . . . in touch with the 'really real.'" The desire for authenticity was pervasive, informing the activism of everyone from SDSers to left-wing Christian students and politically inclined hippies. It certainly was a driving force behind the militancy of the 1960s.

Activists increasingly embraced militant action partly as an answer to the perceived limitations or even debilitating effects of language. Phoebe Hirsch, who attended the University of Wisconsin, recalls a professor challenging her during a semester in Paris in 1965 to "take a stand" on the budding conflict in Vietnam. Back at Wisconsin, she found herself put off by the ceaseless debating of the male-dominated campus left. Deciding that one "just couldn't talk" any longer, she and several other women activists took the bold step of lying down in front of buses carrying troops eventually bound for Vietnam. However strong her fear, the act felt like "totally the right thing to do."[49]

Bill Ayers, contrasting the militancy of the New Left with the theoretical wrangling and complacency of the Old, juxtaposed words and action, theory and practice in the following way:

> You had a responsibility to link your conduct to your consciousness. . . . If you believed something, the proof of that belief was to act on it. It wasn't to espouse it with the right treatises or manifestos. We were militants. That's what we were. We were militants before we were thinkers. . . . Militancy is a stance in the world, a way of being in the world that says that I'm going to put my body somehow in the way of the normal functioning of things, and I'm going take the consequence of having done that. . . . The statement is my body standing in the way, and once that statement is made, you open up a public space where lots of people have to think and act differently. . . . *Militancy was the standard by which we measured our aliveness.*[50]

Ayers first experienced the power of militancy directly while participating in a sit-in at the Ann Arbor Draft Board in 1965. Even the onlookers who "wanted to kill us," he recalls, were forced to ask themselves what principle would drive him and other students to risk their educations and futures. Hirsch's experience and Ayers's reflections describe well the ethic of resistance that began in the defiant acts of the civil rights movement and ran through various forms of nonviolent direct action practiced by the New Left and the antiwar movement, such as sit-ins, blocking traffic, and burning draft cards. The rapid mobilization of millions of people into the civil rights, antiwar, and student movements testified to the educational and catalyzing effect of action. In short, 1960s activists practiced a kind of "body politics," in which the body functioned both as a potent means of transforming the public sphere and as the ultimate marker of political engagement and individual vitality.

The New Left established the connection between militancy and authenticity, or "realness," in its use of language. In their fascinating "Lexicon of Folk-Etymology," Ralph Larkin and Daniel Foss describe the values and spirit of the New Left by defining its key terms.[51] The entry for "real" is instructive. To be "real" for New Leftists meant "being what one becomes upon rejection of the conventions" learned through one's mainstream socialization. "From one's current perspective," these "amounted to 'bullshit,' 'lies,' 'brainwashing,' a 'phony-mindfuck,' etc." The existentialist premises of this formulation are striking. In his preface to Frantz Fanon's *The Wretched of the Earth,* Jean-Paul Sartre wrote: "We only become what we are by the radical and deep-seated refusal of that which others have made of us."[52] For New Leftists, militancy enhanced or expedited that process of becoming. According to Larkin and Foss, to be real also meant in radical parlance to be "brave, courageous or tough." These attributes applied especially to those who embraced confrontations with authorities that held legal or physical risks. Militancy, in short, was an experiential crucible for the forging of one's authentic self.

The New Left's skepticism about language intensified toward the end of the 1960s. With whatever irony, young activists responded to the escalation of police violence and the war in Vietnam with a dizzying explosion of discourse, in which they exhorted one another to greater resistance. Guns and bombs entered the imagery of the more radical sectors of the movement and became standard in the graphics of underground newspapers. It was as if the New Left were trying, through the sheer accumulation of subversive words and images, to will a new world into being. But New Leftists also expressed impatience with the perceived limits of their largely verbal protest. A great part of the frustration was practical. "The need to fight . . . came out of many demonstrations in which you'd talk and talk and . . . they'd essentially say, 'Nice boy, go away,'" the Weatherman Scott Braley explained.[53] Some felt that their discourse amounted to mere verbiage bereft of agency—tokens of an inauthentic and ineffectual politics, removed from edifying danger and of little use to those whose suffering was immediate and severe. In Rossinow's phrasing, merely "talking about change was somehow unreal."[54]

Marcuse persistently pleaded with the young not to sacrifice critical thought to impulsive action. Yet even he acknowledged that the argument against words could appear "overwhelming." He elaborated:

> Bertolt Brecht noted that we live at a time where it seems a crime to talk about a tree. Since then, things have become much worse. Today, it seems a crime merely to *talk* about change while one's society is transformed in to an institution of violence, terminating in Asia the genocide which began with the liquidation of the American Indians. Is not the sheer power of this brutality immune against the spoken and written word which indicts it? And is not the word which is directed against the practitioners of this power the same they use to defend their power? There is a level on which even the unintelligent action against them seems justified. For action smashes, though only for a moment, the closed universe of suppression.[55]

Weatherman tried to overcome the limitations of discourse in part by instrumentalizing language. The quasi-scientific analyses in its founding manifesto issued a call to arms. Its crude talk vilifying "pig Amerika," triumphant slogans, and speeches like those made at the Days of Rage all aimed at strengthening the resolve of its members to use militant action to accomplish what words alone could not. Ono practically sneered at the impotence of language:

> Words, words, words. Mere words, however persuasive, mere ideas, however true, cannot make even a dent in an ingrained psychic structure like racism. To see a group of other whites willing to fight to the very end on the side of blacks will be a shocking experience for most whites. . . . Actually seeing [us] fight will hit hard at the core of their racist being in ways no words or analyses alone can do.[56]

Granting violence singular power to transform thought, Ono echoed the revolutionary wisdom of his day. Frantz Fanon, the lodestar of revolutionaries worldwide, had said with respect to anticolonial rebellion: "Violence alone . . . makes it possible" for "the people" to "understand social truths."[57] Violence, in sum, *realized* social theory by consummating the revolutionary word in the radical deed.

Weatherman's indictment of the reluctance of whites to assume physical risks points to another important dimension of militancy. Part of the frustration with discourse for New Leftists lay in the perception that they had the luxury of words without accountability—that in light of the violence suffered by the Vietnamese and American blacks there was something disingenuous about rhetorical and other forms of passive support for the struggles of America's most obvious and abused victims. That sense, as Weatherman converted it into a call to arms, formed the basis of the common accusation that Weatherman's politics were rooted in "white guilt."

The charge of "white guilt" held that Weatherman's violence was only secondarily motivated by a desire to help blacks and Third World liberation movements, and that it sprang primarily from the Weathermen's own need—whether conscious or not—to alleviate the psychological burden of their social and economic privilege. Violent action, insofar as it promised absolution, was something the Weatherman did, in essence, *for themselves.* By extension, the critique of "white guilt" held that violence failed as a form of genuine solidarity or even resistance; based in self-serving motives, it remained of a piece with the individualism of liberal, capitalist culture. In this vein, the former SDS president Greg Calvert criticized the Weathermen as exemplars of what he called "the politics of proving," whereby New Leftists preached or engaged in violence to demonstrate that they were "as revolutionary" as "the blacks, Cubans, or Vietnamese."[58] As part of a "politics of proving," violence implied an ultimately false and potentially offensive equivalence between white militants and the various groups they sought to join in combat.

But beyond guilt, one can discern in those adopting violence more conscientious efforts to determine the nature of their responsibility to aid the plight of others and to reconcile their actions with their beliefs. David Gilbert recalled that his transition from pacifism to support for violent revolution, had been

> incredibly difficult. I'll use the word traumatic. I don't like psychological terms that much, but it was traumatic for me because being a pacifist gave me a certain moral certitude as an individual. I know that I'll never do anything that's wrong, living my life as an individual purely. That's fine . . . if the main thing you want to say is, I'm a morally pure person. But what had motivated me was the conditions of life of most people . . . and not to be willing to fight against the forces who actively use . . . violence to maintain these social conditions, was acquiescing to more violence. . . . I identified enough with other people that I said, well, if it's right for them to fight and die and it's my government and the businesses here that are the main source of the problem, I can't just say, well it's all right for them. . . . If that was my position it also had implications for how I acted.[59]

Reversing the terms of "white guilt," Gilbert presents *non*violence as a means of remaining pure and accepts that violence holds the possibility of a fall from grace. To him, the charge of white guilt signaled primarily "how far people are from being able to identify with one another." He added: "If you live in an empire, I guess to feel guilty about that is a little more progressive than to feel arrogant about it, right?"[60]

Max Weber's meditation on political morality helps to frame Gilbert's views. Weber describes the "ethic of ultimate ends" and the "ethic of responsibility" as the competing moral foundations of politics.[61] The first ethic, which seeks to bring means and ends into harmony, privileges the moral integrity of the act and the actor. But by restricting the available means to morally acceptable ones, it risks forestalling the desired ends. It may therefore be only a poor servant of justice. The ethic of responsibility concerns itself solely with the consequences of action. Sanctioning unsavory means in the service of moral ends, it too may sacrifice justice— this time in the here and now—to its overarching calculus. For Gilbert, the nonviolence practiced by pacifists represented the ethic of ultimate ends. The ethic of responsibility, with its heightened moral risk, was the domain of those who, like the Weathermen, chose violence.

Robin Palmer began bombing buildings in New York City in 1969 before joining Weatherman in the summer of 1970. When asked years later why he had opted for armed struggle, he recalled the lines of a song of a San Francisco humor troupe that parodied what it saw as the hypocrisy and parasitism of white radicals: "Pull the trigger nigger / I'm with you all the way / right across the Bay." (The Panthers were based in Oakland, on the other side of San Francisco Bay.) Speaking more soberly about the pressure exerted by his own rhetoric, Palmer added, "I felt the only thing I could do was either shut up or start bombing, so [I] started bombing."[62] For Ono, violence transformed solidarity into a visceral sense of identification. As the Weathermen merely contemplated fighting in the Days of Rage, Ono reports, "the abstract phrase 'international solidarity' began to have a real meaning. We began to feel the Vietnamese in ourselves."[63] Fighting, in Ono's fanciful view, made solidarity concrete in the medium of the body.

In light of Gilbert's and Palmer's testimony, violence appears less a way of achieving personal purity than of establishing consistency of thought and action; less a way of relieving guilt than of making a "real" contribution to the struggle of others. (Weatherman's opponents, in their own way, credited the group with meeting the demands of revolutionary practice. Describing his shock at the Days of Rage, a Chicago official confessed: "We never expected this kind of violent demonstration. There has always been a big difference between what [the protesters] say and

what they do.")[64] Gilbert's and Palmer's reflections challenge, in addition, the notion that Weatherman equated the struggle of white radicals
with that of blacks or the Vietnamese. On the contrary, Weatherman's
sense of unity with other guerrillas was based on the reasoning that because blacks and Vietnamese had little choice but to fight, white radicals
should actively choose violence to destroy the system responsible for their
oppression. Within this logic, solidarity was driven by the recognition
of the differences between the forms of adversity faced by American
whites and other racial and national groups.

The challenge of "proving oneself" as a white activist could take on
disturbing forms. Among radicals, physical courage served as a crucial
measure of one's commitment and capacity for solidarity. The practice
of "gut check," performed by a host of movement groups, ritualized this
connection between risk and personal dedication. Gut check was a way
of pressuring members who opposed or hesitated to participate in an action, whether violent in intent or not, that held the prospect of arrest or
injury. Palmer, who was arrested no fewer than seventeen times for protest
activity, recounted the substance and tone of a gut check:

> If you don't do it, you're a coward. If you don't do it, you're not thinking
> of the Vietnamese. . . . You're a racist because the blacks have to live like
> this in the ghetto all the time. You're a racist because the Vietnamese are
> getting bombed like crazy all the time. Children mangled, women raped. . . .
> And you're worried about getting arrested?! And you're worried about
> getting hit by a cop over the head with a billy club?![65]

In Palmer's account, gut check used the themes of race and privilege to
shame and intimidate those experiencing doubt about taking some risk;
heeding that doubt amounted to cowardice, hypocrisy, or even complicity
in oppression. Shortly after the Days of Rage, Jeff Jones drove this race-
based imperative to be militant to confounding extremes. Because of their
oppression, blacks should be free to pursue a variety of political strategies, he said. "But for white people, there's only one form—only one
form—and that's to pick up the gun."[66] Because of their privilege, whites
must not merely match but *exceed* the daring of blacks. Militancy, at its
best, served as a way for activists to draw closer to one another, overcome personal barriers, and honor their deepest commitments through
acts of self-sacrifice. But for those who succumbed to the pressure of gut
check and took risks for which they were not properly prepared, militancy was a cause of self-estrangement.

Reflecting years later on Weatherman's politics, Gilbert affirmed many of the charges of the group's early critics. He described gut check as an unfortunate expression of "macho culture," which issued the core challenge: "Are you man enough to stick your head in the lion's den? Do you have the courage to do this?"[67] He also saw in the Days of Rage "a strange moralism," in which the Weathermen sought to prove they were "better" than the rest of the white left.[68] That conviction lay at the heart of Weatherman's "arrogance" and active "contempt" for whites who did not join the armed struggle. Criticism of the group only reinforced that contempt. In its most dogmatic phase, Gilbert concedes, Weatherman addressed the movement by saying: "We're ready to fight and die. We're ready to do anything, and you're either on our side or you're on the side of the pigs."[69] In Hirsch's characterization, the message was "either you take this stand with us, or 'fuck you'"; if they didn't, "it was their problem, it was never our problem."[70] Militancy, in this unforgiving dichotomy, failed to inspire, enlighten, or produce unity. It functioned instead as the basis for a crude dualism that separated the saved from the damned.

Crude dualism

Not unity)

. . . .

The truth was obscure, too profound and
    too pure, to live it you have to explode.
In that last hour of need, we entirely agreed,
    sacrifice was the code of the road.
        Bob Dylan, "Where Are You Tonight?
        (Journey Through Dark Heat)"

Militancy allowed New Leftists to get at what they understood as the "real" of politics. Many young radicals viewed power and violence as the foundations of capitalism, as both Marxism and experience had taught them to do. These were manifest not only in wars, police brutality, the treatment of prisoners, and the oppression of people of color, but also, if less openly, in market and class relationships, in ideology, and in the modes of authority and discipline in schools, workplaces, and even families. Todd Gitlin, a former SDS president, drew on these premises to convey the role of militancy for the New Left:

> Confrontations were moments of truth . . . bisecting life into Time Before and Time After. We collected these ritual punctuations as moments when

the shroud that normally covers everyday life was torn away and we stood face to face with the true significance of things. Each round was an approximation of the apocalypse, in the original meaning: the revelation of things the way they actually stand.[71]

By making what was latent or obscured apparent, militancy could induce a near-religious revelation of *social* truth—moments of potentially terrifying clarity in which the real nature of "the system" and the stakes of political conflict were laid open to be experienced and understood.

For Jeff Jones, the protests at Columbia University had precisely this effect by showing that,

> If you could create a confrontation with the University administration, you could expose . . . the interlocking network of imperialism as it was played out on the campuses. You could prove that the University was working hand-in-hand with the CIA, that ultimately the campuses would resort to the police to resolve their problems, . . . when you really pushed them they . . . would call upon all the repressive apparatuses to defend their position from their own students.[72]

Jones's experience mirrored Louis Althusser's view—one influential among leftist intellectuals in the 1960s and 1970s—of the relationship between capitalism and the state. According to Althusser, capitalism reproduces itself through the combined functioning of "Ideological State Apparatuses," such as schools, the family, and the media, and "Repressive State Apparatuses," such as the police and the court system.[73] The primary role of such presumably benign institutions as universities is actually to maintain established patterns of ideological hegemony and political authority. But when they fail in their mandate or their true function is exposed, the state intervenes with repression. Violence, from Althusser's perspective, thus serves as the ultimate basis of institutional authority. Militant confrontation at Columbia made that "truth" apparent to Jones.

Confrontation could also reveal something fundamental about inner reality and human existence generally. Susan Stern reported having a profound catharsis at the 1968 Democratic Convention, akin to a conversion experience. Observing rows of riot police attacking protesters, bloodied from the previous days' battles, Stern recalled:

> I lay down shuddering on a piece of blanket, and looked at the clouds gauzy in the blue sky. I thought about bullets ripping through flesh, about napalmed babies. I thought about Malcolm X and lynching and American Indians. Lying there, sweating from doses of speed and terror, I thought about Auschwitz, and mountains of corpses piled high in the deep pits dug

by German Nazis. . . . A new feeling was struggling to be born in me. It had no name, but it made me want to reach beyond myself to others who were suffering. I felt real, as if suddenly I had found out something true about myself; that I was not helpless, that life meant enough for me to struggle for it. . . . [N]ow I would fight.[74]

In her trembling mind, a continuum of oppression linked past evils with the aggression in Vietnam. The grim images and the vision of impending battle evoked in her an uncanny sense of compassion, purpose, empowerment, truth, and realness. Fighting, which the hobbling Stern would do during the remainder of the convention, consummated her epiphany. She emerged from her awakening convinced that life became meaningful in struggle—*that life itself was struggle.*

Art Johnson, reflecting on a somber march ringed by armed National Guardsmen following the battle over People's Park, reflected:

Fifty thousand people marched under the guns of death in the streets of Berkeley on Memorial Day[,] ready to lay down their lives. . . . The scene was a death trip for us all. We had been through death before, sure, on acid, in motorcycle wrecks—but here it was, our real blood, baked dry on the white flags of hope. Brother James [Rector] is dead, the first white youth to die in our fight to defend our own emergent culture. [His death] was the turning point [that] marks for white youth the transition from rebellion to Revolution—the emergence of a sense of common destiny, of a common culture, value system and life style which is dramatically opposed to the materialist, individualist, and corrupt values of this society.[75]

Creating a hierarchy of experience, Johnson contrasts the abstract or figurative death of a bad LSD trip with the materiality of "real blood." Violence, culminating in literal death, realized the meaning of death—and life—for the demonstrators. The stains of blood, much like stigmata on their white bodies, marked their resistance as genuine. Marching "under the guns of death," they also felt an unprecedented sense of cohesion and purposefulness. Violence, finally, induced in Johnson a Manichean illumination of two sides in total conflict with each other.

Johnson's comments also reveal the hazards of militancy. After recommending armed self-defense of "our way of life," he echoes Weatherman's extreme pragmatism, which was suspicious of words and privileged acts: "We must trust our real brothers—those we are bound to through real life activity—working, eating, fucking, doping, brawling—not to those who would involve us in some ego-media-power-theoretical bullshit! We don't need to be 'organized' and 'radicalized' by any theoreticians. We can learn from our brothers who are Doing It!"[76] The clumsy opposition of "real" and "unreal" life virtually annihilates the capacity for critical reflection by declaring it irrelevant, or worse; theory becomes the mortal enemy of practice—conceived as *pure vitalistic activity*—by destroying the budding revolution. Johnson ultimately provides an impoverished vision of the New Left's body politics. In a more or less indiscriminate celebration of the body, he lists a series of activities—each implying a related appetite—that have no intrinsically political substance. They offer, as primitive expressions of eros, only crude compensation for the alienation from the body seen by leftists as defining mainstream culture. Moreover, he ignores the fact that eating, having sex, and fighting were hardly exclusive to the counterculture, making the image of the total opposition of cultures a mirage. Militancy promised to yield true knowledge of society and the nature of political conflict; when promoting reductive analyses, it clouded the New Left's understanding of its own rebellion.[77]

perils

The themes of courage, danger, violence, realness, and death abounded in the theory and practice of the New Left. Focusing on how these terms functioned within the language of the New Left helps us understand their connection to one another. Since to be "real" meant to be "brave, courageous, or tough" according to Larkin and Foss's dictionary, showing physical courage was a way of demonstrating one's realness. New Left ideology enhanced this linkage between militancy and reality. If, as many young radicals held, power is the foundation of social existence, then courage—which impels face-to-face confrontation with power—allows one to participate in that *essential* reality; one becomes, in the process, "real." But the term "real" was also used to describe situations that were "*excessively* dangerous" (Larkin and Foss's emphasis).[78] In this rendering, "realness" reflected the more anxious perspective that "objective reality in the USA was a mere generalization of South Vietnam and Watts, that is, violent and perilous, with the outbreak of civil war imminent." Excess and peril, chaos and conflict, *constituted* reality. To access this volatile and precarious reality required, in turn, embracing *extreme* danger.

death trip

The association of reality and peril becomes more vivid still in the idea of the "death trip." A death trip, in radical parlance, was "a course of action" believed "to eventuate in catastrophe" and "with no counterbalancing gain" to show for it. The New Left, this definition makes clear, assessed acts of militancy by how well they served their political goals, measured against the sacrifice they demanded. The Days of Rage, were a "death trip" in that they courted excessive danger for doubtful gain. But Foss and Larkin list "excessive danger" as one of the definitions of "real"; in this way they establish an equivalence between the terms "real," "objective reality," and "death trip." To the extent that radicals conceived of reality in terms of violence and danger, militancy tended toward death. Black Panther leader Huey Newton spoke to this aspect of militancy with his concept of "revolutionary suicide." For Newton, in an oppressive society, the purest or most decisive revolutionary act—one that answered the violence of the system with violence of one's own—was necessarily a suicidal act. In existential terms, militancy represented a kind of "abiding with death" (Martin Heidegger's phrase) as militants tried to live in acceptance of the perilous structure of reality as they saw it.

militancy
↓
death

Given these high stakes, being militant was extremely demanding both politically and psychologically. Some activists developed the sense of being on a personal "death trip" as their protest evolved. Scott Braley had grown up in a small, straight-laced town in rural Michigan dominated by Dow Chemical. Drawn as a teenager to jazz (putting a "Diz [Dizzie Gillespie] for Prez" bumpersticker on his car was one of his earliest acts of rebellion), marijuana, and other deviant pleasures, he quickly graduated to more robust passions: stronger drugs, hitch-hiking west, and, while back in East Lansing, working with Michigan State SDS. From the Vietnam War, he concluded that America was "completely corrupt" and rapidly "destroying the world," demanding militant protest. "You might win, you might lose, but you have to fight," he believed, to defend and advance your principles. Where the fight would lead, however, Braley did not know, and he developed early on the grim suspicion that he would likely not survive to find out. Even before joining Weatherman, he recalls, "I had had a pretty deep feeling" that "23 was going to be my cut off."[79]

fatalism

A sense of impending doom, though rarely so overtly expressed, laced the imagery of the New Left. A remarkable aspect of the 1960s was the intensity with which young people communicated with one another and the world. With its articles, poems, cartoons, and other graphics, the underground press proved a potent vehicle, not only for political analysis, but also for the projection of young leftists' fantasies and desires. Overwhelmingly, the message was one of enthusiasm for the cause, contempt for the enemy, and confidence in eventual victory. Yet creeping into this presentation were morbid images, at once frightening and fatalistic, that provided a subterranean commentary on the New Left's increasingly hazardous rebellion.

New Left morbidness

The cover of *RAT*'s January 1969 issue pictures a reaper standing in a barren landscape, while an Asian sun rises—or sets—on the horizon. One hand holds a scythe, stuck in a corpse wearing a sash marked "1968"; the other holds a chain encircling the neck of a frightened, vaguely Asian-looking baby labeled "1969."[80] The optimism of 1968—when each month seemed to mark a new victory for the left globally—here vanishes in the projection of the dominance of death and suffering in the year to come. A February 1969 cover of Detroit's *Fifth Estate* shows a skeleton peering down from the center of a sun, in whose rays appears the text, "A Philosophy of Life and Death: wars, crimes, divorce, prejudice and insanity are mirrored on a river of blood whose trickling is the music of a skulled violinist and it washes into the sea of fear within your own mind."[81] The synesthetic images describe mainstream American culture as one of violence, hatred, and separation from which there is no psychic escape.

Fifth Estate's cover a year later is even bleaker. A grotesque reaper, naked except for a tie in the pattern of an American flag, holds the severed head of a "longhair," while dancing over e. e. cummings's lines: "I don't want to frighten you/but they mean to kill us all."[82] The overt "message" is one of fear that the state will increasingly use lethal violence against the movement. Yet the image exceeds this sober prediction, providing instead the fantasy of an encroaching holocaust. The projection of limitless annihilation also has a self-punishing quality, revealing both narcissistic and masochistic impulses within the New Left. The implication of the graphic, on one level, is that the New Left's rebellion is so threatening that it could elicit a response of mass murder. On another level, the graphic potentially conveyed young radicals' unconscious guilt over their rebellion against the system—the great, impersonal societal father—and the attending "desire," surely covert, to be punished. Extending the psychoanalytic model closes the circle. The desired punishment is only the introjection of New Leftists' "original" anger at the authorities presiding over a world deemed rotten.[83]

The Days of Rage highlight, finally, the relationship between militancy and ethics. Some leftists condemned the protest politically while praising it as an act of principle. Most provocatively, Stew Albert declared the Weathermen morally "perfect" by comparing the United States to Nazi Germany, the Vietnamese to the Jews, and Nixon to Hitler. He thus cast the Days of Rage as an expression of the Weathermen's desire, voiced by Dohrn, not to be the equivalent of "good Germans." At the same time, in its evident hyperbole and slippage between historical settings, his anal-

ogy illustrates the dubious extremes to which the left went in commu-
nicating its sense of moral urgency. (Young militants were not the only
ones drawing such analogies. John Fernandez, co-director of a prominent religious antiwar organization, commented that Nixon "may be
worse than" Hitler, making Americans "worse than the good Germans."
Rabbi Heschel, another antiwar leader, confronted Henry Kissinger in
1969 by suggesting that America would "look more and more like Nazi
Germany" if it continued attacking Vietnam.)[84] By any measure, the
United States of the late 1960s was not the equivalent of Nazi Germany.
The left's comparison of the two societies might therefore be dismissed
as a specious conflation of contexts, or even political abuse of the memory of the Holocaust.[85]

The invocation of the negative icon of the "good German" did not,
however, depend entirely for its validity on a comprehensive similarity
between the United States and Nazi Germany. Rather, it could express
the conviction that the morality of assassination and atrocity is absolute,
not relative. These crimes were persistent features of the war in Vietnam
and, to a lesser extent, of the state's campaign against black radicals. The
very existence of such crimes—in whatever quantity—issued a categor-
ical imperative, such as the Germans had faced and overwhelmingly failed
to honor under Hitler, to take an emphatic stance of opposition. Palmer
stressed the role the Vietnam War played in inciting the forceful language
and radical acts of the left:

> It was the Vietnam war that really triggered what happened in the 60s. . . .
> Without the Vietnam war I think the civil rights movement would have
> gone through with its relatively staid and almost monotonous seriousness
> and would not have involved "taking up the gun." . . . The war was so
> outrageous. . . . There was nothing more hypocritical, there was nothing
> more devastating to the sense of patriotism, the sense of American con-
> sciousness. . . . We compared the United States to Nazi Germany. We
> compared Lyndon Johnson and Richard Nixon to war criminals. . . . We
> were behaving as a country the same way as Nazi Germany behaved—
> a war criminal way.[86]

Palmer conceded that the Vietnam War was not neccessarily the greatest outrage in U.S. history, let alone world history. (Slavery, he stressed,
was likely more horrible.) But the war was so compelling for the 1960s
generation "because it was happening NOW!" It instilled in Palmer the
sense that "this is the testing time for all mankind. This is the testing time
for all Americans."

The comparison of the United States and Nazi Germany also suggested that <u>one had a duty to engage in resistance to injustice *regardless* of its ability to alleviate suffering or even move the public.</u> "I don't expect to have an effect," the antiwar leader Bettina Aptheker remarked. "I thought you protested something because it was wrong. Even if nobody listened."[87] New Leftists reasoned: Were the "good Germans" not the "silent majority" in their own country? Conceived in absolute terms, the morality of resistance escapes comparative and utilitarian considerations. As a result, one could speak of the moral statement made by the Days of Rage, despite the action's political failure.

<u>The Weathermen themselves were generally loath to stress the ethical current of their politics. They saw moralizing about the war as the domain of pacifists and liberals and promoted militancy primarily on political and strategic grounds. Ethical discourse clashed also with the ultramilitant style Weatherman initially projected.</u> One journalist observed that "the Weathermen think that anything on the moral level is 'sissy talk.'"[88] Hindsight has shifted their perspective. In the 1980s, Jeff Jones counted the Days of Rage among the group's greatest political failures, joking, "Thank God the Vietnamese weren't counting on us" to actually stop the war.[89] Yet he implicitly defended its moral impulse:

> The point of [the action] was that if they're going to continue to attack the Vietnamese and to kill the Panthers, then we as young white people are going to attack them behind the lines. . . . That's why we . . . smashed up people's private property, their cars, their windows, and fought the cops. . . . The situation was so grave, what the U.S. was doing—this of course was true—that we had to take extreme measures.[90]

Wilkerson used a language of paradox to describe how political senselessness and moral sense combined in the Days of Rage:

> It was just pure insanity. . . . [F]rom the standpoint of rational politics and organization we were out of our minds. We were as bad as the most psychotic religious . . . sects. Some brainwashed bunch of lunatics. On the other hand, as a response to what was going on in Vietnam, it was a response of total outrage. . . . At the time it didn't seem like we were having any impact at all, and it was a gesture of total frustration, which was to go bananas, and as such was a very sane response. And so even though it was totally crazy as a political act, history can't, doesn't, hasn't condemned it.[91]

For her, the Days of Rage were a desperate spasm, at once ludicrous and just, in the midst of a moral and political crisis. Her testimony, read against Gilbert's reflections, reverses the application of Weber's terms to New Left activism. As an act of moral outrage, violence conforms to the ethic of ultimate ends, whose main obligation Weber describes as "seeing to it that the flame of pure intentions . . . protesting against the injustice of the social order" burns brightly.[92]

Whatever the judgment of history, Wilkerson's contradictory verdict illustrates how militancy raised vital questions regarding the ethical and political limits of protest. The Weathermen certainly had no monopoly on moral indignation. Activists whose passion was just as strong could question not only the political sense but also the *ultimate* morality of righteous acts that hurt the goals of the movement or that increased repression and suffering. Was an ethically courageous act necessarily a good act? Could any act of rebellion—whatever the consequences and whoever its victims—be justified by pointing to the greater violence of the state? Weber's meditation on the morality of politics is once again relevant. In distinguishing the ethic of ultimate ends from the ethic of responsibility, Weber speaks of the "abysmal contrast" of these "irreconcilably opposed" orientations.[93] One privileges justice in the present over that in the future; the other privileges justice in the future over that in the present. Each contradicts the other, and neither can bring ends and means into harmony. Violence, which Weber describes as the "decisive means" of politics, makes the distance between the two ethics infinitely great.[94] In converting their outrage into violence, New Left radicals suffered the tragic measure of that irreconcilability.

Max Weber

· · ·

Well, I sure don't know
What I'm going for,
But I'm gonna go for it,
That's for sure.

The Grateful Dead, "Saint
of Circumstance" (lyrics
by John Perry Barlow)

Additional insight into the power and seductiveness of militancy for New Leftists comes from an unlikely source. During the upheavals in Paris in May 1968, Michel Foucault was in Tunisia on an academic assignment. While there, he witnessed the political struggle of students, for whom "physical commitment was implied immediately" by the oppressive con-

Foucault

ditions of neocolonialism.[95] Foucault found himself "profoundly struck and amazed" that the students, who faced years in prison simply for distributing leaflets, would put their "freedom," "bodies," and "lives" at risk in such a radical way. For the students, Marxism was not "merely a way of analyzing reality; it was also a kind of moral force, an existential act that left one stupefied." Foucault contrasted their passion with the sterile "hyper-Marxistization" and "indomitable discursivity" of French student radicals, trapped in endless debate and essentially free of any consequences for their dissident ideas. The Tunisians ultimately inspired in Foucault the desire to have a "total experience" and "accomplish a series of actions that would imply a personal, physical commitment that was real."

These are striking reflections from an intellectual who, in his sweeping criticisms of humanism and modern morality, did so much to retire the vision of "existential man" that informs his description of the Tunisians. Like American militants, he attributes integrity and "realness" to risk and physical courage; he indicts abstraction as a sign of inauthenticity and privilege; and he yearns to commit himself politically in a *total, physical* way that honors the great sacrifice of others. The Weathermen, radicalizing each of these views, made violence the measure of authenticity. Doing so, they appeared to champion Sartre's provocative dictum that revolutionary violence "is man re-creating himself," with the Days of Rage serving as a dramatic occasion for that re-creation.[96] Following the action, Jones insisted that "carrying out acts of armed resistance against the state [is the mark of] the highest form of human being."[97]

Despite such statements, the Weathermen never saw militancy as an autonomous value, fully divorced from political goals. It remained a means to a revolutionary end, not an end in itself. When later admitting to having glorified violence, they would speak primarily of being caught up in a "Debrayist myth" that led them to grossly misstate the benefits of actions like the Days of Rage.[98] Given Weatherman's concern with strategy, the denunciations of the Days of Rage as a political failure appear fitting responses. Indeed, militancy of Weatherman's sort threatened to shut down political reflection, render the message of the movement incomprehensible to those outside it and many within it, and make protesters even more vulnerable to attacks by the state. Marcuse, though able to sympathize with even "unintelligent action," cautioned that "escalation is built into the system" and "accelerates the counterrevolution," which might end up crushing the New Left's rebellion.[99]

Some critics went so far as to charge that, in insisting that fighting was the *only* relevant political act, the *only* expression of genuine commitment, Weatherman had corrupted the movement's values. The middle-aged pacifist Dave Dellinger was no stranger to militancy. He had been arrested numerous times for protest, and he repeatedly defended young militants against the admonitions of older leftists. Yet he urged the Weathermen to see that militancy did not have to be violent to be effective, as Gandhi and Martin Luther King Jr. had shown. Greg Calvert, a gay man admirably critical of the sexism suffusing the New Left, insisted:

> Socialism isn't about trying to "prove" one's manhood. . . . Socialism is about the discovery and struggle of a new manhood and a new woman-hood in which proving, warriors and domination become irrelevant relics. . . . Revolution is an act and process of love in which people become whole again because . . . passion and gentleness, human need and human possibility become so integrally merged that there is nothing left to "prove."[100]

Such responses to Weatherman were not, however, the final word on what was best for the movement. With their abundant calls for more political education, organizing, and coalition-building, critics seemed to offer few *existentially* compelling alternatives to the group. As if trying to answer Weatherman's passion, RYM II spoke of feeling "high on the people" (a phrase of Hampton's) when rallying with strikers and marching with blacks and Puerto Ricans. In unity, one RYM II partisan insisted, the left experienced the true meaning of militancy. Praising this kind of militancy for the *absence* of violence at RYM II events, he explained: "When we don't have to fight, when the pigs are afraid to attack, it's a victory, not a defeat."[101] Yet the RYM II demonstrations were noteworthy to many for their blandness, as they featured the standard fare of marching, chanting, and speech-making. RYM II's rapid demise following the October actions testifies, in part, to its failure to speak to people's passion and anger.[102] The *Guardian* seemed to want to put the genie of militancy back in the bottle altogether, as it condemned the Weathermen for doing their best to turn what should have been "the year of the heroic organizer" into the "year of the heroic fool."[103] Its recommendation of more grassroots organizing may have represented a rationally appropriate statement of What Was to Be Done for a movement sorely lacking adherents. But it did not appeal to the militant spirit responsible for much of the New Left's success. And if there was something far-fetched about

the notion of Weatherman leading an army of working-class youths, there
was an equal measure of implausibility to student radicals, often bred in
more than modest comfort, serving as humble champions of the American masses.

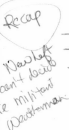

Recap

New left can't decide re militant Weatherman

The debate surrounding the Days of Rage reveals the New Left at a
profound impasse. To many, the Weathermen had taken militancy to a
point of diminishing and even dangerous returns. Yet New Left 1969 had
few resources besides its militant spirit. "We have created the slogan 'All
Power to the People,'" Calvert lamented. "We have not organized or cat-
alyzed 'People's Power.'"[104] After nearly a decade, the New Left had
barely begun to build a genuinely popular revolutionary movement.
Calvert answered Weatherman's vision of violent insurrection with his
own wishful scenario. He advocated "the revolution which does not need
vanguards because it is so deeply grounded in the lives of the majority
of the people that the governing classes will have lost before they know
what happened to their power."[105] Concentrating agency in the left's own
"silent majority"—awakened to revolution through diligent organizing—
Calvert envisioned a seamless transition of power. For others, lacking
confidence in the prospects of a Velvet Revolution in America, militancy
remained the favored way.

crisis in reality

The debates that raged in the late 1960s reflected not only political
divisions within the New Left but also a crisis in its understanding of reality. Weatherman, RYM II, PL, and countless other groups debated, in
essence, what the *real* nature of the system was, what constituted *real*
revolutionary politics, *real* militancy, *real* solidarity, and who the *real* SDS
were. Feminists, growing in numbers and momentum, charged that pa-
triarchy was the real source of oppression, rendering irrelevant much of
the New Left's analysis. People of color accused all manner of white activists of neither understanding nor adequately confronting the reality
of racism, both in society and in their own organizations. As if in an
infinite regress, each perspective pushed reality beyond the reaches of its
rivals. The instability of the very construct "reality" was evident in the
New Left's language. According to Larkin and Foss, young radicals employed the word "really" almost compulsively, sometimes in serial repetition or to begin and end a single sentence (i.e., "Like, that's really really fucked," and "Really, you know that's bullshit, really").[106] The
intended effect of this linguistic intensifier was to add weight to one's
views—to drive home where things were *really* at. Yet "the semantic impact of this redundant usage of 'really' was the communication—or in-

tersubcultural fortification—of a sense of nebulosity, that is, the uncertainty as to just what 'really' was or wasn't." Larkin and Foss thus disclose an autodeconstructive quality to the discourse of New Leftists: the more insistently they invoked notions of reality, the more the concept (or its referent) eluded them, with debilitating results. Endless political and ideological debates did not yield anything like a consensus analysis of the system or ultimately clarify the movement's task. On the contrary, it went hand in hand with the dizzying multiplication of revolutionary factions, ideologies, manifestos, and strategies, and the breakdown of a sense of common purpose.

Others within the protest culture did not try to mask confusion about "reality" with ideology. Instead, they openly testified to and even celebrated reality's uncertain or illusory quality. Larkin and Foss cite the Beatles' 1968 "Strawberry Fields Forever"—in which John Lennon professes, "Nothing is real / It's nothing to get hung about"—as a prime expression of the "deepening ambiguity" of reality, reinforced by the song's "dissonantly hideous conclusion." The Beatles, one might add, amplified this effect with their entirely dissonant "Revolution 9" and chaotic "Helter Skelter." Both became anthems for Charles Manson, who felt they foretold an imminent apocalypse, which his "family" would hasten with its murderous rampage. The songs were recorded in 1968, not long before SDS's collapse, the fraying of the antiwar movement, Altamont, and other events that appeared to turn the dream of the 1960s into a nightmare that refracted "reality" through the disorienting prisms of disillusionment, cynicism, and hate.

Within the psychedelic subculture—which was highly critical of the hyperseriousness of the "ideological" left—there had for several years been a form of testing that explored the ambiguity of the real. In the mid 1960s, the novelist Ken Kesey and his Merry Pranksters held bacchanalian LSD parties, called "Acid Tests."[107] The motto of these events, and the explicit challenge they issued to their participants, was "Can You Pass the Acid Test?" The differences between the Acid Test and gut check as two kinds of personal trials are striking.

The purpose of gut check was for an individual to overcome fear and, through confrontation, embrace the violence at the foundation of capitalist society. The challenge of the Acid Tests, by contrast, was to withstand the massive disorientation induced by the drug and the chaotic environment—to endure and even revel in the decomposition of the psychic and sensory frames of reference through which one conventionally apprehended reality. As potentially harrowing psychological and quasi-spiritual ordeals, they could induce a "death trip" all their own—one that demanded its own kind of courage to survive.[108] One possible insight from the experience was that reality—contrary to what the "normal" mind perceived—was at root chaotic; or one might sense that reality was a matter of perspective and could be creatively refashioned. For some, this revelation had political implications. Abbie Hoffman claimed that he made the decision to become a full-time activist while on an LSD trip, the drug having imbued him with a sense of near-infinite power and possibility.[109] And, in the ultimate experience of danger, one could take the drug in such a way as to combine the spirit of gut check and the Acid Tests. Hoffman reports that he took several hits of acid on the most violent night of the 1968 Democratic convention. The drug made the encounter with the raw power of the state all the more terrifying and exhilarating—a sensation that Hoffman, who suffered from mental illness, likened to the rush of manic depression.[110]

The New Left's politics of reality, much like militancy, was a source of both strength and weakness. On the one hand, the efforts of young leftists to define and connect with reality reflected their core desire to break out of what seemed an artificial world of superficial comforts and estrangement from their political and moral potential. Trying to discern "reality" behind the haze of the ideology of the status quo, they sought to find in politics and life something truer and more meaningful than what mainstream society offered them. On the other hand, the very attempt to demarcate reality with dogmatic certainty disempowered the New Left. So many in the movement contrasted to the "inauthentic" world they rejected some purportedly definitive understanding of the true nature of "the system." This effort, as it tended toward ideological absolutism, militated against an appreciation of the sheer complexity of a society like the United States, as well as of the monumental challenge of changing it. The result was a loss of humility and, with it, of the healthy sense of pluralism that had once been the New Left's hallmark. Such a pluralism, had it survived the late 1960s, might have encouraged New Leftists to see the value of a variety of approaches to political change. The tragic aspect to the dissolution of the New Left, in this light, was not so much the erosion of an always tenuous unity as the loss of its ability to deal constructively with diversity in its ranks.

·   ·   ·

The wheel is turnin' and you can't slow it down
Can't let go and you can't hold on
Can't go back and you can't stand still
If the thunder don't get you then the lightning will

> The Grateful Dead,
> "The Wheel" (lyrics by Robert Hunter)

The challenge of what to make of the Days of Rage was greatest for the Weathermen themselves. They had in advance assigned the action a decisive place within a projective mythology of revolution in America. Yet rather than reassessing their fantastic expectations in light of the disastrous results, the Weathermen mostly tried to force perceptions of the Days of Rage back in line with their expectations. The result was a tortured blend of exuberant claims of victory, frank admissions of failure, and subtle revisions in their self-understanding that made possible Weatherman's entire history as an "armed struggle" group. Weatherman had come to Chicago hoping that violence would somehow speak for itself—transcend, as a form of pure practice, the realm of language or representation. Weatherman's own conflicted response to the Days of Rage shows, however, that violence was itself an ambiguous text, whose meaning the Weathermen could not fully master.

After the Days of Rage, Weatherman collectives held intense criticism-self-criticism sessions to analyze the event. The first public pronouncement on the action came on October 21 in the SDS newspaper. Weatherman shortened the title of the last edition, *The Fire Next Time*, to simply *FIRE!* With this change, the group suggested that the Days of Rage were just the conflagration it had desired. Consistent with its neofuturist aesthetic of speed and raging chaos, Weatherman favored images over words to tell its exploits. The single-sheet issue was designed as a wall poster that featured pictures from the action, including protesters smashing windows and a Weatherman hitting a policeman. A cartoon word bubble had the fighting Weatherman saying, "Taste the Sweetness of Destiny, Racist Pig!!" with the words "Bloody Melee," "Rampage in Loop," and "Violent" dotting the collage.

On the reverse side, a National Liberation Front (Viet Cong) star sat in the middle of more battle pictures, over which Weatherman wrote:

> On Monday, October 6, a pig statue honoring the murderers of Chicago strikers was blown to bits. On Tuesday, October 7, the head of the Chicago Pig Sergeants Association said that "SDS has declared war on the Chicago Police—from here on in it's kill or be killed." On Wednesday, October 8 a white fighting force was born in the streets of pig city. . . . We came to

Chicago to join the other side—to stop talking and start fighting . . . to destroy the motherfucker from the inside.

There were only 500 of us, but we forced Pig Daley to call in the Guard. . . . We did what we set out to do, and in the process turned a corner. FROM HERE ON IN IT'S ONE BATTLE AFTER ANOTHER— WITH WHITE YOUTH JOINING IN THE FIGHT AND TAKING THE NECESSARY RISKS. PIG AMERIKA—BEWARE: THERE'S AN ARMY GROWING RIGHT IN YOUR GUTS, AND IT'S GOING TO HELP BRING YOU DOWN. DID THAT PIG SAY KILL OR BE KILLED?[111]

Judging from *FIRE!* the Weathermen emerged from the Days of Rage jubilant and filled as never before with enthusiasm for combat. Their statement reads like an imitation of the Panthers' defiant street speech combined with a rhetoric of relentless showdown. The group's imagery—or imagination—of battle soon grew still more fantastic. The front page of a subsequent issue of *FIRE!* featured a medieval etching of corpses hanging from trees and littering a battlefield, with the legend: "The above photograph was taken at the SDS National Action last month in Chicago. The figure at the left, drinking from the wine skin, is youth culture freak Marion Delgado."[112] The paper also showed an eerie charcoal drawing of a woman, her face blackened with ashes, sitting near a pile of skulls, while a battle rages in the distance.

The group stressed the transformation of the Weathermen themselves in the crucible of battle. The first issue of *FIRE!* shows Brian Flanagan, who faced attempted murder charges, leaving a Chicago courthouse with a clenched fist. Below his picture an explanation ran, "When we used to ask for a war to end wars . . . there was a kind of protection we got from the man. . . . Nobody in the 'white movement' had to do a lot of jail time. Our people haven't got offed yet. . . . But we've changed. We're not trying to end wars. We're starting to fight a war."[113] Weathermen exalted Flanagan, who appears more frightened than defiant in the photo, as a virtual martyr, who proved their willingness, as whites, to suffer jail or death. Yet Weatherman's display was conspicuous in what it left out. *FIRE!* made no reference to the virtual boycott of the action by working-class youths, the denunciations by the Panthers, and the avalanche of criticism from the movement. All this, in Weatherman's overheated imagination, melted into irrelevance, leaving the Weathermen and the police alone to play a deadly game of King of the Mountain, governed by the stark challenge to "kill or be killed."

Weatherman's more analytical statements on the Days of Rage echoed the self-congratulation of *FIRE!* while confronting some of the action's obvious shortcomings. On one level, the group tenaciously clung to the notion that it represented the beginnings of a phase of militant mass struggle in America. Shin'ya Ono, assessing the action a month later, restated Weatherman's view that "without this leap" into violent, galvanizing action, "the movement will continue to be a mere aggregate of individuals who may wish things to be otherwise . . . but who really have no concrete idea of how to make a revolution."[114] The Days of Rage, he claimed, forced "millions of kids" to "grappl[e] for the first time with the existence" of a white fighting force and helped those already in the movement to "re-examine the nature of their revolutionary commitment . . . and struggle harder."[115] At the same time, Weatherman tried to come to terms with its inability to field the army it had promised. The Weatherbureau officially blamed "the sectarian and dogmatic spirit that permeated every aspect of our work" and the "humorless franticness which we mistook for seriousness" for driving youth away.[116] Weatherman ultimately dealt with its failure by reconceiving the priorities of its supposed white army: the toughening of the group's own cadres was now the main goal. Two anonymous Weathermen claimed: "Our failure to attract thousands of kids turned into an important victory. . . . [The action] fixed in us a very deep part of our politics: being a revolutionary means fighting as hard as we can with whatever strength we've got."[117]

Weatherman's insistence that the Days of Rage had been a success had a tangle of roots. Some participants privately judged the event a failure and left the group, taking their criticisms with them. Among those who remained, strong personalities dominated the dissenting voices inclined to argue that Weatherman should rethink its fundamental approach.[118] Certain troubling issues, such as the destruction of "working-class" cars in Chicago, were neither resolved nor even seriously discussed.[119] To the extent that Weatherman retained faith in its capacity to lead a revolution by violent example, it became a prisoner to both its ideology and the myth it had created about itself. The self-imposed isolation of the members in tight-knit collectives, where doubts were taken as signs of weakness, served to reinforce their questionable assumptions.

And yet there is a sense in which the Days of Rage conformed to at least some of Weatherman's basic premises and goals. Beneath its bluster, the group recognized that the system was powerful, that identification with it ran deep, and that it would be incredibly difficult to persuade people in positions of privilege of the need to fight. Hirsch explained that Weatherman felt "allied with the world's struggle [but] separated from a lot of white people." The group's isolation in Chicago—far from causing the Weathermen to abandon what could seem a dangerously false and lonely path—only affirmed their sense of being "exceptional" whites. She continued, "We wanted to create havoc . . . not meaningless havoc [but] with a clear sense of why we were doing it. . . . We wanted to shake up day-to-day life and we certainly did that."[120] Another Weatherwoman allowed that "public officials' negative response was always a barometer of how" the Weathermen viewed themselves, adding to their self-congratulation over Chicago.[121] Some Weathermen looked past the problems with the protest because they were already so strongly focused on the next step—one so big, so bold, and so demanding that it seemed scarcely to permit eruptions of doubt and equivocations of will. Braley reports: "We had already made a commitment to build armed struggle on some level. We didn't know what it meant at that point, but I had personally made that decision. [The action] came, it went, it didn't affect what I thought about things because at that point I felt the development of clandestine work . . . was the primary thing to do, and whether there were 50 of us or 100 or 40,000 of us wasn't the question."[122]

The place of militancy within the ethos of the New Left suggests that the cathartic experience of combat itself substantially drove Weatherman's estimation of its achievement. So much of the preparation for the Days of Rage consisted of conditioning the members' courage. Two anonymous Weathermen asserted: "For each one of us . . . Chicago would be a crucial test. We knew that some of us might be killed. . . . We understood that to say we dug the Viet Cong or the Tupamaros or the Black Panthers and yet not be willing to take similar risks would make us bullshitters and racists."[123] Years later, Jones judged the Days of Rage an unequivocal political failure, but he observed that the Weathermen had overcome "tremendous personal fears." Given the courage he had summoned up to lead the march on the first night, he counted the action as one of his proudest experiences as an activist.[124] Jim Mellen not only acknowledged, but also questioned, the group's courage. As he walked to the Weatherman action on the last of the Days of Rage, a policeman threatened to attack him later in the day. Yet he could not say to his fellow Weathermen, "'Sorry gang. They're gonna hurt me so I'm not gonna show up today,' because all our people knew they were going to get hurt. It was sort of a collective puberty rite. We're all out hunting the simba; out hunting the lion and nobody can say to the other, 'I don't want to do it. . . . We don't need a lion.'"[125] The Days of Rage were, in short, the ultimate gut check—one the Weathermen passed.

Yet fear persisted, affecting the group's outlook in profound ways.

Gitlin described the "willful suspension of disbelief" as the "spiritual heart of the new militancy" that emerged with the turn from "protest to resistance." Suspending critical judgment about the weakness of the movement and the strength of the state worked against the potentially "imprisoning sense of isolation" and "paralyzing fear" as New Leftists pushed "to the outer rim of what [their] generation, by itself, could accomplish." The Weathermen were easy prey to this denial. To Braley, the Days of Rage were "like a train you grabbed onto." Though some of Weatherman's expectations were "completely unreal" and "self-deceptive," he recalls, "it was too scary to believe that no one else was going on that train."[126] To Larry Weiss, looking back, by the time of the Days of Rage, "all connection with reality was over."[127]

The New Left further tried to neutralize fear by believing, in Gitlin's words, that it had "outdistanced known reality [and] therefore also the judgment . . . of cool heads and internal restraints."[128] Hirsch recalled: "We were stepping out of the norm. . . . You had Old Left–New Left; this was a new New Left," intent on confounding conventional assumptions about what a rebel movement should do or be.[129] Yet Ayers confessed that behind the group's apparent confidence there was

> a sense that we were not only going out in unmapped territory, but [that] it was unmapped territory that was deeply mined and that we were likely to hurt ourselves badly. And the feeling of dread . . . was growing in my stomach and I think in our collective stomachs. . . . We were steeling ourselves for intense action. We felt that we would die, that some of us would die, and we looked at ourselves with an edge of both determination and a kind of despair.[130]

In light of this grim undercurrent, the variously campy and gruesome imagery in *FIRE!* can be read as a way of refracting the trauma produced by the decision to fight—a form of psychic defense, similar in function to gallows humor, that at once alluded to and provided distance from the mortal seriousness of Weatherman's undertaking. Projecting themselves into cartoon land by portraying their actions in collages and word bubbles, the Weathermen could de-realize the possibility of their own deaths. Invoking visions of annihilation, they could express an anxiety over their chosen paths that would be difficult to acknowledge either privately or in their public statements. However great their courage or yearning for "reality," the Weathermen hesitated in confronting the perilous reality of their endeavor head-on.

That hesitancy took on increasing relevance as the Weathermen assessed the "military" lessons of the Days of Rage. Ono insisted, incred- ibly, that "militarily and tactically, the action was a victory" by virtue of the extensive property damage and the relatively minor injuries to the Weathermen. Yet he also concluded that the Days of Rage had proved that "mass street action is a necessary, but a losing tactic."[131] Retiring the model of street fighting, the group soon explored a strategy of sabotage, in which bombs, not fists and bricks, were to provide the desired conflagrations. Just weeks after the Days of Rage, Weatherman's New York collective quietly began assembling an arsenal of explosives with which it would try to take the armed struggle further.

CHAPTER 3

"Hearts and Minds"

The Antiwar Movement, Violence, and the Critical Mass

While Weatherman was attempting to fashion itself into a revolutionary vanguard by fighting in the streets and planning for sabotage, other activists were devoting their energies to the more immediate goal of ending the war in Vietnam through mass mobilization. Demonstrations in October and November of 1969 were the centerpieces of the antiwar movement's fall strategy to show that the public had turned decisively against the war. Despite the desire of the organizers for unity around the message of peace, the demonstrations served as an occasion for intense debate among protesters over the nature of the war, strategies for ending it, and the ultimate goals of antiwar activism. The demonstrations also had an important bearing on the growing impulse within the left to violence. The Weathermen and other aspiring revolutionaries shared with less radical or risk-prone activists the concrete objective of ending the war. Doubting the efficacy of peaceful protest, however, they promoted violence as a vital, even necessary, means to that end. In addition, the war elicited a groundswell of anger, particularly among the young, which radicals tried to tap and further politicize. Opposition to the war, in short, was the main impetus for New Left violence, and it was from the antiwar movement that any larger push by whites toward armed struggle was most likely to come.

Mass demonstrations were among the defining acts of the antiwar movement and 1960s protest in general. They functioned as complex signs—events that everyone could regard as significant, but whose fun-

damental meaning and impact defied any single interpretation. Like the
Days of Rage, these demonstrations posed challenges to representation,
as activists and others argued over what they accomplished and labored
to fit them into competing ideological and strategic assumptions. More
specifically, the fall protests revealed the interdependent relationship between violent and nonviolent protest—how each was supported against
the perceived limitations or even dangers of its alternative. For some, the
size and intensity of the protests enhanced the hope of ending the war
through peaceful, democratic channels, while strengthening fears that violence would undermine their efforts. For others, the very size of the
protests, given that they produced no obvious change in war policy, only
enhanced the sense of the futility of nonviolence. These debates raged,
even as the line between purely violent and nonviolent protest blurred.
Discerning the reality behind activists' warring rhetoric sheds light on
the important question—one central to any judgment on Weatherman—
of what role militancy and violence played in the successes and failures
of the antiwar movement.

In addition, mass demonstrations elicited from their participants, observers, and critics alike a vocabulary of "the people," "the masses,"
"hearts and minds," and "the majority." These were the key terms with
which the war's supporters and opponents sought to justify their positions. In the fall of 1969, each side claimed that it was the majority—that
it had won Americans' hearts and minds. This rhetorical standoff represented more than the predictably contrasting claims of opposing political interests or the challenge of accurately measuring public opinion.
Rather, it reflected the instability of the entire vocabulary of democratic
legitimation with which political opponents laid claim to a popular mandate. That instability was rooted, in part, in the inherent difficulty of giving voice to such amorphous entities as "the people" or "the masses."
Whatever the faith commonly placed in them, these groupings can only
be represented symbolically, making the domestic battle over Vietnam a
war of symbolisms, in which each side developed an arsenal of images,
words, and actions by which it asserted itself as the bearer of the public's
will. More deeply, the volatile nature of the debate on the war raised the
possibility that the very notions of "the people," "the masses," and "the
majority" are inventions of language. The persistent ambiguity regarding
just what Americans thought about the Vietnam War signals an indeter-
minacy at democracy's core. The bitter conflict over the war—a seemingly exceptional domestic struggle born of exceptional circumstances—

thus exposes the fragility of democratic assumptions under "normal" political conditions.

Ambiguities in democratic theory and practice powerfully affected the efforts of radicals to articulate a rationale for "bringing the war home." Their efforts yielded competing visions of resistance, divided chiefly over whether antiwar activists felt they were fighting on behalf of or against the American people. This tension tapped into a broader crisis in the political imagination of the left, for which appeals to "the people" and "the masses" have held a special place.

.   .   .

Then they'll raise their hands,
Sayin' we'll meet all your demands,
But we'll shout from the bow your days
        are numbered.
And like Pharaoh's tribe,
They'll be drownded in the tide,
And like Goliath, they'll be conquered
        Bob Dylan, "When the Ship Comes In"

On October 15, 1969, more than two million people participated in local and regional antiwar demonstrations known collectively as "the Moratorium." The demonstrations were organized by the Vietnam Moratorium Committee (VMC), which had formed in the early summer for the purpose of staging the protests. Hatched by two former youth organizers for the antiwar presidential candidate Eugene McCarthy, the idea of the Moratorium was to show that antiwar sentiment had spread far beyond major cities and campuses and was now everywhere in America. All manner of campus groups and civic, religious, and professional associations joined in the organizing, giving the Moratorium an aura of "respectability" and the reputation among some radicals of being a "liberal" protest.[1]

The hard organizing work of the summer and early fall paid off beyond anyone's expectations. The Moratorium events were impressive for their grassroots focus, size, scope, and involvement of politicians and celebrities. Coretta Scott King, the widow of the recently slain Martin Luther King Jr., led candle bearers encircling the White House. Tens of thousands gathered in New York City to hear speeches by Shirley

MacLaine, Woody Allen, and Senator McCarthy. Organizers in New Haven called everyone in the phone book, producing a demonstration of 30,000 people. Detroit's mayor called on Nixon to "commence immediately the withdrawal of U.S. forces from Vietnam." Liberal congresspersons engaged the House of Representatives in hours of debate about the war, and thousands of federal employees joined in the day's protests. High school students throughout the country boycotted classes. Two New Jersey teenagers even took their own lives on the evening of the Moratorium, apparently in anguished protest of the war.[2] The Moratorium was an "outpouring of public dissent unprecedented in American history."[3] In its peacefulness and mainstream cast, it was also the first major antiwar protest with which the mainstream press sympathized.

The Moratorium, immensely successful in showing the breadth of antiwar sentiment, served as a rehearsal for mass rallies in Washington and San Francisco exactly one month later. The November demonstrations were organized by the New Mobilization Committee to End the War in Vietnam (New Mobe), a coalition of prominent antiwar groups that had for several years organized protests under the name "the Mobe." In its composition and reputation, the New Mobe was more radical than the VMC; young militants, radical pacifists, and various left-wing groups gravitated to the November demonstrations as the occasion for their voices to be more forcefully heard. VMC leaders endorsed the New Mobe protest with great hesitation, as they feared that violence in Washington would undermine the statement made by the Moratorium.

Though the New Mobe repeatedly announced its peaceful intentions, the issue of violence hovered over the November protest in a double sense. On the one hand, the Nixon administration sought to portray the event as far more threatening than the October Moratorium, despite the fact that many activists drew no sharp distinction between the two protests and attended both. The administration's claim was that the November demonstration would attract violence-prone elements with an anti-American agenda. Vice President Spiro Agnew, as part of a coordinated campaign to smear the demonstration, denounced the "anarchists and Communists" in the New Mobe leadership for preying "upon the intentions of gullible men" and turning their "honest concern" into something "sick and rancid." In a televised address on November 3, Nixon announced the support of America's "silent majority" for the war and proclaimed that the "vocal minority" of demonstrators threatened the country's "future as a free society." In response to loudly advertised fears of violence, 9,000 troops were brought to Washington and Marines set up machine guns on the Capitol steps.[4]

On the other hand, some antiwar forces were indeed hoping for militant action in Washington. The Yippie leaders Abbie Hoffman and Jerry Rubin called for a demonstration on the evening of November 15 at the Justice Department to protest the ongoing Chicago 8 conspiracy trial, in which they were defendants. Though Hoffman publicly pledged that the action would be nonviolent, Rubin privately told one alarmed organizer that the plan was to attack the building.[5] A rally on the evening of November 14 at Dupont Circle also provided a likely occasion for violence. The rally was sponsored by the "Revolutionary Contingent in Solidarity with the Vietnamese People," which included the Weathermen, militant New York activists calling themselves "the Crazies," and independent SDS chapters. Weatherman had at one point envisioned a prominent role for itself in the November demonstrations. The plan was to hold small, regional demonstrations on November 8 and then lead droves of youth in a violent rampage in Washington, much like in the Days of Rage. Politically isolated and burdened by legal and financial difficulties, Weatherman scaled back its ambitions. Though the group insisted that the war would be ended by military defeat and not by demonstrations, Ayers conceded at a press conference in Chicago shortly before the protest that "any motion against the war in Vietnam is significant at this point. Anything that stops the killing of Vietnamese people . . . we're supporting; so we're going to Washington, D.C." Weatherman also announced that it would leave its helmets at home and refrain from violence.[6] Yet some remained suspicious of Weatherman's true intentions. The FBI, aided by wiretaps and informants, tracked the Weathermen's push toward Washington. The New Mobe, for its part, would deploy thousands of marshals to keep order and deter violence throughout the weekend.[7]

On November 11, a final, ominous sign came when a collective headed by Sam Melville bombed the offices of Chase Manhattan Bank, Standard Oil, and General Motors in New York City. One day later, it bombed the Criminal Courts Building. The collective had made headlines over the summer and early fall for bombings in New York of a Marine Midland Bank, the Federal Building, and the Whitehall Street Military Induction Center. The explosions did hundreds of thousands of dollars' worth of damage, temporarily disabled the Whitehall center, and caused New York radicals to speculate about who had so boldly turned talk of revolutionary violence into action. The group also attracted the interest of the FBI, which set up a twenty-person unit to investigate the bombings.[8] The November bombings would be the collective's last. On the evening of November 12, Melville was apprehended by nearly two dozen armed agents while attempting to bomb military trucks in the company of a police informant. Authorities quickly arrested two co-conspirators, Jane Alpert and David Hughey, and issued a warrant on a third, Patricia Swinton, but missed the involvement of Robin Palmer and three others (among them an Ivy League professor) whose identities were never publicly revealed. Melville was sentenced to thirteen years in prison. He would later be killed in the 1971 Attica prison uprising, making him one of the New Left's few and most beloved martyrs.

After Weatherman, the New York City collective was at the time the most significant New Left group engaged in violence. Its activities testify to the growing volatility of the antiwar movement as the war ground on and the tension between violence and nonviolence sharpened. Capturing this unsettled climate, on November 12, the front page of the *Washington Post* featured a story about the issuing of a permit for the peaceful New Mobe march two days later alongside a report on the collective's latest strike, headlined "3 Bombings in N.Y. Tied to War Foes." The collective also affirms what focus on the Weathermen can obscure, namely, that the Weathermen were neither alone among New Leftists in pursuing armed struggle nor represented the only way of doing things.

Sam Melville defined the spirit of the collective, even if he was a unique personality within it. Born Sam Grossman, the son of a Jewish communist, from whom he had become estranged, he changed his name to Melville because of his love of Herman Melville's novel *Moby Dick,* rife with the themes of adventure and lonely obsession. Friends describe him as the quintessential man of action: handsome, charismatic, and emanating an enticing sense of danger, he seemed something of an American archetype. (His girlfriend and fellow bomber, Jane Alpert, said of him: "Radical politics, an air of masculine authority, and a delicious illicit sense about sex—Sam mesmerized me.")[9] Unlike the Weathermen or other members of his collective, Melville had no need of complex justifications for violence and elaborate training to sharpen his courage. Instead, he gravitated, as if by instinct, to violence as an expression of political principle or simple common sense. He bitterly complained, for instance, that protestors remained too passive when under attack by police at street demonstrations.[10] Political friends, alluding to both his name and character, called him Ahab. Explaining the moniker, Palmer confessed that though Melville was quite smart, he was at root "an anti-intellectual [who] much preferred doing something to giving a speech about it. . . . Sam didn't like to talk, he liked to act. He was Ahabian."[11] Melville, in short, appeared to embody Weatherman's ideal of militancy that exalted decisiveness and disparaged mere rhetoric.

The New York collective did not, however, share Weatherman's rigid ideology, seemingly single-minded commitment to revolutionary violence, or tight group discipline. Its members remained active in their careers and in a range of activism, including alternative education, underground journalism, and guerrilla theater. They neither adopted the toughened personas of "stone-cold revolutionaries," as the Weathermen had done, nor kept a low profile, as caution would seem to dictate. Two members, Palmer and a female friend, were in fact famous in Greenwich Village's radical scene for their Yippie antics. On Halloween night of 1968, the two had run naked through a high-profile gathering in New York City of recently declared Humphrey Democrats and then presented the severed head of a pig to John Kenneth Galbraith, while supporters brandished Viet Cong flags and chanted revolutionary slogans. They continued these spirited disruptions, which often entailed arrest, well into their careers as bombers. Being so conspicuous as theatrical troublemakers, they figured, would discourage police from thinking they could conceivably be involved in bombings. For added measure, they strictly separated their activities in New York's West Village, where much of the guerrilla theatre was planned, from those in the East Village, where the dynamite was stored and the bombings planned.

The life of the Melville collective, unlike that of the hyperdisciplined Weathermen, had a haphazard, make-it-up-as-you-go-along quality, punctuated by moments of exhilaration and great danger. The impulse to commit bombings came partly from two Canadian "Quebec Liberation Front" fugitives, whom Melville and Alpert had harbored in New York and then helped in hijacking a plane to Cuba. The Canadians, impressing their American hosts with their intelligence and commitment, made the guerrilla life seem appealing. The New York group secured its dynamite when three members robbed a Bronx explosives company. Elated, they kept the dynamite for weeks in a kitchen refrigerator (having heard that it stayed "fresh" that way), while they debated what to do with it. The first strike proved inauspicious. On July 26, 1969, the anniversary of an important date in the Cuban revolution, Melville bombed a warehouse of the United Fruit Company, which had backed the Cuban dictator Fulgencio Batista. The bomb, however, was placed near soft dirt, greatly muffling the explosion and earning it only a small mention in the *New York Times*. With neither great forethought nor the group's clearance, Melville then, in the late evening, bombed a Marine Midland bank. A warning, which Alpert had begged Melville to phone in, was ignored by a night watchman. Nearly twenty people, mostly female secretaries working the night shift, suffered minor injuries, leaving Melville devastated and determined never again to so recklessly endanger people. The group soon grew more efficient. In September, Alpert planted a bomb on the floor of New York's Federal Building, which housed U.S. military. Describing the process of transporting the bomb, Alpert reports having felt hyperaware of her surroundings, at once fearful and "absolutely happy," nervous and oddly calm, "as when the first rush of an acid trip subsides." Watching the massive explosion at 2 A.M. from a distant building, she and the others stood in silent awe and then erupted in jubilation at having slowed the war machine and, in her mind, "brought the revolution an inch or two closer."[12]

Though ostensibly pledged to communist revolution, the collective framed its rebellion more in existential than in narrowly political terms. The communiqué accompanying the bombings on November 10, which the *Washington Post* called "highly literate," read "corporations have made us into useless consumers, devouring increasing quantities of useless credit cards and household appliances. Jobs are mindless. Vast machines pollute our air, water and food."[13] Explaining the deepest roots of his actions, Melville later wrote from prison: "We must move to a place beyond all known issues. . . . What we want is salvation from a meaningless annihilation. To not be cremated for coka-cola and plastic flags . . . on the moon."[14] He also conceded soon after his arrest what Weatherman as an organization would take years to admit: that guerrilla activity in America was scarcely destroying the U.S. power structure or world imperialism. Melville defended his activities, at last, in strongly ethical terms, writing, "In a time when all action seems meaningless at least we won't be good Germans."[15]

Whatever the illicit pleasures of the collective's improvised rebellion, the group's lack of discipline would cost it dearly. An aspect of Melville's imperious personality was his refusal to adhere fully to group decisions. By early November, the collective had nearly fallen apart, dividing precisely over the question of whether it made political sense to commit bombings so close to the November 15 demonstration. Melville pressed on, winning half the collective back to bombings. Yet over the group's strenuous objections, he recruited George Demmerle, the informant responsible for the collective's demise. Demmerle, as was standard for provocateurs, had spent months proving his stripes among radicals (he had been arrested for protest activity and tirelessly staffed a Yippie booth at Woodstock); talked loudly and even crazily of the need for violence; and slowly won the trust of his main target, Melville, who was seeking collaborators not prone to second thoughts.[16] Despite its doubts, the group did not subject Demmerle to the presumptuous and potentially degrading tests—such as drugging and verbally abusing the "suspect" to see if he would crack—that Weatherman used to root out informants.

The collective was distinct from Weatherman in a last important way. While Weatherman was talking boldly of its desire to wage an all-out guerrilla war, the New York collective engaged strictly in what it dubbed "pacifist bombings." Attacking property only, and, after the Marine Midland explosion, issuing warnings to prevent injury, it pioneered a style of attack that would only later become Weatherman's signature.

The recent bombings, along with the Dupont Circle and Justice Department actions planned for November, conveyed the skepticism of antiwar radicals as to what large, peaceful demonstrations could accomplish. For five years, the antiwar movement had had to contend with the sense that activities such as marching, petitioning, and lobbying Congress had little effect on war policy. Wells documents a "broad historical pattern," evident already by 1967, in which "[p]erceptions of powerlessness were especially prevalent among antiwar activists in the weeks after big national protests."[17] By the end of the 1960s, many activists were tired of the cycle of exhilaration and disappointment associated with large demonstrations. Pointing to the movement's apparent legacy of failure, some denounced the continued pleas for civility by mainstream antiwar leaders and engaged in such militant actions as burning draft cards, closing down military induction centers, stopping troop trains, "trashing" property at demonstrations, and, at an extreme, bombing military and corporate targets.

Such acts were hardly the exclusive doing of the young. Long before Weatherman formed, older activists pledged to pacifism and driven by religious conviction were committing sabotage against the war machine. Most notably, in May 1968, in Catonsville, Maryland, nine activists, including two Catholic priests, Philip and Daniel Berrigan, took 1-A files designating young men for service from a Draft Board office and burned them with crude napalm made from a recipe in a U.S. military handbook. They prayed while waiting for the police, who arrested them on the charge of interfering with the administration of the Selective Service Act.[18] At

their trial, they argued that it was their moral duty, given the accumulating horror of the war, the futility of appeals to the powerful, and the
nature of their faith, to transcend symbolism and hinder the U.S. military in "an actual physical way."[19] In this they succeeded, as the files had
to be laboriously reconstructed. But it was precisely the symbolism that
gave the act its greatest power. The napalm did not burn human beings,
but only pieces of paper—files that stood "for the death of the men they
represent." To the charge that they were sowing disorder, the defendants
answered that they had violated only that "public order which is in effect a massive institutionalized disorder . . . killing is disorder." Addressing the court and the country, they intoned: "When at what point
will you say no to this war? We have chosen to say with the gift of our
liberty, if necessary our lives: the violence stops here, the death stops
here . . . this war stops here." They were convicted and given sentences
ranging from two to three and a half years in prison.

The deeds of the Catonsville 9, as the group came to be called, gave
rise to similar actions. Over the next several years, close-knit groups of
faith-based activists—nearly all strict pacifists and a great many devout
Catholics—raided Draft Board and other government offices in over a
dozen cities. The early model for these actions was to wait for capture
and use the resulting trial to challenge the war publicly. As stiff sentences
were handed down and the war escalated, the raiders operated more and
more clandestinely. Better to mute the symbolism and live free to fight
another day, some reasoned, than to spend months or years behind bars,
where one's value to the antiwar cause was not nearly as great.[20]

These raids, which meant taking on extraordinary levels of risk, were
motivated very much by the desire to match deeds to words. In this respect, despite their pacifism, spiritual conditioning, and ethical rigor, the
militants of the religious left strangely mirrored the equally small, close-
knit cadres of young radicals exploring subversion by violent means.
Their actions also underscore how difficult it became to strictly separate
violent and nonviolent protest. The Berrigan circle took as its mandate
the premise that "certain property has no right to exist: concentration
camps, slums, and 1-A files."[21] To destroy these was therefore not violent at all. Even so, the cumulative, material damage to the war machine
caused by pacifists—priests, nuns, and clergy among them—may have
rivaled or even exceeded the damage done by New Leftists fancying themselves guerrillas pledged to violent insurrection.

The escalation of tactics reflected not only a heightened sense of urgency but also ideological shifts within the antiwar movement. Toward

the end of the 1960s, increasing numbers of activists saw Vietnam as an
imperialist war. This view opposed more limited understandings of the
war as an expression of the stubborn pride of President Johnson and his
advisors, perpetuated by his duplicitous successor; an overzealous anticommunism that misinterpreted America's true security interests; or the
deep-seated militarism of American society. Instead, anti-imperialists
viewed the war as a logical extension of the American economic and political system—as something that America's corporate, political, and military leadership both *wanted* and *needed*. The reluctance of the U.S. government to end the war in the face of unrelenting opposition from the
National Liberation Front in Vietnam and widespread protest at home
compounded the impression that the war was no isolated foreign policy
mistake but a structural necessity for American capitalism.

As anti-imperialism gained ground, many protesters also began to express their active support for the NLF. In doing so, they came into conflict
with activists whose goal was peace and whose principal objections to
the war were its political and financial costs to the United States and the
tremendous suffering it caused on both sides. Support for the NLF became conspicuous in the symbolism of radicals. Some displayed, often
at considerable risk of censure within the movement or attack by police,
NLF flags and chanted at rallies "Ho-Ho-Ho Chi Minh, NLF is gonna
win!" In one incident, a contingent marching in Philadelphia in 1967
provoked the United Veterans for Peace by carrying NLF flags; tensions
got so high that police had to separate the flag holders from the other
marchers.[22] Behind these overt gestures of solidarity with the NLF lay a
deeper, more personal sense of identification with the Vietnamese. Some
American activists saw the sacrifice of the Vietnamese as the wellspring
of their own protest and comparatively modest sacrifice. Palmer, who
zealously promoted the use of the NLF flag as the antiwar movement's
most powerful symbol, wrote in 1967, "We protest because the NLF
fights; we march in broad daylight, because the NLF crawls through jungles at night; we get our heads cracked and our knees clubbed because
those in the NLF die." Defending the NLF politically, he added, "the war
will end sooner (America will withdraw) when more Americans realize
that they are fighting something good they cannot defeat instead of something evil they cannot defeat."[23]

Imperialism was also a way of describing the distribution of power in
the United States, with important implications for antiwar resistance. The
charge of imperialism, with its Marxist premises, suggested that American foreign policy served the interests of a more or less coherent capi-

talist class that was only superficially committed to democracy at home. Radicals were therefore leery of democratic appeals to a power structure intent on fighting the war for its financial and political gain. Within an anti-imperialist framework, resistance to the war translated easily into a desire for the radical redistribution of political and economic power in the United States. In its most ambitious rendering, the call to "bring the war home" meant trying to bring down the whole system responsible for the war in Vietnam.

The sense that something more than demonstrations was needed coursed through radical circles on the eve of the November march. In *FIRE!* Weatherman charged that, "Marches on Washington won't end the war because peace marches . . . can't work in a fundamentally anti-democratic society." According to Weatherman, the antiwar leadership "constantly held back the political and tactical growth of the movement" by believing that massing large numbers of people would persuade the "small class of corporate imperialists" responsible for the war to relinquish its power.[24] Here the Weathermen approached Marcuse's provocative assessment of the function of sanctioned dissent in a regime of "repressive tolerance," such as he felt the United States to be:

> Within a repressive society, even progressive movements threaten to turn into their opposite to the degree to which they accept the rules of the game. . . . The exercise of political rights . . . in a society of total administration serves to strengthen the administration by testifying to the existence of democratic liberties which, in reality, have changed their content and lost their effectiveness. In such a case, freedom (of opinion, of assembly, of speech) becomes an instrument for absolving servitude.[25]

Insisting that "the real terms of the struggle are set by the most advanced actions," like the Days of Rage, Weatherman endorsed the New Mobe march mainly as an opportunity to radicalize young demonstrators. Weatherman declared bluntly, "It's not so much that we're against the war; we're for the Vietnamese and their victory."[26]

Less strident voices issued similar criticisms of the march. Seattle's underground newspaper *The Helix* had freshly denounced the Days of Rage. Yet it too complained that "mass actions of peaceful protest, in and of themselves, do little to achieve substantial change in American society." Alluding to the Nixon administration's comments following the October Moratorium that it would not be influenced by the fall protests, the *Helix* flatly predicted that the November demonstrators would "see how useless their actions have been when once again they are ignored by Nixon and baited by Agnew and Mitchell" (Nixon in fact told reporters that he planned to watch college football on TV in the White House on the day of the November march, which he then did). Condemning the antiwar leadership for its efforts to court liberal support and to "isolate militants," the *Helix* called for "massive militant action" to "raise the social and political cost" of the war.[27] As the antiwar movement approached the greatest public display of its size and strength, it suffered its sharpest divisions.

.   .   .

We own half the world, oh say can you see
The name for our profits is democracy
So like it or not you will have to be free
'Cause we're the Cops of the World, boys
We're the Cops of the World
                Phil Ochs, "Cops of the World"

The November demonstration was a series of events stretching over three days, in which the initiative toggled between the peaceful majority and the militant minority. The "March against Death" began the protest on Thursday evening. Buses from all over the country deposited demonstrators, noticeably young, at the west end of the Arlington Memorial Bridge. There, they were given candles and placards bearing the name of an American GI killed in Vietnam or a Vietnamese village attacked by the United States. They marched for two and a half hours, often in rain and hail, to the White House, where they read the names on their placards into a microphone. The march ended at the Capitol, where to the beat of a drum, they dropped their placards into coffins adorned with flowers. Forty-five thousand people completed the march, which lasted forty hours.[28]

In the March against Death, the antiwar movement conveyed its message of peace in the starkest terms: youthful eros marching past the masters of war, life protesting death. The march's solemnity and quiet determination was a moving experience for its participants and deeply impressed the mainstream press. Yet for some on the left, the march seemed depressingly futile. The Liberation News Service commented that it didn't

> tell you where to go from here, how to fight against this abomination. But still somehow it was impressive. Macabre, deathly and medieval, making

you think of a society in decay, plague-stricken or destroyed by famine or war. And it made you think too about the kids . . . many of whom didn't really know where the war had come from or what to do about it other than offer up their sense of sorrow. It seemed strange that they could really think their frail candles would affect the power that rested comfortably behind [the White House's] blinding floodlights.[29]

The column lamented not only the naïveté of the marchers but, more fundamentally, the seeming exhaustion of the forms of protest and the symbolism on which the movement had so long relied.

Friday evening spotlighted the militants. The Weathermen vacillated on their role in the protest to the bitter end, first trying a scheme of extortion. On Thursday, Ayers and three other Weathermen, desperately needing money for the group, marched into the offices of the Vietnam Moratorium Committee and demanded $20,000.[30] In return, Weatherman would refrain from violence the following night. Turned away by incredulous VMC representatives, the Weathermen then geared up for battle. On Friday, several thousand demonstrators tried to march from Dupont Circle to the South Vietnamese Embassy. They met a blockade of policemen, who fired tear gas at them. Marchers retaliated by throwing rocks, bottles, and bricks. Weathermen and others broke windows and started small fires. The melée did not have the aggressiveness of the Days of Rage, and the Weathermen privately complained that the demonstration was too timid.[31] Yet something of the fighting spirit that Weatherman had quickly come to symbolize surfaced within the crowd. "People who had six weeks ago called us crazy adventurists were now running in the streets with VC flags and smashing windows," Weatherman proudly observed.[32] The Quicksilver Times concluded from the battle that "many demonstrators [who] had peacefully marched for years . . . finally learned that peaceful marches would not end the war. . . . They now understand, 'You don't need a weatherman.'"[33] New Mobe leaders, fearing that the violence of a small minority would discredit their protest, disclaimed the Dupont Circle action.[34]

The New Mobe demonstration on Saturday drew more than half a million people in Washington and several hundred thousand in San Francisco, making it the largest concentrated antiwar demonstration up to that point. In the capital, the majority of the demonstrators were young, white, and middle class, prompting comparisons with the summer's gathering at Woodstock. For hours, they marched, rallied, sang, and listened to speeches, while Military Police in Army jeeps roamed the streets near the Mall. Placards ranged from the straightforward ("Peace Now") to the earnest ("Computer Professionals for Peace"), the insistent ("Return to Sanity"), the clever ("Save Lives, Not Face"), and the brazen ("Agnew—Shut Up!").[35]

The tremendous size and urgency of the protest made it a compelling political statement, like the March against Death. Yet it too pulsed with a tension of hope and despair. The New Left reporter Sherry Reeder compared the protest to the medieval Children's Crusade led by Peter the Hermit to regain the Holy Land from the Muslims. "Very much like the earlier crusade," she observed, "the youth that gathered in Washington were there for a purpose without a real means of gaining that which they sought. . . . Chanting the holy word of peace, the largest youth crusade in history started down the Mall to recapture the land of Amerika for the people. [Among the crowd] there prevailed that beautiful faith in believing that something can be done." Upon reaching the Mall, the sense of expectancy was dampened by endless speeches to the converted. Reeder commended the singer Arlo Guthrie—son of the folk legend Woody Guthrie and a great balladeer for justice in his own right—for his desperate admission from the speakers' platform: "I don't need to say anything. It's all been said before." In an echo of Weatherman's rhetoric, Reeder concluded her report forebodingly: "Was anyone [in power] listening after all, or is it true that, as one demonstrator's placard proclaimed: 'This is the last march, the fire next time.'"[36]

The novelist Sol Yurick had come from Brooklyn with a rag-tag group of working-class youths, who, in a makeshift collective, shared their frustrations with the war, their economic prospects, and their frequent harassment by police. Seeing the plaintive mass of demonstrators, Yurick thought of the "workers of St. Petersburg in 1905 led by Father Gapon, petitioning the Little Father for redress and bread and getting shot for their faith."[37] From the rote speeches and peace songs, he concluded that, in five years, "We've gone nowhere." Yurick's image of the vulnerability of the mass turned into one of its power—if it had defied the Mobe leaders and loosed itself in violent rage:

I think that we were very close . . . close enough to terrify even those who hated the war but believed in the system . . . and were fighting against the war that they had supported last year because they were no longer making money from it. Who knows what hurried conferences took place, who knows what their estimation of the danger was . . . If we had all to run, to charge, we could have swept those sentries aside like nothing . . . and stormed through that white mausoleum of American dreams till we came to that figure, crouching by the T.V. doing magical obeisance to a quiescent and absent public that gave him life, and we could have torn the heart out of that manifestation of an old America . . . they knew it better than we did. It was close: we were all there: we might have done it: they know it: we blew it.[38] [ellipses his]

A small contingent chanting "War, war, one more war, revolution now" had in fact tried to break through the line of marshals and rush the White House, but to no effect.[39] Yurick, having flickered between fantasies of tragedy and triumph, left the march with a sense of wasted opportunity.

"Fire" came in the early evening as thousands of protesters broke away from the main demonstration and set out for the Justice Department. Some demonstrators marched behind a banner reading "Power to the People" over a Black Power fist; further back was a banner for the "Nat Turner Brigade." Among the sea of Viet Cong flags, signs read "Stop the Trial," "Beat Nixon into Ploughshares," and "The People of Vietnam Have Made Their Choice—Support the NLF!" The Weathermen felt like kings for the day. Jim Mellen recalls that thousands of people "did the same thing we did [in Chicago] in front of the Justice Department. . . . [I] hollered, 'Let's go this way,' and, Jesus, you should see the crowd that followed me. The reason they followed me was because I was a Weatherman."[40]

Yet the same tensions that plagued the Days of Rage were present in Washington. As the crowd made its way toward the Justice Department, Mellen recalled:

> It was an astonishing situation. People thought that we were really revolutionary heroes and that we were greater than life. We went down this street and we surrounded a black motorcycle policeman. . . . so many people you couldn't even see them all. . . . [H]e pulled his gun out and pointed at me and said, "If you guys comes one step closer I'll shoot!!" All these people . . . really thought we were just going to overwhelm this policeman and take away his gun from him. I thought this was madness because not only might he shoot me, but also, he was a forlorn character. Why would you want to hurt this guy? He was scared to death. . . . [A] lot of people were asking me afterward, "Why didn't you off that pig?"[41]

As the crowd traversed a commercial district, demonstrators smashed store windows and even beat up a random shopper because they were "so inflamed with the idea of doing something."[42]

When at the Justice Department, some protesters tacked "Building Condemned" signs on the building's enormous, medieval doors. Others stoned the edifice and smashed windows with red flags, providing the week's second image of a society in turmoil. At one point several helmeted demonstrators—Weathermen or Weatherman-types—took down the American flag from the building's flagpole and put the Viet Cong flag in its place. Police quickly restored the original flag, keeping guard over it in battle-ready posture. Rows of police in riot gear soon moved in to clear the area. Tear gas wafted into the upper floors of the building, where officials nervously watched the riot. Attorney General John Mitchell reported that he felt as if he were witnessing the storming of the Winter Palace in Saint Petersburg in 1917.[43]

The fall protests, though designed to present an image of unity, exacerbated existing divisions within the antiwar movement. Some activists stressed the importance of bringing large numbers of people into the movement and, in the wake of such a show of force, appealing once more to the relevant powers to end the war. Within the framework of those goals, New Mobe leaders declared the protest a resounding success, despite Nixon's insistence that he would not be affected by it and the boycott of the protests by the great majority of Congress.[44] The New Mobe highlighted the "beauty and meaning" of moments of peaceful togetherness, such as the "quiet and self-discipline" of those waiting to participate in the March against Death and the "joyful swaying of uncounted thousands" singing "Give Peace a Chance."[45] Other activists with broader ambitions saw the antiwar movement as an opportunity for building a mass socialist base in the United States and accepted the need for strategic alliance with antiwar liberals. The *Guardian,* for instance, praised the New Mobe's efforts at building a coalition and denounced the "left-wing adventurism" of those committing violence. But the *Guardian* warned also of the movement's susceptibility to the "right-wing opportunism" of liberals that threatened to submerge anti-imperialist politics within the movement. Both extremes, it felt, reflected the "pessimism and frustration" of a left that had failed to build a sizable anti-imperialist following.[46]

A final strain in the movement, though internally divided on the ideal form and ultimate ends of militancy, advocated direct action to impede the actual prosecution of the war and provoke a broader sense of political crisis. In postmortems on the march by the radical left, anger with the antiwar leadership at times rivaled anger over the war itself. To Abbie Hoffman, the demonstration looked like "a huge mess begging the president, the state department, the pentagon, all these war criminals 'Just Give Peace a Chaaance. . . .'" Criticizing both the restraint of the New Mobe and what he saw as the planned violence of the Weathermen, Hoffman celebrated the spontaneous violence of Yippies and others as an authentic expression of political anger. He declared, "You cannot express outrage at the policies of the Amerikan government by raising a V [peace] sign. Outrage takes on meaning when you see someone throwing a rock through a window."[47] In the days following the march, an insurgent, youth-dominated "Radical Caucus" within the New Mobe pushed for a campaign of massive civil disobedience.[48] At an extreme, the Weathermen concluded with some merit that the "most important tension" in the demonstration was not over the war but over "the question of violence." Jeering at those who pleaded for peace in an orderly fashion, the Weathermen gloried in their Dionysian romp in Washington, in which they "moved through the streets in groups, marching, dancing, running, chanting, singing, downing jugs of wine."[49] The group's main "commentary" on the protest was a multipage cartoon in *FIRE!* showing smiling, helmeted Weathermen marauding through the city.

Judging from these assessments of the protest, each grouping appeared certain of the superiority of its approach, resented the others for jeopardizing its efforts, and battled for the allegiance of antiwar protesters. At the heart of the division, viewed less in ideological than in strategic terms, lay the question of whether the movement was to succeed by using the legal, democratic channels available to it or, by recognizing the limitations of those channels, "bringing the war home." The *Washington Post*'s editorials praised the peacefulness of most demonstrators, gushed over the D.C. police's purported restraint, denounced those carrying VC flags and throwing rocks as hatemongers, and mentioned the Weathermen only to dismiss them as extremists.[50] Yet the *Post* columnist Nicholas von Hoffman all but predicted "fire" if Nixon ignored the protesters' pleadings:

> It was the best, it was the biggest, it was the last of the antiwar demonstrations. If it cannot convince the men who make war and peace that they can't safely go on with the conflict, no amount of marching, praying or singing will change their minds.
>
> The young people will turn to other tactics because they've come in supplication and politeness; they've walked like pilgrims, holding candles in the windy night, and, one by one in front of the White House, begged for their lives. . . . There's nothing more they can do to win the minds and hearts of the men who run the government. Either these men understand the shame and reproach of having tens of thousands of people implore them for life and clemency on the streets, or the youth will turn to other ways to stop the killing.[51]

The November protest did not of course persuade those in power to end the war. Some activists, mostly the young, turned to more drastic forms

of protest. The November march was the last national demonstration in
which the Weathermen publicly participated before committing bombings from the underground. The New Left press openly called for violence
and even the overthrow of the government, while bombing collectives
sprang up from coast to coast to attack the war machine.

The November demonstration did not by any means, however, mark
the *wholesale* turn to illegal or violent resistance. Mostly, the same tension between nonviolence and violence, persuasion and disruption continued to play itself out in antiwar organizations and in demonstrations
in Washington and other cities. In early May 1970, the antiwar movement was poised for mass militancy. On May 1, Nixon announced the
hitherto secret bombings of Cambodia, which he described as necessary
for cutting off enemy supply lines. The nation's campuses immediately
erupted. Among them was Ohio's Kent State University, where on May 4,
the National Guard—called in following the burning of the campus
ROTC building—killed four unarmed students, prompting another wave
of outrage and disruptions. On May 9, more than 100,000 people again
gathered in the capital. According to organizers, as many as 20,000 were
willing to commit civil disobedience, with no guarantee that their protest
would remain peaceful. Five thousand armed soldiers lay in wait in the
basements of government buildings, including the White House. Yet internal bickering and confusion over what to do reigned among the Mobe
leaders. The rally remained overwhelmingly peaceful and lawful, leaving many disgusted that only a tepid demonstration had emerged from
their boiling anger.[52] The Mobe, long the mainstay of national antiwar
organizing, dissolved in the protest's wake.

One year later, in the "May Day" protests of 1971, the militants took
the lead. Rallying behind the slogan, "If the government won't stop the
war, we'll stop the government," thousands of demonstrators massed in
Washington to *literally* shut down the government by blockading roads
and bridges, city streets, and government buildings. Yet police and soldiers outmaneuvered the demonstrators, whose numbers were far too
few to pull off the audacious plan. The protest resulted in more than 8,000
arrests, most of them illegal; those arrested were jammed into the D.C.
Armory, converted into an open-air jail. Sustaining the imagery of a war
at home, buttons commemorating the protest read, "I was an American
P.O.W. Camp Nixon, May '71."[53] In the aftermath of this last and most
spectacular mass protest in Washington, factionalism and demoralization in the movement grew deeper still.

Government repression and internal disagreements were scarcely the only causes of the movement's decline. Nixon used strategically timed troop withdrawals, the phasing out of the draft, and, ultimately, the "Vietnamization" of the war to feed hope for its end and deflate domestic opposition. The antiwar movement, for all these reasons, never achieved a unity of purpose and action, nor experienced any clear epiphany, even as it drew closer to its goal of ending U.S. involvement in Vietnam.

.   .   .

The people, they know
But the people don't care
    The Grateful Dead, "Black
Peter" (lyrics by Robert Hunter)

mass politics

Mass mobilization is its own kind of body politics. Rather than the act of "throwing oneself on the gears of the machine" that defines militancy, a mass demonstration requires only large numbers of comparatively passive actors. By assembling bodies in public spaces, it seeks to issue a unilaterally declared referendum that affirms or withdraws consent from the actions of government. Paul Goodman, the author of the counterculture classic *Growing Up Absurd* (1960), captured the basic function of mass demonstrations like those in the fall of 1969 by speaking of "the heady sense of being the sovereign people, the body politic" they afforded.[54] Indeed, the strength of the fall protests lay primarily in their sheer size. The *Washington Post* alluded to the inert quality of the mass—the importance of its simply being there—by saying of the November 15 demonstration, "it was a happening in which nothing happened except that a young crowd, whose numbers will never be known, was there."[55] The *Post* additionally described the demonstrations as heralding an era of "plebiscitary democracy" in America.[56]

   In *The Nationalization of the Masses* (1975), George Mosse demonstrates the historical importance of mass politics in democratic societies by tracing the genealogy of fascist ritual. He begins by stating the Rousseauian premise that in democracies, legitimacy is rooted in popular consent, or the general will. "The people" or "the masses," both as a statistical majority and a unified construct, function as agents of legitimacy. In addition, democracy conceives of the national community in terms of universal citizenship, not loyalty to a royal dynasty. Yet no precise way exists to ascertain or represent the popular will; to the extent that that will remains elusive, democracy and the broader conception of the nation are rooted in an abstraction. Democratic societies have therefore since their inception faced the challenge of somehow staging the presence of "the people" to secure mandates for particular activities of the state, to affirm the institution of popular government, and, most fundamentally, to help unify the nation. Civic rituals in democracies, such as those of the early French Republic, exalted the people themselves as the primary objects of worship within a secular religion of the state and quickly became an integral part of the political culture of the democratic West. (They also, according to Mosse, provided the historical basis for fascist mass gatherings that only appear to be wholly antithetical to democratic impulses: while fascism disdains pluralism and restricts membership within the national community, it adheres to the democratic assumption that governmental authority derives from the popular will, and it well understands the importance of symbolism.)[57]

Antiwar activists faced their own challenge of staging the "will of the people" in a manner that would undercut intermittent elections, poll data, the press, and political representatives as the conveyors of public preferences. None of these, by and large, favored the antiwar cause for most of the war's duration, despite the movement's accumulating size and strength. Large demonstrations, like militant direct action, sought to address those in power "directly." They were a way, in short, of having the people speak.

Yet the movement, never able to field a literal majority in a single protest, had to rely on logics of equivalence and the signifying acts of the media to convey that it stood in for a majoritarian whole. In its crudest form, that principle of equivalence held that for every demonstrator who had the opportunity and the initiative to show up, there were many others who could take her place. The *Guardian* invoked precisely this logic in its coverage of the November protest when it wrote, "For every person who traveled many miles under difficult circumstances . . . there were dozens, scores, who for some reason were unable to attend the massive demonstrations."[58] For such a claim to be credible, it was crucial that the crowd appear more or less representative of the American populace as a whole. The common emphasis among the leaders of large antiwar demonstrations on respectability, lawfulness, and even displays of patriotism, such as the waving of American flags on the speakers' platform, sought to encourage the public's identification with the protesters and thereby geometrically expand their numbers. In a perfect illustration of this gesture (if one out of keeping with the sentiments of many in the audience), Senator George McGovern declared from the November 15 stage "We love America enough to call her away from the folly of war. . . . We meet here today because we cherish our flag."[59] Conversely, organizers feared violence partly because it permitted politicians, the media, and the public to think of the demonstrations as dominated by "extremists," out of touch with "ordinary" Americans. Even while condemning the government, demonstrations could be quasi-nationalistic rituals: their very existence celebrated America's tradition of sanctioned dissent; their message, "We are the majority! We are the people!" affirmed the principle of popular sovereignty.

The fall demonstrations, according to their organizers and supporters, succeeded precisely by rallying a *symbolic* majority. "It is obvious that the majority has spoken," the *Guardian* proclaimed, despite the disproportionately young and white character of the crowd.[60] The New Mobe's Sidney Peck similarly concluded, "the great majority of Americans opposed this war."[61] The next step in the democratic process, the organizers determined, would be to translate that freshly evident majority opinion into congressional action.

Exploiting the heavily mediated nature of the movement's message, the Nixon administration claimed just the opposite. In the wake of the November protest, one Nixon aide, Herbert Klein, commented that the "small" demonstration should be ignored because, "all measurable devices . . . indicate that there is no question but what [*sic*] the American people do support the President."[62] To buttress this claim, officials pointed to the 80,000 pro-Nixon telegrams and letters the White House allegedly received following Nixon's "silent majority" speech, poll data backing the president, the continued support of most congresspersons for the war, and the D.C. police's low estimate of the crowd's size at 250,000 (the organizers estimated 800,000). Attorney General Mitchell characterized the protests as, on the whole, violent, unlawful, and un-American; the demonstrators could therefore not possibly speak for the public. Vice President Agnew added for good measure that the media were biased in favor of the protestors. "It has been so important that thousands of silent Americans are beginning to speak out, so that a government which misjudges American public opinion—and it's obvious that Hanoi does—isn't deluded in its own feeling that the only real Americans who speak out speak against the President's policies," Klein said.[63] To believe that a majority opposed the war was to aid and abet the communist enemy!

Nixon's invocation of the "silent majority" was, however, the administration's masterstroke. The use of the phrase on the heels of the Moratorium and the eve of the November rally struck at the heart of the demonstrations' purpose.[64] Those abstaining from protest, Nixon implied, sided with his policies, making *inaction* the essence of his own plebiscitary politics. The alibi was perfect. By definition, the silent majority could not express itself nor be demonstrated to exist in the manner of the antiwar movement's vocal constituency. For it to exist, Nixon only had to declare that it did.

Was there any truth to Nixon's proclamation? More fundamentally, what *did* the majority of Americans think of the war in the fall of 1969? No clear answer shines through the thicket of competing claims. U.S. participation in the war was a mistake, 58 percent of Americans polled in October 1969 thought, but a poll the very next month found that 65 percent backed Nixon's Vietnam policy. As the question subtly changed, so too did the result. The preferences of the working class, commonly considered the backbone of the silent majority, were equally hard to decipher. Separate polls suggested that workers were by turns more hawkish *and* more dovish than the rest of the country.[65] Beyond public opinion research, the waters remained muddy. The millions who protested could not plausibly be dismissed as politically insignificant, and neither was it remotely credible that everyone who did not demonstrate against the war approved of it, as Nixon suggested. Yet the number of Americans who agreed with the demonstrators could not be known, and many among the silent no doubt did support the president. So intent was the patriotic businessman Ross Perot on proving this that in the fall of 1969, he ran prowar newspaper ads with coupons that sympathetic readers could return to the ads' authors. The (aborted) plan was to dump the coupons in front of the White House for news cameras to see.[66] To the movement's mass rally—promoted as the voice of the people—the war's supporters thought to counter with a mass of letters through which the silent majority murmured.

Behind the passion, partisanship, and occasional absurdity of the debate over the war lay a contradiction approaching paradox: in 1969, both pro- and antiwar forces claimed with some credibility that they were the majority. The judgment of which side was right—and logically, they both could not be—was scarcely a matter of applying some perfect measure of public opinion. None existed, or could exist. Rather, it lay in the highly subjective choice of *which code* (polls, bodies, legislation, letters) one took as the truest measure of the people's will. In this battle of codes, perceptions counted for more than an ultimately inscrutable reality. It did not necessarily matter, for example, whether Nixon's silent majority was real or imagined.[67] As Rhodri Jeffreys-Jones asserts, Nixon's speech enforced "the idea that a good leader ignored raucous minorities and heeded instead virtuous majority opinion"; thus, "the conjectural incoherence of the invisible masses [became] a conspicuous political asset."[68] Researchers testing Nixon's claim shortly after it was made concluded that the idea of the silent majority was a "cleverly designed symbol" that might "become more important for the reality it creates than the reality it describes."[69] That is, the impression that the public supported the war might, in circular fashion, lead individual Americans and their political representatives to support the war. Most disturbingly, Nixon appeared to believe in his own myth of the silent majority and used this purported mandate to justify continuing the war.

As argued in chapter 2, the New Left experienced a crisis over where political reality lay. Militancy of an extreme sort provided one response by assuming that force was the essence of politics, that violence was the essence of force, and that to engage in violence was therefore to experience the "real" of politics. But these assumptions were neither universally shared on the left nor always held with great consistency or confidence; "reality" remained something of an impossible object of political and existential desire. Debate over the war pointed to a broader-reaching crisis of the real within specifically democratic politics, whose essence is popular sovereignty. Questions abounded: Which was the *real* majority? Who was a *real* American, and what did he or she *really* think about the war? As the antiwar movement struggled with these questions, it developed very different conceptions of its task.

Two possibilities haunted the antiwar movement, with crucial implications for those pursuing violence. The first was that the government might ignore its demands, even if it organized a clear antiwar majority. The movement would then have to find strategies other than mass mobilization to bring the war to an end. Weatherman, in arguing for violence, presupposed that most Americans opposed the war. Ayers explained that by 1968,

> [We felt] that we'd reached the end of a certain road, that we'd convinced the majority of the American people—or so we thought—to oppose the war, that we'd won the battle of hearts and minds. . . . And yet the war pounded on with an escalating madness [and with] no end in sight. And no matter how many people we could convince, no matter that we drove a president from office [Johnson] and defeated the guy who carried his water [Humphrey], we still couldn't stop it.[70]

In assuming the existence of an antiwar majority, radicals, however tenuously, claimed a popular mandate for their militancy and violence, despite the widespread condemnation of such tactics inside and outside the movement. For the most part, the Weatherman imagined itself to be fighting a "People's War" in America against U.S. imperialism. Like the insurgencies in Vietnam and Latin American countries, their war was to have the support and active involvement of the masses. Weathermen who met with North Vietnamese officials in Cuba in 1969 were particularly moved by accounts of their resistance, in which the whole of North Vietnam seemed to rally as "one heart, one mind" in opposition to the United States.[71] The Vietnamese in fact communicated to American activists that it was their duty to organize as many people as possible into the antiwar movement and keep using institutional channels (such as lobbying Congress), even while engaging in more radical protest. Militancy, within this model, would accent a larger, domestic struggle against the war that included many levels of participation.[72]

The second, more disturbing possibility was that the antiwar movement might not secure a real or even perceived majority. Throughout the movement's life, the dominant faith held that opposition to the war would necessarily shift from the stance of an insurgent minority to that of a majority. Paul Goodman explained in 1967: "We assume that Americans do not 'really' will the Vietnam war but are morally asleep and brainwashed . . . that there has been a usurpation by a hidden government which makes policy, and that an awakened populace can throw it off."[73] Whatever their diligent efforts to awaken the populace, activists had to contend with the war's sustained popularity and the widespread dislike of demonstrators among large segments of the public. (A fall 1969 poll showed that 69 percent of Americans thought that antiwar protesters were "harmful to public life.")[74] In the absence of a popular mandate, the rationale for "the war at home" changed; no longer could it be tethered to an antiwar majority.

Apparently taking for granted the existence of a prowar majority, the Yippies and other New Leftists stressed the need to build a youth rebellion that, given the structural importance of young people for the war, would be able to end it without widespread "establishment" support. Weatherman went so far as to argue at times that it was fighting not only an entrenched power structure but, potentially, the tens of millions who supported it. Protest violence, in this understanding, did not gain its legitimacy from the America people. This does not mean that the Weathermen dispensed with appeals to the majority altogether. Instead, they redefined *which majority* commanded their loyalty. The largest share of northern and southern Vietnamese, their thinking went, wanted a unified, communist Vietnam, or at the very least freedom from U.S. aggression; violence served this international mandate. More broadly, Weatherman justified its conduct by pointing to the anti-imperialism of the peoples of the Third World, who could be seen as a *global* majority.[75]

Reflecting on the fate of the slogan "Serve the People," Robin Palmer more viscerally expressed the ambiguities in "the war at home." "Serve the People" was a rallying cry for leftists throughout the globe, from Chinese communists to the Black Panthers, SDS, and Germany's Red Army Faction. It placed faith in the common man and woman and announced activists' ultimate accountability to their needs and desires. In the United States, the slogan was particularly relevant for radical minority groups, such as the Panthers and the Puerto Rican Young Lords, whose community programs sought to provide services for those whose basic needs the economic and political system did not meet. The slogan also implied that conservative forces in the government and among the public were the greatest obstacles to the success of popular progressive movements. Palmer described how in 1968, with the assassinations of Martin Luther King Jr. and Robert Kennedy, it appeared that "the right, the reactionaries, had more guns than we did, had more power than we did" and "knew how to get what they wanted better than we did, in spite of the fact that it didn't seem that they were as numerous as we were. . . . When Nixon talked about the silent majority, we scoffed." In 1968, Palmer took part with other Yippies in running a pig for president behind the slogan "Take heart, good people, Rome wasn't destroyed in a day" and derisively exposed with his guerrilla theater what he felt was the illegitimacy of an electoral process that, failing to yield a serious antiwar candidate, did not represent the apparent antiwar majority.

Yet as the continued popularity of both Nixon and the war sank in, Palmer concluded,

> Nixon was right. We'd all go home to our parents and they'd say "Of course Nixon is right. We like Nixon, we don't like you, even if you're our son and daughter. . . . Get a haircut, get a job!" . . . The silent majority supported the war. They did. . . . There's no way we could say that the people of the United States had a good heart, and that if only the people, the true voice of the people . . . had been able to express itself, there would have never been a war in Vietnam—that's bullshit.

Weatherman's J. J. echoed Palmer's cynicism in an irreverent adaptation in 1969 of the left's vaunted slogan. At a 1968 SDS convention, J. J. had proposed half-seriously that the group adopt the slogan "Serve the People

Shit." Bill Ayers later suggested that Weatherman adopt "Fight the People," insofar as its enemies included all those Americans supporting the status quo. (Ayers, Jim Mellen recalls, would quip to his critics: "You're supposed to serve the people. . . . What ya gonna do? Open a restaurant?")[76] Years later, Palmer explained the meaning of J. J.'s slogan and why he identified with it: "That's all [the people] deserved. The people didn't deserve shit because of segregation. The people didn't deserve shit because of McCarthyism. The people didn't deserve shit even because of capitalism and the great disparity between the wealthy and the poor. The people deserved shit because of the Vietnam war, because we were behaving as a country the same way as Nazi Germany behaved."

Arriving at this view was a disillusioning journey. In the early 1960s, Palmer had been confident, in his words, in the "perfectibility of man" and in the virtues of the democratic process. His optimism was affirmed by Lyndon Johnson's position on civil rights. Palmer reports being so overjoyed hearing on the radio Johnson's speech before Congress urging passage of the 1964 Civil Rights Act that he got out of his car in busy New York City traffic to cheer his hero. Yet Palmer's "sentimentalities" about democracy and respect for Johnson were soon destroyed by the Vietnam War. By the late 1960s, he directed his outrage at the entire system, whose people *chose* to fight the Vietnam War. When asked years later on whose behalf he had protested, Palmer leapt up to say: "The Vietnamese! The Viet Cong!"[77]

Antiwar radicals, in short, advanced two dramatically opposing visions of the "war at home." In one version, it was to dislodge a policy that flouted the public's will. In another, fought by a minority within a minority, it was to use any means necessary to end the aggression in Vietnam, irrespective of the public's wishes. The tension between these versions can be recast with respect to democracy: Was the Vietnam War a failure of democracy because the government steadfastly refused to heed the people's call for peace? Or did democracy fail because an "immoral majority" decided, in democratic fashion, to support a war that was nonetheless unjust? Proponents of the "war at home" never came to a consensus on which was the case; indeed, it was possible for activists to sustain both views at once or to move between them as their faith in the good will of that elusive entity "the people" ebbed and flowed. Mellen complained of this confusion, "[T]o take the slogan Serve the People made little sense [but] to just take the slogan, turn around, and say, 'Fight the People' made even less sense. What we really needed was a clear-cut, strategic conception of who we were fighting for and who we were fighting against, or to what extent we were fighting against somebody . . . [or] against what they conceived to be their interests."[78]

In his essay "In the Shadow of the Silent Majorities," the French philosopher Jean Baudrillard sheds light on these ambiguities by refocusing attention on the vocabulary animating debates over the war. Baudrillard, like Mosse, asserts the constructed status of "the masses." Absent any precise "attribute, predicate, quality and reference," the masses have no "sociological 'reality'" in any "*real* population, body, or specific social aggregate."[79] They are, for Baudrillard, the ultimate signifier without a referent—the empty center of a whole "code of analysis" used to interpret wide-ranging social phenomena. For Baudrillard, however, the absence of empirical masses is more than a case of their social construction. In a loose periodization, he accepts the validity of an earlier, eighteenth-century political vocabulary that invoked "the people"— though technically inaccessible—as still a more or less meaningful and representable referent. Under the dominance of what Baudrillard calls "the social," codified with the rise of Marxism, "the masses" have replaced or transcended "the people" and are seen as the bearers of the final transparency of politics, economics, and history. Their fictional status is qualitatively worse. They can neither express themselves nor even figuratively be made to speak. Yet Baudrillard grants the masses a special kind of agency. They repel attempts to inspire them with a moral, political, or historical calling, to unlock their explosive potential, to charge them with "the sublime imperative of *meaning*." Defeating every effort at their excitation and representation, they are a fundamentally implosive construct that absorbs meaning—an *essentially* "silent majority" whose very immobility, indifference, and silence are its revenge on those who claim to speak in its name.

Baudrillard directs a portion of his argument against the left, for whom the masses have functioned as both the object and subject of emancipation. The masses "drift somewhere between passive and wild spontaneity, but always as a potential energy . . . today a mute referent, tomorrow, when they speak up . . . a protagonist of history." Despite efforts to awaken them, they have remained "inaccessible to the schemas of liberation, revolution and historicity" and resist even more modest efforts to incite their moral and political interest. The French public's overwhelming preference in 1977 to watch a qualifying match for football's World Cup rather than the news—quite dramatic at the time—of the extradition of an attorney for the Red Army Faction to Germany typified this refusal of meaning for Baudrillard. As if to break the left's conspiracy of silence about the masses' historical failure, Baudrillard queried:

> Can anyone ask questions about the strange fact that, after several revolutions and a century or two of political apprenticeship, in spite of the newspapers, the trade unions, the parties, the intellectuals, and all the energy put into educating and mobilizing the people, there are still (and it will be exactly the same in ten or twenty years) a thousand people who stand up and twenty million who remain "passive"—and not only passive, but who, in all good faith . . . frankly prefer a football match to a human and political drama?[80]

For Baudrillard, the episode was not an example of "ideology," in which elites or a culture of distraction dulled the public's critical faculties. Rather, it reflected the "authentic" inertia of the masses, which Baudrillard regards as the true source of their power.

Baudrillard's analysis suggests that the antiwar movement invested the masses with false promise. Militants confronted the inertia of the masses in several ways. Like other opponents of the war, they experienced disappointment that the population did not mobilize in even greater numbers. The masses, conceived of as a *social totality,* resisted the antiwar movement's moral and political charge. The numbers the antiwar movement manage to field never rendered it the unequivocal victor in the battle for America's hearts and minds. However, within Baudrillard's analysis, the problem was not insufficient numbers, Nixon's cunning, or Americans' approval of the war. Rather, the movement overestimated the expressive power of the masses—the very possibility that their univocal voice could be heard or represented. The image of Nixon watching American football on TV on November 15 while half a million people marched outside his house evokes Baudrillard's example of the French public's enthusiasm for the soccer match. Nixon's actions only superficially functioned as a calculated boycott of the event. In this conventional model, he remains the representative of the silent majority as a prowar constituency; by watching TV—and college football at that, whose fan base is largely working and middle class—he led Americans in their indifference to, or contempt for, the march. From a more probing perspective, Nixon was the cynical champion of the majority he invented. With a still sharper lens, Nixon seems to embody the very immobility of the mass, its *constitutive* indifference. He serves now as the banal champion of the true, vexing silence of the silent majority that made it *impossible for either pro- or antiwar forces* finally to win the allegiance of "the masses."

passivity
of antiwar
recruits
frustrating

Antiwar militants were also frustrated with the seeming passivity of the mass of people the movement did manage to assemble. The Weathermen and the Yippies upbraided the November crowd for not rioting in greater numbers. Others pitied the naïveté of pilgrims armed only with candles. Yurick cursed the marchers for failing to storm the White House, tear Nixon from the TV, and expose the fiction of the "absent and quiescent public" whose support he claimed. Yurick's scenario almost perfectly enacts Baudrillard's description of the unfulfilled vision of the left: it exactly pictures the moment when the masses, on the verge of seizing power and fulfilling their destiny, hold back. In assessing the reasons for that restraint, militants typically criticized their fellow activists' insufficient appreciation of the imperialist character of the war, naïve faith in American democracy, or failure of courage. Baudrillard's model suggests that militants were ultimately foiled by the implosiveness of the mass, *evident even in their own mighty ranks.*

Baudrillard's analysis, however, is vulnerable on two grounds. The first is political. In a muted, postsocial populism, Baudrillard celebrates the radical loss of meaning, as the silent majority repels attempts to impose on the masses values and opinions they do not possess. Indifference becomes a new form of the Great Refusal. He thus transforms a presumed vice into a virtue. The masses, failing as bearers of liberatory meaning, are redeemed as the agents of meaninglessness. To be sure, it may be valuable to demystify notions of "the people" or "the masses" as preexisting unities, capable of issuing unambiguous mandates or of fulfilling an historical mission of liberation. With such terms, New Leftists and other radicals obscured the diversity of the actual groups they sought to empower and pinned their hopes of victory on abstractions. Their highly general language of emancipation collapsed, in a sense, under the weight of its own vagueness.

It is harder to see the desirability of the broader loss of meaning and the kind of silence Baudrillard champions. It remains imperative that communities of common interest enter public spaces and agitate on behalf of political values. Their success presupposes both the capacity for group initiative and a political system that considers itself accountable to some conception of popular sovereignty. Relatedly, Baudrillard so thoroughly exults in the masses' power of stubborn silence that he seems to deprive principled public statements of all importance. It is still important to speak up, even if through one's voice, the masses don't also speak. And though the slogans "Serve the People" or "Power to the People" may be rooted in reductive abstractions, they still make basic sense as ways of indicting the disproportionate power of the few, stressing the need for inclusiveness and equality, and expressing an enabling faith in the goodness of humanity.

Baudrillard's analysis is also vulnerable in a descriptive sense. The 1960s were an era of extraordinary mobilization. Rather than grapple with the challenge of 1960s protest to his narrative of the rise of the silent majority, he simply issues the transhistorical axiom that one thousand will stand up while millions remain passive. In the United States alone, millions stood up against the war. It is not just that Baudrillard has his numbers wrong. There is an obvious sense in which it *did* matter, with the stakes of life and death, how many people were in the streets and what, so to speak, they were doing there. For Baudrillard, the 1960s are a blind spot that prevents him from seeing in "the masses" the capacity for both silence and expressiveness, implosiveness and explosiveness, absence and presence.

Applying Baudrillard's analysis to the antiwar movement leads to consideration of the impact of protest, and violent protest in particular, on the war itself. Was violence, as is almost always claimed, essentially a product of impatience with the slowness of the democratic process? Did it unequivocally hurt the movement?[81] Or did it in any sense advance the antiwar cause? The historical reputation of the Weathermen and others using violence hinges greatly on the answers to these questions.

role of antiwar violence? impact?

If the antiwar movement was at a crossroads at the end of 1969, it was the government and military officials who planned and prosecuted the war who were largely responsible for the movement's dilemma. While some activists were convinced of the futility of nonviolent protest, most still believed in the ability of peaceful, legal mechanisms to end the war. But the government, by conducting its war strategy in secret and often willfully misleading the public, left activists to argue somewhat blindly with one another about their actual impact on policy and about which antiwar strategy was best.[82]

Tom Wells's mammoth *The War Within,* widely considered the definitive work on the antiwar movement, helps to glean the reality behind the activists' perceptions. By meticulously studying how key government officials responded to individual protests, Wells offers what amounts to an independent assessment—one benefiting from hindsight, detachment, and breathtaking research—of debates within the movement. He concludes that antiwar activity "played a major role in constraining, deescalating and ending the war."[83] The movement's achievements included influencing Johnson to scale back the air and ground wars and Nixon to

Tom Wells's theory

antiwar o HAS an effect

withdraw troops and limit attacks on Cambodia and Laos. Most dramatically, the October Moratorium and the pending November 15 demonstration played a role in Nixon's withdrawal on November 1, 1969, of an ultimatum he had secretly issued to North Vietnam in the summer. It warned of "savage" attacks, possibly including tactical nuclear strikes, should the North refuse to surrender. Finally, Wells holds that the antiwar movement contributed to Nixon's decision to phase out America's military involvement in Vietnam.[84]

This impressive record ultimately yields a mixed set of lessons, if one reads Wells against the grain. Wells presents the situation of the movement as one of profound irony, whose consequences proved costly. Though activists had more power than they commonly recognized, their "failure to appreciate their actual political power hurt their cause."[85] That injury took several forms: limits on the display of antiwar feeling, caused by some activists' antipathy to traditional legal demonstrations; bitter internal dissension in the movement, which limited its size and strength; and the inactivity of countless individuals who became convinced that their protest would make no difference. Wells uses knowledge of the movement's influence to indict, if often implicitly, antiwar militants who lost faith in the democratic process. He targets their excessive cynicism about the responsiveness of the American political system to dissent and their dismissive attitude to peaceful protest.[86] For Wells, the Weathermen were a misguided fringe and erred chiefly in believing that violence helped the antiwar cause and in drastically overestimating its appeal among the war's opponents. (Former Weathermen do not necessarily reject these criticisms wholesale. In the 1980s, Jeff Jones described the November 1969 march as "one of the most important demonstrations of the whole antiwar period." Recounting how it influenced the withdrawal of Nixon's ultimatum, he explained, "People went home from the demonstration [saying,] 'Half a million mobilized in Washington, and it has no effect.' But years later we realized that, in fact, it was significant."[87] Larry Weiss went so far as to say that Weatherman "made a significant contribution to destroying the antiwar movement" by insisting, in essence, "that either you fight with a metal pole and a helmet or you are 'objectively' on the side of Nixon.")[88] The great moral of Wells's story is that activists would have done better to stick with peaceful protest, no matter how ineffective it may have appeared.

Yet Wells also presents material that helps us to understand the frustration and anger underlying so much radical protest. He consistently shows, for example, that conventional forms of public pressure on the government limited only the *magnitude* of the destruction in Vietnam. He thus undermines his central claim that antiwar activists should have been more satisfied with their comparatively subdued efforts and less inclined to pursue highly confrontational forms of resistance. Moreover, government officials kept from the public information about the scope and destructiveness of the war, such as the bombing of Cambodia (conducted in secret for over a year) or the massacre in Mai Lai (knowledge of which the government long suppressed). In short, U.S. conduct in the war *was often far worse than the war's opponents had been led to believe.* Having known the "hidden truth" might not so much have convinced protesters that they were making a difference as sharpened their sense that they were not making nearly enough of a difference. The escalation of protest, not moderation, might have been the result of more complete information.[89]

More significantly, Wells provides evidence to suggest that militancy and even violence played a role in the movement's success as well. In his telling, government officials feared more than the loss of a popular mandate for the war; they also feared the threat to the legitimacy of their power and to domestic stability that militants posed. The fierce rhetoric of protesters, the violence at demonstrations, the sabotage, the numerous trials, the need for troops to guard government buildings, the campus turmoil, and, eventually, the numerous bombings all bespoke a national climate, not merely of dissatisfaction with a policy, but of hostility to the government and authority generally. The high-level administration officials Wells interviewed were typically unable to say in hindsight what kinds of antiwar actions were most influential. Instead, they stressed the impact of antiwar protest as a whole. For some, however, the militancy made a strong, even terrifying, impression. From their experience with protests, Secretary of Defense Robert MacNamara (under Johnson) and CIA Director Richard Helms developed an acute sense of the danger of the "mob." In 1969, one official warned of "internal physical turmoil," including the widespread rioting of whites and blacks, should Nixon deliver on the November ultimatum given the North Vietnamese.[90] Another described existing levels of violence as "the most severe internal threat" the country had faced since the Great Depression.[91] Henry Kissinger, the German-born secretary of state under Nixon, conveyed his sense of the danger antiwar radicals posed by making repeated comparisons between the America of the 1960s and Germany's Weimar Republic of the 1920s and 1930s, which collapsed under the pressure of internal dissension and violence.[92] This somewhat different model of the movement's effectiveness suggests a second, competing level of irony that Wells never fully acknowledges: activists' perceptions of their powerlessness also led to a ratcheting up of protest; insofar as the resulting strife and fears of broader instability adversely affected the war effort, the antiwar movement's "ignorance" and attending "excesses" had benefits after all.

The two versions of the movement's influence drawn above recall the two conceptions of the masses' power that Baudrillard rejects as illusions: their capacity to speak and to explode. Baudrillard's skepticism proves instructive when discouraging unqualified praise for the politics of mass mobilization and misleading when denying "the masses" agency altogether. In his introduction to Wells's volume, Todd Gitlin describes the antiwar movement as one of the outstanding "triumphs in the history of democracy," in which "what had started as a rivulet, the protest of a few, grew into the torrent of a vast and representative majority."[93] Gitlin appropriately lauds the movement for its civic initiative, as millions of people with no special political endowment influenced deeply entrenched military and political powers in the prosecution of a war. The magnitude and even heroism of that feat is indisputable. Gitlin errs, however, in assuming the ultimate transparency of the democratic process. In his formulation—one standard in tributes to antiwar activism—the movement succeeded by finally winning American's hearts and minds and then forcing the war to an end. One may ask, at what point did that "vast and representative majority" finally materialize? When did the public unequivocally reject the war?

Doubting the existence of such a plebiscite or the emergence of an antiwar consensus is not to deny that the movement had an impact. Failing any clear victory, the movement was nonetheless able to establish a limit to what government officials felt they could do abroad. That limit still relied on the notion of "the masses" as arbiters of governmental action. Over time, the antiwar movement both threatened prowar politicians with the loss of electoral majorities and eroded public confidence—that elusive requirement for effective policies—in the war. In this sense, the movement did achieve critical mass. Even if the American "masses" never rejected the war, the movement benefited from the assumption that the war was something the masses *could* reject. In this way, they attained a "real" agency.

The same logic holds when assessing the impact of militancy and violence. These may never have functioned as the voice of "the people," and neither were they even the preferred tactics of the antiwar movement. But they did seem to inspire fear among the political and military establishment of a popular uprising that would cripple the government and force intolerable degrees of national division. Militancy had practical value less as a hindrance to the war in a literal, military sense than as the expression of a *possibility* presumed to be latent in the masses. Violence, promoted as the most direct form of direct action, itself functioned as a symbol. Militants appear at times to have been aware of this symbolic aspect of their activism. Commenting on the November 15 march, the Weatherman Shin'ya Ono speculated with some validity that "the more [government officials] drag their feet in admitting defeat and getting out of Vietnam, the more the candle-holding type [of demonstrator] will join the ranks of the crazies on the street."[94] Abbie Hoffman, in defense of Yippie rioting, warned that the Mobe might turn into "the Mob" should the war persist.[95] In short, the primary contribution of "the crazies" to the antiwar effort lay in the threat that the violence would spread.

Wells ultimately contends that there is no way to gauge the *precise impact on U.S. policy* of the antiwar movement as a whole, let alone that of its different strands. Scholars could likely debate the effectiveness of the diverse forms of activism ad infinitum without settling on any definitive judgment. I doubt whether a method could even be devised for rendering such a judgment.[96] The experiences of a single figure convey my sense of the role militants played in the antiwar movement.

· · ·

So do your duty, boys, and join with pride
Serve your country in her suicide
Find the flags so you can wave goodbye
But just before the end even treason might be
     worth a try
This country is too young to die
I declare the war is over, it's over, it's over
                    Phil Ochs, "War Is Over"

In the mid 1990s, Robin Palmer described the high-point of his long career as an antiwar activist. Though he was already well over thirty during the glory years of the 1960s, he immersed himself in New Left politics and had an uncanny knack for participating in the era's storied events, making him something of the Zelig of the era's radicalism.

Palmer was born in 1930 in Harlem, across the street from the Audubon Ballroom, where Malcolm X would be assassinated; thirty-five years later, he attended a memorial for the slain Black Power leader not far from his birthplace. He was the son of a Cornell University professor and recalls going as a child to football games and proudly singing the national anthem and Cornell's alma mater. Despite this patriotic upbringing, as a young man, he developed very unconventional views; though he was trained as an Army paratrooper, when called to serve in Korea, he became one of a handful of conscientious objectors to the war.

In 1965, Palmer attended the first large antiwar demonstration in Washington, D.C., organized by SDS. During this time, he met weekly with a veterans group that sent letters to politicians and circulated petitions demanding an end to the conflict in Vietnam. On July 4, 1966, the group marched some fifty miles from Valley Forge to Philadelphia's Independence Hall protesting the war. The following year, Palmer was among those at the Pentagon who broke through a police cordon and laid siege to the building, for which he was arrested on the serious felony charge of assaulting a U.S. marshal. Dr. Benjamin Spock, the renowned pediatrician and antiwar leader, helped bail Palmer out of jail. A picture of him being beaten by police on the Pentagon steps made the front page of the *Washington Post* and was used as the back cover of the paperback edition of Norman Mailer's *Armies of the Night,* which described the protest. (The *Post* somewhat fatuously captioned the photograph of the thirty-seven-year-old Palmer: "Prone boy, center, protects girls beneath him.")[97] Palmer drove back to his home in New York City with Abbie Hoffman, a newfound friend, with whom he collaborated on Yippie provocations.

Like many other 1960s activists, Palmer narrates his political history by recounting key moments or epiphanies in which he, the movement, the country, or all three seemed to cross some vital threshold. One such moment took place in 1968 at Columbia University. Palmer had temporarily left his "straight job" as a deep-sea diver (working in a submarine owned by the first mate on Jacques Cousteau's *Calypso*) to join the student uprising. The liberal faculty, as Palmer describes it, played an ambiguous role in the protests, as they ringed the occupied Low Library both to keep conservative students from attacking the rebels and to keep more people from joining the occupation. Palmer, as a professor's son, had always looked upon faculty with near reverence, esteeming them as the "heart and soul" of an enlightened university. So it was a moment of high Oedipal drama when at Columbia he became so enraged at a professor's efforts to physically prevent him from climbing into a window of Low Library that he literally spat in the professor's face. "Who have I become?" he wondered in that instant. Fazed, but undeterred in his radicalism, he participated later that year in the mayhem at the Democratic National Convention, for which he was named an unindicted coconspirator in the Chicago 8 trial.

The year 1969 was a pivotal one both for the movement and for Palmer. Just as Weatherman was forming, Palmer became active with the Melville collective. He personally carried the briefcase that held the bomb that exploded at the Criminal Courts Building in New York where the trial of the "Panther 21" was being held. Chance also intervened to enrich his life as a radical. While walking home in late June, Palmer stumbled, quite by accident, on the Stonewall riot that inaugurated a new phase in the gay liberation movement; seeing police beating a drag queen, he entered the fray and spent the night in jail with the rioters.

In 1970, he joined Weatherman and was arrested trying to firebomb a Citibank office in New York City. He was sent to Attica prison and participated in the 1971 uprising, during which his best friend, Sam Melville, was shot by a state trooper and died in his arms. Palmer can be seen standing naked, herded through the mud with other vanquished and abused inmates, on the cover of Tom Wicker's harrowing account of Attica, *A Time to Die*. At a trial about events there, Palmer offered his views on the war and his methods of protesting it. A state prosecutor, trying to discredit Palmer's testimony praising Melville and condemning his murder, asked in leading fashion if Melville had a nickname among the Attica inmates. Indeed, he was called in prison "the Mad Bomber," and friends privately confessed that depression and insecurity partly drove his actions. (In Attica, Melville was also called "the Weatherman," which seems to have been a catch-all name for white bombers.) Palmer answered the prosecutor, "Yes, [Sam] did have a name. He was referred to as the 'Sane Bomber.'" Johnson and Nixon, in Palmer's view, were the mad bombers.

Palmer was released from prison in 1973 and then visited Cuba, during which a profound disillusionment with communism began to set in. He gained a measure of ignominy in 1975 when Jane Alpert denounced him as a "dull-witted misogynist" in a widely read essay she wrote for *Ms.* magazine that blasted the sexism of Sam Melville, the Weather Underground, and the left as a whole.[98] More favorably, Dave Dellinger described Palmer in a memoir as one among a group of New Leftists who had fallen into the "trap" of violence but never lost their "humanity and sincerity."[99] Though only a minor historical figure, Palmer is a striking personification (one could choose others) of the movement's evolution from protest to resistance and then to revolution—a narrative arc that powerfully shaped postwar American history.

In 1975, Palmer attended a ceremony in a Manhattan church in which North Vietnamese officials personally thanked scores of antiwar activists. After waiting in line several hours, the activists had the chance to address the Vietnamese and shake their hands. Palmer, overwhelmed at the time with joy, recalls feeling that "they did it [defeated the U.S.]. . . . But we helped them."[100] Palmer's "we" is significant. It includes no doubt the petitioners, the candle holders, the marchers, the conscientious objectors, the draft resisters, the GI resisters, the clergy and the churchgoers, the college and high school students, and many of their parents. But it includes also the NLF flag wavers, the rock throwers, and the bombers— all those disparaged so often and so loudly in the antiwar movement. They "did it" too.

CHAPTER 4

The Excesses and Limits
of Revolutionary Violence

Following the Days of Rage and the antiwar demonstrations in Washington, notions of space—distance, height, location, and boundaries—defined the experience of the Weathermen. One Weatherman explained, "[W]e felt we had to be undaunted; if we ran into an obstruction, we had to leap over it or go around it; we could never just fall back."[1] The group now sought to "bring the struggle to the next level" by inflicting "material damage" on America's military-corporate apparatus. The transition from street fighting to bombing entailed more, though, than a tactical shift in an improbable war of liberation. Weatherman also intensified a politics of transgression that was not reducible to its anti-imperialist ideology or its strategic goals. Weatherman thus made its own vivid contribution to the ethos in the 1960s of "going further" that pushed political and cultural rebellion to exhilarating, disorienting, and often dangerous extremes.[2]

bombings

politics of transgression

Two events signaled the extent and perils of Weatherman's provocation. In December 1969, in Flint, Michigan, Weatherman held its last public meeting, at which the group finalized plans for going underground. The meeting, called the "War Council," was most conspicuous for its rhetoric. The Weathermen lauded Charles Manson and projected a scenario of virtually random violence, meant to consume the country in chaos. The "vision" of Flint, as it gloried in defiance and subversion without limits, was seemingly realized when two months later a Weatherman collective accidentally blew up a New York City townhouse while making bombs, killing three of its own members. Following the townhouse explosion, Weatherman quickly completed its descent underground. As fugitives pledged to violent insurrection, the Weathermen were now both

Flint meeting
going underground

accidental explosion townhouse

literally and figuratively outside the boundaries of the law and the norms governing civic life.

The townhouse explosion was a watershed for the Weathermen, causing them to confront the hazards of their path. The group began to rethink not only its purpose and methods, but also a sense of political and ethical limits. As a result of these deliberations, the Weather Underground would engage exclusively in "armed propaganda" actions aimed at property, whose main effect was to dramatize opposition to the state's violence abroad and at home. Once called "the id of their generation" by Tom Hayden, the Weathermen tried to refigure themselves as something closer to America's conscience by punishing the state for *its* continued transgressions.[3] In its new guise, the group also became in part the kind of symbol it had once denounced. Initially intent on making a "real" or "material" contribution to anti-imperialist struggles, the group now functioned largely as a shadowy reminder of the resentment U.S. policies bred internationally and at home, and of an anger and alienation among white American youths that would not fully dilute with the passing of the Vietnam War and the waning of the New Left. In a sense, the greatest achievement of the Weather Underground in the mid 1970s was that it avoided capture.

Both the Flint meeting and the townhouse explosion have had important places within the historiography and the broader mythology of Weatherman, the New Left, and the American 1960s in general. For most, they represent the fruition of aggressive, self-destructive or even nihilistic tendencies in the New Left—striking instances of "going too far." Yet Weatherman's escalating violence was far from a simple case of zealotry or excess. It was also an outraged or even traumatized response to the Vietnam War, to racism, and to domestic repression. Equally important, the Weathermen pulled themselves back from a kind of abyss; where they stopped powerfully defined the entire journey.

.   .   .

Oh but you who philosophize disgrace and
       criticize all fears,
Bury the rag deep in your face
For now's the time for your tears.

                              Bob Dylan,
        "The Lonesome Death of Hattie Caroll"

Even before the Days of Rage, Weatherman's leadership had planned to submerge parts of the organization and develop a clandestine capability

to complement the group's aboveground work.[4] The legal fallout from
the Days of Rage made the move underground all the more pressing. Up
until the October protest, the FBI had done with respect to Weatherman
largely what the movement had done: pore over the group's public statements, try to determine its ideological orientation, and assess what its
future actions might be; the FBI's early "intelligence" on the group, judging from its reports, consisted mostly of excerpts from New Left publications and the (often clumsy) summaries of the speeches of Weatherleaders by agents who had simply attended public meetings.[5] By the end
of the Days of Rage, many Weathermen faced jail time, mostly for felo-
nious assault and "mob action," for their actions in Chicago. Equally
important, the FBI was now convinced that Weatherman represented a
significant threat to the nation's security. On the basis of the Days of Rage,
the federal government indicted Weatherleaders for interstate travel to
induce riots, speculating that the charges might well "mark [the group's]
demise."[6] The Weathermen also became the objects of intensive federal
investigations and harassment by local police. In late October, the FBI
alerted its field offices that New York City's Weathermen were "going
underground and forming commando-type units which will engage in
terroristic acts, including bombings, arson, and assassinations."[7] Within
days, it ordered all offices to "follow the activities of any Weatherman
group in their respective areas" and opened cases on all known or suspected members, citing the group's "past violent activities and continued advocacy of revolutionary measures to overthrow the United States
government."[8] Local law enforcement was quick to respond. In mid November, twenty-three Boston Weathermen were arrested on spurious attempted murder charges after someone fired shots at a Cambridge police station. Though the charges were dropped when the only witness, a
teenager, confessed that the police had coerced his false testimony, local
Weathermen continued to face trumped-up indictments and stiff penalties for protest activity.[9]

    Police hostility was most intense in Chicago, home to Weatherman's
leadership in the SDS National Office. Plain-clothed "Red Squads" followed, threatened, arrested, and, on occasion, beat Chicago Weathermen.[10] Fearful of a police raid on its office, the collective obtained firearms
to defend itself. In the fall of 1969, the Red Squad indeed busted down
the doors—with the Weathermen wisely deciding not to resist with
gunfire—and hung Weatherman Robert Roth out the window by his an-
kles.[11] However intimidating, police treatment of the Weathermen paled
in comparison to the assaults on Chicago's Black Panthers. Gunfights

between the police and the Panthers periodically erupted, claiming lives on both sides. In late November, police shot dead a Panther, "Jake" Winters, in a warehouse, and the Panthers charged that he had been killed in cold blood. Russell Neufeld and Robert Roth later recalled feeling in Chicago that they were "in a war zone," in which Weatherman's survival depended on its developing a clandestine capacity.[12]

In the late fall and early winter, two events deepened Weatherman's conviction that there was an immediate need for armed struggle. Each highlighted the dominance of race in Weatherman's ideology and self-conception. The Chicago 8 conspiracy trial had begun on September 24, prompting demonstrations at Chicago's federal courthouse in which dozens of protesters, including several Weathermen, were arrested.[13] To the left, the trial was a transparent attempt to weaken the movement by imprisoning its leaders on essentially fraudulent charges. The defendants responded by lampooning the trial process, while also using it to indict the Vietnam War and racism.

A month into the trial, the Black Panther leader Bobby Seale was literally bound to his chair and gagged after repeatedly interrupting the proceedings to demand representation by an attorney of his choice. (He had wanted to be represented by his personal attorney, who was ill at the time, and not by the lawyers defending the Chicago 8 collectively.)[14] Seale, who blasted the judge as racist in his courtroom rant, was the only black among the defendants; at the time of the August 1968 Convention, he had never even met most of those with whom he had allegedly conspired to engage in violent disruptions. The image of a black man physically restrained in an American courtroom startled people across the political spectrum. For leftists, it affirmed their view of the trial as a grim farce. To the Weathermen, the alleged lack of solidarity shown Seale by the seven white defendants and the failure of demonstrators outside the courtroom to erupt in outrage further proved that whites were not sufficiently committed to aiding the black struggle. With stepped-up violence, the Weathermen would show their superior commitment.

Then, on December 4, the Illinois Black Panther Party chairman, Fred Hampton, aged twenty-one, and a fellow Panther, Mark Clark, aged twenty-three, were murdered during their sleep in a pre-dawn raid by Chicago police on a Panther house, just blocks from the SDS office. The raid had been coordinated by the FBI, relying on a paid informant for floor plans and other details to plot the attack. Though the authorities claimed that the Panthers had provoked a gunfight, the latter quickly established that the police story was entirely fallacious and opened the building for the community to see evidence that Hampton and Clark had, in plain language, been assassinated. (Preposterously, the seven Panthers who survived the raid, all of whom were shot by police, were initially charged with attempting to murder their attackers, even though they had offered no resistance.) Especially disturbing was the sight of Hampton's blood-drenched bed, in which he had been shot at close range. The informant, who had suspected but not known that the FBI was planning a hit on Hampton, was paid $300 for his services.[15] That the youthful Hampton had been such a dedicated and inspiring figure compounded outrage at the attack. Under his leadership, the Chicago Panthers had developed a "Breakfast for Children" program, provided work and hope for scores of poor young blacks, and worked to forge a truce between rival Chicago gangs. An overflow crowd attended Hampton's church funeral, and thousands publicly mourned his death.

Relations between the Chicago Panthers and the Weathermen were at once close and strained. The groups saw each other on a daily basis, and the Panthers used Weatherman's printing press to put out their newspaper. Yet Hampton had publicly denounced the Days of Rage. Jeff Jones recalls the Panthers being "infuriated" by Weatherman's refusal to function simply as a support group of theirs.[16] Bill Ayers confessed feeling that the Panthers' "serve the people" ethic, by making resource-poor communities responsible for the distribution of social welfare, amounted to a "gun-toting liberalism" that failed to address the structural inequities of capitalism.[17] Tensions between the groups reached a head following the police killing of Winters. In Neufeld's recollection, the Panthers had wanted Weatherman to print their memorial poster for him; but Weatherman, lacking money for the materials, was unable to provide that help. So the Panthers, led by Hampton, stormed the Weatherman office and beat members with two-by-fours, while muttering lines from Stalin. The Weathermen were stunned by the Panthers' eruption, attributing it to the immense pressure the Panthers were under. Neufeld was clubbed by Hampton and bears the scar on his head to this day. Asked years later if there might have been a masochistic element to the Weathermen's relationship with the Panthers, given Weatherman's concern over its "white skin privilege," he answered calmly, "No, they were getting killed. They were literally under siege and they weren't prepared to deal with it."[18] Just days after the incident, Hampton was dead.

Hampton's murder deeply affected the Weathermen, underscoring a basic premise of theirs and the New Left as a whole: that race constituted a primary basis of oppression and vastly separated the experiences of white and black activists.[19] Reflecting on the shock he felt, David Gilbert highlighted the apparent failure of whites to do enough: "There are Panthers being shot to death in their beds [and if] we're a revolutionary movement worth its salt we can't just say, 'Oh we sympathize with them.' We have to create pressure. . . . In terms of my personal experience, it was the murder of Fred Hampton more than any other factor that compelled us to take up armed struggle."[20] At the same time, the murder led the Weathermen to wonder if the limited protection from police violence they had by virtue of being white would soon erode. Wilkerson recalls, "we were terrified" and felt "we had to mold [a] fighting force that would be effective or everybody would be killed. . . . Someone woke me up at five o'clock . . . and said 'Fred's Dead.' And probably, if there's one moment that the [Weather Underground] was born, it was that moment. It was so brutal."[21]

Going underground was an ultimately ambiguous turning point for Weatherman, owing largely to a tension in the group's basic outlook. On the one hand, the Weathermen saw themselves as "the handful of exceptional whites" or even "race traitors" who alone among the New Left understood the imperative to support the struggles of people of color with violence.[22] The result was the group's intentional isolation from the white movement. On the other hand, Weatherman continued to believe, even as its numbers dwindled and criticism mounted, that its violence would awaken the militancy of young working-class whites, still thought vital to a successful revolution. Was the underground, then, to be part of a militant mass movement, or the final sign of the futility of trying to build such a movement?

This tension had a deeper basis in the group's analysis. As Naomi Jaffe explained, Weatherman saw most white Americans as embodying a "real historical contradiction" in their dual identities as both "oppressors and oppressed." The Weathermen, like others on the left, puzzled accordingly over whether whites were potentially agents of, or overwhelmingly obstacles to, radical change. Unlike others, the Weathermen asserted that this question could be answered only through violence—that violence alone had the power to force whites to resolve their dual identities either in favor of "the oppressed" or their roles as "oppressors." Disappointed by the response to the Days of Rage, Weatherman now looked to a clandestine fighting force to establish clear lines of battle and reduce complex issues of social and political identity to a single choice.

Compounding the confusion, the group spoke of violence with a double or even triple voice. "Bring the war home," Weatherman's slogan in 1969–70, ostensibly called for armed socialist revolution in the United States, but as Dohrn suggested years later, it much more plausibly implied hastening the end of the war in Vietnam by raising its social cost through militant protest. Individual Weathermen may have been committed to the latter, while overtly pledged to the former.[23] Neufeld confessed to just this, believing deep down that "the most" Weatherman "could do was disrupt the empire."[24] Finally, as Ayers suggested, the whole idea of "bringing the war home" may have ultimately been a metaphor. Like the slogan "The Vietnamese will win," it conveyed New Leftists' outrage, their naïvely optimistic view of the direction of world history, and their threat to the U.S. establishment—figured as a "doomed and helpless but temporarily destructive giant"—that it would face the escalating wrath of the young unless it did the right thing.[25]

The move of individual Weathermen into the underground came in different ways and meant different things. According to Neufeld, to avoid arrest while doing even legal things like printing *FIRE!* eventually required the Chicago Weathermen to function surreptitiously. In such a climate, "trying to have a legal, mass movement" seemed "foolhardy and delusional." For him, "there was never a decision to go [underground]. It just kind of happened."[26] Roth, although seized with horror by Hampton's murder, was also gripped by a sense of personal responsibility: "It was like I was on a path . . . scared but determined. I thought this is going to make a difference . . . and if not us, who?"[27] For Scott Braley, the die had been cast the previous summer. He recalls walking in the woods with a dear friend, a future Weatherwoman, and the two saying to each other, "'This is leading to revolutionary struggle, probably armed struggle. . . . We might or might not live through it.' . . . We acknowledged we weren't sure it was right, [but we] made a vow that we would go down this road [and would never] be any of these horrible people that write turncoat books, 'I was a dupe of the Communist Party.' We were doing this consciously."[28]

.   .   .

Never could read no road map
And I don't know what the weather might do
But hear that witch wind whinin'
See that Dog Star shinin'
I've got a feelin' there's no time to lose.

> The Grateful Dead, "Saint of Circumstance"
> (lyrics by John Perry Barlow)

If the Days of Rage were, at least in Weatherman's design, a moment of pure or unmediated action, Weatherman's "War Council" in Flint, Michigan, was a massive indulgence in symbols, a dizzying play of signs, mostly exhorting Weatherman's own members to more intense action. The meeting, held in late December 1969, in a black-owned ballroom in a poor neighborhood, was still technically a meeting of SDS's national council. By that point, however, few SDSers recognized Weatherman's leadership or participated in the conference. The handful of non-Weathermen at Flint included representatives of Detroit's White Panthers (a militant group that advocated cultural rebellion and armed resistance), the Bay Area Revolutionary Union (a theoretically minded Marxist-Leninist cell), and RYM II, as well as several unaffiliated teenagers. The "War Council" also attracted the interest of the FBI, which just days before the meeting compiled its initial field reports on the Weathermen, identifying approximately 270 members, 85 of whom were already on its special "Security Index."[29] At Flint, agents diligently recorded the identities of most of the 300 or so people in attendance and established who had written checks to rent the auditorium.[30]

Weatherman had advertised the Flint event as a political and cultural happening—in the words of the Liberation News Service (LNS), an "out-asight international youth culture freak show."[31] The Weathermen would try, in a familiar and frequently vexing gesture of the New Left, to blend militant politics with the libertine spirit of the counterculture. According to the Weatherwoman Susan Stern, Flint was Weatherman's "attempt to give the movement and the counterculture another chance before [giving] up on white-skinned Americans altogether."[32] Yet the event disappointed anyone expecting a genuine interest in making allies on the part of the Weathermen.

Weatherman had two very serious agendas at Flint. Midway through the gathering, the Weatherbureau announced the plan to go underground. Materials distributed at the conference gave an initial sense of Weatherman's vision of underground combat, stating: "Our strategy has to be geared towards forcing the disintegration of society, attacking at every level, from all directions and creating strategic 'armed chaos' where there now is pig order."[33] After the announcement, much of the conference focused on the practical aspects of clandestine armed struggle, such as the choice of targets, the procurement of weapons, and the building of secure cells. Equally important, the group's leaders sought to strengthen the resolve of the rank and file in preparation for the descent underground, making Flint, in Kirkpatrick Sale's description, one of "the most bizarre gatherings of the decade."[34]

The Weathermen transformed the ballroom into an environment to further incubate their enthusiasm for violence.[35] They decorated the walls with posters of their slain heroes, such as Che Guevara and Malcolm X, and pictures of Fred Hampton arranged to form the words "Seize the Time." The Weathermen also displayed images of their adversaries— Nixon and Agnew, certainly, but also pages of the *Guardian,* over which they drew gun sights and wrote the words "P-I-E-C-E N-O-W." At the center of the room dangled a giant papier-mâché pistol. Activities included karate exercises (one session was led, remarkably, by Tom Hayden), performances from a "Weatherman Songbook" that replaced the lyrics of popular songs with variously campy or morbid doggerels, the taking of large doses of LSD, and wild evening dances in which Weathermen chanted "Explode!" Typical of Weatherman's songs was "White Riot," sung to the tune of "White Christmas," which praised the Days of Rage: "I'm dreaming of a white riot/Just like the one October 8/When the pigs take a beating/And things start leading/To armed war against the state."[36] With a humor that had turned plainly sick, another song derided Chicago official Richard Elrod, paralyzed in the Days of Rage, to the tune of Bob Dylan's "Lay, Lady, Lay": "Stay Elrod stay/Stay in your iron lung/Play Elrod play/Play with your toes awhile."[37] The Weathermen also repeatedly invoked the notion of "barbarism," as they saw themselves, like the Visigoths, wreaking havoc on a tottering empire. In an especially perverse conversation, the Weathermen debated the ethics of killing white babies, so as not to bring more "oppressors" into the world and denounced American women bearing white children as "pig mothers."[38]

Speeches by Weatherleaders most forcefully defined the themes and emotions of Flint. Dohrn began by excoriating the white conspiracy trial defendants and the left generally for not tearing up the courtroom when Seale was bound and gagged.[39] According to Dohrn, this passivity had encouraged Chicago's police to kill Hampton.[40] She then presented the ideal Weatherman not simply as a determined revolutionary but as an unruly agent of disruption and offense. After relating an anecdote of how she and J. J. had recently torn down the aisle of an airplane, grabbing food from the plates of shocked passengers, Dohrn proclaimed, "That's what we're about, being crazy motherfuckers and scaring the shit out of Honky America."[41] Dohrn then gave praise to an unlikely hero, uttering a phrase she and the Weathermen would come to dearly regret. Referring to the Manson gang's Tate–La Bianca murders of the previous summer, Dohrn exclaimed, "Dig it; first they killed those pigs, then they ate dinner in the room with them, then they even shoved a fork into pig Tate's stomach. Wild!"[42] For the remainder of the conference, Weathermen greeted each other by holding up four fingers to represent a fork and chanted periodically "Free Charles Manson!"

In his speech, Mark Rudd stressed the need for a single-minded commitment to revolution by invoking Captain Ahab from Melville's *Moby Dick*. Rudd was hardly the first leftist in the 1960s to draw on *Moby Dick* for political metaphors. Several years earlier, Chairman Mao Tsetung had written presciently that Southeast Asia was, geopolitically speaking, America's white whale: the U.S. obsession with military victory in the region would cost the country dearly.[43] Eldridge Cleaver had argued that whiteness itself would prove to be America's fatal lure, as it had been for Ahab. But for Rudd, Ahab was less a figure of self-destructive obsession than an object of emulation. Rudd declared himself "monomaniacal" and demanded that the Weathermen pursue revolution with the same zeal as Ahab in his hunt for the whale. The Weatherman Howie Machtinger presented a second American icon, Superman's indefatigable nemesis Lex Luthor, as a role model, because he was "willing to fight forever."[44]

J. J. concluded the conference by explaining that the "personal pacifism" in which middle-class white youth are bred reflects how thoroughly they have been sheltered from the violence that victimized American blacks and the world's poor. J. J. was encouraged, however, by the increasing turn of white youth "away from a low energy culture . . . that robbed people of their passion" toward a new culture "of high energy and repersonalization through dope, sex, acid, revolution."[45] He boasted that the Weathermen are "against everything that's good and decent in Honky America. We will loot and burn and destroy. We are the incubation of your mother's nightmare."[46] According to one reporter, J. J.'s oration left the few non-Weathermen remaining at the conference "stunned."[47]

Flint devolved into a spectacle of political and emotional fervor, at once disturbing and surreal. Those attending the conference drew on figures of madness in describing it. Jeff Jones characterized Flint in retrospect as the apex of Weatherman's "group psychosis."[48] To Wilkerson, who recalls spending Flint in a "kind of blur," the event was "horrible," "total insanity."[49] Another Weatherwoman described Flint as "a very sad and alienating scene" that seemed like "some kind of a nightmare."[50] Carol Brightman, an antiwar activist mostly critical of Weatherman, recalled that the meeting "was grotesque, but it was like theater, [because] it didn't seem related to anything real."[51] Jonah Raskin, a radical professor, found the Weathermen at Flint at once "cogent and mad, penetrating and ludicrous."[52] One left-wing journalist titled his column on Flint "Abstract Barbarians?" concluding, "I wanted to write an article on how to think about Weatherman. It can't be done."[53] Another paper used the headline, "The Year of the Fork?"[54]

For much of the left, Flint compounded questions about Weatherman raised by the Days of Rage. Did the group intend to mount a principled campaign, built around comprehensible and potentially popular goals, or would it indulge "violence for its own sake"? However far-flung its vision, did Weatherman at least represent the promise of a society more just and humane than the one it sought to destroy? Though a gathering of only a few hundred among a movement of hundreds of thousands, Flint also raised important questions about the New Left as a whole: Was Weatherman simply an aberration that would burn itself out? A false and dangerous turn, demanding that the group be actively isolated? Or an extreme expression of tendencies present throughout the movement, with which the New Left as a whole had to come to terms?

Reflecting on Flint in a pacifist magazine, Hendrik Hertzberg asked "Is this our movement?" and answered, sadly, yes. He saw Weatherman as a "logical consequence of [the] intellectual flabbiness and dishonesty" of the left, which "stripped language of meaning" through "verbal overkill" (as in descriptions of America as "fascist"), spread the reckless idea that revolution was imminent, and more and more thoughtlessly endorsed violence.[55] The issue of violence extended beyond political protest. The movement had recently confronted its capacity for brutality in the disaster at Altamont—a California rock festival that shared nothing of Woodstock's magic and ended in the stabbing death of a black man by Hell's Angels—and, to a lesser extent, in Charles Manson, who conceived of his murderous cult partly in countercultural terms.[56] Yet the challenge the Weathermen posed to the self-conception of the New Left was greater.

<u>They were neither seasoned rogues like the Hell's Angels nor sociopaths</u> <u>like Manson. On the contrary, they were dedicated, well-educated ac-</u><u>tivists, several of whom had been elected the leaders of the New Left's</u> <u>most important organization.</u>

The Weathermen, looking back on their histories, identify the violence of the state as the ultimate source of the rhetoric at Flint. Gilbert, though denouncing the talk of Manson and killing babies as "sick," explained that it had "happened in the context of something that was like a com-plete radical change from anything that we had dealt with before. . . . <u>We were psyched up, freaked out, upset . . . but it was a very political</u> <u>thing.</u> Panthers were being murdered [and] most of the white movement was sitting by and letting it happen."[57] Stern insisted that "the Mansonite trip was born out of despair and frustration" and "in no way corre-sponded to the quality of the rest of Weatherman politics."[58] Jaffe re-called that by the time of Flint:

> We were so enraged by the war and by the distance between what we
> wanted to be able to do and what we were able to do. . . . We weren't
> interested in mollifying anybody's taste at that point. We really were inter-
> ested in turning ourselves into effective instruments to destroy imperialism.
> We weren't going to stick any forks into anybody. [Manson] might have
> been a stupid choice of metaphors, but we . . . were trying to make the leap
> to be people that could [destroy imperialism]. . . . Could we have made the
> leap in a way that was more principled and less insane? I don't know. That's
> what we felt we needed at the time—to say to ourselves we're ready . . . to
> do anything. And that didn't seem so crazy to me at the time.[59]

In addition to stressing outrage and frustration, these accounts allude to the fundamental *alienness* and traumatic impact of violence for the Weathermen. Todd Gitlin described how New Leftists experienced a kind of "violence shock" as the Vietnam War and physical attacks on dissi-dents intruded upon their previously safe worlds.[60] Noting that violence was virtually absent from the childhoods of most New Leftists, the psy-chologist Kenneth Kenniston reasoned that they could therefore initially see violence as something existing "'out there' . . . in their adversaries, in American Racism and American foreign policy."[61] The University of Wisconsin Professor Harvey Goldberg, defending in court the bomber of a campus building, described the youth of the 1960s as a "trauma-tized generation."[62] Gilbert's sense of the Weathermen having "freaked out" in the context of the "complete radical change" caused by the state's violence affirms these models of trauma.

Violence was also disorienting for the Weathermen as they tried to develop their own capacities for aggression. The heavily ritualized atmosphere of Flint seemed designed to help the Weathermen make that transition. The pattern of Weatherman's role models is telling. Two that they "honored," Lex Luthor and Captain Ahab, were drawn from fiction and had to be thoroughly recontextualized to serve Weatherman's narrative of armed revolution. The radical abolitionist John Brown, whom the Weathermen also praised at Flint, was the closest thing the Weathermen had to a genuine historical exemplar indigenous to white American culture.[63]

Manson could be attractive to the Weathermen of late 1969 at a variety of levels. Lacking precedent or seeming purpose, the murders by his "family" were nihilistic, summoning Doestoevsky's formula of distinctly modern crime: "Nothing is forbidden, everything is permitted."[64] To elevate Manson was to take on the mark of radical otherness, to announce oneself, in Jaffe's words, as at least "*capable* of doing anything," even if the Weathermen had no intention of repeating his acts. Praising Manson, Weatherman rhetorically blurred the revolutionary imperative to use "any means necessary" for political ends with a fascination with normlessness and total license.[65]

The status of the Weathermen as largely middle-class whites was essential to their politics of transgression. The Weathermen were not, like the Panthers, the self-described representatives of poor urban blacks, whose claim that they were oppressed was transparently credible to the American mainstream. To enhance their menacing image, militant blacks frequently played up a host of long-standing stereotypes of blacks as irrational and violent, codified in the image of the "crazy nigger." Cleaver exploited racist fears of black male sexuality by infamously describing in *Soul on Ice* the rape of white women as an act of political rage.[66] In addition, he dubbed Huey Newton the "baddest motherfucker ever to set foot inside of history" for his audacious, face-to-face confrontations with police on the streets of Oakland.[67] Most provocatively, the Panther's David Hilliard threatened the life of Richard Nixon from the stage of the massive November 15, 1969, antiwar protest in San Francisco. His obscenity-laced speech concluded, "Nixon is an evil man . . . responsible for all the attacks on the Black Panther Party. . . . Fuck that motherfucking man. We will kill Richard Nixon. We will kill any motherfucker that stands in the way of our freedom."[68] Indicted for advocating the president's assassination, Hilliard explained that his comments were essentially a "metaphor" uttered within the "language of the ghetto," where profanity and hyperbolic threats are common.[69] Whatever the status of such rhetoric, the government certainly saw the Panthers as a source of peril. In September 1969, FBI Director Herbert Hoover declared the group the "greatest threat to the internal security of the country."[70]

White radicals, to put it crudely, had comparatively little means of being "bad motherfuckers," regardless of their stated hatred of the status quo and the dubious notion, originally asserted by Norman Mailer, that the deviant white was a "white negro."[71] Weatherman's talk at Flint of frightening "Honky America" appears a rather transparent and forced mimicry of a black radical idiom. Manson, however, was a product of white culture, whom the Weathermen could rally around to code their rebellion as genuinely menacing and, through their tortured mediations, narrow their distance from black radicals. The *Ann Arbor Argus,* while denouncing Manson as a contemptible "mindfuck," explained that Manson might lead Americans to fear the counterculture "as people who murder and torture with IMPUNITY!"[72] The LNS stated bluntly that Weatherman "digs Manson" because "he's a 'bad motherfucker.'"[73]

By the same token, the increasing hostility of "the establishment" to the New Left encouraged white rebels to see themselves—and to celebrate their roles—as despised outsiders in their own right. "We are waste material," Jerry Rubin announced in 1969. "We fulfill our destiny by rejecting a system which rejects us."[74] The use of the word "freak" echoed Rubin's sentiment. An originally derogatory term that condemned the dropout culture as degenerate, "freak" became a popular self-description among the young. Daniel Foss explained: "It may disturb some Americans to discover that a number of youths (as of 1967–1968) have been referring to themselves with pride as 'freaks.'. . . But that is part of the whole point."[75] As the lines between the hippies and the politicos blurred at the end of the decade, the word "freak" was worn broadly as a badge of honor. Rock bands did their part in promoting the freak image and giving it a political edge. In 1969, The Jefferson Airplane released "We Can Be Together"—a lush anthem to the rebel culture on the album "Volunteers," whose cover shows the group dressed as a deranged militia. Composing the lyrics from graffiti in Berkeley and other slogans of the left, the Airplane sang: "We are all outlaws in the eyes of America / In order to survive we steal, cheat, lie, forge, fuck, hide, and deal / We are obscene, lawless, hideous, dirty, violent, and young . . . / And we are very proud of ourselves / Up against the wall / Up against the wall motherfucker / Tear down the walls."[76] Along these lines, some in the movement took apparent pride in the Weathermen as the left's audacious,

if crazed, answer to state hostility. A cartoon in an underground newspaper shows Vice President Agnew deliberating over what epithets to hurl
at the November 1969 antiwar protesters. He giddily suggests "Egregious
claque of despicable snots" and "Syphilitic morons with shit for brains."
In the corner of the cartoon a wild-eyed freak stomps away from a bomb
blast, next to the caption: "Meanwhile—in a series of nighttime raids
the sinister and incredible WEATHERMAN strikes again!!! What's this
crazy bastard up to, anyway?"[77]

Yet an air of unreality hung over the Weatherman's menacing performances, further confusing just what to make of their "message." To
Carol Brightman, the theatrical quality of what she called Weathermen's
"shenanigans" at Flint provided some comfort, as she assumed the Weathermen to be playacting identities they had neither the intention nor the
means of realizing.[78] Others were less assured. A reporter for the *Berkeley Tribe,* after showing how closely Dohrn's comments matched the recent court testimony of the alleged Manson gang murderer Susan Atkins,
commented indignantly that neither Dohrn nor Atkins, "has any comprehension of the horror they speak of. Both endorse horror in a weird,
lame way, straight out of a Crumb cartoon. Bernadine [*sic*] is proud of
it. Understanding that killing is necessary is one thing. Reveling in it is
another."[79] For the reporter, Flint was a spooky episode in an elaborate
fantasy life, so dangerous precisely because of Weatherman's detachment
from its content. In such moments, the Weathermen seemed to declare
themselves the progeny of a sick society now turning on its creators, and
to strive, however unselfconsciously, to make what was monstrous in
American society apparent by themselves becoming monstrous. Attuned
to this dynamic, the middle-aged journalist I. F. Stone said of the young
radicals, "To understand their irrationality is to become aware of ours."[80]

The *Tribe* felt Weatherman's potential for cruelty was signaled also
by what it called "the horror of inhuman logic." While asserting that "on
a perfectly logical level" killing white children is "correct" as a means
of eliminating racism, it nonetheless declared Weatherman "fucked up
on an emotional, supra-rational level."[81] Here the *Tribe* alluded to a pro-
tototalitarian impulse in Weatherman to at least *conjure up* its own "final
solutions." At Flint, a woman pointed out that Weatherman's cynical view
of white workers created problems for Weatherman's desired scenario
of Third World peoples overrunning the United States. If the country were
vanquished before "the masses" were fully organized into revolutionary
consciousness, she argued, then fascism would seem to be required to

keep whites in line. The Weatherman Ted Gold replied sharply, "If it will take fascism, we'll have to have fascism."[82] Susan Stern had answered an exasperated friend:

> "Are you going to fight everyone who doesn't agree with you? . . . Do you really think every white person in this country should die, Susie, do you really?" . . .
>   "If they're not going to do shit, well . . . yes, I do. If people won't join us, then they are against us. It's as simple as that. That includes the working class, and kids, if necessary."
>   "Everybody has to die?"
>   "Everybody has to die."[83]

Gold's and Stern's comments were hardly official statements of Weather ideology. Gold, in fact, was among those who argued shortly after Flint against putting a picture of Manson on the cover of *FIRE!* he felt, and most concurred, that there was ultimately nothing progressive or even political about Manson's violence. Even so, their comments reveal how the group could be bedeviled by a conspicuously instrumental rationality absent any moral compass. Gold had actually *lauded* fascism, while Stern sanctioned virtually infinite murder. Viewed historically, such "inhuman logic" echoes Arthur Koestler's "grammatical fiction"—the cold reasoning used by the Stalinists in Koestler's novel *Darkness at Noon* to measure the value of individual lives based on how well they "objectively" served the unfolding of the laws of History.[84] Weatherman, in short, added its own iteration to a dystopian formula, all too familiar to the twentieth century, that combines shrewd reasoning with a morbidly transgressive imagination.

    Marcuse's notion of the "Great Refusal" offers additional perspective on Weatherman's transgressions. Convinced that "administered societies" quickly neutralized or assimilated all forms of local resistance, Marcuse counseled the rejection of "the whole."[85] Yet neither Marcuse nor the New Left had any fixed sense of when one was being authentically radical, rejecting the system in its totality, truly subverting the mainstream. The escalation in militancy over the course of the 1960s was, in part, an experiment with new and more provocative forms of refusal. The Weathermen appeared intent on being the opposite of everything they felt the dominant culture valued. Years later, Roth described Weatherman's core message at Flint: "We spit on all your values, on all your sensibilities."[86] Stern conveyed the intensity and narcissistic quality of the group's "refusal" in the threat made at Flint that "there would be no peace in America as long as one Weatherman was left standing."[87]

From a deconstructive perspective, Weatherman's "refusal" seems a rather crude strategy of reversal. In opposing chaos to order, destruction to the status quo, the Weathermen simply inverted the hierarchies within a binary structure, leaving the structure intact. In a Marcusean vocabulary, the Weathermen practiced a *non*dialectical form of negation that naïvely equated *transgression* with *transcendence*. Marcuse defined negation, most broadly, as the refusal to accept the rationality and necessity of the given.[88] But according to Marcuse, truly dialectic negation also had to contain a moment of affirmation—a vision, however prefigurative and itself negated by prevailing "reality," of liberated utopian possibilities. Marcuse developed this view mostly with respect to aesthetics, but his aesthetic theory provides useful analogies for politics.[89] To Marcuse, emancipatory art must express, through its commitment to form, a beauty that testifies against and transcends the contradictions, ugliness, or even the obscenity of the established order. He therefore praised certain works of "high" bourgeois art and some of the creativity of the counterculture, such as Bob Dylan's more soulful songs, for pointing toward a transcendent realm.[90] (As if in agreement, the folksinger Phil Ochs penned the line, "In such an ugly time, the true protest is beauty.")[91] Marcuse was, by contrast, highly critical of the ostensibly radical "anti-art" of the 1960s that seemed to attack all aesthetic forms as pejoratively "bourgeois" and tried to dissolve entirely the distance between art and life. Criticizing Antonin Artaud's "theater of cruelty," which influenced the experimental theater of the decade, he wrote:

> Today, what possible language, what possible image can crush and hypnotize minds and bodies which live in peaceful coexistence (and even profiting from) genocide, torture, prison? And if Artaud wants . . . "sounds and noises and cries, first for their quality of vibration and then for that which they represent," we ask: has not the audience . . . long since become familiar with the violent noises, cries, which are the daily equipment of the mass media, sports, highways, places of recreation? They do not break the oppressive familiarity with destruction; they reproduce it.[92]

Beyond a critique of art, Marcuse offers a model of failed resistance as the repetition or mirroring of the very tendencies the resistance seeks to oppose. Flint, as Weatherman's own grisly theater, conformed to this model, insofar as it failed within the terms of Marcuse's analysis to *truly* shock and gloried in a destructiveness the Weathermen presumably sought to overcome.

Marcuse, in addition, suggests the importance of a tension between "acting out" and "working through" for the New Left. In their narrowly psychotherapeutic usage, these terms indicate different responses in an individual to trauma. Acting out is a way of remaining within trauma by falling into melancholic inertia or by blindly repeating the source of the trauma. (A clear case of the latter would be an abused child then abusing his children or spouse.) Working through entails coming to terms with trauma by acknowledging its impact and resisting troubling or dangerous tendencies associated with it, while not aspiring to fully overcome it. The terms, though initially developed by Freud to interpret psychic phenomena in the individual, may illuminate the response of groups to instances of trauma or crises within politics and culture. More generally, they may aid in understanding the relationship of critical modes of thought and action with the objects of their criticism.[93]

Kenneth Keniston, in one of the few intelligent psychoanalytical analyses of the New Left (facile tales of Oedipal revolt abounded), implicitly drew on the categories of acting out and working through by describing the "genuine agony" of the New Left as "the discovery that violence lies not only within the rest of American society, but in the student movement itself."[94] Keniston had praised the optimism and vitality of the New Left in his 1968 book *Notes on Committed Youth;* by 1971, he sought to account for the malaise and relative inactivity into which it had fallen. According to Keniston, that malaise owed not only to the grinding violence of the war and racism but also to the traumatic confrontation of the New Left with its own capacity for violence, typified by groups like Weatherman. Interpreting this violence in psychocultural terms, he surmised that the rebelliousness of the 1960s provided a context for the desublimation of a "rage, anger and destructiveness" among middle-class white youth that they had previously denied or channeled into less obviously violent forms.[95] Such aggression, he felt, was "no less a symptom of the pathological violence of American life" than police repression and the bombings of Vietnam.[96] He counseled that the left neither fall into a melancholic form of political resignation nor plunge deeper into violence. Rather, he urged that New Leftists work through their disturbing discovery by renewing their commitment to social change in full recognition of their own destructive impulses.[97]

New Leftists were at times alert to this danger of assuming the likeness of their enemy. Jerry Rubin complained of the New Left's debilitating competitiveness by asking, "Are we creating a New Man, or are we a reflection ourselves of the bullshit we hate so much?"[98] Dave Dellinger asserted that Yippie culture was, in its pronounced egotism, "distressingly like the mirror-image" of the dominant culture.[99] To the *Berkeley Tribe,*

Altamont revealed that "we were the Mother Culture," that the "the horror show is in all of us."[100] The White Panthers proclaimed that their goal was to "kill the inner pig."[101] Stern characterized the Manson comment as an expression of "the last putrid drop of American poison still flowing in the blood of the Weathermen."[102] A Weather collective admitted, "to change the pear we had to bite into it, but in our overeagerness, we often got some bad mouthfuls."[103] The Rolling Stones' "Sympathy for the Devil," sung by Mick Jagger just before the Altamont murder, was widely seen as a kind of negative anthem to demonic tendencies in the movement. Robin Morgan, a leading feminist, charged that the militancy of the New Left reproduced the aggressiveness and will to dominate of the reigning chauvinist culture.[104]

Nearly all these formulations cast the left as suffering from a bad immanence, in which features of its adversaries were recognizable in itself and vice versa. There is, however, some variation in the images, conveying different levels of self-awareness. By implicitly arguing that the corruption of the New Left reflected the corruption of America, New Leftists acknowledged that they remained products of their society, inevitably marked by deficiencies such as "racism" and "egoism." By extension, New Leftists saw themselves failing politically to the extent that they did not eliminate or distance themselves sufficiently from those deficiencies. As a corollary, New Leftists were generally loath to credit any of their virtues to their "Amerikan" socialization. Instead, they rooted their strengths in the inspiration of African-American and Third World revolutionaries, in the cathartic experience of protest itself, in the devious sensuousness of drug and sexual experiences, and in the new forms of community they created with one another. Some appeared to believe in the possibility of *complete* self-reinvention—of a kind of purification or exorcism of their "Amerikanness" achieved through transformative rituals such as criticism-self-criticism and the passage through "good" otherness. Abbie Hoffman gave that otherness figurative boundaries by insisting at the conspiracy trial that he was a citizen not of the United States but of a "Woodstock Nation." Rubin drew more dramatic lines of separation, stating: "Our search for adventure and heroism takes us outside America, to a life of self-creation and rebellion. In response America is ready to destroy us."[105]

For the left, however, to attribute everything troubling or repellent within it to the "dominant culture" was to shift the blame for its own failings onto its enemies. The New Left can therefore be accused of participating in at least the *logic* of scapegoating. Conventionally, scapegoating entails the denigration of the corrupting influence of the "outsider," figured as an absolute other, a source of impurity and contagion. But in fact it is the dominant group that projects *its own undesirable qualities* onto that other, whose attack or destruction it sees, in sacrificial terms, as enhancing its vitality or even ensuring its survival.[106] In contrast to this model, the New Left remained a minority sub- or counterculture, closer in position to the denigrated "outsider." New Leftists felt less anxious about contagion than about wholesale ruin at the hands of the American mainstream. Their condemnation of America, following the Panthers' lead, as a "pig" order sought rhetorically to reverse their own outsider status and to cast their enemy, in a typical gesture of scapegoating, as subhuman. For all its fury, the New Left never had the strength to reproduce the power dynamic that makes scapegoating so destructive. Yet even in its "weak" position, the New Left subtly disavowed responsibility for its own destructiveness and used the awareness of its own limitations to vilify its adversary further.

There are problems, however, with Kenniston's analysis. Sympathetic to young leftists, Kenniston is careful to point out that their violence was dwarfed by that of the state. Nonetheless, he contends that the state's war makers and the militants drew from the same well of violence and rage. Here Kenniston fails to acknowledge that violence varies greatly in its origins and function. Most important, he suggests that the New Left's violence was only, or essentially, an unfortunate mirroring of the violence of the larger society. From this premise, it is a small step to a blanket denunciation of protest violence—one that may obscure its complexities and confound judgment of it.

New Left violence can be seen as a form of mirroring that resists Kenniston's criticisms. Robin Palmer invoked Newton's basic laws of physics to insist that the force of the state, relatively unimpeded by peaceful dissent, met an opposite (though unequal) reaction in the counterforce of its opponents. Protest violence, in this blunt account, was an attempt to answer and ultimately stop the violence of the state. When not entirely rejecting their national roots, New Leftists could also present their violence as a positive expression of their American heritage. Palmer saw armed support for the Viet Cong as an assertion of America's own revolutionary past—captured in the self-description of some radicals as the "Americong"—and an *affirmation* of the American values of freedom and self-determination.[107] New Left violence, in these formulations, is not reducible to "unconscious complicity" with the destructiveness of the adversary. Rather, New Leftists explored in violence the utility or even integrity of force as a means of defending themselves and their allies, expressing outrage, and, most broadly, asserting their political principles and interests.

Kenniston, finally, pays little attention to the efforts of groups like Weatherman to reflect critically on violence. It was they who learned most immediately both its power and its dangers. They struggled to develop a militant practice that was politically coherent, ethically defensible, and existentially self-aware. The Weathermen's reckoning with their excesses was prompted by a tragedy of their own making. It is that event to which we now turn.

Weathermen reflect critically re. violence.

·   ·   ·

This wheel's on fire,
Rolling down the road,
Please notify my next of kin,
This wheel shall explode!
> Bob Dylan,
> "This Wheel's on Fire"

Going underground initially meant different things for different Weathermen. In January 1970, Weatherman finally closed the SDS National Office in Chicago. Under a plan the Weatherbureau called "consolidation," the collectives then engineered emotionally painful "purges" of those they suspected of being police agents or whose commitment they deemed less than total.[108] Only one informant, the Vietnam veteran Larry Grathwohl, survived the purges. Most dramatically, he passed a Weatherman "acid test" by, he claims, cleverly feigning taking an LSD tab; although berated for hours as a homicidal "pig," he failed to crack.

Though most of the movement wanted nothing to do with Weatherman, some individuals desperately sought to be part of the group and were crushed by the prospect of being told they did not measure up. This intense desire to belong had reasons both bad and good. Dohrn conceded that Weatherman "did have a cultish quality that made it hard to leave." Yet, she felt, most people were "in it for authentic and genuine reasons and wanted to be found worthy of participating."[109] Others close to Weatherman, doubting their own courage, or the wisdom of "armed struggle," or both, never resolved their relationship to the group and remained at its edges. One such activist confessed: "Part of me that thought that maybe I wasn't a good revolutionary, maybe I just wasn't committed enough. . . . I was willing to give up a lot of my life and my time but I wasn't willing to make bombs. . . . Did I not believe in it or was it too scary for me? Part of me believed that it was OK to do physical violence where you didn't kill people [but] quite a few people believed . . . that killing was part of the program, and I certainly couldn't . . . jump that [line]."[110]

Jim Mellen, author of the original Revolutionary Youth Movement statement giving rise to Weatherman, had grown more and more vocal after the Days of Rage in criticizing the group's direction. He recalls pleading with his friends and comrades:

> The important thing to understand about people like Fidel Castro and Ho Chi Minh and Mao Tse Tung is that they survived: they didn't go out in a blaze of glory. I was always told that I was from the Two-Months-in-the-Library School of Revolution, . . . and I kept trying to tell them that going out in a blaze of glory is just another way of going out. They argued that my approach was too staid, too stodgy. . . . I was constantly trying to figure out where I failed [in convincing others to] continue with above-ground political action and long range planning, and not become personal existential heroes.[111]

When talk of consolidation began he concluded, "This is the limit. This is ridiculous." Unsure of how to exit the group, he simply left a Weatherman house one afternoon and did not come back. Still puzzled years later by the process of his disengagement, he admitted, "I think I probably decided to leave after I left. I mean, it's very hard to leave anything like this . . . I was very close to [the Weathermen]. They were my whole world."[112]

By the end of Weatherman's consolidation, the group had 150 or so members—fewer than half as many as during the Days of Rage. (The group had no official membership, making it difficult to fix its numbers at any given point.) Members of the Weatherbureau, weary of one another after nearly a year of intense collaboration, split the organization into three parts. Collectives based in San Francisco, New York City, and Chicago and Detroit were to experiment more or less autonomously in devising underground strategies. Members of the West Coast collective, headed by Dohrn and Jones, spent time in Berkeley and San Francisco's Haight-Ashbury district, but avoided public political activities and quietly plotted bombings. The Midwest collective, headed by Ayers, built an arms cache and fabricated crude bombs with Grathwohl's help. The most dangerous of the bombs, dynamite with a burning cigarette as its trigger, was placed outside a Detroit police station, putting at risk both police and passersby, but failed to detonate.[113] The New York collective was the most militant. Its leaders, J. J. and Terry Robbins, thought that whites would move in a revolutionary direction only through the prompting of dramatic acts of violence, and they were dead set on providing the drama.[114] The collective was headquartered in the fashionable Greenwich Village townhouse of Cathy Wilkerson's father, a broadcast executive, while he was on vacation in the Caribbean. Though not technically underground, members of the collective virtually disappeared from public life and built a large stockpile of dynamite, purchased by Weathermen using false names from demolition supply companies in New England.[115]

Former Weathermen, though generally refraining from talking about personalities in the group, identify Terry Robbins as a main source of the group's most aggressive tendencies. Robbins had been an important organizer in the Ohio-Michigan SDS region and was a contributor to Weatherman's founding manifesto. He had excelled in the organization by virtue of his militant line and fascination with explosives. In his memoir, Ayers describes Robbins as at once a best friend, a partner in mischief, and a dangerously driven figure—"smart, obsessive," inhabiting an "anarchic solitude," and wedded to a strategy of "the bigger the mess, the better."[116] In a private interview, Ayers elaborated: "I don't want to demonize Terry . . . but Terry did have a very apocalyptic view of himself. . . . I used to say to Terry that if there hadn't been a movement [he'd] be the guy up in the Texas Tower" (a deranged sniper who opened fire on university students, killing over a dozen people). Ayers added, "But it wasn't just Terry. Terry's extremism was an impulse in all of us."[117] Palmer recalls that Robbins "scared the shit out of him" when they first met in early March 1970 in a recruiting session for Weatherman. Listening to Robbins talk wildly, with an embarrassed J. J. present, of plans to bomb an Army dance, Palmer responded, "I don't agree with what you're saying. You're going to get yourself killed." To Palmer, Robbins appeared a victim of "gut check" and what he proposed was "crazy."[118] Days later, Palmer's prediction would come true.

On March 6, 1970, a massive explosion leveled the Wilkerson townhouse.[119] Kathy Boudin, entirely naked, and Cathy Wilkerson, clad only in jeans, emerged in a daze from the wreckage. On the street they met Anita Hoffman, Dustin Hoffman's wife (whose house was next door) and Susan Wagner, Henry Fonda's former wife, who took the women to the Fonda house. Clothed by their hosts, Wilkerson and Boudin then vanished. Three dead bodies lay among the wreckage. The police soon identified two as Diana Oughton, aged twenty-eight, and Ted Gold, aged twenty-three, from New York City. Pieces of another body could not be identified, but the Weathermen later announced that Robbins had also died in the blast. Among the rubble, police found more than eighty sticks of dynamite; experts estimated that had it detonated, it would have "leveled everything" on the entire block.[120]

The Weathermen have refrained from disclosing in detail what the internal life of the collective had been and for years concealed the intended target of the bombs, leading to rampant speculation among the authorities and the left alike. Yet an outline of events can be gleaned from official communications of the group and the recent comments of former members. In late February, four New York Weathermen had bombed the New Jersey home of the judge presiding over the trial of the Panther 21—a group of New York City Black Panthers spuriously accused of a conspiracy to blow up department stores, city landmarks, and police and subway stations. With Robbins likely in the lead, the four insisted that the action had not been extreme enough: injuring no one, it did only "symbolic" damage. Planning what Weatherman would confess was a "large-scale, almost random bombing offensive," they built antipersonnel devices (explosives wrapped in nails) and persuaded the collective to bomb a dance at an Army base at Fort Dix, New Jersey.[121] Robbins apparently crossed live wires while preparing the bombs in the townhouse basement, causing the blast.

The townhouse explosion was one of the crucial junctures in an era full of dramatic turning points. It certainly frustrates any attempt to give a narrowly structural account of New Left violence in the United States and would likely fascinate anyone trying to determine the role in history of chance events. One can begin to assess its importance by speculating on what might have unfolded had it not occurred. If the collective had succeeded in its plan to kill Army officers and their dates, the "war at home" would have instantly become more volatile. The bombing might have inspired some small number of Weathermen and others to commit similar acts. The government, which often disregarded civil liberties in pursuing dissidents, and two months later at Kent State would again break the taboo against killing white demonstrators, might have abandoned all restraint in its efforts to destroy Weatherman.[122] Mass arrests or even murders of suspects might have been followed, in turn, by movement reprisals, conceivably kidnappings or assassinations. In short, had Fort Dix been attacked, it is possible that Americans would now speak of the 1970s as a "decade of terrorism," as do people in countries like Germany and Italy, where "Red Armies" clashed with their governments in grim cycles of lethal violence. By the same token, those responsible for the murderous plan might have been denounced and marginalized by other Weathermen, effectively stopping the escalation of the group's violence.

The consequences of the explosion that can be determined in less speculative ways are also immense, but tangled in a complex chronology made more complicated by the differences between the Weathermen's public acts and their private deliberations. The media and the public reacted with shock and outrage. The *New York Times* scrambled to provide background stories on the Weathermen, printed timelines of recent bombings, reported extensively on the March 12 explosions perpetrated at three Manhattan buildings by "Revolutionary Force 9" (a collective that apparently took its name from the Beatles' song "Revolution 9"), noted the *hundreds* of idle bomb threats made that week, and tracked the efforts of officials to tighten restrictions on the sale of dynamite. Echoing indignant politicians, the *Times* pronounced the Weathermen to be "criminals, not idealists."[123] Thomas Powers elaborated that view in a series of Pulitzer Prize-winning articles that chronicled what he saw as Oughton's transformation from a sensitive, midwestern child of privilege to a zealous assassin.[124] For much of the country, the blast turned the Weathermen into an instantaneous symbol of the antisocial violence into which the New Left had apparently descended. For historians, it has provided the seemingly perfect bookend for narratives of the New Left beginning with the earnest optimism of SDS's founders and ending with the movement's fiery self-annihilation.[125]

Law enforcement increased its efforts to eliminate Weatherman. A month before the explosion, FBI Director Hoover had characterized Weatherman as the "most violent, persistent and pernicious of revolutionary groups" (a distinction usually reserved for the Panthers).[126] The FBI immediately began to search for Wilkerson and Boudin, as well as for Weathermen who were free on bond or under consideration for prosecution. Nearly two dozen Weathermen were named as targets for "intensive investigation," in which designated field offices were to report weekly on their whereabouts or efforts to locate them.[127] A memorandum explained that "identification of all Weatherman activists," which permitted sustained surveillance and the preparation of charges, "is the key to smashing the movement."[128] The discovery in late March of a stash of dynamite in Chicago and fears that the Weathermen would react to pending indictments with a "final, desperation outburst of violence" increased the FBI's sense of urgency.[129] A measure of paranoia seemed to accompany the FBI's efforts. In late March, the Bureau informed Nixon's aid John Ehrlichman that a federal employee had a daughter in Weatherman, who had allegedly told him that the group planned to bomb airline passenger planes.[130]

On April 2, Attorney General John Mitchell personally announced a fifteen-count federal indictment of twelve Weatherleaders and named twenty-eight unindicted co-conspirators for the Days of Rage, making many of the elusive Weathermen fugitives from U.S. law.[131] (In late December 1969, a Cook County grand jury had issued thirty-seven indictments against sixty-four Weathermen for alleged breeches of Illinois law.)[132] The main federal charges were for "conspiracy" and "interstate travel to incite riots"—the same charges brought against the Chicago 8 defendants. Each charge held a maximum sentence of five years in prison. In May, the FBI publicized that "one of the most intensive manhunts in [its] history" was under way for nine of the Weatherleaders.[133] To aid in its pursuit, the Bureau schemed to have Richard Starnes of the Scripps-Howard News Service write a "special visual feature story" on the nine fugitives, making use of the FBI's own "Identification Orders" and emphasizing the Weathermen's violent nature.[134] On May 7, Starnes's article appeared in the *Washington Daily News,* replete with descriptions of the fugitives provided by the Bureau.[135] Hoover personally thanked Starnes for his "excellent article," and the FBI noted with satisfaction that a congressman—unaware of the story's origin—had placed it in the *Congressional Record.*[136]

The FBI was, however, unable to locate most Weathermen. It complained, with unintentional humor, that their "degenerate living habits, their immoral conduct, and their use of drugs" made it "extremely difficult to find informants who fit this mold and are willing to live as they do."[137] It also recognized that hundreds of communes throughout the country provided potential havens for the Weathermen. Desperately needing an arrest, on April 15, the FBI captured two Weatherwomen, Dianne Donghi and Linda Evans, but in the process blew the cover of its sole deep informant, Larry Grathwohl.[138] (As part of the deception, Grathwohl had been arrested with the others, but was observed in the police station talking on friendly terms with police.) Weathermen who were more heavily sought escaped the FBI's grasp, as dozens of sympathizers throughout America provided them with safe housing, disguises, and money.

For the left, the townhouse explosion was another chilling eruption in a climate of escalating confusion and violence. I. F. Stone, at the liberal end of opinion, saw in the blast a cautionary tale for a society apparently willing to sacrifice its youth in a war they had rejected.[139] Left-wing critics took the blast as decisive proof of the poverty of Weatherman's approach. Detroit's *Fifth Estate* offered a "Eulogy for SDS," accusing Weatherman of having finally "lost touch with political reality" altogether.[140] Andrew Kopkind, still ambivalent about Weatherman, concluded that the budding armed struggle was far too small and disorganized to actually threaten state power. Yet he suggested that it might enhance the current "sense of crisis" that would force "real, existential choices" upon Americans.[141] Other radicals, closer still to the Weathermen, memorialized the dead in anonymous poems. The most evocative began, "How does it feel / To be inside / An explosion / Was there time / To flash upon / The way we came?"[142]

For all the acrimony heaped on Weatherman, enthusiasm for revolution had been building for months and would rush toward a crescendo in the spring of 1970, just as the group met disaster. A May 1969 graphic in DeKalb's *News from Nowhere* captured radicals' sense of the inexorable march toward violence. It begins by showing two "kaleidoscope" eyes next to a hand holding a sunflower under the label "1966." The image for 1967 has peace signs in the eyes. By 1968, the eyes bear the "ohm" symbol for resistance. "1969" features blackened sunglasses next to a revolver and the ominous caption, "Mine eyes have seen the coming . . ."[143] In November, New York City's *Leviathan* announced its goal of transforming itself from a "magazine of the movement" into one "of the revolution." It explained, "We began life as Jonah . . . inside the great whale that devours us all. We're still not sure exactly . . . how to get out . . . but we're going to learn how to rip that whale's guts apart."[144] The following month, twenty-two-year-old David Hughey, recently captured for involvement with the Melville collective, issued his own cosmic call to arms: "Our little individual consciousness whose main concern is to be protected . . . has to start giving way to a collective consciousness . . . where the individual, rather than constantly escaping life and death . . . let's go and flows into life and death. And in the context of repressive America this flow into life and death amounts to a very deep and strong desire to fight."[145] As such rhetoric proliferated, so too did the means for acting on it. In December, Berkeley's "International Liberation School" published *Firearms and Self-Defense: A Handbook for Radicals, Revolutionaries, and Easy Riders,* which covered such topics as "Shotguns" and "Gun Laws."[146]

The *Berkeley Tribe* wove together the militancy, exuberance, and conceit of radicals, as well as their international outlook. The cover of its late February–early March issue pictures a snarling globe topped by Cleaver's proclamation: "We call for total chaos in the capitalist countries . . . we will have war."[147] Dotting the globe are reports of violence: the bombing of a Select Service office in Arizona; the destruction of a municipal building outside of Cleveland; the attack by Venezuelan guerrillas on a Mobil Oil pipeline; and the trashing of the U.S. embassy in Manila. An editorial called for the immediate building of a "People's Militia" to combat what it described as the "Final Krackdown" allegedly planned against local radicals.[148] Later in the month, radicals answered the conviction of the Chicago 8 defendants on charges of contempt of court (they were acquitted of the more serious charges, but still potentially faced years in prison) with semi-planned rioting throughout the country.[149] In both word and deed, echoes of Weatherman seemed everywhere.

Nixon's announcement on May 1 of the hitherto secret bombings of Cambodia and the subsequent shooting of students at Kent State and Jackson State universities threw the nation's campuses into chaos. Students shut down hundreds of universities and for a week bombed or burned ROTC buildings at a rate of four a day, amid calls for revenge or civil war.[150] According to government figures, there were 281 attacks on ROTC buildings alone and a staggering 7,200 arrests on American campuses from June 1969–June 1970.[151] In a special issue on "Guerrilla Warfare in the United States," *Scanlan's* magazine documented close to 500 acts of arson or bombings (attempted or successful) of government, corporate, police, military, and university targets in the first six months of 1970.[152] In August, the New Left took its first life when four radicals bombed the Army Math Research Center at the University of Wisconsin at Madison, accidentally killing a postdoctoral student, Robert Fassnacht. A month later, Susan Saxe and Kathy Power were sought for the murder of a Boston police officer during a bank robbery meant to secure funds for radical activities. Activists of every sort fleeing prosecution or imprisonment fed the burgeoning underground—among them Jane Alpert and Patricia Swinton of the Melville collective; the former SNCC president Rap Brown, wanted for incitement to riot; Angela Davis, suspected of involvement in the bloody takeover of a Marin County courthouse by Jonathan Jackson (brother of the Soledad inmate and author George Jackson); the radical pacifists Daniel Berrigan and Mary Moylan, convicted of antidraft activities; the Madison bombers; and Saxe and Power.[153] By October, Saxe, Power, and Bernardine Dohrn were on the FBI's "Ten Most Wanted Fugitives" list.[154]

The release from prison of Huey Newton following his acquittal of murder charges and the Black Panthers' convening of the "Revolutionary People's Constitutional Convention" in the summer of 1970 promised to provide leadership and focus for the left. In September, the Weathermen helped break Timothy Leary, serving a ten-year sentence for possession of small amounts of marijuana, out of a California prison. An exultant Leary exclaimed in a Weatherman communiqué: "There is no compromise with a machine. You cannot talk peace and love to a humanoid robot whose every Federal bureaucratic impulse is soulless, heartless, lifeless, loveless. . . . Resist lovingly . . . passively . . . physically. . . . To shoot a genocidal robot policeman in the defense of life is a sacred act."[155] Leary then fled to Algeria, where he and Eldridge Cleaver forged an apparent alliance, fueling new hope of a merger of cultural and political radicals—the revolutionary marriage of acid and guns. Back in the United States, the Black Liberation Army, which had evolved from the Black Panther Party and was supported by its "International Section," headed by Cleaver, became increasingly active; its clandestine cells robbed banks, attacked police stations, and engaged on occasion in deadly ambushes of police.[156] In a nonviolent vein, the growing feminist and gay rights movements drew more young people into activism and radically expanded the meaning of revolution. The Weathermen, long denounced as poison in the New Left's waters, marveled at the rising tide of militancy. Taking refuge there, Dohrn recalls, "We became part of a sea of us; we were not at all the only ones."[157]

The Weathermen initially gave little public indication that either their goals or tactics had changed after the townhouse explosion. Most immediately, the explosion both hastened and made more total the move underground. Those living semi-underground or awaiting indictments vanished overnight. Braley explained, "every FBI agent for a million miles was on every person"; everybody "had to be grabbed off the streets and put somewhere."[158] In the panicked process, some members were simply left behind.

News of the blast reached some Weathermen in surreal ways. Johnny Lerner was in Cuba on a "Venceremos Brigade" with three other "borderline" Weathermen when he heard reports of the explosion. The stranded Weathermen then went to Europe with fake ID's and returned to the United States; though initially meaning to reconnect with the underground Weathermen, Lerner never completed the last step.[159] Another of the stranded members, long conflicted about the group, did meet with Weatherleaders when back in the United States. If anything, her experience in Cuba cutting sugarcane increased her distance from the group. She explained, "It was very hard work and I liked it. . . . You had the satisfaction of a big pile of sugarcane at the end of each row. . . . it felt very satisfying after the life I had been living" with the Weathermen. At the meeting, she told the Weathermen that she was "going to find a different direction in life," and left the organization.[160]

Russell Neufeld had long been bothered by Weatherman's inability "to connect with real peoples' lives." Concluding that it was "ultimately mass movements that change society," he quit the group when it submerged more deeply underground. Neufeld was walking in New York City to meet a friend when he learned of the townhouse explosion, and he then watched the details unfold on television in a hotel room with his parents (in town for a professional conference). His brother called from an apartment in Madison, Wisconsin, with Grathwohl present, leading to his spurious arrest for having allegedly bought the dynamite in the townhouse.[161] Like other Weathermen, he had no idea of the existence of the New York collective, let alone its plan to attack human targets. The explosion and the arrest, Russell confessed, left both him and his parents, "in shock" and took "a long time to accept and internalize."[162]

And then there was Bill Ayers, already underground, waiting for two days near a dusty truckstop in rural America for some word from the Weatherbureau, learning finally that his best friend, Terry, and his girlfriend, Diana, were dead. His mind reeled with fantasies of consolation: Robbins, he convinced himself, was the group's demon, who had pushed for the reckless assault; his beloved Diana, in his guilt-wracked imaginings, was the group's angel, who had pleaded with Robbins and the others to stop.[163]

Underground did not mean inactive. On May 21, 1970, Weatherman issued its first communiqué in which Dohrn, now the group's main leader, made a declaration of war. Describing all efforts at reform as futile, Dohrn announced that revolutionary violence "is the only way" for American rebels. The Weathermen also flaunted their success at hiding, taunting the FBI to find them "in every tribe, commune, dormitory, farmhouse, barracks and townhouse where kids are making love, smoking dope, and loading guns." Praising the growing militancy of the youth culture, they proclaimed: "All freaks are revolutionaries, and all revolutionaries are freaks." The communiqué concluded with the warning that within two weeks, Weatherman would attack a symbol of "Amerikan injustice." A few days past the deadline, Weatherman claimed responsibility for the bombing of New York City police headquarters in retaliation for police violence against blacks and other minorities. In July, the Justice Department issued a new round of federal indictments, based on the Flint "War Council," of twelve Weatherleaders for weapons possession and a conspiracy to commit bombings and murders.[164] The Weathermen responded by warning Attorney General Mitchell: "Don't look for us, Dog; we'll find you first."[165] Subsequent communiqués in the first nine months of Weatherman's underground existence accompanied the bombing of the National Guard headquarters following the shootings at Kent State; bombings of the Marin County and Long Island City courthouses; the bombing of the rebuilt Haymarket statue in Chicago; and the Leary escape.[166] In the communiqués, the Weathermen were as brash as ever. That accompanying the Haymarket bombing, which a Chicago Police Superintendent denounced as "an insane act perpetrated by psychopaths," ran: "students and hippies who now hear peace talk from the white man must remember how talk of peace was used against the Indians and preached to the Blacks. Don't be tricked by talk. Arm yourself and shoot to live. . . . We are not 'attacking targets'—we are bringing a pitiful giant to his knees. . . . [G]uard your planes. Guard your colleges. Guard your children."[167]

.   .   .

Crimson flames tied through my ears
Rollin' high and mighty traps
Pounced with fire on flaming roads
Using ideas as my maps
"We'll meet on edges, soon," said I
Proud 'neath heated brow.
Ah, but I was so much older then,
I'm younger than that now.
                    Bob Dylan, "My Back Pages"

Behind their bravado and audacious bombings, the Weathermen were deeply affected by the townhouse explosion. In late April, many Weathermen, including Boudin and Wilkerson, made their way to a secluded location in northern California for a meeting to discuss what had happened in New York and what the future of the organization should be. This would be Weatherman's first, crucial reckoning with its initial vision of armed struggle. Jeff Jones had gone home after the explosion to assure his parents that he had not been killed and to say his good-byes before completely vanishing underground. He came to the Weatherman summit intent on defeating the more extreme politics in the group or leaving and taking others with him. For Jones, the Weathermen had strayed "far away from the essential humanity and commitment to democracy that had fueled us in the first place." He, with Dohrn and several others, successfully argued that radical politics "wasn't about big bombs" and "terrorist acts."[168] Dohrn recalls that the meeting was different also in *how* the Weathermen argued—"not by staying up for 72 straight hours and seeing who was still on their feet, but actually trying to bring everybody back to . . . how you change hearts and minds."[169]

J. J., in charge of New York operations, was held responsible with the late Robbins for the townhouse catastrophe and sent on indefinite leave, never to rejoin the group. He wandered for a couple years in northern California and Mexico, eventually settling under an assumed name in Vancouver, Canada, where he died a natural death in 1997. Once a great champion of the revolutionary motto "Audacity, audacity, and more audacity," he confessed to Rudd in an unsent letter that he had "lost, killed, alienated, or driven away" all his friends, and that life was "sad and lonely," whether he was a fugitive or not.[170] Other Weathermen voluntarily made what Ayers described as an "honorable retreat from the craziness" and left the organization, paring it down to well below one hundred.[171]

On December 6, 1970, Weatherman made public the results of its self-evaluation in a lengthy communiqué, signed by Dohrn, titled "New Morning—Changing Weather." It began:

> We want to express ourselves to the mass movement, not as military leaders, but as tribes at council. It has been nine months since the townhouse explosion. In that time, the future of our revolution has changed decisively. A growing illegal organization of young men and women can live and fight and love inside of Babylon. The FBI can't catch us; we've pierced their bullet proof shield. But the townhouse forever destroyed our belief that armed struggle is the only real revolutionary struggle.[172]

Admitting that "something had been wrong with our direction besides technical inexperience," the Weathermen then tried to account for their misdirection.

"New Morning" chiefly criticized the "the military error," which Weatherman defined as "the tendency to consider only bombings or picking up the gun as revolutionary, with the glorification of the heavier the better." Under the influence of "the military error," and racked by sleeplessness and fear, the New York collective "acted as if only those who die are proven revolutionaries." Weatherman frankly admitted confusing martyrdom with commitment and reducing radical politics to a fatalistic end game, consummated in death. In a striking revision of its ideology, Weatherman then urged the Movement to engage in aboveground activities such as demonstrations. Echoing earlier communiqués, the statement also proclaimed the fundamental progressiveness of the youth movement and described "grass and organic consciousness expanding drugs" as "weapons of the revolution."

In praising the youth culture, the Weathermen both expressed a more expansive concept of radical politics and reasserted their roots. In conversations after the explosion, members reflected on their first demonstrations, their early efforts to persuade friends, and their "talents, interests, differences." Abandoning notions of being America's Zero Children striking out at a society that had misshaped them, they now saw themselves as part of a robust, if still naïve, counterculture. In this spirit, Weatherman memorialized Oughton and Gold as teachers (they had taught in Guatemala and New York City respectively) and Robbins as a community organizer (he had worked with SDS in a Cleveland ghetto). The Weathermen also revised their appreciation of other revolutionaries, lauding the Vietnamese "not as abstract guerrilla fighters, slugging it out with U.S. imperialism," but as people with "parents and children and hopes for the future." Finally, "New Morning" reflected the growing feminist consciousness in the organization. It concluded with a list of "exemplary" women revolutionaries throughout the world. And, after Weatherwomen protested the sexism of the name Weather*man*, the group renamed itself in the communiqué the "Weather Underground."[173]

"New Morning" conveyed both the tragic-comic aspects of Weatherman and how much the group had matured since going underground. Weatherman conceded virtually all of the major charges of its critics since its founding—its glorification of violence, its dismissal of conventional protest, and its dangerous belief that a revolutionary group can succeed or even survive without any kind of genuine popular base. Yet even in confession, the Weathermen spoke with a conspicuous arrogance, as though the revolution were somehow theirs to lead and as though they alone could assert the widely held "truths" that *they* had recently discovered. Particularly awkward was their declaration in the name of the movement of a faith in the value of public, nonviolent protest—a faith that most activists had never fully lost. By the same token, the Weathermen could lay claim to an authority that comes with having learned certain things themselves, from beyond a boundary others could only imagine. The group was, in a sense, the New Left's canary in a coal mine, alerting others to the dangers of at least a certain approach to armed struggle.

The Weathermen now sought to lead largely by example. "New Morning" intended only to correct for the "military error" and not, as one might infer, to signal the group's withdrawal from violence altogether. Crucially, Weatherman had decided, following the townhouse explosion, not to engage in actions aimed at killing police—actions, Jaffe has recently indicated, that the group "could have and would have done" had it not been forced into sober self-reflection.[174] In addition, teams of Weathermen toured the country to persuade independent radical collectives not to engage in the kinds of all-out assaults Weathermen had once favored. Dohrn, who took part in this effort, explained that the basic goal was to turn "people away from thinking 'the more damage the better,' from thinking that it was ok to hurt or kill civilians," and to argue that "kidnapping and assassinations were off the table." The Weathermen gave political, practical, and ethical reasons in urging restraint.[175]

Attacks on property were another story. Shortly after "New Morning," the Weather Underground planted several small bombs in the Capitol to protest the recently announced U.S. invasion of Laos. Ayers explained that the attitude among the group was, "'We've corrected for the townhouse, now take this, BOOM!'"[176] Weatherman's change of approach was already evident in its bombings since the townhouse. In each, the Weathermen issued a warning to prevent injury—a practice they continued throughout their existence. Capturing the universal sentiment among former members, Jaffe said: "We were and continue to be very proud of the fact that we didn't injure anybody in any of those actions."[177]

Not everyone on the left was pleased with "New Morning," including some Weathermen. Braely confessed, "I did think it was backpedaling on armed struggle, but I wasn't all that clear on what we should do." Though he counted himself as "one of the organization's hippies," he was less than enthusiastic about Weatherman's effort to bust Leary out of jail and the group's newfound love of the counterculture. Equally important, some of Weatherman's apparent allies sharply criticized the statement.[178] Two months after the publication of "New Morning," members of the Panther 21 issued an open letter to the Weathermen.[179] By February 1971, the situation of the Panther 21 was doubly desperate. Arrested in April 1969, the members had been given extremely high bail, such that most of the group had been in prison for eighteen months as their trial for at-

tempted murder and other serious charges slowly unfolded. (The trial, ending in the acquittal of the defendants, lasted until May 1971, making it
the longest trial in New York State up to that point.)[180] In addition, the
New York Panthers were in the process of being expelled from the national Black Panther Party by its increasingly paranoid West Coast leadership for alleged breaches of solidarity.[181] In their statement, the Panther
21 singled the Weather Underground out for praise among white groups
because it had gone beyond lip service and "related to action—the
unequivocal truth by which revolutionaries gauge one another." Yet they
also expressed strong misgivings about the direction outlined in "New
Morning"—in particular the Weather Underground's praise of the counterculture and apparent retreat from violence. Their criticisms echoed
Weatherman's own earlier grievances about the counterculture: that it was
escapist, indulgent, and racist, because it was more concerned with the
individual freedom of whites than with the "group freedom" of African
Americans. Though acknowledging the need for political education, the
Panthers rejected as naïve the belief that transforming the consciousness
of young whites would have any impact on the conduct of the Panthers'
oppressors. And, reminding the Weathermen that blacks were suffering
daily, the Panthers insisted that violence remained the only viable strategy for black liberation. In ways principled, desperate, and heavy-handed,
they implored the Weathermen not to abandon the armed struggle.

The Panthers' letter was one of the few direct public communications
between black and white revolutionary groups. It is hard to overstate the
significance of the dilemma it posed for the Weathermen, given the status of race in Weatherman ideology. The Weathermen had justified their
violence largely by asserting the need for whites to join blacks and other
people of color at the front lines of combat; disidentifying with much of
the New Left, the Weathermen had declared themselves accountable, in
effect, to the most militant of militant blacks. With the Panther 21 statement, the Weathermen finally received the kind of endorsement that most
radical blacks had previously withheld. But the statement, by insisting
that violence was *the* essential ingredient of revolutionary politics, potentially tempted the Weathermen back to the narrow conception of radicalism behind the "military error"—an error to which black militants
were hardly immune. For the Weathermen to curtail their violence was,
however, to risk losing their identity as "exceptional whites" and undermine their ethic of solidarity. Striking a balance between the two impulses proved difficult. On December 4, 1970, two days before the publication of "New Morning" and exactly one year after the murder of Fred

Hampton, Robin Palmer led five others in an ill-fated attempt to avenge Hampton's murder by firebombing a First National City Bank office in New York City after business hours. (The group had also planned to attack two police stations, the Bolivian Consulate, a research building at New York University, and a New York law firm with which President Nixon was affiliated.) The Weatherbureau, doubting the security of the action, urged Palmer not to go through with it. Its sense of caution proved well founded, as Palmer had unwittingly recruited a police agent, who had the cell arrested.[182]

The Weather Underground did not respond publicly to the letter from the Panther 21—a decision many Weathermen later regarded as a horrible mistake.[183] Gilbert recalls that the Weathermen privately concluded that the Panthers had misinterpreted "New Morning" by failing to see that they retained an armed struggle strategy.[184] The group's continued bombings would make that plain, and the Panthers were not owed further clarification. But the Weather Underground's new modus operandi *did* represent a step back from the kind of violence favored initially by the Weathermen and still by the Panther 21, designed to instigate a civil war. In effect and likely intent, the group's "armed actions" in the 1970s were transparently "symbolic." Most notably, the Weather Underground bombed the California Department of Corrections in August 1971 in response to the killing of George Jackson during a prison escape; the New York State Department of Corrections following the massacre at Attica prison a month later; and the Pentagon in May 1972, after the U.S. bombing of Hanoi. In each case, the Weather Underground reacted to instances of state violence against people of color—violence it felt compelled to censure with more than just words, but that it was powerless to prevent. "New Morning," in this light, represented the Weathermen's reassessment of what was possible given the political climate and what kind of action was valid and desirable for white radicals.

Some in the group felt that the Weathermen redrew the bounds of race too sharply. Gilbert explained, "There's a way in which the Weather Underground . . . was still the white, middle-class underground. It wasn't a situation in which our own communities [were] being killed. And so there was a way in which we comfortably also limited the level of violence we took on . . . which limited the amount of solidarity we provided Third World struggles."[185] The group's restraint, in this view, partly reflected political weakness and the retreat into race and class privilege. Others, likely the majority, saw the group's moderation more positively. In the early 1990s, Dohrn described the Weather Underground's violence as an "extremely restrained and highly appropriate response" to the state's violence.[186] Gilbert's and Dohrn's comments outline, beyond poles in a tactical debate, very different ways of negotiating a politics of solidarity. Praise for restraint, when read as a muted commentary on issues of race, implicitly signals the acceptance of certain limitations imposed by one's identity. Part of the difficulty Weatherman had in attracting whites to violence reflected precisely the *experiential* barriers dividing the worlds of black and white and the very different kinds of adversity each community faced. Attempts to artificially collapse those differences could be disastrous. Larry Weiss recalls being briefed that the New York City townhouse collective had believed that to use safety mechanisms on its bombs would be to assert its "white skin privilege."[187] With this ludicrous assumption, Weathermen looked past the fact that the vast majority of American blacks hardly joined the Black Panthers and the BLA in "picking up the gun."

The Weather Underground never settled on a single conception of the ideal role for white revolutionaries or of the form that their violence should take. Positions such as Gilbert's and Dohrn's were enunciated by various members at various times, with every view subject to intense internal debate. Over the course of the 1970s, the clear trend was towards the deescalation of violence and support for a wide range of political activism—much of it nonviolent and legal. The group not only developed an aboveground support group but also engaged in conventional forms of political agitation on such issues as unemployment and the racial integration of northern schools through busing. As the 1970s ground on, underground members even questioned the wisdom of maintaining a clandestine organization whose military capabilities and political effectiveness were severely limited, and whose raison d'être —in an era of waning militancy—was increasingly tenuous.[188]

·   ·   ·

Though I could not caution all,
I still might warn a few
Don't lend your hand to raise a flag
Atop no ship of fools.
>   The Grateful Dead, "Ship of Fools"
>   (lyrics by Robert Hunter)

For all their Sturm und Drang, the Weathermen were most notorious for something they had planned to do but did not—take the lives of others in a deliberate act of political murder. Their political and historical significance, by extension, lies not only in the extremes to which they went but also—if less often acknowledged—in the boundaries they never in fact crossed. Seen in this double light, the townhouse explosion looms so large in the history of the New Left both as an emblem of "going too far" *and* as the catalyst for pulling back.

In political terms, "New Morning" came too late: too late to salvage SDS or make up for Weatherman's role in its destruction; too late to win the Weathermen a sufficient following to make them a broadly influential force in American politics; and too late, as the social movements of the 1960s declined and new ones gained strength, to do much more than shift the emphasis of an armed struggle that in any version was destined to fail in its goal of toppling the U.S. government. Yet, as an articulation of limits, "New Morning" shaped the group's fundamental identity for most of its existence.

Central to Weatherman's transformation was its meditation on the ethics of violence—whom it was willing to harm and to what ends. By the decade's end, these questions set the ultimate stakes in the tension within the New Left between "acting out" and "working through," transgression and transcendence. Young radicals received eloquent counsel from their elders as they struggled over how to channel their outrage. Daniel Berrigan, while himself a fugitive in 1970, wrote an open letter to the Weathermen, cautioning:

> The mark of inhuman treatment of humans is a mark that also hovers over us. It is the mark of the beast, whether its insignia is the military or the movement. No principle is worth the sacrifice of a single human being. That's a very hard statement. At various stages of the movement some have acted as if almost the opposite were true, in that we got purer. . . . A revolution is interesting only insofar as it avoids like the plague the plague it hopes to heal . . . and will be no better and no more truthful than those who it brought into being.[189]

Berrigan begged the Weathermen to see themselves as givers of hope, like Che Guevara or even Jesus, and to view their lives as about "something more than sabotage."[190] Dave Dellinger similarly implored, "compassion, rejection of violence, refusal to treat other human beings as objects or as means to our own good or bad ends, these are all necessary virtues. To reject them *during* the struggle to create a good society is to reduce dangerously the possibility of achieving them *after* the revolution has apparently triumphed."[191]

Marcuse was no pacifist. Beyond defining a "natural right" of extralegal and even violent resistance, he distinguished between reactionary and emancipatory violence, "white" and "red" terror, based on their differing goals and emancipatory violence's quality of implying its own abolition.[192] While all forms of terror, he insisted, were equally condemnable from a *moral* standpoint, "in terms of their historical function," much separated the violence "of the oppressed and the oppressors."[193] The "terror employed in the defense of North Vietnam," for example, he thought "essentially different from the terror" used against it.[194]

Yet in his 1969 *An Essay on Liberation,* Marcuse discussed the creation of a "new sensibility" instinctively resistant to "cruelty, ugliness and brutality" *as both the means and the end of liberation* in the developed Western world.[195] "Our goals, our values, and our own new morality— our *own* new morality, must already be visible in our actions," Marcuse explained to an approving New Left audience in 1969. "The new humans who we want to help to create—we must already strive to be these human beings right here and now."[196] Marcuse never wavered in his belief that the New Left's most urgent tasks were political education and the creation of this new sensibility, and he never saw the development of a military capability as an appropriate or desirable goal for white American radicals.

Advocates of violence countered by describing pacifism as the luxury of privilege and by arguing the futility of peaceful protest. For some, revolution required the creation of a shrewdly instrumental or even callous subjectivity. Criticizing Marcuse for emphasizing "the new, humane consciousness and sensibility," Harold Jacobs, a sociology professor at Berkeley, insisted: "We indeed have to remake ourselves but not only in the humane ways we might wish. We have to learn to discipline ourselves, to hate, to destroy, and to kill. This society will be liberated, but at the cost of much blood."[197] Such sentiments echoed, consciously or not, the 1869 *Catechism of a Revolutionist* written by the Russian student radical Sergei Nechayev, perhaps the best-known text of a generation of Russian anarchists widely regarded the pioneers of modern-day "terrorism." Within a global rebel culture, it has functioned for decades as a psychological and existential template for aspiring guerrillas seeking to train themselves in the cold "science of destruction." With unflinching conviction, Nechayev declares the revolutionary "a doomed man" who must suppress any trace of "attachments," "belongings," "feelings," "pity," and "love," all of which may stand in the way of his "single passion— for revolution."[198] With rituals and a dogma all their own, the Weathermen of 1969 and early 1970 sought to cultivate this lethal discipline.

The townhouse explosion prompted the Weathermen to reflect on how dehumanizing their experiences had been and to consider whether inhumane conduct was a valid or necessary dimension of revolutionary politics. Evaluating their histories, former members stress the importance, and also the difficulty, of balancing competing imperatives. One demanded militant, even violent responses to injustice; the other required conscientiousness and compassion. For Gilbert, the townhouse explosion indicated that

> it isn't a game. It is real. I mean, yes, we had seen that [with] the Panthers. . . . But then there was someone very close [to us who died]. It is life and death, and it's a big, big decision to try to be a revolutionary. It's not just this romantic thing of being in the mountains, or this morally pristine position. . . . And part of the risk of being a revolutionary is not just personal harm, but making mistakes that will hurt [others]. But to me the risk of not doing anything when so many people are being destroyed . . . that's even worse. But there's no neat sort of easy choice there.[199]

Gilbert described the Weather Underground's restraint: "It's not accidental that [in] over twenty or thirty [actions] no one got hurt. . . . There are some situations of revolutionary struggle where people do get hurt, but the point is that revolutionary morality has a very high standard. You don't want innocent bystanders hurt. You try to minimize casualties. It's not like reactionary violence, ruling class violence, that's napalm on villages."[200] Naomi Jaffe, reflecting on the townhouse, confessed:

> I was a little dazed by that time. I must have been repressing a lot of my feelings because it was really years before I even cried about it. I didn't really experience it when it happened. . . . It seemed like what we had to do was so hard . . . [that] we had to put aside everything else, repress everything else. We were young. It doesn't seem like that to me now. I feel more vulnerable than I've ever been to all the pain of what's going on in the world. But at that time I didn't know how you could be vulnerable to all that pain and still do the work.

For Jaffe, militant action seems to have required psychic and emotional numbing, which robbed her of the ability to mourn even the death of her friends, let alone the potential targets of their violence. With distance from armed combat, Jaffe now rejects the trade-off she once felt necessary. Still an activist, she praises the vulnerable and sentient warrior—however she may fight—whose very conviction that "*every* life is precious" guides her efforts.[201]

When asked if the Weathermen had considered the political and moral consequences of their early vision of armed rebellion, Larry Weiss answered, "Hell no! . . . To actually have killed somebody else—you can't grasp it." The group, he insisted, was prepared only in "the stupid, adrenaline sense—ready in . . . that you don't actually think about what it means in any real sense, any human sense."[202] Other New Leftists gearing up for violence appeared equally unprepared. One message the Weathermen privately conveyed to radical collectives throughout the country following the townhouse explosion was, in Dohrn's words, that "you can't do political kidnappings"—as some Latin American guerrillas had recently done and American radicals imagined doing with figures like Kissinger—"unless you're willing to kill somebody, so if you're not willing to kill somebody, don't even play around with it."[203] Whether heeding such pleadings or their own consciences, American New Leftists never made kidnapping part of their arsenal.

In retrospect, Bill Ayers contrasted the Weathermen to the Vietnamese revolutionaries and to the South Africans who had toppled apartheid, whose achievements had been forged in generations of political struggle: "We were a group of very half-cocked twenty year olds. We had no past, no history, no knowledge . . . I don't think we thought it through, no, and . . . had we continued down a certain road . . . not only all of us would have died, but the things we believed in . . . would have been set back deeply."[204] Reflecting on what it might in fact mean to kill, Ayers stressed the importance of mourning one's own violence:

> I often think and wonder: to be the guy who slips into the general's tent and slit his throat—can you do that and still grieve about what you're doing, . . . about what a horrible, hideous asshole you are? It seems to me to not be able to act, even in an extreme way . . . is a kind of paralysis [and a way of saying] it's OK if *they* fight, but I can't possibly because I'm too good. . . . On the other hand, to get yourself to the point where it means nothing to you, where you just say, "Fuck it," is to sell out the revolution.[205]

Struggling to find a middle ground between passivity and callous violence in the service of a "just" cause, Ayers invokes a language of morality—long explored by philosophers and ethicists—that tries to reconcile rebellion and restraint, the imperative to act against injustice and the limits on action that the commitment to justice imposes.

Albert Camus, though not a direct influence on Weatherman, was one such thinker. In his play *Les Justes* (translated as *The Just Assassins*), Camus used the experiences of a Russian anarchist cell in 1905 to explore precisely the conditions in which a political murder may be regarded as just. The anarchists eventually kill a wicked nobleman, while going to great lengths to avoid harming his children. Once captured, the assassin, Stepan, refuses the Grand Duke's wife's offer of clemency and spiritual absolution, provided that he renounces his act and condemns his comrades. He then goes willingly to the scaffold. The point of the play, in Camus's words, is to show "that action itself has its limits. [That] there is no good and just action, but [that which] recognizes limits and, if it must go beyond them, at least accepts death."[206] (Camus's concept thus has nothing to do with terrorist "martyrdom"; Stepan dies to repay a debt to humanity, not to express the depth of his sacrifice, nor to serve any God in hope of a divine reward.) Here Camus goes to the heart of his understanding of rebellion. In his philosophical writings, he describes rebellion as an act of radical solidarity—an affirmation of a principle or value that transcends the self and implicitly unites all human beings. The true creed of the rebel is: "I rebel, therefore we exist."[207] Killing another human being, however, is a breach of that solidarity, a shattering of the human bond, that negates one's identity as a rebel. To accept one's own death is to accept the loss of the claim of solidarity, even as one rebels in its name. Alluding to the violence of the twentieth century, Camus lamented, "Our world of today seems loathsome to us for the very reason that it is made by men who grant themselves the right to go beyond those limits, and first of all to kill others without themselves dying."[208]

These may appear tortured constructions from Ayers and Camus. Grief for one's own violence, compassion for the victim, and even the acceptance of one's own death do not, in themselves, make violence just; that determination depends also on the motivation, target, kind, and consequences of the violence. Conversely, Camus may appear to make impossible demands of rebels. Accepting that violence is valid means accepting that people will be killed; for combatants to dwell on that loss, let alone cede their lives, would cripple their struggle. Yet Ayers's and Camus's reflections can be read less as a literal code of conduct and more as an injunction that political violence, whatever its aim, not be conceived of as a purely instrumental act or as something that ennobles and redeems its perpetrator.

Robert Roth, also reflecting on the townhouse explosion, spoke directly to the question of limits. Absorbing the deaths of his friends and comrades as "a tragedy," he conceded that it also "would have been a tragedy" if they had succeeded in their plans. Their deaths led Roth and the Weathermen to ask,

If you're going to fight, how are you human as you fight. . . . How do you treat people who have doubts [and] fears, how do you examine who you are fighting against and who you're not? . . . What's your own morality? Do you have morality? Do you care about other people? Do you think really long and hard before you put people in danger? Who do you put in danger? . . . If you try to change the society, how are you changing yourself? How are you becoming more human? . . . If moving towards armed activity means steeling yourself and hardening yourself in this way that cuts out all human feelings and emotion and care, then what kind of movement are you going to build? . . . Are you going to build a real community. . . . Are you going to build a culture of resistance . . . without turning on each other, without burning to a crisp within a second.[209]

Roth's commentary provides a striking counterpoint to Nechayev's "Catechism." As against Nechayev's cold-hearted certainties, which judge everyone and everything based on utility to the revolution, Roth offers a series of questions driven by concern for others, which amount to a "catechism of the rebel" in a Camusian sense: conviction is complicated by doubt, and the ultimate standard for judging action is how well it both serves *and reflects* the values in whose name one rebels.

How deeply the Weathermen should be credited for drawing sane conclusions from a disaster of their own making is debatable. At least some in the group *had* sought to attack "civilians," and it was only their recklessness that spared them from becoming killers. Even after the townhouse explosion, the Weathermen minimized but did not eliminate the risk of injury; luck intervened to ensure that only property was harmed. In addition, in the mid 1970s, the Weather Underground lent support—rhetorical and perhaps more—to the Black Liberation Army (BLA) and the Puerto Rican independence group Fuerzas Armadas de Liberación Nacional (FALN), each of which engaged in lethal actions.[210] However one may judge these groups—whose violence was very different from that of white radicals in its causes and character—the Weather Underground's support for them potentially reveals that the Weathermen wanted to have it both ways: on the one hand, to continue to claim an exceptional status among whites by backing the militancy of people of color; on the other hand, to steer clear of the greatest hazards of armed struggle and to claim as their greatest defense that their own violence did no "real" harm. And some Weathermen, unwilling to abandon violence when the group disbanded in 1976, participated with remnants of the BLA in armed actions—such as a 1981 robbery of a Brinks armored truck to secure funds for "revolutionary" activities—that had deadly results.

Weathermen want it both ways military without fatalities

Finally, the political concept behind the Weather Underground's armed struggle may appear so flawed, so drastically out of touch with political reality, that it would seem hard to speak of the "morality" of the Weathermen's violence. As Ayers repeatedly asserts in his memoir, metaphors may matter, and the Weather Underground may ultimately have functioned as one giant metaphor or symbol.[211] But bad metaphors—ones that reduce the world to a comic-book morality—can be destructive, and some metaphors, to the extent that they serve as calls to arms, can wound and kill ("Off the Pig!" as opposed to "We Shall Overcome"). Furthermore, societies and governments are not simply monsters, even when they do monstrous things, and the struggle against them is not just a matter, as Ayers described Weatherman's "metaphorical" understanding of the world circa 1970, of playing heroic Odysseus against the great Cyclops.[212] Wilkerson, in a sharply critical response to Ayers's memoir, focused precisely on the confusion in the group over what to make of the extreme language of its leaders. Ayers himself, she charges, "was one of the architects of much of the insanity he blames on others" by virtue of his incendiary speeches during Weatherman's formative months. Wilkerson now believes that he "never took seriously [such] language himself," but she says that most of the Weathermen "did not realize that he meant it only as talk."[213]

The Weathermen *did*, nonetheless, assert the value of limits and restricted their violence accordingly. In this, they set a constructive example. The importance of limits is everywhere and tragically evident: in the tendency of revolutionary movements to perpetrate violence serving no emancipatory end or to perpetuate violence long after "liberation" has occurred; in the mass murders of the twentieth century, driven by the reduction of the victim to a thing and the exaltation of killing as a way of purifying the individual or the group; and in the recent rise of global terrorisms, executed with increasing brutality. The question of limits has relevance for Germany's RAF, which in the 1970s embraced forms of violence that the Weathermen had long rejected. It has great relevance, finally, for U.S. conduct in Vietnam, which must figure into any comprehensive assessment of the Weathermen's actions. The U.S. military and its political commanders institutionalized normlessness in the frequent commission of atrocities in Vietnam: the bombing of civilians, the use of chemical weapons such as Agent Orange, and still uncounted Mai Lais. Much of the world judged the war criminal, and part of the private struggle of many Vietnam veterans has been to grieve over their own violence. That struggle became public through the efforts of some veterans to convince the nation that an aspect of their post-traumatic stress was what the war had turned them into. In one of the most disturbing "protests" of the era, some veterans actually tried in 1971 to turn *themselves* in for war crimes to the Pentagon. (A nervous Pentagon official referred them to the Justice Department.)[214] It took America years to recognize the multifaceted suffering of the veterans. And the prosecutors of the war and their supporters, so concerned in the last years with achieving "Peace with Honor," failed to acknowledge, let alone memorialize, the Vietnamese victims.[215]

Tom Hayden, in defense of New Left radicalism, commented in early 1970 that its combined violence did not equal that of one bomb dropped from a B-52. Dellinger responded angrily that Hayden's remark missed the point—that the left should hardly be proud that it had never developed the resources to do more damage.[216] But here Dellinger dismisses Hayden's point too quickly. The violence of the Weathermen and other New Leftists consisted, by and large, of bombing buildings, destroying offices, and breaking a great many windows. The death toll resulting from the thousands of violent acts, stood at three—Robert Fassnacht, killed in the Madison bombing; the Boston policeman killed in 1970; and a prison guard killed in 1972 by the small California-based group "Venceremos."[217] In all three cases, the deaths were unintentional. In contrast, the state violence that New Leftists opposed involved countless deaths, the toppling of governments, and deliberate assaults on domestic dissidents.

Even if, as Dellinger suggests, from his principled pacifist standpoint, the far greater violence of one's adversary does not justify one's own, Dellinger misrepresents the New Left's relationship to violence. Overwhelmingly, New Leftists restricted their violence *by choice* and showed concern for the victims. The deadly Madison bombing led to a public declaration of grief by Karl Armstrong, the main perpetrator of the act. On the witness stand, Armstrong defended the bombing and, to his lawyers' dismay, insisted that under similar circumstance—believing, as he had, that the building was clear of people—he would do it again. But Armstrong also confessed that his "mind was literally devastated" by the death of Fassnacht, *which he felt could never be justified.*[218] With Fassnacht's death, the virtue of "doing no harm" had vanished. The last honor left to Armstrong was a public expression of sorrow and the private torment of regret. In his reaction lies a piece of the New Left's honor.

The triumphant Weathermen, now in charge of the Students for a Democratic Society, at the podium of the June 1969 SDS National Convention. Bernardine Dorhn is in the center; Mark Rudd and Susan Stern are to her left. [David Fenton]

Weathermen marching at the October 1969 Days of Rage. J.J., the main author of the "Weatherman" statement, is at the center, wearing a helmet. Terry Robbins, who died in the townhouse blast in March 1970, is to his left. [David Fenton]

Weatherwomen marching through Chicago's Grant Park during the "Women's Militia" action at the Days of Rage. Kathy Wilkerson is on the left, wearing a white helmet and holding a Viet Cong flag. [David Fenton]

Arrest photos of Bill
Ayers, Bernardine Dohrn,
and Jeff Jones. [Chicago
Historical Society]

Weatherwoman being arrested during the Days of Rage. [David Fenton]

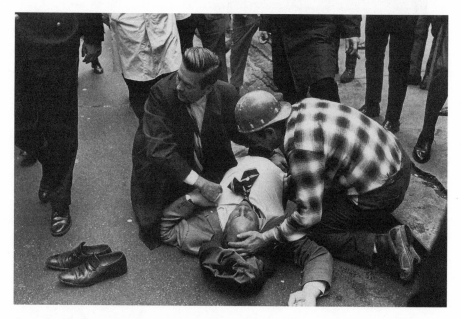

Assistant Corporation Counsel Richard Elrod just after suffering a paralyzing injury on October 10, 1969, the most violent of the Days of Rage. [David Fenton]

Illinois Black Panther Party Chairman Fred Hampton addresses a Chicago rally in 1969. Bobby Rush, who later became a U.S. congressman, is to his right. [Paul Sequiera]

The bed in which Fred Hampton was shot and killed by Chicago police on December 4, 1969. Hampton's assassination prompted the Weathermen to go underground in the weeks following. [Paul Sequiera]

Anonymous Weatherwoman during the Days of Rage. [Paul Sequiera]

Chicago Police Department poster from April 1970 identifying eight Weatherman fugitives, sought for charges stemming from demonstrations the day the Chicago 8 trial began and for the Days of Rage. [Chicago Police Department]

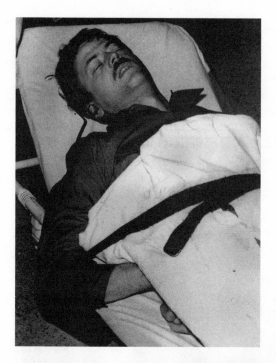

LEFT: Benno Ohnesorg after being shot by police on June 2, 1967, at a demonstration against the visit of the shah of Iran to West Berlin. He soon died from his wounds, and his death instantly radicalized the West German New Left. [dpa]

BOTTOM: Horst Söhnlein, Thorward Proll, Andreas Baader, and Gudrun Ensslin (left to right) in court on October 31, 1968, to hear the verdict in their trial for the Frankfurt department store arsons of April 1968. Baader and Ensslin would go on to form the RAF. [dpa]

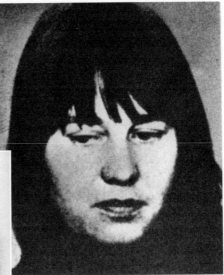

Photographs of Ulrike Meinhof,
Andreas Baader, and Gudrun Ensslin
used by police in its search for RAF
fugitives. [dpa]

RAF Wanted poster. Andreas Baader, Ulrike Meinhof, Holger Meins, Gudrun Ensslin (first row, left to right); Jan-Carl Raspe, Ilse Stachowiak, Axel Achterath, Ronald Augustin (second row); Bernhard Braun, Heinz Brockmann, Albert Fichter, Klaus Jünschke (third row); Irmgard Möller, Brigitte Mohnhaupt, Ralf Reinders, Ingeborg Barz (last row). [dpa]

Damage from the RAF's bombing of the headquarters of the U.S. Army
Supreme European Command in Heidelberg, on May 24, 1972. Three U.S.
military personnel were killed in the attack, the deadliest of the RAF's 1972
"May Offensive." [dpa]

March following the funeral on November 18, 1974, of Holger Meins, nine
days after his death in prison as the result a hunger strike. Gudrun Ensslin's
father, Pastor Helmut Ensslin, is second from the left. The sign reads: "The
guerrilla Holger Meins was murdered by State Security and Justice." [dpa]

LEFT: Jean-Paul Sartre visiting Stammheim prison on December 4, 1974, to discuss the treatment of RAF prisoners with Andreas Baader. The RAF attorney Klaus Croissant is on Sartre's left. [dpa]

BOTTOM: Weapons seized by West German police in a raid on RAF cells in Frankfurt am Main and Hamburg on February 2, 1974. The cell, known as the "Gruppe vom 4.2" (the date of its capture), was plotting to free RAF prisoners. [dpa]

Ulrike Meinhof's funeral on May 15, 1976. Authorities said that Meinhof had hanged herself in her cell in Stammheim prison, but many on the left believed that she had been murdered. Some of the mourners are wearing masks to avoid identification. [dpa]

Hanns Martin Schleyer, photographed on October 13, 1977, thirty-eight days after being kidnapped by the RAF. Six days later, following the deaths in Stammheim prison of Andreas Baader, Gudrun Ensslin, and Jean-Karl Raspe, Schleyer was found murdered near the French-German border. [dpa]

Deadly Abstraction

The Red Army Faction and the Politics of Murder

Over the course of the 1970s, what turned out to be West Germany's only war—that between the Federal Republic and self-styled "urban guerrillas" seeking its overthrow—grew dramatically in intensity. By 1976, the year the Weather Underground dissolved, the RAF's leaders had been in prison for nearly four years. They were charged with bombings, attempted murders, and murders, stemming mostly from the 1972 "May Offensive," in which the RAF targeted officials of the West German state and U.S. military personnel. Several dozen more members of the RAF and other guerrilla groups were in prison, accused or convicted of acts of terrorism. Their capture and the passing of the Vietnam War hardly served to quell the conflict. As opposition to the war and imperialism receded, the focus of the guerrillas' strongest anger shifted to the criminal justice system—in particular to the systematic abuse inmates alleged they suffered in prison. Prisoners from the RAF and other groups engaged in a series of hunger strikes to protest their treatment, culminating in the death by starvation in November 1974 of the RAF's Holger Meins and a new explosion of anger on the left.

In the mid 1970s, the RAF and other groups committed brutal acts of violence, most often aiming to win the release of jailed members. These include the June 2nd Movement's killing in 1974 of a West Berlin judge just after the death of Meins; its kidnapping in February 1975 of the Christian Democratic official Peter Lorenz, ending with the exchange of Lorenz for ten imprisoned guerrillas; and the RAF's brief seizure in April of the same year of the German embassy in Stockholm, Sweden, during which two diplomatic staff and two RAF members died. The conflict further escalated in May 1976 with the death of Ulrike Meinhof by hanging in her cell in Stammheim prison. State officials, playing up speculation that she was in bitter conflict with the rest of the group, insisted that her death was a suicide. Many on the left contended that she had been murdered, giving rise to the great "Mord oder Selbstmord" ("Murder or Suicide?") debate that raged for years in Germany.[1] In retaliation, the RAF killed the federal prosecutor Siegfried Buback and Jürgen Ponto, chairman of the board of Dresdner Bank.

In April 1977, the two-year-long trial of the RAF's Andreas Baader, Gudrun Ensslin, and Jan-Carl Raspe ended, with the defendants being found guilty of four murders, of twenty-seven attempted murders, and of forming a criminal association, for which they were given life sentences. With legal options for the prisoners' release exhausted, RAF commandos committed their most desperate and provocative acts. On September 9, the RAF kidnapped Hanns Martin Schleyer, president of the Employers' Association of the Federal Republic and of the Federation of German Industry. It demanded the release of Baader, Ensslin, Raspe, and eight other RAF guerrillas. To his captors, Schleyer was a doubly appropriate target: not only was he an embodiment of "capitalist oppression"; he had been a member of the Nazi Party and an SS Hauptsturmführer in Czechoslovakia, where he served under the direction of the Sicherheitsdienst chief Reinhard Heydrich—one of the architects of the "Final Solution"—until Heydrich's assassination by Czech partisans in May 1942. Schleyer appeared, in short, to be a living symbol of what the RAF asserted was the continuity between the Nazi Reich and the Federal Republic.

Chancellor Helmut Schmidt refused to meet the kidnappers' demands. Facing an apparent stalemate, RAF raised the stakes five weeks later. On October 13, in alliance with the RAF, a Palestinian commando hijacked a Lufthansa Boeing 737 departing from Majorca for Frankfurt. The hijackers took ninety-one hostages (including the crew), and demanded the release of the German prisoners, as well as of two Palestinians held in Turkey. After traveling to Italy, Dubai, and Bahrain, the plane went to Aden, Yemen, where, on October 16, the hijackers shot and killed the plane's pilot, dumping his body on the tarmac. It then traveled to Mogadishu, Somalia.

Schmidt chose to end the standoff by force six weeks after the kidnapping of Schleyer. On the evening of October 17–18 a special security force, Grenzschutzgruppe 9 (GSG 9), raided the plane in Mogadishu, killing three hijackers and wounding the fourth, with no loss of life to their captives. In the wake of the raid, what would be called the "forty-four days in autumn" rushed toward a chilling crescendo. The evening after the raid, Baader and Raspe died of gunshot wounds in their Stammheim cells, Ensslin died by hanging, and a fourth RAF inmate, Irmgard Möller, was nearly killed by a stab wound to her chest.[2] The government, as with Meinhof's hanging, claimed their deaths were suicides and voiced indignation that guns had apparently been smuggled into the prison. And, again, RAF supporters and others charged the government with murder—a claim some maintain to this day.[3] On October 19, Schleyer's kidnappers announced that they had killed their hostage, whose body was later found in the town of Mulhouse along the French-German border. At Schleyer's funeral, Bundespräsident Walter Scheel declared that the six weeks of the kidnapping "have clearly been the worst in the history of the Federal Republic."[4]

The events of the fall of 1977, however evidently dramatic, only begin to convey the bitterness of the conflict. Statistics of the dead and injured belie that intensity. By late 1978, forty-three people had been killed. Of the dead, twenty-eight were victims of left-wing violence, including ten policemen and four members of the judiciary, and fifteen guerrillas had lost their lives.[5] The number of people killed in a single year in auto accidents, a clichéd observation ran, dwarfed this seven-year tally of casualties.[6] Nor did the intensity of the conflict derive from any military threat the RAF posed. Pleading publicly for mercy for Meinhof shortly before her arrest in June 1972, Heinrich Böll, the winner of the 1972 Nobel Prize in Literature, described the RAF's struggle as that of "six against sixty million."[7] His estimate was not that far off. A year into its existence, fourteen of the group's thirty or so members were incarcerated; by the end of 1972, only one person considered by police to be a member of the RAF's "hard core" *(harte Kern)* was still at large.[8] The RAF would rebuild itself several times during the next two and a half decades, but only a few dozen RAF guerrillas in all its "generations" participated directly in the most destructive of its armed actions.

The meaning and intensity of the West German conflict must be sought neither in its body count nor in the roster of destruction, but in its symbolic impact and how it functioned as a symptom of larger political, social, and historical tensions. To recognize that both the threat the RAF posed and the response to it were largely symbolic, "psychological and not physical," in a common formulation, is to assert an interpretive axiom—one acknowledged by the guerrillas themselves, those charged with defeating them, countless German commentators, and scholars of "political violence" or "terrorism" in general. Determining just how the RAF's violence functioned symbolically is a formidable task, however, because the conflict involved competing symbolic logics, articulated by a host of actors.

The RAF's violence was *by design* symbolic, insofar as it meant primarily to convey a spirit of resistance, which the RAF hoped would spread; its bombs were to "detonate also in the consciousness of the masses."[9] More broadly, the RAF saw itself as a positive expression of the political situation, both globally and in West Germany. It attributed its own existence to what it saw as the weakness of imperialism, the discontent pervading German society, and the growing determination of the left to finally do what was necessary to seriously challenge state power. The state, in sharp contrast, perceived the RAF not only as a threat to internal security, but also as a broader, largely figurative challenge to its legitimacy and to the democratic principles for which it stood. The RAF represented a political poison—intolerable in any dose—that was reminiscent of the militarism and contempt for pluralism characterizing fascism. The state thus did battle with the RAF as "Hitler's children," haunting postwar society.

Independent observers throughout the political spectrum assessed the symbolic stakes very differently. Though the RAF never remotely enjoyed broad public support for its "armed struggle," its members did for a time elicit some sympathy as underdog outlaws persecuted by an overbearing state. In a widely publicized 1971 poll—taken during the first great hunt for RAF fugitives, but before the deadly 1972 "May offensive"— 40 percent of respondents described the RAF's violence as political, not criminal, in motive; 20 percent indicated that they could understand efforts to protect fugitives from capture; and 6 percent confessed that they were themselves willing to conceal a fugitive. Interpreting these data, Sebastian Scheerer explained that "the RAF became less a symbol of popular aspirations than of victimization by the state's security apparatus and by authoritarian measures that were felt to be highly problematic."[10]

In 1977, Walter Boehlich invoked a deeper sense of the symbolism inherent in the conflict:

> Hitler's children aren't the political criminals, but rather Schleyer's children. It isn't what happened under Hitler that motivates them, but what the Schleyers of this world do today . . . : that they represent a democratically organized society just as easily as they did a fascistic society; that they have remained in the new Germany where they were, namely, on top; that they are implicated in a continuity, which wouldn't be the case if fascism had been apprehended as the horrendous crime that it was.[11]

Rejecting the RAF's charge of the thoroughgoing similarities between the Nazi state and the Federal Republic, Boelich nonetheless presented the RAF as a symptom of the confusion, shame, and outrage of a generation coming of age politically in a society that had too comfortably asserted its distance or even redemption from Nazism.

Horst Mahler broke with the RAF in 1974 and affiliated with traditional Marxism-Leninism. Following the events of 1977, he described the RAF as a symbol of the weakness of the socialist left, insofar as its violence made apparent the left's failure to develop power through legitimate and politically constructive means. Mahler ultimately lumped terrorism with unemployment, alcoholism, drug addiction, and criminality as expressions of a society in crisis.[12] Far from being the "cure" for capitalism's pathologies, the RAF was *itself* one of capitalism's pathologies. (Mahler has since become a nationalist reactionary of the far right.) To the philosopher Günter Rohrmoser, speaking from the political center, terrorism was a disturbing manifestation of a different sort of estrangement: that of the German people from the state. That the RAF existed in a democratic society made it "a symptom of a profound loss of reality and a new, radical form of alienation."[13] At root, the Federal Republic had failed to establish or maintain the full, positive identification of the population with its authority and its founding principles. Terrorism was therefore "a signal, a sign . . . of the extent to which [West Germany's] collective ethos has eroded," requiring, above all, the renewal of a near-spiritual sense of West German unity.[14]

Hitler's children, Schleyer's children, Lenin's children, Nixon's children, Guevara's children: such were the labels that explicitly or implicitly attached to the RAF during its early history. Protecting or itself endangering democracy, repudiating or sustaining the fascism of the past: such were the competing views of the conduct of the state.

·   ·   ·

The question of what would have happened if . . .
is ambiguous, pacifistic, moralistic.

> RAF, "Das Konzept Stadtguerilla"
> ("The Concept of the Urban Guerrilla")

To capture their sense of the form that protest violence should take, West German militants of the late 1960s voiced the slogan: "Violence against things, yes; violence against people, no." Honoring the slogan meant re-

stricting violence to small-scale destruction of property at street demonstrations and occasional attacks on buildings, such as Berlin's Amerika
Haus. When militants did appear to target people, their actions were often
merely theatrical. In April 1967, members of Berlin's Kommune 1 had
planned to "attack" U.S. Vice President Hubert Humphrey while he was
visiting West Germany. Uncovering the plot, police arrested several
members of the radical collective with much fanfare. What the authorities had originally alleged were bombs, however, prompting the conservative media to denounce the plotters as "terrorists," turned out to be
harmless sacks of pudding.[15] Commenting on the episode in *konkret,*
Meinhof castigated the outraged reaction to the phantom assault: "Drop-
ping napalm on women, children, and the elderly is not criminal, but
protesting against it is. . . . It is considered impolite to aim pudding and
oatmeal at politicians, but not to roll out the red carpet for politicians
who have villages wiped out and cities destroyed. . . . Napalm yes, pudding no."[16]

Kommune 1 soon added a sardonic twist to its provocative brand of
political humor. On May 22, 1967, arson in a department store in Brussels killed 253 people. Two days later, two commune members, Rainer
Langhans and Fritz Teufel—whose name, perfect for his role as trouble-
maker, means "devil"—issued a leaflet asking, "When will Berlin's department stores burn?" It explained:

> The Yanks have been dying for Berlin in Vietnam. We were sorry to see
> the poor souls shed their coca-cola blood in the jungles of Vietnam. So
> we started by marching, throwing the occasional egg at America House,
> and we would have liked to see HHH [Humphrey] die smothered in pud-
> ding. . . . A burning department store with burning people conveys for the
> first time in a major European city that crackling Vietnam-feeling . . . that
> we in Berlin up to now have missed. . . . Brussels has given us the only
> answer: Burn, Warehouse, Burn![17]

Langhans and Teufel were arrested for their incendiary rhetoric. Ten
months later, a Berlin judge found that the leaflet, however offensive,
was a "literary statement designed to shock," not a literal threat, and
cleared the two of the charges.[18]

The department store arsons committed in Frankfurt by Andreas
Baader and Gudrun Ensslin eight days after the acquittal of the communards may appear a chilling effort to answer the leaflet's grim query—
to bridge the gap between imagination and action and make the militant
metaphors of the New Left real. (Baader and Ensslin had, in fact, visited
Kommune 1 just prior to the action to see if anyone wanted to join them;

only Thorward Proll, a friend of the two, agreed.) The arson was partly that bridge. Meinhof praised the assailants for having broken both the law and internal restraints. Ensslin, in a perfect echo of American militants, defended the arson by proclaiming, "We have found words are useless without actions."[19] But the arson, examined in its specifics and the justifications provided for it, was much more an instance of "symbolic violence" rooted in the injunction against harming people than an attempt to act out the kind of genuine terror the communards had rudely envisioned.

At their trial, Baader, Ensslin, Proll, and Söhnlein confessed to having committed the arson as a protest against the Vietnam War and contrasted their destruction of a few commodities in a small fire set after hours with the use of napalm against civilians. They also indicted, in ways both playful and defiant, what they charged was the wholesale corruption of the West German justice system and the society it defended. In court, they declared that they "would not defend themselves against a justice" that "in 1933 unapologetically threw itself into fascism and in 1945 equally unapologetically rose from fascism"; that "did not dismantle authoritarian structures, but instead built them anew"; that "protects property and wealth more than it does human beings"; and that "speaks in the name of the people, but acts in the name of the ruling class."[20]

Berward Vesper, Ensslin's one-time fiancé and a budding counterculture author, issued his own diatribe following the announcement of sentences of three years' imprisonment for the arsonists. To him, the prosecution defended commodities, while implicitly condoning violence in Vietnam against humans. "Commodities," he asserted, "take on human traits, while the dead, once and for all destroyed and never interchangeable, are denigrated by being considered mere statistics."[21] Vesper also charged that indignation at the arson was evasive or disingenuous if it ignored the violence that was "permanently and everywhere manifest" in West Germany. For him, the real threat was "the violence in the family, the violence in the schools, the violence in the factories, the violence in the home, the violence in the prisons, the violence of suicide, the violence of the violent criminals, the violence of the police, the pervasive violence that destroys countless lives and diminishes all lives."[22] The motive for the arson, in light of statements by the defendants and their supporters, appears to have been this: by eliciting outrage at a small act of destruction, it was meant to turn critical attention to truly damaging forms of violence and, ideally, expose the hypocrisy of its denouncers. It sought, in short, to transform consciousness, while permitting leftists, in their minds, to take the moral high ground.

To Meinhof, the protests following the May 11, 1968, attack on Dutschke were of a piece with the arson. Supporting the transition from "protest to resistance," evident in the injury of scores of police in street battles, she wrote: "Those who from their positions of political power condemn the throwing of stones and acts of arson . . . but not the bombing of Vietnam, terror in Iran, or torture in South Africa . . . [are] hypocritical."[23] Meinhof held fast to the basic formula of her response to the "pudding attack," even if pudding had since given way to stones, fists, and fire.

Determining what drove some radicals to cross the line from "violence against things" to forms of "armed struggle"—whether arsons, bombings, or armed robberies—that intended or held a great risk of injury is an imposing challenge. Frustration with peaceful protest, the escalating conflict with police, the attraction to Third World struggles, and perceptions of the Federal Republic as quasi-fascist—all these played roles in that transformation. These "causes" did not, however, render armed actions simply a next step in a linear progression toward "terrorism." Rather, armed struggle represented a radical leap—a fundamental shift in one's politics and sense of self—taken as the pressure of events, beliefs, and feelings built to a breaking point. An article in the West Berlin anarchist paper *833*, printed just a week before the freeing of Baader, conveys how radicals experienced that pressure.

In mid April of 1970, *833* ran a lengthy piece on the American movement, highlighting the early history of Weatherman. Mirroring the rhetoric and imagery of America's underground press, the article was headlined in English "Blow Up Amerika, Blow Up Berlin!" and surrounded by pictures of Weathermen fighting police and drawings of dynamite.[24] From the rash of bombings in America, the authors concluded that the Weathermen and other radicals there had succeeded in threatening "the capitalist establishment where it is most vulnerable—at its center." Unaware of Weatherman's efforts to rethink its approach following the townhouse explosion, the authors insisted: "The political debate over the Weathermen will continue. But their commitment and devotion force every American revolutionary to examine his own relationship between who he is, what he thinks, and what he does." In chiding and even aggressive tones, the article put the challenge to German radicals:

> Remember the good old days of the movement, when we talked up
> Mao, Che, the Viet Cong, and Revolution, without ourselves being
> Mao, Che, the Viet Cong, or revolutionaries? . . . Do you remember
> the nice, comfortable, bourgeois, hippieish, counterrevolutionary, anti-
> communist, boring, empty, deadly, disgusting days? Those days are,
> thank God, over. For us "movement people" there are only two possi-
> bilities. Either we press on to become fighters in the global revolution
> or we slink back into our bourgeois holes and become anticommunist
> swine.

This passage is striking in the assumptions it makes and the urgency it
conveys. The movement and the world had moved rapidly through whole
phases, such that what had made sense even a few months before was
no longer adequate. Some fateful hour had been reached at which revolutionaries faced the stark duty to fight. The alternative, presented with
self-disgust approaching self-hatred, was to lapse into the misery of counterrevolutionary complacency. Salvation from this wretched condition
ultimately meant one thing: to "pick up the gun." The choice was no real
choice at all, but an act of political and existential necessity.

The decision to move from resistance to "armed struggle" brought
new, more destructive forms of violence, and with them the sharper challenge of arguing their legitimacy. The RAF faced this challenge in its
founding act, the freeing of Baader on May 14, 1970, from a Berlin research institute, during which two security guards were shot and an elderly staff member, George Linke, was nearly killed. The shooting of Linke,
though clearly not analogous to the violence in Vietnam, was nonetheless an injury to a "civilian," making the RAF vulnerable to the charge
that it had engaged in the same kind of callous victimization of "ordinary people" of which the left accused capitalism.

For Baader and his comrades, the sense of triumph at pulling off the
audacious act overshadowed the problems raised by the shooting. In its
founding communiqué, printed in the May 22 issue of *833,* the RAF
lauded Baader's "liberation" as the first crucial step in the building of a
bona fide "Red Army" and made no direct mention of the injury to
Linke.[25] The statement, printed under an image of a black panther taken
from the Black Panther Party logo, ran:

> Did the pigs really believe that we would let comrade Baader sit in jail for
> two to three years? Did the pigs really believe that we would forever fight
> with paintballs against bullets . . . ? Did any pig really believe we would
> talk about the development of class struggle . . . without arming ourselves
> at the same time? Did the pigs who shot first believe that we would allow

ourselves to be gunned down like slaughter-cattle? Gandhi and Martin Luther King are dead. The bullets that killed them, the bullets that hit Rudi [Dutschke] . . . have ended the dream of nonviolence. Whoever does not defend himself will die. Whoever does not die will be buried alive: in prisons, in reformatories, in the hovels of Kreuzberg, Wedding, Neuköln, in the stony wastelands of the new housing developments, in the overcrowded kindergartens and schools, in the perfectly furnished, newly built kitchens, in the mortgaged bedroom palaces. . . . START THE ARMED STRUGGLE! BUILD UP THE RED ARMY!

In a tape-recorded message printed in *Der Spiegel* on June 5, Meinhof brazenly defended the RAF's conduct during the escape: "Those in uniforms are pigs, not human beings . . . there is no use in talking to them, and naturally they can be shot."[26] In a second communiqué, which appeared two weeks later in *833,* the group confronted its critics:

It makes no sense to tell the wrong people what is right. We have been doing that for too long. We do not have to explain the Baader Liberation Action to the intellectual windbags, nervous Nellies, and second-guessers but only to the potentially revolutionary portions of the population—those who understand the action immediately because they understand themselves to be prisoners as well. . . . [It is to them]—not the petit-bourgeois intellectuals—[that] you owe the explanation that enough is enough, that the time for action has come. . . . Behind the supervisors stand the shop foremen, the personnel office, the security force, public relief, the police. Behind the janitor stand the building manager, the owner, the marshal, the eviction notice, the police. . . . Without a buildup of the RAF, the bastards and pigs can do what they want and go on doing it: incarcerate, fire, fine, take kids away from parents, intimidate, shoot, rule. To bring the conflict to a head means stopping them from doing what they want and making them do what we want.[27]

It is hard to know quite how to assess these statements. Whatever their claims, the authors were certainly conscious that they were speaking to multiple audiences and that what they said about their acts was integral to the acts themselves and to how the group was perceived. But if the statements were composed with some care, they also seem born of the heat of the violent moment, suffused with an associative mixture of defiance, exhilaration, and foreboding.

The communiqués reverse the logic of earlier militancy. If, for example, the moral substance of the department store arson lay in the gaping distance between it and the violence the arsonists protested, the value of Baader's freeing lay precisely in the use of equivalent force against the enemy—bullets, and not "paintballs," against bullets. The RAF piles up the justifications, as if it is at once explaining itself to the world and convincing itself of the virtue of its act. The "liberation action," it insists, conveys the depth of its commitment to revolution and its loyalty to its "comrades." Aimed at a "subhuman" adversary who seeks the annihilation of all who resist, it is also an act of self-preservation and a way of claiming dignity. In an echo of Weathermen's slogan "Kill or be killed" following the Days of Rage, the RAF declared that the choice now was to fight or die. The indictment of German society, finally, is total, mandating its destruction. Wherever the RAF looks—whether at prisons, schools, bureaucracies, or workplaces—it sees only coercion, violence, and living death.

The statements' aggressive tone counts for more than braggadocio. According to Mark Juergensmeyer in his study of religious terrorism, virtually all terrorist violence, especially that which is horribly destructive, is at root "symbolic."[28] That is, it offers its assailants primarily forms of symbolic empowerment in the place of more tangible political gains; this grant of the "illusion of power" defines terrorism, even when it does achieve some limited strategic purpose or temporarily changes the political and psychological landscape by exposing the vulnerability of the power it attacks. Juergensmeyer's model suggests that there was a symbolic or compensatory aspect to the RAF's actions, no matter the group's stated goals and self-understanding. The RAF's language oozes with self-aggrandizement, from the gloating over the action to the taunting of the police and the claim that the system must now bend to *its* will. The intent behind the RAF's call to build a literal guerrilla army may well have been to transcend symbolism and turn the illusion of power into "real" power by waging a popular campaign of violence. Yet the great danger the RAF faced was that this "symbolic empowerment," far easier to achieve than a genuinely popular revolt, would become an end in itself. In the absence of such a revolt, violence of an increasingly destructive sort would be required to sustain the *illusion* of power.

The RAF did not issue its first extensive manifesto, "Das Konzept Stadtguerilla" ("The Concept of the Urban Guerrilla"), until nearly a year after its formation. Meinhof had privately confessed regret for having said, following the freeing of Baader, that the police were mere "pigs, not human beings," and the RAF sought with the new statement both to clarify its position and to improve its image.[29] Written by Meinhof, working day and night in a Hamburg apartment, the lengthy tract finally addressed the shooting of Linke:

As for the question, asked often enough, whether we would have liberated Baader if we knew that Linke would be wounded—the answer to this question can only be no. The question of what would have happened if . . . [ellipses in original] is ambiguous, pacifistic, moralistic, and whoever asks it is just sitting on the fence. . . . It is an attempt to trivialize the question of revolutionary violence and give [it] and bourgeois morality a common denominator, which isn't possible. . . . There was no reason to believe that a civilian would intervene. The idea that one can perform an unarmed prison liberation is suicidal. . . . We shoot only when someone shoots at us; the pig who lets us go, we let him go as well.[30]

Meinhof's statement is grossly ambivalent. On the one hand, it articulates limits to violence, such as a prohibition against needlessly endangering civilians. Had the RAF known it would violate this limit, it would not have tried to free Baader. On the other hand, Meinhof obscures the fact that in the action, the RAF had violated its own creed: even if the security guard had shot first, the unarmed Linke—hardly a "pig"—had *not* shot at them. In addition, the statement denounces any inquiry by "outsiders" into the legitimacy of the act as an expression of a "bourgeois" worldview that has no right to judge the group's conduct. The RAF thus declared itself to be the sole arbiter of the morality of its actions, accountable only to itself. Finally, Meinhof suggests that concern with the ethics of violence is a sign of indecisiveness about the validity of armed struggle. In the RAF's unforgiving judgment, indecisiveness on this question virtually amounted to complicity with oppression. By equating scrutiny of the morality of violence with betrayal of the struggle, the RAF further invalidated the reservations of its critics and pushed aside ethical questions.

·   ·   ·

For capitalists, profit is everything and the people who
produce it for them are no better than dirt.
                                                            RAF communiqué,
                    "Erklärung vom 20. Mai 1972, Kommando 2. Juni"

In its first two years of existence, the RAF, along with other "urban guerrilla" groups in West Germany, appears to have broadly adhered to the principles Meinhof had laid out. In a series of bank robberies in the fall of 1970, the RAF stole more than 220,000 marks without firing a shot. From late 1969 on, radicals committed dozens of bombings and arsons of banks, police stations, administrative buildings, and U.S. military facilities. Some were carried out by established groups like the "Tupamaros–West Berlin" (which soon became the June 2 Movement), but others were committed by anonymous ad hoc collectives. In virtually all these attacks, the damage was limited to property.[31]

The early serious injuries and deaths associated with the armed struggle occurred in shoot-outs between police and suspected terrorists, with the guerrillas claiming that they had fired only in self-defense. A gunfight in Berlin in February 1971 prompted the first nationwide hunt for RAF fugitives. A second security operation six months later, in which 3,000 heavily armed police patrolled cities in northern Germany, produced the armed struggle's first martyr. On July 15, in Hamburg, police shot and killed the RAF's Petra Schelm, a twenty-year-old hairdresser from Berlin. Her death, captured in a newspaper photo of blood pouring down her face, outraged the left and led some among the broader public to question the aggressive tactics used in pursuing suspected terrorists. In October, the RAF killed its first policeman, thirty-three-year-old Norbert Schmid, in a shoot-out in Hamburg from which the gunman, Gerhard Müller, and Meinhof narrowly escaped. Margrit Schiller was captured, quickly becoming a lightening rod for the public's growing hostility to the RAF.[32] In the next six months, police shot and killed two more radicals, twenty-four-year-old George von Rauch in Berlin and Thomas Weisbecker, aged twenty-three, in Augsburg. Both had been leading figures in the rebel youth scenes in their cities, and their deaths spurred small protests throughout West Germany. In Hamburg, on the day of Weisbecker's shooting, the RAF and police exchanged gunfire, during which the RAF's Manfred Grashof and Police Commissioner Hans Eckhardt were severely wounded. Both soon died from their injuries.

The plight of the RAF fugitives gained even greater notoriety when in January of 1972 the author Heinrich Böll wrote an article in *Der Spiegel* addressing Ulrike Meinhof's fate. Böll asserted that "Meinhof has declared war on this society, she knows what she is doing and what she has done," but asked " who can say what she should do now?"[33] Though pleading that she suspend her futile struggle, he nonetheless expressed some understanding of her motives and painted the RAF as victim of the demagoguery of the Springer Press. He then suggested that German society extend to Meinhof the offer of "forgiveness or at least safe return" *("Gnades oder wenigtens freies Geleit")*.[34] Böll was immediately condemned by some as a "sympathizer" of the RAF and himself put on public trial to defend his controversial views

The radicals' resolve to shoot only when fired upon progressively crumbled, despite leftists' claims to the contrary. "Bommi" Baumann, a member of the June 2 Movement who was present when police killed von Rauch, originally alleged that the police had fired without provocation (though von Rauch was armed, Baumann insisted that his gun had not been drawn). The left took this version as the truth and depicted von Rauch as a defenseless victim. Years later, however, Baumann confessed:

> I no longer know who first pulled the trigger . . . one thing that I find really shitty is that the left simply begins with the assumption that George didn't pull the trigger at all. The left has made a real Christian martyr [of him]. . . . The guy wasn't like that, he was the kind of guy who said, "Of course we'll shoot." We had the guns so that we wouldn't be arrested anymore . . . the climate among the bulls [police] had gotten to such a place that they always "knew" that we would be armed and that there would be shooting.[35]

In Baumann's account, a relationship of hunter and hunted and a shared ethic of "shoot or be shot" prevailed between the police and the guerrillas. Confirming this view, an officer of a Special Commission pursuing the RAF later admitted that the police's attitude also was, "If you shoot first, you survive."[36] On two occasions, police in fact killed people erroneously suspected of being RAF fugitives. The first victim was Richard Eppel, a seventeen-year-old driving without a license who had sped nervously past a checkpoint. The second was a Scottish businessman, Ian Macleod, gunned down in June 1972 as he stood naked behind a bedroom door in a Stuttgart apartment that the police mistakenly believed harbored RAF members. In both cases, as in the many shoot-outs between fugitives and police, judges and investigators ruled that the police had acted in self-defense and should not be subject to legal penalty.[37]

For the guerrillas, the imperative of survival and the simple desire to avenge fallen comrades appeared to take precedence over ideological and moral considerations. Much of the early violence of RAF and other guerrillas was therefore oddly depoliticized, driven not by any grand design but by the pressures of illegality and the intense loyalties the underground bred. In the shoot-outs, the guerrillas interacted with the police as their lethal pursuers, reinforcing their image of the state as essentially predatory and its agents as their chief enemies. In this way, street confrontations hardened the ideological conflict between the guerrilla movement and the state.

The RAF gave its violence a decidedly political and deadly cast in its 1972 "May Offensive." In a span of two weeks, the group bombed two

U.S. military bases, police stations in two cities, and offices of the Springer Press. The attacks, carried out by "commandos" bearing the names of slain guerrillas, were audacious in their design and grimly spectacular in their destruction. To begin the campaign, on May 11, the "Kommando Petra Schelm," consisting of Baader, Ensslin, and Holger Meins, bombed the Headquarters of the U.S. Fifth Army in Frankfurt, killing an officer and injuring thirteen American servicemen. The following day, the RAF set off a bomb outside the Augsburg police station, injuring one person; later that day, a blast in front of the Bavarian Federal Police Headquarters in Munich demolished twenty-five cars. Four days after that, the RAF bombed the car of Wolfgang Buddenberg, the Karlsruhe judge who had signed most of the arrest warrants for RAF members. His wife, and not he, was in the car, and suffered serious injuries. Then, on May 19, the RAF bombed the Hamburg offices of the Springer Press, injuring seventeen workers. To conclude the offensive, on May 24, two RAF members drove a car carrying more than 400 pounds of TNT onto the site of the Headquarters of the U.S. Army Supreme European Command in Heidelberg (cars with U.S. license plates were let through, and the RAF had obtained such a car); the car later exploded near an officers' clubhouse, killing a captain and two GIs and wounding five others.

In its communiqués, the RAF offered a variety of justifications for its bombings and, if only implicitly, for the deaths and injuries they caused. The attacks on the military bases were responses to the United States's recent mining of North Vietnamese harbors and stepped-up bombings of North Vietnam—acts that hurt Vietnamese civilians—escalated with harrowing intensity a war the United States insisted was winding down and drew international condemnation. The RAF denounced the U.S. bombings as "genocide, the murder of the people, annihilation, Auschwitz."[38] Its message to the United States was clear: "West Germany and West Berlin will no longer be safe bases" for the U.S. military.[39] The RAF demanded the immediate withdrawal of U.S. troops from Vietnam and threatened continued "attacks against the mass murderers in Vietnam until the Vietcong are victorious."[40]

The RAF similarly presented its assaults on the police and the judiciary as forms of counterviolence. With the bombing in Munich, it meant to avenge the death of Weisbecker and to convey the broader lesson that the police "can't kill any of us without reckoning that we will hit back."[41] The RAF targeted Judge Buddenburg because it held him responsible, by virtue of his legal rulings, for the recent death in prison of the RAF's Manfred Grashof. The bombing of the offices of the Springer Press raised the greatest difficulty. Injuring workers clearly violated the RAF's insistence that "urban guerrilla actions are directed against the institutions of the class state, imperialism and capitalism [and never] against the working people."[42] (Immediately after the bombings, some radicals in fact speculated that it must have been the work of police agents, intent on discrediting the left.)[43] So the RAF blamed the injuries on Springer, arguing that its urgent pleas to have the building cleared—phoned in shortly before the bombs detonated—had been willfully ignored. The initial communiqué explained that "Springer would rather take the risk of his workers and clerical staff being injured by bombs than risk losing a couple of hours working time. . . . For capitalists profit is everything and the people who produce it for them are no better than dirt."[44] For the RAF, the injury to the workers only strengthened the validity of the Springer Press as a target.

The May actions illustrate that the RAF's violence was not—as common denunciations of the group as fanatic, nihilistic, or sociopathic suggested—entirely without scruple or rationale. It had chosen its targets with precision and defended the bombings in strongly political terms. American military bases in Germany were important staging points for the shipment of troops and matériel to Vietnam and provided tactical support for operations there. To attack them was to strike at the American war machine. More broadly, the RAF intimated a logic of reciprocal force, in which U.S. soldiers on foreign soil—trained for violence and members of an "imperialist" army—were appropriate objects of lethal attacks, especially as the Vietnam War persisted. By potentially chipping away at the U.S. military's confidence, the bombings transcended symbolism and had practical value both as a blow to the American empire and an act of solidarity with the Vietnamese. The RAF's tacit model was that of a just war fought by unconventional methods and within borders the RAF defined. This "war," as the RAF presented it, drew its legitimacy from the moral ends it served and its restriction of violence to military targets. The RAF's evocation of Auschwitz suggested that Germans had both a special imperative and right to protest the Vietnam War by drastic means.[45] With the bombings directed at the police and the judiciary, the RAF extended the notion of reciprocity to its conflict with the state. Violence against state agents no longer needed to be strictly self-defensive. Retaliation was a sufficient motive.

No matter their stated rationale, the May actions posed serious problems for the group. The RAF's model of anti-imperialist struggle always presupposed that the West German masses, however defined, would applaud armed actions. Extending this assumption, the RAF confidently announced that "the people in West Germany do not support the security forces in their search for the bombers . . . because they know that the bomb attacks against the mass murderers in Vietnam are just, and because they know from experience that words and demonstrations against the crimes of imperialism are no use."[46] But here the RAF erroneously interpreted the limited and largely fleeting public sympathy for RAF fugitives in prior police hunts as an endorsement of its violence. Overwhelmingly, the May bombings produced outrage and fear among the public, whose great majority now saw the RAF's violence as decidedly criminal and not "revolutionary."

The RAF, in addition, remained evasive on the issue of the human toll of its violence. Its communiqués, which scarcely even acknowledged the victims, failed to specify the political value of injuries and deaths or define precisely whom it considered a legitimate target. Did the group consider *any* American serviceman or official in West Germany fair game by virtue of the war in Vietnam or "U.S. imperialism" in general? Did *anyone* associated with West Germany's security forces or judicial system bear criminal guilt, punishable by injury or death, for the state's pursuit of the RAF? And who or what empowered the RAF to make such judgments, especially in the absence of any popular mandate?

To the extent that the ethics of the RAF's violence was connected to its political consequences, the RAF courted additional hazards. If, as it hoped, its violence were to serve as an example to others and contribute to America's defeat in Vietnam, then the casualties would have served some political goal (however one may judge either the ends or means). If, however, this scenario *did not* come to pass, the deaths of people like the American military personnel—who bore no direct responsibility for U.S. aggression in Vietnam—would be rendered politically meaningless. The ethical calculus, in short, could not be separated from the political future; and this future, though subject to speculation, could not be known in the present, when the RAF made the decision to kill. The RAF also failed in other ways to recognize that violence was a precarious enterprise, not easily controlled by force of the good intentions it insisted it had. Its silence about the "accidental" injury to Judge Buddenberg's wife, along with its specious blaming of the Springer Press for the injury to workers *its* bombs had caused, signaled the group's inability to assume true responsibility for its actions.

The May Offensive was a turning point for the RAF in additional senses. The West German left sharpened its objections to a program of violence that now included planned political murder and, if unintentionally, injuries to civilians. In separate conferences in late May and early June, leftists debated the current state and future course of liberation struggles in Germany and abroad. The near-unanimous view of the RAF was one of condemnation.

The first and more radical of the conferences was held by the Frankfurt chapter of Rote Hilfe, an organization that formed in Berlin in 1970 to offer legal aid to leftists, among them RAF members. (Rote Hilfe took its name from the KPD's legal aid organization in the 1920s and 1930s.) Described as a "Teach-in Against State Repression," the conference was banned at the last minute from the University of Frankfurt by university and city officials who objected to materials issued in preparation for the meeting. When the conference took place at a new Frankfurt location, student groups, Marxist-Leninist organizations, and independent radicals heatedly discussed the RAF's recent bombings and the issue of violence more broadly.

Rote Hilfe gave the most charitable assessment of the RAF. In a preconference flyer, the group defended the bombings directed at the U.S. military, asserting, "If imperialism is a worldwide system, and that it is, then the struggle against it must be waged worldwide. It will and must be a violent and armed struggle, or it will not be waged at all."[47] Rote Hilfe also described the IG-Farben Headquarters in Frankfurt, once a center for the financial leaders of the Nazi Reich and now used by the U.S. military in its strategic planning, as a doubly appropriate target of RAF's May 11 bombing. In a final show of solidarity, Rote Hilfe played at the conference a tape-recorded message from the underground by Meinhof encouraging leftists to continue the struggle. Yet Rote Hilfe balanced its praise for the RAF with sharp, if comradely, criticisms. It insisted that the attacks in Augsburg and Karlsruhe had been driven by emotion, not political sense, and that the May actions as a whole hindered the growth of the West German left.

In defending the RAF, Rote Hilfe was in the distinct minority. Most participants denounced the RAF for alienating "the masses" and prompting greater repression of the legal left. Typical of the criticisms by the "K-groups" was that of the Kommunistischer Studentenverein, which said that the RAF's violence was "neither practiced by the masses . . . nor is it understood by the masses as an expression of their interests. The masses, on the contrary, perceive the actions as a threat, and therefore identify with the reactions of the state apparatus. . . . This violence is not revolutionary. It sabotages the struggle against state repression in that it helps to conceal the class character of this repression and encourages the isolation of communists."[48] In making the response of the masses the ultimate measure of the RAF's credibility, communists judged the RAF a grievous failure.

The "Angela Davis Conference" held on June 3–4 at the University of Frankfurt featured less dogmatic but no less forceful indictments of the RAF. As in the United States, New Leftists in West Germany saw radical African Americans as a vanguard of the global movement. Angela Davis, on trial at the time for the Marin County courtroom takeover, was a hero among German leftists as well. The purpose of the conference was to express support for Davis and the black movement, but also to explore the meaning of solidarity.

Oskar Negt, one of several prominent left-wing intellectuals at the conference, used part of his address to denounce the RAF. Describing its actions as "unpolitical," he warned: "Whoever turn politics into a test of individual courage, without being able to specify its goals and program for change, becomes more and more a victim of his own illusions. . . . Whoever believes that he can, with exemplary action, spectacular prison breaks, bank robberies, and bombings, create a revolutionary situation . . . erects an impenetrable wall between himself and social experience."[49] According to Negt, the RAF had committed the May bombings on the basis of horribly mistaken premises: that the current situation in West Germany was one of "open fascism," that violence against individual policemen or Springer executives could weaken capitalism, and that the group's violence expressed the popular will. At root, the RAF had lost touch with the "lived experience of human beings" and therefore had no "objective corrective for the evaluation of the political effectiveness of its actions."[50] Negt concluded by voicing the essence of socialist criticism of the RAF: that "without the active support of the working class, there can be no fundamental change in our society."[51] In the wake of the May actions, the RAF suffered a double marginalization: first, from the mainstream of German society and, second, from the very movement to which it looked for support.

The "May Offensive" ultimately spelled the doom of the RAF's founding generation. The bombings prompted a massive hunt for RAF fugitives, in which more than 130,000 police patrolled West Germany's highways, checked its borders, and combed key quarters of its cities. Up to this point, the public had experienced the terrorist conflict almost exclusively through the media. As citizens now encountered roadblocks and checkpoints, endured searches, and responded to pleas for information to aid state investigators, they became direct participants in the drama.

The police generally enjoyed the public's cooperation. Baumann, underground at the time, reports that after the injury to the Springer workers, even "liberal sympathizers" withheld support from fugitives, and some threatened to turn them in.[52] In late May, a Frankfurt resident became suspicious of three male neighbors as they mixed some unknown materials outside their house. He alerted police to what turned out to be the hiding place of Baader, Meins, and Jan-Carl Raspe, who had been preparing explosives. The three were arrested on June 1, following a firefight during which Baader was shot in the leg. On June 7, a clerk in a Hamburg boutique grew suspicious of a nervous-looking young customer who had what appeared to be a heavy object—in fact, a gun—in her bag. The clerk called the police, who arrested fugitive Gudrun Ensslin. Two days later, police captured the RAF's Brigitte Monhaupt and Bernhard Braun in Berlin.

Shortly after midnight on June 14, a young woman knocked on the door of a left-wing teacher and trade union member and asked if two people could stay with him. Though he agreed, he suspected that the visitors were RAF fugitives. He called the police, who lay in wait at his house and on the 15th captured two suspects, Gerhard Müller and a woman whom they believed was Ulrike Meinhof. Unable to verify initially the suspect's identity, investigators took an X-ray of her skull and compared it to an X-ray of Meinhof's skull—tucked in a *Stern* magazine article about the RAF found in the apartment—showing evidence of a brain surgery she had undergone years earlier. The X-rays matched. When the police captured Irmgard Möller and Klaus Jünschke three weeks later, virtually everyone in RAF's "hard core" was now in custody. The "people" had spoken by rejecting their self-appointed leaders, and the career of the RAF's first generation as a clandestine armed struggle group was over.

·   ·   ·

Clear awareness that your chances of surviving are none.
Ulrike Meinhof, "Brief einer Gefangenen aus dem
Toten Trakt" ("Letter of a Prisoner from the Dead Tract")

The incarceration of the RAF's founding members brought about the formation of new underground cells and a decisive shift in the means and ends of the guerrilla movement. In one commentator's description, the "'anti-imperialist struggle' transformed into a battle against the Federal Prosecutors' Office and Federal Police."[53] The scene shifted accordingly from the networks of the underground to the prisons and the courtroom. Virtually all the major acts of violence of the mid and late 1970s had one main goal, the freeing of imprisoned guerrillas. These actions were frequently brutal, signaling another escalation in the intensity of left-wing violence.

The immediate cause of this escalation was RAF and other political inmates' insistence that they were being subjected to systematic mistreatment in prison. Though often ignored or minimized in histories of the RAF, the controversy over prison conditions was among the most important aspects of the conflict. The charge of abuse, which the state resolutely denied, dominated the RAF's politics for much of the 1970s and 1980s. The issue of the prisoners' treatment was also among the most vexing dimensions of the conflict. The RAF and the state made wildly different claims of fact and interpreted the same facts very differently. So divergent were their perceptions that it seemed as if they were describing fundamentally different realities, with no mediating force able to settle which version was truer. The prison controversy thus serves as a microcosm of the ambiguities and even inscrutability characterizing the conflict more broadly.

The overarching complaint of RAF prisoners was that they were subject to special, highly punitive handling *(Sonderbehandlung)* on account of their politics. Their chief objection was to being held for months or even years in isolation both from one another and from the general prison populations in the various facilities in which they sat. These conditions could apply even while they were in pretrial detention *(Untersuchungshaft)*. Contact with lawyers and relatives was also severely restricted. At an extreme, some prisoners languished in "dead tracts" *(tote Trakte)*, prison floors almost entirely lacking in stimuli and on which they were the only inmates. The RAF decried a host of other measures: the denial or heavy censorship of reading materials, the inspection of personal and legal correspondence, "acoustic isolation" from external sounds, fluorescent lights left continually burning in the cells, frequent cell and body searches, and meticulous, around-the-clock surveillance of their actions, including by cameras *(Spione,* or "spies") peering into their cells. To the RAF, these practices amounted to deliberate, modern, and "hygienic" forms of physical and psychological torture.[54] To buttress their claims, the RAF and its support groups cited the findings of American and German researchers concluding that isolation was in fact an effective method of manipulating and seriously degrading the psyche, the emotions, and the will.[55]

Though the accusation of "isolation torture" *(Isolationsfolter)* was intentionally provocative and hotly contested, the toll of isolation on some prisoners appears to have been very real. The RAF's Astrid Proll was arrested in May 1971 on charges (from which she was later cleared) stemming from a shoot-out with police. In 1971–72, she spent a total of more than five months of near-complete isolation in the Women's Psychiatric Section of the Köln-Ossendorf prison. The attorney Ulrich Preuß, who represented Proll and her fellow inmate Ulrike Meinhof, complained that his clients "lived practically 24 hours a day in a completely undifferentiated environment."[56] Utterly silent, nearly all white, and entirely unadorned, it was "acoustically and visually desolate," with the inmates "totally bereft of social contact," save brief encounters with corrections officers at mealtimes.[57] He likened their treatment to shock therapy used on psychiatric patients. The attorney Henning Spangenberg described Proll's ordeal in more sadly poetic terms, insisting that "the only contact [she] had was with her torment."[58] The conditions proved so debilitating to Proll that a judge ordered her release from prison altogether and suspended her trial. For years thereafter, confined spaces and perfect silence brought back terrifying memories of her cell.[59]

Meinhof, kept for eight months in 1972–73 under similar conditions in the same facility, wrote from her cell a poem, "Aus dem Toten Trakt" ("From the Dead Tract"), that conveyed the sensory confusion, dementia, and consuming rage that isolation wrought: "You can no longer identify the meanings of words, only guess. . . . Guards, visits, the yard seem as if they are on celluloid. . . . Raw aggression, for which there is no outlet. That is the worst. Clear awareness that your chances of surviving are none. . . . Visits leave behind no trace. . . . The feeling that time and space are interlocked . . . that you move in a time loop."[60] Meinhof's poem, widely circulated by the RAF, induced other inmates to fear extreme isolation. Margrit Schiller, incarcerated in Lübeck prison in 1974, came to the horrifying conclusion that she too was on a "dead tract" as the other inmates were removed, one by one, from her floor. Surrounded only by a "vast emptiness," she, like Meinhof, became unable to "distinguish internal perceptions from external reality."[61]

In a 1973 report widely cited by the RAF and its advocates, the Dutch psychiatrist Sjef Teuns asserted in scientific language what the inmates' testimony intimated: that isolation and sensory deprivation induced the "progressive disorientation," the "deformation of the personality," and, ultimately, the "destruction of the sense-deprived individual." His report concluded ominously: "Sensory deprivation—because it can only be produced through human manipulation—is at once the most human and inhuman method for the protracted degradation of life. Applied for months or years, [it] is the proverbial 'perfect murder' for which no one—or everyone, except the victim—is responsible."[62] An even more damning perspective came from Heinz Brandt, an Auschwitz survivor who had also suffered extended periods of solitary confinement in an East German prison. In a 1973 interview, he asserted,

> As crass and paradoxical as it may sound, my experiences with strict, radical isolation were worse than my time . . . in a Nazi concentration camp *[KZ]*. . . . [I]n the camp, I still had the bases for human life, namely, communication with my fellow inmates. . . . We were able in the camps to see, not only outrageously fascistic and sadistic mistreatment, but also the possibilities for resistance and collective life among the prisoners, and, with this, for the fulfillment of the fundamental need of a human being: social existence.[63]

The self-described "political prisoners" charged that the practical intent of their mistreatment was to induce confessions, force betrayal within their ranks, and, in keeping with Dr. Teuns's research and Brandt's testimony, literally destroy individual prisoners. The state's larger purpose, as they saw it, was to dispirit and destroy anti-imperialist resistance. The inmates protested by engaging in a series of well-coordinated hunger strikes, starting in January 1973. Dozens of prisoners from the RAF and other groups participated in the first three major strikes, carried out over a twenty-month period. The strikers were supported by their attorneys, legal aid organizations such as Rote Hilfe, and the "Committees against Isolation Torture in the Prisons of the FRG," which formed in 1973–74 in Berlin, Hamburg, Frankfurt, Stuttgart, and other cities.

The hunger strikes sought most immediately to improve prison conditions, chiefly by ending the isolation of inmates and related deprivations. Though they gained considerable attention and some public support, they generally failed to win the inmates any of their core demands. With each new strike, the resolve of both the inmates and the government grew, as did the stakes. The first strike had forty participants and lasted a month. In the second, running nearly seven weeks in the spring of 1973, officials introduced the controversial practice of force-feeding the inmates in an effort to break the strike. The strike ended with isolation being lifted for only two inmates. That winter, responding to their clients' enduring despair and the media's skepticism about their complaints, the RAF's attorneys organized a controversial teach-in at the Technische Universität Berlin titled "Torture in the Prisons of the FRG." Family members of the inmates spoke out as well, holding press conferences in which they blasted the government for the inhumane treatment of their loved ones.

The third strike, beginning in September 1974, involved eighty inmates and lasted a grueling 140 days (some inmates suspended their strikes as others joined). Determined to win their demands, but anticipating the state's intransigence, the inmates squarely faced the prospect of their deaths. A month into the strike, thirty-five mostly young activists occupied the Church of the Holy Cross in Berlin's Kreuzberg neighborhood as an act of solidarity with the inmates. Marathon discussions took place, yielding a resolution, signed by twenty-seven pastors, that described the occupation as an act of conscience and called for an impartial inquiry into prison conditions.[64] Berlin's *Justizsenator* Horst Korber dismissed RAF's reports of torture in Berlin's Moabit prison as "fairy tales" *(Märchen)*, prompting bitter demonstrations against him.[65] As the strike wore on, several dozen people engaged in brief "solidarity hunger strikes," among them the author Peter Schneider and the renowned German-Swedish prison advocate Brigitta Wolff, while many others publicly endorsed the strikers' demands.

On the fifty-fourth day of the strike, the seemingly inevitable happened: an inmate, the RAF's Holger Meins, producer of a notorious 1968 film showing how to make a Molotov cocktail, died of starvation in Wittlich Prison Hospital. His death prompted a level of outrage on the left not hitherto seen during the RAF's existence. Meins had been something of an exception in the RAF. As a student in Berlin, he had shown considerable promise as a filmmaker, and as the youth movement grew, he was drawn most strongly to its graphic expressions. A poster of his depicting a flower with a grenade at its center and the names "Vietcong," "El Fatah," "Black Panther," and "Weatherman" shooting from the petals, with the words "Free All Prisoners" below it, had been widely used in the 1970 May Day demonstration in Berlin. The poster was also left at the site of an anonymous bombing of an IBM office, and it was soon condemned as a criminal incitement to violence, leading to the prosecution of its publishers, 833.[66]

Former friends and associates uniformly describe Meins as sensitive, sympathetic, and warm—quite unlike SDS's ideologues and the others in the RAF, who seemed obsessively focused on their dangerous work.[67]

As if alluding to his character, in prison the RAF gave Meins the nickname "Starbuck" from Melville's *Moby Dick*. Described by Melville as "earnest" and "conscientious," Starbuck had tried in vain to keep Ahab from seeking revenge against the whale.[68] Though Meins's experience in the RAF and in prison hardened him, he apparently retained a certain softness and abstract longing, evident in his art; beside his deathbed sat a very accomplished collage he had made in prison in which simple colored shapes floated over a black background.

In response to Meins's death, angry protests took place in Frankfurt, Cologne, Hamburg, Stuttgart, and other cities, in which demonstrators charged that Meins had been murdered by the state. Central to this claim was the charge that Meins had deliberately been force-fed an insufficient amount of calories; medical evidence marshaled by the RAF's defenders suggested that the intake of small amounts of nutrients was actually more debilitating than no intake at all, and that force-feeding had therefore hastened his death.[69] In West Berlin, up to 2,500 people gathered in university auditoriums to discuss possible responses, while demonstrations— despite being officially banned—choked sections of the city.[70] A resolution circulated at the Technische Universität asserted: "The motive behind the special treatment of political prisoners in the FRG is clear: to silence them . . . to make them renounce their political beliefs and, as a necessary means to that end, to destroy their souls and rob them of their identities."[71] Rudi Dutschke, though not a supporter of the RAF's violence, attended Meins's funeral and, standing over the grave, exclaimed: "Holger, der Kampf geht weiter! ("Holger, the struggle continues").[72] More radical voices still, such as the Committees against Torture, insisted that Meins "died for the liberation of the people from imperialist exploitation" and unequivocally endorsed the RAF's "armed struggle against the imperialist system of the multinational corporations, which sustains itself through open fascism and genocide."[73] At the extreme, guerrillas responded to Meins's death with violent retaliation.

For the prisoners, the ultimate purpose of the hunger strikes was to sustain their political struggle with the only mode of resistance left to them. The RAF described the strikes as "the last weapon of our prisoners for the propagation, mobilization and organization of anti-imperialist politics."[74] Underlying this assessment of the strikes was the RAF's belief that repression inside prisons epitomized the oppressiveness of the West German state and imperialism as a whole. The RAF inmate Siegfried Haag charged that "the direct violence of the state is carried out in your cell"; to resist in prison was therefore to take on the state in the most direct manner possible.[75] The RAF and its supporters also linked the campaign against prison conditions to a larger sense of struggle in other ways: by attributing Meins's death to "class justice"; by portraying Stammheim, the high-security prison where the RAF's leaders were eventually lodged, as the densest concentration and most vivid symbol of state power; and by lauding Meins, Baader, Meinhof, et al. as heroes of the "international class struggle" for their defiance in prison. The RAF thus asserted the continuity of its resistance in prison with its founding vision of revolutionary anti-imperialism and of the guerrilla as an icon of unending resistance. Far from destroying the RAF's sense of collective purpose, the prison experience provided a new context in which it carried its politics forward and crafted a heroic self-image.

The state and its defenders dismissed the RAF's allegations of mistreatment as exaggerations or outright fabrications, whose shrewdly instrumental purposes were to draw new recruits into terrorism, manipulate public opinion, and provide justifications for more acts of terror. The state defended any "special treatment" of the prisoners on the basis of its suspicion that they conferred from their cells about violent plots on the outside. Much evidence supported the state's skepticism about the complaint of torture. Only small numbers of prisoners experienced severe isolation and only for limited periods of time. After objecting to the absence of stimuli, inmates were allowed to have radios, phonographs, and television sets in their cells. They were also permitted newspapers and extensive libraries, which included even manuals on the technical aspects of guerrilla war. At the start of 1975, Baader had more than 400 volumes in his cell.[76] Neither was human contact in short supply. Baader had 58 meetings with lawyers in January 1975 alone and more than 500 such visits from November 1974 to January 1977.[77] According to one account, imprisoned terrorists (convicted or alleged) received a staggering 12,664 visits from lawyers and others between 1975 and 1977, during which charges of "isolation torture" raged.[78] Moreover, RAF members in Stammheim and other facilities were eventually allowed to meet with one another for portions of the day. One conservative commentator, observing all this, remarked wryly that if RAF inmates were subject to any "special treatment," it consisted of the enjoyment of immense privileges.[79] The liberal news weekly *Der Spiegel,* which investigated prison conditions in advance of an interview it conducted with prisoners during the third hunger strike, came to a similar conclusion.[80]

The prisons themselves proved quite porous. Through the semi-secret "Info-system," lawyers shuttled messages among RAF inmates and from the inmates to the world outside; with these, the group was able to engage in collective discussions of political and strategic matters, maintain some sense of cohesion, and, for a time and to a degree still unknown, give instructions to the underground. The most dramatic security breaches took place in Stammheim prison. Starting in 1974, officials began moving RAF's leaders, among them Meinhof, Ensslin, and Baader, into the newly refitted, high-security wing of the Stuttgart facility. The state also built, at a cost of millions, a special courthouse next to the prison capable of handling what officials saw as the stringent security demands of the impending trial.[81] Eerily drab and designed for maximum efficiency, Stammheim earned the reputation of being West Germany's most secure prison, in which techniques for the control of inmates had been perfected. Yet the RAF's attorneys managed to bring in all manner of contraband: first, messages from other prisoners; then cameras, with which the inmates photographed their Spartan cells to document their alleged abuse; and, finally, the Colt revolvers that Baader and Raspe presumably used to commit suicide.

In addition to misrepresenting the extent of their isolation, RAF members made what seemed incompatible accusations against the state. They denounced, for example, both the denial of water to *and* the forced feeding of inmates as inhumane attempts to break the hunger strikes (drinking water, the inmates claimed, greatly enhanced the ability to survive without food).[82] Moreover, RAF members in prison *had* in fact conferred—at least in 1973 and 1974—with those on the outside about possible violent acts to win their freedom. And to those in the underground, their freedom was initially thought essential to the *continuation* and *strengthening* of the armed struggle.[83] Finally, some on the radical left contended that the campaign against "torture" was politically driven deception, more or less as the state had asserted. In 1978, Horst Mahler, who had split from the RAF while in prison, described the charge of torture as a "propaganda lie" intended to "morally blackmail" the left and "legitimate the brutal form of struggle" employed by guerrillas trying to extort the prisoners' release. With the chiding and, some prisoners felt, condescending remark that "an Indian brave doesn't cry," Mahler recommended that imprisoned guerrillas accept the consequences of their actions without specious complaints.[84]

The government's position had, however, its own profound biases and blind spots. The state consistently downplayed or dismissed outright the damaging effects of isolation broken only by intermittent visits and highly mediated "contact," such as that which radio listening offered. It refused to accede to demands for more conventional conditions of confinement whose fulfillment—while hardly threatening "national security"—would have alleviated the prisoners' hardships and might have prevented the prison deaths. The state also failed to understand the hostility that its techniques of discipline and punishment bred in the prisoners. In force-feeding, doctors strapped inmates to their beds, pried their mouths open with painful clamps, and pumped nutrients into them through tubes running through their nostrils or down their throats.[85] Some force-feedings, Schiller alleges, were administered with deliberate brutality, leaving the mouths of the inmates bloodied.[86] The inmates found more subtly offensive such things as the placement of extra locks on their cell doors; the mandatory taking of meals in isolation; the barring of timepieces from the cells; and the maze of procedures—described in numbing detail in official prison documents distributed by the prisoners' advocates—governing their confinement, observation, and movement.[87] Such practices formed the experiential basis of the prisoners' denunciations of the Federal Republic as a terroristic state, determined to destroy them by means of torture. There was, in short, a Foucauldian subtext to the inmates' broadly Marxist charge that their treatment showed the lengths to which a capitalist society would go in liquidating militant communist resistance. More than anything else, the prisoners seemed to resent and rebel against the highly nuanced and invasive ways that power functioned in the prisons as "total institutions." Betraying no appreciation of the ordeal of the prisoners and how it might affect their mind-set, the Christian Democrat leader Helmut Kohl announced before the Bundestag just after Schleyer's murder that "the suicides in Stammheim were no admission of defeat. . . . They were only an expression of the boundless fanaticism driving the terrorists' assault on every humane and peaceful order."[88]

The RAF's dubious presentation of its campaign against "isolation torture" as the epitome of an "anti-imperialist" politics testifies, in part, to the group's self-absorption. Consumed by the issue of prison conditions, the RAF failed in the mid 1970s to address imperialism in anything other than a highly general sense. Nor did it articulate exactly how its battle against prison conditions would help the peoples of the Third World. For the most part, the RAF simply asserted that since it was, in its self-description, an anti-imperialist group, support for the group necessarily advanced the anti-imperialist cause. By this logic, RAF prisoners virtually equated their fate with the destiny of global anti-imperialism. The shift in the RAF's language was an index of the group's involution. By the mid 1970s, the RAF had virtually ceased producing anything ap-

proaching a systematic geopolitical analysis or program of action.[89] Its
statements had become increasingly shrill, defensive, fragmentary, repet-
itive, and jargon-laden. Asked by a *Der Spiegel* interviewer in 1975 to
describe the Federal Republic, RAF prisoners responded: "Imperialist center. U.S. colony. U.S. military base. Leading imperialist power in Western Europe, of the European Community, second greatest military power
in NATO," and so on.[90] Speaking in this blunt, semi-private language,
the RAF increased its internal cohesion at the expense of its ability to
apprehend, and communicate effectively with, the outside world.

In broadly political terms, the RAF's self-absorption in prison was an
outgrowth of a problem that had long afflicted the New Left in both West
Germany and the United States: its lack of a strong connection to "the
masses" or "the people." In developing a radical politics not rooted
strictly in class conflict, New Leftists in both countries sought to liberate themselves and their movements from narrow Marxist conceptions
of how social change happens. Yet in this freedom, they faced the
prospect of operating without the benefit of a sizable and energized
base—of being self-appointed leaders without a large mass of followers.
Efforts to make their revolts fully popular ones repeatedly failed, however much they may have tapped into common dissatisfactions and desires. The more dogmatically, or desperately, New Leftists insisted upon
their connection and service to "the people," the more awkward their
separation from "the people" became.

Revolutionary internationalism allowed New Leftists to reconceive
what popular struggle meant, such that solidarity with the *global* masses—
the world's majority—could take priority over winning mass appeal at
home. But New Leftists in First World societies had very few direct links
with liberation movements in the Third World. Those that did exist, such
as the relationship between West German and Palestinian guerrillas, were
often strategic, revealing perhaps more a mutual interest in tactical alliances than any deep and enduring political kinship. The solidarity New
Leftists offered, in sum, was for the most part ideological and moral, predicated on an intuitive but underelaborated sense of being involved in a
single, global struggle against imperialism. The internationalism of the
West German New Left was particularly attenuated, as it was based largely
on a critique of U.S. power and a view of the Federal Republic as a proxy
for U.S. interests. Moreover, most New Leftists in West Germany and elsewhere seemed to agree that building a mass socialist movement at home
was the key to building socialism internationally. The New Left's inability to convert its democratic and egalitarian ideals into an unambiguously

popular domestic revolt could not, in the last instance, be rationalized through appeals to internationalism.

The RAF pursued a decidedly unpopular brand of radicalism, as it came, on occasion, close to acknowledging. Asked in a prison interview to account for its "absolute lack of influence on the masses and connection to a base," the RAF replied that there remained within West German society at least "the *trace [Spur]* of the politics of the RAF."[91] At other times, RAF inmates tried to work against this isolation by *making a metaphor of themselves*—by presenting their fate as conjoined with that of the forces with which the RAF insisted it was aligned. In so doing, the RAF sought to compensate for its chief political failure: the absence of a sociopolitical referent beyond itself. Yet, as the RAF's near-exclusive focus became the freeing of its prisoners, its self-referentiality became all the more apparent.

The RAF's self-image while in prison reflects the effects of isolation in a more literal sense. For activists, one's location in a particular environment can dramatically affect one's perceptions. What might be called the "politics of location" had a profound impact on the New Left. Activists' more or less total immersion in radical organizations and in highly politicized settings, such as universities and anarchist "scenes," fed their belief in their own power. But it also led them to overestimate popular dissatisfaction in their own countries and to exaggerate their strength. Conversely, their segregation in self-enclosed worlds, whose boundaries were reinforced by public and state hostility, fed a sense of isolation and the conviction that desperate measures were required in the face of the overwhelming power of the adversary. The very emergence of the violent underground testifies to both this extreme optimism and fatal pessimism born, in part, of isolation.

Life underground enhanced the distorting effects of location. Members of the underground were estranged from normalcy, cut off from much of the legal left, and radically dependent on one another. As a result, they lacked external checks on their perceptions. Comparing left-wing violence in Germany and Italy, Donatella della Porta spells out the hazards of the underground:

> the organizational model of the underground groups evolved towards more centralized . . . forms, thereby increasing the vicious circle of increasing isolation. The risks of being discovered induced members to concentrate decision making in the hands of a small group of clandestine leaders. . . . When repression increased and support from social movements decreased, the organizations withdrew into themselves. . . . Even in front of several

signs of defeat, the choice of clandestinity remained *imprinted* on these
groups [such that] they virtually ensured that their development would
be shaped by internal dynamics rather than interaction with a broader
environment . . . survival and solidarity rather than political effectiveness.[92]

Mahler put things more starkly: "In clandestinity . . . you see the world
only from within a military model, as a free zone or as a dangerous territory. You do not see human beings so often anymore."[93]

Prison was a total, rarefied, and highly constricting environment that
further limited the guerrillas' already narrow worldview. The conditions
of extreme hardship and absence of external points of reference reinforced
the tendency of the guerrillas to use their own circumstances as a basis
for claims about their society as a whole. Herein lies the paradox of the
RAF in the mid 1970s. With imprisonment, the boundaries of its world
literally and drastically shrank. The group's isolation became complete
with the *Kontaktsperre,* or "contact ban," initially imposed on seventy-
two inmates from the RAF and other groups two days after the kidnapping of Schleyer in September 1977. Under the *Kontaktsperre,* the inmates
were placed in solitary confinement, stripped of reading material, and
deprived of *all* human contact, including meetings with their attorneys.
This practice, whose constitutionality was not at first certain, drew sharp
criticisms from the RAF and others. The Bundestag soon sanctioned the
ban by passing the *Kontaktsperregesetz* (Contact Ban Law), which made
legal the total isolation of prisoners in response to conditions of "national emergency." The *Kontaktsperre,* ostensibly put into place out of
fear that the inmates were orchestrating violence outside the prison
(highly implausible at this point), declared the RAF to be so dangerous
that it demanded quarantine.[94] With the ban, the state sought literally
to excise the RAF from the body politic by totally depriving its members
of visibility, publicity, community, and voice.

Yet in the face of isolation, the RAF expanded its own significance by
presenting its experience as illustrative of the *essential* reality of West German society. Since its inception, the RAF had practiced a kind of anti-
carceral politics, distributing at least its verbal assaults among institutions and settings whose ultimate function, it felt, was to constrain,
control, and oppress: prisons, certainly, but also schools, reformatories,
factories, bureaucracies, even places of middle-class comfort. Actually,
being in prison enhanced RAF members' sense of the purpose and reach
of the system's power. In their perception, the abuse they suffered in
prison epitomized the state's disdain for radical dissent; the meticulous

regulation of their lives in prison bespoke the perniciousness of the administered society, which made everyone an object of social control; and the alleged attempt at their destruction laid bare the fascistic nature of the Federal Republic. In short, prison became the dominant metaphor for society as a whole. At the 1974 trial for her involvement in the freeing of Baader four years earlier, Meinhof described the act as "exemplary," because "anti-imperialist struggle is really about liberation from prison—from the prison that the system always already is for the exploited and oppressed . . . from the prison of total alienation and self-estrangement."[95] Seen in this light, Schiller's comment that isolation had blurred the distinction between "internal perceptions" and "external reality" is a broad description of the RAF's politics.

In making a metaphor of itself, the RAF developed an oddly immaterial cast, even as its imprisoned members experienced the most material operation of power—the infliction of physical suffering, holding the body in a constant state of pain—and even as its active commandos murdered and injured to win the prisoners' release. The operation of the metaphor depended on the RAF's prisoners successfully representing their situation as one of true abuse. But this is precisely what was so difficult, given that the prisoners were concealed behind the veil of the prison walls.

The state, by virtue of this circumstance, held a distinct advantage in its war of representation with the RAF. Chiefly, the prisoners could never confirm forensically that their alleged suffering—always described as mental as much as physical—was real. Skepticism could parry every public charge. Did the state do with the prisoners what they claimed, and were the effects of their "special handling" really so dire? When the inmates' suffering was undeniable, as from the hunger strikes, just who was to blame remained unclear. Did the inmates, as the government and its defenders asserted, willfully misrepresent prison conditions in order to justify the hunger strikes and ultimately coerce the prisoners' release? Against this wall of doubt, the prisoners' rhetoric pulsed with the desperation of their being subject to some grotesque, private horror that the world was largely unable or unwilling to see.

The concealment of the prisoners' experience did not, however, guarantee the state's victory in the battle over the public's perceptions. If the RAF's allegations could not be proved, neither could they be definitively *dis*proved. Some among the public greeted the state's defense of its conduct—often expressed in the bureaucratic language of the official denial—with skepticism of their own. The more the prisoners claimed to suffer and the more the state denied their charges, the greater that skepticism grew. "The facts," themselves indeterminate and intensely politicized, hardly seemed capable of settling the matter. One's judgment hinged, it seemed, on how one was inclined to view the state and with whom one identified.

Elaborating for *Der Spiegel* what it meant by the "trace" of its politics, the RAF stated:

> It isn't a matter of supporters, fellow travelers and allied organizations; the issue is the RAF and the impact of its politics—in the sense that the measures the government has taken against us are changing many people's perception of the state and pushing them to recognize it for what it is: the imperialist bourgeoisie's apparatus for oppressing the people—in the sense that many people identify with our struggle and change the way they think about, feel about, and ultimately act toward the power of the system, which they once perceived as absolute—in the sense that people have the power to act, that a feeling of impotence does not conform to objective reality— in the sense of proletarian internationalism, the awareness of the connection between liberation struggles in the Third World and those here, the awareness of the possibility and the necessity of joint action, joint work, legal and illegal. On the level of praxis, that it is not enough to debate but that it is possible, necessary, and feasible to act.[96]

This pronouncement appears, most obviously, emblematic of the RAF's heavy-handed, highly projective, and even wishful thinking in the mid 1970s. The RAF plainly failed to instigate the kind of broad-based revelation of capitalism's oppressiveness and of the glories of class solidarity; its example hardly empowered its sympathizers to engage, en masse, in "revolutionary" action. But the RAF *did become* the occasion for some indeterminate number of West Germans to question more rigorously the identity of their state and to strengthen at least their attitude of resistance to it. Understood in these terms, the trace the RAF left cut deeply into the psyche of Germans, especially of the young, giving substance to the RAF's conspicuously symbolic and even ethereal politics.

In essence, the RAF redefined its "place" in German politics by asserting that despite its apparent marginalization, it was at the nerve center of state power. It in fact proved irrepressible while in prison. The more intensely the state tried to isolate the group, the more the RAF became a matter of public concern and controversy—a symbolically dense object of national fixation. Tellingly, the RAF's apparent self-annihilation— the alleged suicide of its leaders in Stammheim—was in ways the group's most provocative, public, and visible act. As the media, investigators, and West German citizens endlessly debated whether the ambiguous deaths

were suicides or murders, the RAF continued to haunt and even dominate public dialogue.

The close relationship between experience and perception helps to
account for what critics of the RAF have described as the group's
Realitätsverlust—its distancing from or loss of reality. That distance
widened greatly in the mid 1970s, when the RAF's leaders were literally
cut off from the conventional world. Most disturbingly, the prisoners
seemed incapable of seeing past their pain and remotely acknowledging
that they had themselves caused immense suffering through violence that
killed and maimed.

Their isolation also helps to explain the tremendous defiance they displayed in prison. Behind that defiance lay both a political and, one can
assume, personal sense of despair. With their impending convictions, they
faced lifetimes of confinement in miserably lifeless institutions such as
Stammheim. Their desolation also powerfully affected the RAF's internal dynamics. Whatever the image of unity, RAF prisoners were beset by
schisms and recriminations, especially during the hunger strikes. Through
the Info-system, RAF practiced a crude and at times vicious form of
"criticism-self-criticism," in which its leaders, above all Baader, accused
the others of being "traitors, collaborators, bulls, and swine."[97] Those
wavering in their commitment to the strikes risked being denounced;
those abandoning the strikes risked being formally shunned by the others, deepening the misery of their isolation. One exasperated participant
in the prison dialogue pleaded, "The purpose of our questions is not to
conduct an Inquisition."[98]

In light of these grim circumstances and crushing prospects, the
deaths of RAF inmates, whether by starvation or apparent suicide, can
be seen as acts of self-sacrifice or martyrdom. In an analysis of the role
of suicide in religious terrorism, Juergensmeyer describes martyrdom as
a "rite of destruction" designed to ennoble death and make the dying
holy.[99] It accomplishes this by integrating death into a vision of "cosmic
war," a conflict conceived as a "great encounter between cosmic forces—
order versus chaos, good versus evil, truth versus falsehood," as well as
"a defense of basic identity and dignity."[100] The saga of suffering and
death is made ultimately meaningful within the terms of cosmic war;
though the martyr may be vanquished in the here and now, his or her
death nourishes that larger struggle, settled in some greater scale of time.
Martyrdom, in converting the "failure" of death "into a victory," is therefore a form of symbolic empowerment, much like terrorism itself.[101]

Though the RAF certainly had no overtly religious dimension, the group did assert the utter corruption or fallenness of the capitalist world and promoted socialism as a near-redemptive ideal of perfect justice. It likewise gave its struggle a near-sacred cast as a battle between good and evil, between the great defenders and enemies of life. The RAF's sense of being locked in a cosmic struggle intensified as its "real power" diminished and its situation grew more desperate. Nearly delirious from starvation, Meins wrote from his deathbed: "The only thing that matters is the struggle—now, today, tomorrow, whether we eat or not. . . . Either a pig or a man / Either survival at any price or struggle unto death / Either problem or solution / There is nothing in between. . . . Everyone dies anyhow. What matters is how, and how you lived. It's simple. Fighting the pigs as a human being for the liberation of man . . . , fighting to the last, loving life, disdaining death."[102] With these variously sad and severe pronouncements, Meins makes his own "struggle unto death" the ultimate sign of the triumph of his humanity and his limited victory over death.

The apparent suicides of Baader, Ensslin, and Raspe—though denounced by some in the mainstream as cynical ploys to make the state *appear* murderous—may be also be viewed in sacrificial terms. By taking their own lives, the inmates potentially sought both to affirm and symbolically overcome their powerlessness in the face of a hopeless situation. That their deaths, and by extension their lives, were locked in a struggle over the sacred was confirmed by their fate in death. Public contempt for Baader, Ensslin, and Raspe was so great that some Stuttgart residents clamored that their bodies be left to rot or thrown into sewers. Gudrun Ensslin's father encountered great difficulties as he searched for someone in the city willing to provide a burial plot for a proper funeral. Behind the desire to deny the RAF's dead a conventional burial, it seems, lay a wish to deny them, not only whatever sanctification and forgiveness the grave might bring, but their humanity. Stuttgart's mayor, Manfred Rommel, son of the famous World War II general Erwin Rommel, feared an extended debate over the matter, and so he quickly decided to have the three buried in a cemetery just outside the city's limits. This compromise appeared to have its own ritual purpose: to ward off whatever impurities their bodies represented. At the funeral, police mounted on horseback chased angry mourners through forest roads, while police helicopters circled overhead. At the actual burial, surrounded by a thicket of police, the caskets of Baader, Ensslin, and Raspe were unceremoniously dumped in the ground, while Gudrun's sister and young child looked grimly on.[103]

. . .

The death of Holger Meins and the decision to take up
arms were one and the same.

    Volker Speital, "Wir wollten alles und gleichzeitig nichts"
    ("We Wanted Everything and Nothing Simultaneously")

Whatever the objective merits of the prisoners' complaints, their fate had
a powerful subjective impact on those forming new guerrilla cells. Some
in these cells were established RAF members who, having been successful in hiding, or been themselves released from prison, were intent on
freeing their friends and comrades. Remarkably, within months of serving more than a year in prison, Schiller rejoined the underground, where
she conspired to engage in "liberation actions."[104] But others among the
reemergent underground, called RAF's "second" and "third generations," were younger than the RAF's founders and had not passed as thoroughly through the activism of the 1960s. To a great extent, they became
radicalized through the issue of the prisoners' treatment.

Siegfried Haag had by no means endorsed the RAF's methods when
he began working on the long-awaited trial of the RAF's leaders in the
mid 1970s as a court-appointed attorney. Immersion in the plight of his
hunger-striking clients, and Holger Meins especially, soon changed his
views. Haag, who was at Meins's bedside just before he died, described
his sense of powerlessness: "I shall never be able to forget this experience all my life. I was so intensely involved [with his situation] at the
time and I felt that as a lawyer I could not defend him the way he needed
to be defended . . . [nor] do anything to prevent [his] death."[105] Nine
months after Meins's death, Haag was arrested for allegedly trying to
procure arms for the RAF. He promptly fled Germany, after which he
conspired to free RAF members.

Hans-Joachim Klein came from the working class and became politicized while serving in the late 1960s as a conscript in the army. In the
mid 1970s, he went from working with Rote Hilfe to joining the semi-
clandestine Red Cells, with whom he engaged in violent actions. He too
described the death of Meins as a "trigger" that forced him to see "the
impotence of legality." Thereafter, Klein carried in his wallet the grotesque
autopsy photograph of Meins, who at his death weighed less than 100
pounds. Klein confessed keeping the picture with him so as "not to dull
the edge of my hatred."[106]

Volker Speital, born in 1950, entered the "anti-authoritarian rebellion" on the countercultural side. In the early 1970s, he lived with his wife Angelika in an "alternative" house, where he took drugs, read Timothy Leary and Wilhelm Reich (not Dutschke or Marcuse), and "dreamt of a farmhouse in the country, of nature, love, and freedom."[107] Though he knew little of the RAF, he felt "oppressed by the pressure to conform," so he cheered the group's assaults on the established order. Speital eventually began working in Stuttgart with Rote Hilfe, whose members' intense political convictions deeply impressed him. Soon he became involved with the Stuttgart Committee against Torture, run out of the office of the RAF's lead attorneys, and began carrying messages between prisoners.

Years later, he described how this work led him underground:

> I saw prisoners in silent cells being literally tortured and slowly destroyed through scientifically researched methods. One felt one was in enemy territory. The opponent was no longer just [Federal Prosecutor] Buback . . . but practically anybody who did not actively protest these methods. I saw only the hunger strike and did nothing else . . . than agitate for fourteen to sixteen hours a day with leaflets, press releases [etc.] in support of it. Then came the day Holger Meins died. . . . For us his death was a turning point. Partly because we had never been so close to such drastic misery and death, and, more important,—truth be told—because we felt morally responsible for his death. Responsible because our strenuous activities to help him could not prevent his death. The death of Holger Meins and the decision to take up arms were one and the same. Reflection was no longer possible; one simply reacted to the emotional power of the prior months.[108]

In addition to describing vividly his sense of despair, Speital indicates the extent to which the focus of the armed struggle had narrowed. Speital employs the near-standard trope by which New Left radicals described their turn to illegality. He recounts working tirelessly through legal means to stop a perceived injustice; sensing himself encircled by the state and isolated within the left; turning contemptuously against anyone not equally consumed by concern; and, crucially, feeling *personally* responsible for suffering and death he was unable to prevent. His decision to adopt violence, at which point emotion replaced reflection, came with the piercing recognition of the apparent inadequacy of conventional forms of protest. Yet the object of Speital's outrage differed from that of radicals, including the RAF's founders, of just a few years prior. It was not the persistence, in spite of peaceful protest, of great global injustices, such as the war in Vietnam. It was not prompted by the murder of an innocent protester, such as Ohnesorg in 1967, or the shooting of a leader, such as Dutschke, in 1968. Rather, Speital's rage stemmed from the circumstances of a small number of prisoners who had been captured after committing lethal acts in what they saw as conditions of war.

Merely working on behalf of the prisoners, Speital suggests, reproduced some of the peculiarities of underground existence, by which the world both was and wasn't the way it appeared. Baptist Ralf Friedrich, who was also involved with the Committees against Torture, explained that surveillance of underground activities was such that one "couldn't take a single step without the police knowing [about it]. For us, the Federal Republic *was* in fact a police state."[109] By the same token, the intensity of the work deformed his perceptions. "We were a closed circle," he allowed. "It was always the same people talking about the same things. A group dynamic set in that blocked certain ways of thinking. We were no longer able to apprehend reality."[110]

The violence designed to free imprisoned guerrillas signaled not only the narrowing of the politics of armed struggle but also the further loss of its moral ballast. The killing on November 10, 1974, of West Berlin's *Kammersgrichtspräsident* (Supreme Court President) Günter von Drenkmann by the June 2 Movement in a botched kidnapping attempt was a chilling case in point. Von Drenkmann was a liberal SPD judge who had had no judicial dealings with guerrilla groups. The day after Meins's death, his killers came to his house posing as flower deliverers (he had just celebrated his sixty-fourth birthday) and shot him when he resisted capture.[111] Von Drenkmann's role as a leading member of the judiciary and, hence, his "exchange-value" as a hostage, would appear to account for his having been the J2M's target. After the shooting, the J2M insisted that its violence hurt only those who "exploit, deceive and betray the people" and portrayed von Drenkmann as a villain who *deserved to be murdered*.[112] To the J2M, he was among the "hard core" of those responsible for Meins's death simply because he was West Berlin's highest-ranking judge.[113] It added by way of justification that, like his father, he had been a judge during the Nazi period, which presumably made him an embodiment of the persistence of fascism.

Other grisly acts of violence followed. The occupiers of the German embassy in Stockholm on April 25, 1975, called the "Kommando Holger Meins," executed two diplomatic staff members and pledged to kill a hostage every hour to convey the seriousness of their demand that twenty-six prisoners be released. The raid ended abruptly when bombs the RAF had placed in the embassy accidentally exploded, killing two RAF members. On May 9, 1976, Ulrike Meinhof was found dead by hanging in her Stammheim cell. Though officials stated that she had committed suicide, leftists charged that she had been murdered by the state. The RAF's Jan-Karl Raspe, standing trial in Stammheim-Stuttgart with RAF's other leaders, announced in court, "I don't have much to say. We believe that Ulrike was executed. We don't know how, but we know by whom and we can imagine the nature of the method."[114] Demonstrations both larger and more militant than those following Meins's death took place across West Germany. In a Frankfurt protest, a policeman was seriously injured. On May 15, some 7,000 people, many with heads covered to avoid identification by police, attended Meinhof's funeral in West Berlin. The following April, the RAF exacted revenge. In Karlsruhe, the "Kommando Ulrike Meinhof" assassinated Chief Federal Prosecutor Siegfried Buback, the official broadly responsible for the prosecutions of the RAF, also killing his driver, Wolfgang Göbel, and a justice official, George Wuster.[115]

With its murder in late July 1977 of Dresdner Bank's Jürgen Ponto, the RAF reached new levels of shocking aggression. Susanne Albrecht and two male companions came with flowers to the door of the Pontos, who were friends of Susanne's parents. Once inside the house, she and her companions pulled guns in an effort to take Ponto hostage. When he resisted, Albrecht and her accomplices shot him five times. His wife watched him die. The fall of 1977 brought more victims. On September 5, in an attempt to free eleven prominent guerrillas from prison, RAF's "Kommando Siegfried Hausner" kidnapped in Cologne Hanns Martin Schleyer, the current president of the Employers Association of West Germany and a former SS *Hauptsturmführer*. In the process the RAF killed Schleyer's driver, Heinz Marcisz, and three police guards, Reinholf Brändle, Roland Pieler, and Helmut Ulmer. (Schleyer had feared he might be a target for the RAF and traveled with a special security detail.) Following the GSG raid in Mogadishu of the hijacked plane and the deaths in prison of Baader, Ensslin, and Raspe on the evening of October 17–18, the RAF executed its prisoner, shooting him three times in the head in a forest on the German-Belgian border (pine needles were found in Schleyer's mouth). In a communiqué sent to the French newspaper *Liberation* on October 19, Schleyer's killers declared that they had ended his "miserable and corrupt existence" and instructed police where they could find his body. Schleyer's corpse was recovered the following day in Mulhouse, France, from the trunk of a green Audi.[116]

Public statements issued by the "commandos" committing these acts are striking in their near-total absence of explicit political content. Those accompanying hostage takings mostly listed demands, made threats, and discussed the mechanics of the proposed exchange of the hostages for the prisoners.[117] Ponto's killers remarked: "In a situation where the Federal Prosecutors' Office and Secret Services are preparing to murder their prisoners, we don't have much time for long statements. As for Ponto and the bullets that hit him . . . we will say that we didn't realize clearly enough how powerless such characters, who instigate war in the Third World and wipe out whole nations, are in the face of violence when it confronts them in their own homes."[118] This statement starkly reveals the mind-set of the most brutal among the armed struggle's new generations, whose actions even the prisoners did not necessarily support.[119] It describes the West German state as literally murderous and the situation of the prisoners as so desperate that it constitutes a self-evident justification for Ponto's murder. It employs a perversely general standard of political guilt, whereby Ponto's status as a prominent banker made him an agent of genocide. With their evasive construction of "the bullets that hit him," the RAF members fail to properly name or assume responsibility for their act. Finally, Ponto's killers appear to take morbid pleasure in their victim's powerlessness.

The RAF began its armed struggle with exalted, if impossible, ambitions. It had hoped to instigate an uprising in West Germany that, in concert with revolutionary movements worldwide, would usher in a global, socialist utopia. Its violence was to be discriminating in its targets and strictly guided by principles, winning the public's acclaim. Yet the group received little support and was overmatched by security forces. Its violence, even in its early phases, was not nearly as circumspect as its rhetoric suggested. Over the course of the 1970s, the struggle against imperialism became more and more a "private war" against the state, and the noble anti-imperialist fighter—always in part a figure of RAF's myth-making—gave way to the "free-the-guerrilla guerrilla," whose modus operandi was hostage taking, extortion, and murder. Following the kidnapping of Schleyer and the murder of his driver and three guards, Jochen Reiche asserted that the people of West Germany "now fear, no longer without justification, being killed by those who once sought to free them."[120]

Throughout the 1970s and into the 1980s, individual guerrillas experienced doubt about the value and legitimacy of armed struggle. Some renounced violence and spoke out about the need for a comprehensive reconciliation of the conflict between the guerrillas and the state. Among an enduring "hard core," however, the sense of the validity and even holiness of the armed struggle persisted. In the 1975 RAF trial, Meinhof repeated the group's mantra that "the actions of urban guerrillas are never, never directed against the people. They are always directed against the imperialist machine . . . [and] the terrorism of the state."[121] The RAF's history, with its deaths of civilians and moments of heedless cruelty, belied her self-righteousness.

The June 2 Movement illustrates just how strong the guerrillas' powers of denial and rationalization could be. The group was composed mostly of West Berlin anarchists, some of whom had working-class backgrounds. Like America's Yippies, they combined an absurdist hippie sensibility with militant politics. Horribly out of place in the colorless world of West Berlin and chronically disgusted with German society, J2M members nicknamed themselves "the Blues." With the name, they seemed to admit the futility of armed struggle and the doomed nature of their lives as improbable "urban guerrillas." Even while underground, some members wore flamboyant clothing and long hair, as if to tempt police to capture them.

The J2M felt that the RAF, despite its socialist rhetoric, was essentially a group of elitist intellectuals. The J2M fancied itself, by contrast, the champion of the common man and woman and made on occasion special gestures to demonstrate its populist bent.[122] In the wake of the RAF's murderous Stockholm embassy takeover, J2M bank robbers gave chocolates to the frightened bank customers to indicate that they meant them no harm. The J2M kidnappers of the CDU official Peter Lorenz treated him with respect in captivity, for which he publicly thanked them after his release. Just days after Lorenz was let go, dozens, if not hundreds, of West Berliners risked arrest in distributing 50,000 copies of the J2M pamphlet *Die Entführung aus unserer Sicht* ("The Kidnapping As We See It").[123] The statement was styled as a tribute to everyday people and to the resentment of the rich by the poor and the working classes. The J2M explained: "We believe that words and arguments are no longer of any use in changing what is rotten in our society. . . . [W]hat does it mean when a man toils all day and comes home so exhausted that all he can do is sit in front of the TV? Where do child abuse, domestic violence, and suicide come from? And why don't we find such things in Berlin's wealthy suburbs but in its low rent districts?"[124] The pamphlet then publicized, based on documents found in Lorenz's briefcase, his considerable salary (20,000 marks a month, earned mostly through his corporate dealings) and the plight of a poor, single woman with a handicapped son whose pleas for help Lorenz had ignored. In Robin Hood–like fashion, the J2M sent the woman the 700 marks Lorenz had in his wallet.

Yet it was the J2M that killed the German shipbuilder Erwin Berlitz when it bombed the British Yacht Club in Berlin in February 1971 in protest of the "Bloody Sunday" killings by British forces in Londonderry. Though treating Lorenz with respect, his captors had planned to execute him should the government refuse to release imprisoned guerrillas. Following its killing of Justice von Drenkmann, the J2M had charged that "the outcry at [his] death . . . is the outcry of the ruling class over the death of one of its own."[125] With this claim, it ignored the fact that the act drew sharp criticism from across the political spectrum, including the far left. Young radicals massing in Berlin following Meins's death typically denounced both the state and von Drenkmann's killers.[126] The left-wing newspaper *Berliner Extra-Dienst* insisted: "The death of Holger Meins demands from every leftist unconditional solidarity with a victim of bourgeois class justice. The attack on the president of the Berlin Court demands unconditional protest against the exercise of violence against a human being."[127] Finally, on the night of June 4–5, 1974, a J2M cell murdered a twenty-two-year-old student, Ulrich Schmucker, as a "traitor," for allegedly having given some mildly sensitive information to the police while in custody. After a cursory review of the "evidence," a J2M "tribunal" found Schmucker guilty and sentenced him to death. Schmucker's body was found in a forest outside of Berlin, where he had been shot in the back of the neck. Echoing the RAF's rhetoric, a J2M flyer denounced left-wing criticism of the act as "whiny, moralistic, pacifistic, and divisive."[128]

. . .

The goal, free human beings, must already be evident
in the means.

> Herbert Marcuse, "Mord darf keine
> Waffe sein" ("Murder Cannot Be a Weapon")

For much of West German society, the guerrilla movement evoked fear, intense loathing, and concern for the nation's security; the overarching imperatives were to find, indict, prosecute, and imprison its members, while incapacitating their networks of support. For leftists sharing some of the guerrillas' broad goals, the RAF and similar groups posed a different set of challenges and questions: how to turn political and moral outrage to constructive ends; how to develop a militant practice that was consistent with one's values; and how to maintain the integrity of one's resistance. As they debated these questions, leftists discerned not only the strategic failure of the armed struggle but also its problems as a politics and ethics of resistance.

Leftists of all kinds denounced the RAF's violence for its ineffectiveness as a political strategy. The RAF mostly alienated those it meant to mobilize and, by provoking state repression, worsened the political climate in which all leftists had to operate. This negative verdict on the *efficacy* of RAF's violence implied a larger judgment on its legitimacy. Herbert Marcuse made this criticism with special force.

In a 1977 editorial following the killing of Schleyer, Marcuse asserted that there exist circumstances in which the murder "of the agents of repression," like Admiral Luis Carrero Blanco, the Spanish prime minister (assassinated in 1973 by Basque separatists), or, hypothetically, Hitler, "truly changes the system—at least in its political manifestations—and mitigates oppression."[129] He also argued that "tyrant murder" *(Tyrannenmord)*, such as that of the SS leader Heinrich Heydrich in Czechoslovakia in 1942, is justifiable on both instrumental *and* symbolic grounds by virtue of the "tyrant's" direct involvement in horrendous crimes.[130] The RAF's violence clearly failed to meet these criteria. Though implicated in a capitalist system Marcuse deemed oppressive, figures such as Buback and Schleyer were hardly villains in any immediate sense, and their deaths could not conceivably help to topple the power structures of which they were a part. In a relatively stable, prosperous society such as the Federal Republic,

> The physical liquidation of individuals, including the prominent and the powerful, does not upset the normal functioning of the capitalist system. Rather, it strengthens its repressive potential, without (and that is decisive) activating or bringing to political consciousness potential opponents of repression. Indeed, these people represent the system: but they only *represent it*. That means, they are reproducible, exchangeable, and the reservoir for their recruitment is inexhaustible.[131]

Given this reality, the RAF violated what Marcuse called the "law of revolutionary pragmatism" that must guide socialist practice. Marcuse additionally rejected the notion that the *structural* guilt of capitalism's representatives necessarily translates into their individual culpability. He pointed out that the idea of structural guilt, taken to its logical extreme, makes workers the chief culprits in oppression, because their labor is singularly indispensable for the reproduction of capitalism.[132] In its facile approach to questions of guilt, the RAF also violated the "law of revolutionary morality" that in essence requires that "the goal, free human beings, must already be evident in the means."[133]

Iring Fetscher was a liberal professor who in the late 1970s assumed the role of the Federal Republic's semi-official critic of the RAF. He consistently defended West German democracy and identified the numerous *Denkfehler*—"errors of insight"—that doomed the RAF's efforts. The RAF's misreading of Marxism was one such error. In *Capital,* Marx describes individuals as *Charactermaske* ("character masks"), insofar as they personify and bear particular functions within a social division of labor. But for Marx, the notion of a character mask is an *analytic,* not an existential, construct. It describes people only with reference to their socioeconomic roles, not in their totality. (Indeed, one RAF member later confessed that though his cell dutifully studied Marx and Kant, they had not understood what they read terribly well.)[134] Furthermore, individuals assume particular roles through pressure exerted by the division of labor, thus mitigating their responsibility for the roles they play. Fetscher protested, "one cannot kill a character mask, but only a living human being in his many-sided complexity. . . . The terrorist who intends to kill a character mask outdoes with his crime the inhumanity of a system that he allegedly fights and wants to change."[135]

More radical voices accused the RAF of a deeper betrayal of socialist principles. The University of Hannover psychology professor Peter Brückner, like Marcuse, vigorously supported New Left protest and was embraced by young radicals as an intellectual patron of their cause. Though not an advocate of armed struggle, he publicly criticized the treatment of RAF prisoners, warned of fascist tendencies in the Federal Republic and, in a biography of Meinhof, situated her rage in relation to what he saw as the hypocrisy and failed potential of West German society. In 1972, at the age of forty-seven, Brückner was suspended from his university post after having been accused at the trial of the RAF's Karl-Heinz Ruhland, who turned "state's witness," of having lent RAF's leaders material support when they were in hiding.[136] Brückner was, however, deeply troubled by the left's violence. In 1974, he and Barbara Sichermann published reflections on the J2M's killing of Schmucker, which implicitly condemned the kinds of political murder more commonly practiced by the RAF and other guerrillas.

Brückner used the assassination to state a kind of first principle of political morality: that "a human being is always an embodiment of hope, of expectation."[137] To Brückner, it is precisely this vision of humanity informed by freedom and possibility that justifies the killing of arch-oppressors like Heydrich. Far from embodying hope, they "live as the death of others, as their hopelessness."[138] This view of humanity should also preclude reducing people to categories and assuming dominion over their fate, as in the Schmucker tragedy. Brückner decried the rhetoric used by both the J2M and its left-wing critics: the description of Schmucker as a "traitor" by his executioners; as a "little pig," not worth killing, by one group; and as a "petit bourgeois," scarcely responsible for his transgression, by another. For Brückner, this kind of abstraction—deplorable in its own right—was quintessentially a quality of the left's adversaries, as the "fascists, the state forces, the executive powers readily reduce humans to abstractions. We demand of the left, which lives by abstraction in its intellectualizing, not to abstract in this case. . . . [T]he left has, in contrast to the right, scruples about death, and knows the relationship between means and ends."[139]

Brückner conceded that not all self-described leftists obeyed the principles he outlined. To Brückner, it was Stalin who had above all practiced a lethal "left-Manicheanism." Brückner, like Fetscher, observed that Marx denounces capitalists only for the economic functions they perform, such that "'capitalist' does *not* mean 'not-human,' and even less 'bull' or 'pig.'" Yet Stalin, by equating one's economic function with one's identity, divided people into a "'world and counterworld,' into a good portion [and] an evil part," for whom "there is truly no place in the world."[140] Essentializing political conflict in this way, Stalinist Manicheanism "is in reality racist [and] turns the class conflict into a race conflict."[141] With their murders of "traitors" and "capitalists pigs," the RAF and the J2M participated in Stalin's legacy, as well as in the inhumanity that defined the far right.

To Jochen Reiche, writing in the left-wing *Jahrbuch Politik,* the RAF's extreme violence was less the product of any ideological position than a consequence of the group's highly abstract and dualistic thinking. According to Reiche, the RAF's worldview had from the start been reductive, dogmatic, and pseudo-theoretical. Its main premises were that things are simple, not complex; that imperialism was the chief enemy of humanity, responsible for virtually all of the world's ills; and that the Federal Republic, despite its apparent "reformism," was in fact fascist. By virtue of these crude theses, the RAF "fought against an opponent who—as the RAF imagines him—does not in fact exist."[142]

The RAF's premises drove the group's violence in two main ways. First, the RAF declared that all the crucial political imperatives concerned practice, not theory. To close its founding manifesto, the RAF quoted Eldridge Cleaver saying: "Either you're part of the problem or part of the solution. There is nothing between. . . . My opinion is that most of what happens in this country does not need to be analyzed any longer."[143] Reiche saw the guerrilla as a "despairing attempt to realize in the individual the unity of theory and practice" insofar as he or she was to put into practice a revolutionary ideology whose main components RAF considered settled.[144] Second, the RAF viewed resistance as a life-and-death struggle against an enemy that was absolute evil. Meins's judgment that one is "either a pig or a man" with "nothing in between" conveyed the RAF's inability to acknowledge anything other than extreme alternatives, resulting in an attitude of kill or be killed. To Reiche, the group's demonization of the Federal Republic as fascist ultimately served to "eliminate the psychic resistance to the murder of human beings."[145] Mahler saw political murder as an extension of the RAF's uncompromising "morality," which he defined the following way: "The world is terrible, unending suffering, murder, death blows. That can be changed only through violence, which also demands victims, but fewer than if the status quo persisted."[146] The RAF's "morality," in this rendering, contained a sacrificial logic that *virtually required* murder. RAF members, that is, participated as killers in what they saw as a continuum of death and suffering. Baader had in fact described "hatred" and the "willingness to sacrifice" *(Opferwillen)* as vital attributes of the revolutionary.[147]

For the left-wing scholar Wolfgang Kraushaar, the RAF's killing of Schleyer's driver and his guards crystallized the group's bankruptcy. These murders, which the RAF did not even acknowledge in its communiqués, served the purely practical goal of carrying out the kidnapping. Worse, the RAF implicitly asserted that by virtue of Schleyer's status as a high-ranking economic official, his life was worth more than those of his subordinates. The RAF thus reproduced the class hierarchy that it meant to destroy. In addition, the RAF made Schleyer's life equivalent to the freedom of eleven prisoners and so constructed a crude logic of exchange between human beings—a logic in which the lives of the drivers and guards did not count. In Kraushaar's judgment, with its proposed exchange of Schleyer for the hostages, the RAF exceeded the purported inhumanity of the West German state. By treating the murders as "an a priori breach of any possible exchange," the state categorically refused to buy into the RAF's system of equivalencies.[148]

The left-wing poet Erich Fried criticized the RAF's killings with greater nuance and some ambivalence. Following the murder of Prosecutor Buback, he asked:

> What should I say / about a dead man / who lay in the street? . . . This piece of flesh / was once a father / full of love / This piece of flesh / believed he was doing right / and did wrong / This piece of flesh was a man / who likely would have been a better man / in a better world. . . . What he had done in life / would make my heart grow cold / Should my heart now be warmed / by his death? . . . It would have been better / if such a man / had not died the way he did / It would have been better / if such a man / had not lived the way he did.[149]

With its description of the slain Buback as a "piece of flesh," the poem may appear to participate in the RAF's baleful reduction of human beings to things. But Fried invokes the image only to qualify it in richly human terms: Buback is also a loving father, who set out to do right. The core complaint is not against the man and his sins, but against the world and its sins, by which good men do evil. For Fried, both Buback's death *and* his life are tragic. To disdain the man does not mean to desire or celebrate his death; it means, rather, to disdain the world and to seek to change it.

On one level, these criticisms disclose in the guerrillas a penchant for abstraction that permitted or even encouraged acts of victimization. Despite its professed fidelity to Marxism, the RAF failed to apprehend its society concretely or to develop a credible assessment of either the culpability of its victims or the efficacy of its violence. Instead, the RAF used blunt analytic categories to vilify the state and dehumanize its representatives. On another level, the criticisms stress the guerrillas' tendency to reproduce in themselves the negative qualities they imputed to their enemies and to the structure of their society. According to Marcuse, the RAF failed to embody the vision of new human beings, indulging instead in its own senseless violence. Detecting a parallel between the RAF and a historical variant of fascism, Fetscher charged that the RAF's "attempt to attack capitalism by killing and kidnapping representatives of the economy or political life recalls in a fatal way the pseudo-concreteness of the so-called 'left Nazis.'"[150] To Reiche, the RAF's struggle amounted to the fight of a "terrorist elite against the power elite of the state apparatus," both of which were cut off from "the masses."[151] Kraushaar described the RAF as ultimately another secretive organization that operated in the Federal Republic, like the Federal Police, the CIA, and the KGB.[152]

The central irony that haunted the West German armed struggle groups was that, at times, they mirrored precisely what they claimed to oppose.

In that sense, their ostensibly radical resistance was self-defeating, beyond its failure as a strategy for political change. Taken together, the RAF and the Weathermen reveal the hazards of New Left radicalism, if not of radical resistance in general. The Weathermen partly succumbed to, but mostly guarded against, the danger of "mirroring" qualities they saw in or projected onto their opponents. The experiences of both groups show that the aspiration to resistance provides no guarantee that one represents a genuine alternative to what one opposes. Furthermore, the very aspiration to total resistance—the presumption of the utter difference between oneself and the oppressive other and the desire to destroy that other—may actually obscure the affinities one shares with one's political enemy.

The charge that the guerrillas mirrored their adversaries was not only made by those outside of the armed struggle. In 1978, Mahler and the former RAF member Jürgen Bäcker asserted that just as the left had responded with outrage to the massacre of civilians in Vietnam, so too should it condemn the RAF's killing of hostages and innocent bystanders. Those who perpetrate such acts, they charged, "betray our ideals and themselves."[153] Baumann described his renunciation of violence in the mid 1970s as the choice of "love" over "terror." He concluded from his years in the underground: "For me, the whole time it was a question of creating human values, which didn't exist in capitalism. . . . And you'll be better doing that than bombing society and creating the same rigid figures of hatred at the end."[154]

In the mid 1980s, additional guerrillas in and out of prison broke with the RAF and issued stunning public criticisms of the armed struggle. These so-called *Aussteiger* ("drop-outs," roughly translated) confirmed much of what the RAF's critics had been saying for years. Siegfried Haag was captured in 1976, convicted of conspiracy to commit murder, and sentenced to fifteen years in prison. In 1986, an interviewer asked if he now recognized that terrorism could cause "unending suffering, because the victims also have families, lovers, friends?" Haag replied: "My current thoughts run in that direction. That is: the experience that a violent act can always kill a human being, but that his death lies beyond the mere function that he performs."[155] Baptist Ralf Friedrich went underground in 1977 and was for three years among the RAF's new "hard core." He left the group in 1980 and then lived in East Germany working in a paper factory with his partner and fellow RAF member Sigrid Sternebeck. In a 1990 interview, he conceded that although he had supported the Schleyer action, "Today it is naturally clear to me that one cannot so eas-

ily kill a man, even if he is one's political archenemy." Although he and
Sternebeck "totally rejected" the killing of Schleyer's guards, he confessed
feeling that "Our souls still suffer the consequences"; while not legally
culpable in the murders, he acknowledged a "moral responsibility . . .
for which I'd like to ask forgiveness from those directly affected."[156] In
1985, Klaus Jünschke, convicted of murder in 1977, led several prisoners in announcing their total separation from the armed struggle. Reflecting on the path of violence, he declared, "Today it is clear that this entire history is destructive, debilitating, that it destroys not only the lives
of those who are engaged in the struggle, but also of those without guilt,
that it deforms society, which should be changed to create more freedom
and less suffering."[157]

.   .   .

They wanted parents without guilt so that they could
be children without shame.

> Jörg Bopp, "Die ungekonnte Aggresion"
> ("The Unacknowledged Aggression")

West Germany was hardly unique among Western societies in having an
insurgent youth movement develop in the 1960s. Nor was it unique in
having an armed struggle movement emerge from the student and youth
protests; in addition to those in Italy and Spain, where violence raged, small
guerrilla groups formed in France, England, Belgium, and the Netherlands.[158] The West German conflict did, however, have a special intensity,
owing both to the peculiarities of German history and to the ways in which
various groups represented and responded to those peculiarities.

The RAF radicalized the tendency of the West German New Left to
see in its society signs of the persistence of fascism. Although it was far
from being a unified and rigorously argued thesis, the *Fascismusvorwurf,*
or "charge of fascism," could express everything from Frankfurt School–
inflected descriptions of late capitalism as a repressive totality to the view,
revived from communist doctrine of the prewar years, of social democracy as a form of "social fascism"; to the denunciation of the Vietnam
War as "genocidal"; to complaints that police violence was "neofascist."
Young Germans even described the conservative sexual morality of their
parents' generation as "fascist." Believing that sexual repression was a
chief cause of the Nazis' aggression, they promoted sexual liberation as
intrinsically antifascist.[159]

Like other groups in the New Left, the RAF used the charge of fascism as a highly emotional language of condemnation announcing the need for greater militancy. References to fascism abounded in its statements. A communiqué from the 1972 "May Offensive" denounced the "*SS-praxis*" of the West German police.[160] That issued with the bombing of the U.S. military base in Heidelberg claimed that the German people supported the action "because they have not forgotten Auschwitz, Dresden, and Hamburg."[161] The RAF likened the failure to clear the Springer building before its bomb went off to the burning of the Reichstag in 1933, thereby suggesting that both were designed to promote social chaos conducive to an assertion of power by the far right.[162] At times, the RAF explicitly equated imperialism with fascism. In a 1972 statement, Meinhof insisted that "National Socialism was only the political and military precursor to the imperialist system of multinational corporations."[163]

In the mid 1970s, the RAF sharpened its comparisons of the West German state to the Nazi regime. Most provocatively, the RAF likened the treatment of its prisoners to the Nazis' extermination policies. In 1973, Meinhof commented that "the political conception of the dead section at Cologne [prison] . . . is the gas chamber. . . . My ideas of Auschwitz became very clear in there."[164] Baader went so far as to charge that the treatment of RAF prisoners was more brutal than the tactics used by the Gestapo.[165] Finally, guerrillas made reference to fascism in describing their victims, for instance, seeing von Drenkmann and Schleyer—both of whom had served under the Nazis and then rose to positions of prominence in the new Germany—as personifications of fascist continuity.

In its mind, the RAF was fighting a new behemoth that bore traces of the old. Its expansive understanding of fascism linked the crimes of the German past with the conduct of the current government of the Federal Republic and the imperialism of the United States in a chain of more or less equivalent evils. To attack any of these was simultaneously to attack all of them. Much as the RAF thought it could attack capitalism by killing capitalism's representatives, it felt that it could sever the perceived continuity with the Nazi past by killing what it saw as the symbols of that continuity. When conceived of as a form of antifascism, RAF's killings were not only just, but heroic.

In equating the current state with the Nazi Reich, the RAF simultaneously did battle with the present and the past. Behind this conflation of contexts lay a psychological motive stemming from the burden of the past experienced by Germany's postwar generation. Illuminating the psychohistorical dimension of the RAF's violence requires probing more deeply

into the intergenerational conflicts of the 1960s and the broader psychopolitical landscape of postwar Germany.

Historians generally concur that postwar Germany avoided systematically confronting its fascist past. Germans in the Western zones, standard
narratives run, invested immense energy in rebuilding their country and
in establishing West Germany as a bulwark against communism. These
commitments, which served the imperatives of the present, encouraged
the evasion of the past. Moreover, Germans tended to view themselves
as among the war's victims, either of the avenging armies of the Allied
powers (especially the USSR), or of Nazi demagogues, or both. Summing
up the postwar mood, one historian wrote, "Like burned children, the
majority turned their backs on an active political engagement after their
stint with National Socialism. Instead of confronting the 'most recent
past,' as the twelve years of Nazi rule were commonly referred to, the
Federal Republic was happy to settle into a general amnesia about this
time and especially about the Holocaust."[166] The past, in short, necessarily remained "unmastered" because it had never been seriously engaged
as a problem.[167]

The psychologists Alexander and Margarete Mitscherlich, writing in
the late 1960s, were among the first to address the issue of German denial. According to the Mitscherlichs, postwar Germans exhibited a striking "inability to mourn" both the victims of Nazi Germany and the collapse of the Reich. At the heart of this inability lay the refusal to accept
the loss of National Socialism as a collective fantasy that had given its
followers a special sense of power and purpose. To the Mitscherlichs,
the identification of Germans with Hitler had been so intense that accepting his defeat and the demise of National Socialism threatened their
identity in a radical way. Unable or unwilling to face this traumatic self-
devaluation, Germans denied the past outright or adopted the attitude
that "bygones are bygones without occasion for remorse."[168] Should Germans continue to repress the past, the Mitscherlichs warned, National
Socialist ideals might persist "within the unconscious."[169]

Years later, the American scholar Eric Santner redeployed the Mitscherlichs' thesis in tracing the impact of the past on what he described as the
psychopathologies of the postwar (West) German family.[170] Santner asserted that the postwar generations had inherited the denial and repression of the past from their parents. Unlike the latter, however, they were
conscious of and consciously troubled by that denial. As a result, they
experienced qualities of melancholy and depression that their parents had
avoided. In addition, because of their compromised pasts, the parents

were not available to their children as totemic resources for the positive constitution of identity. Yet the parents remained indispensable to the process of identity formation. The postwar generations therefore suffered "the double-bind of having to identify with figures of power one also at another level needs to disavow."[171] More broadly, they faced the challenge of developing a sense of identity as *Germans* in a context in which the "cultural reservoir" of national symbols and associations had been "poisoned" and provoked "traumatic ambivalence."[172]

Testimonies by Germans born during or shortly after the Nazi era relate feelings of disappointment, demoralization, and disgust consistent with Santner's model. An especially poignant—and strikingly relevant—recollection reads:

> I am as German as the members of the Baader-Meinhof gang. I belong to their age. We were ashamed of our country. We were told what happened—the marching—the books . . . the people we loved being driven out—Albert Einstein, Thomas Mann. . . . Other people we had never heard of—those nameless millions who so silently went to the camps where their voices were gassed forever silent. This was no country to be proud of. We were also pained, lonesome kids amid adults who could not, must not ever be trusted. How could I trust my parent who, balancing me on their knees, sang "Deutschland, Deutschland, Über alles" with me? Who would make me call after a man in the street, a man I didn't even know, "Jew! Jew!" Who with my father—once a high-ranking officer—would tell me they'd never heard of any camps. And who, when I asked him about the 6 million Jews that had been put to death, insisted that it was 4.5 million—the figure I had quoted, he said, had been made up by the notoriously deceitful Jewish media—4.5 while my heart was counting—one and one and one . . .[173]

Santner, while capturing the agony of the postwar family, obscures the efforts of New Leftists to shatter their parents' silence and force the issue of the past into public consciousness. Young radicals indeed used their parents not as role models but as *negative* icons, from whom one must at all costs differentiate oneself. That desire was acutely felt by those who eventually adopted or endorsed violence. Mahler, who grew up in the early 1950s, confessed that the Nazi past dictated that from an early age, he had to feel "ashamed of being German." He explained: "The essential, highly personalized problem was this: how did your parents behave [during the Nazi period]. The question also had implications for us, namely, that whenever events occur that even in a distant way recall the twelve years [of Nazi rule], we must actively resist them."[174] As Baader's lawyer, he described the 1968 Frankfurt department store arson as a protest, not only against German silence on the Vietnam War, but also against an entire generation that had tolerated the crimes of the Nazi period.[175] Berward Vesper, the son of a mildly famous "Blood and Soil" poet who had extolled National Socialism, defended the arson by declaring that "Vietnam is the Auschwitz of our generation."[176] The Red Cells member Hans-Joachim Klein derisively described the Germans as "specialists when it came to genocide." To him, they "should have been the first to start shouting about Vietnam. All the Germans, not merely a few leftists. They did nothing. Arguing didn't move them, pamphlets didn't convince them, they got used to broken windows. . . . So there came a point . . . when something new had to be found."[177]

The nexus of the fascist past, intergenerational conflict, and New Left protest can be pressed further to help understand the political violence of the 1960s and 1970s. In the mid 1980s, the psychologist Jörg Bopp sought to explain why West German New Leftists turned on their elders and leveled the charge of fascist continuity with such vehemence. His intriguing analysis reveals in the New Left a thicket of competing aspirations, rife with consequences it did not intend.

Bopp identified in German New Leftists a foundational desire to "prove to themselves and to the world that they had overcome the failure of their parents."[178] They served this desire by sharply reacting against anything they saw as recalling fascism. Yet Bopp contends that behind New Leftists' revulsion at Nazism and their parents' involvement in it lay a disquieting fear that they had nonetheless internalized elements of their parents' experience. Opposition to "fascist continuity" only exacerbated this fear. According to Bopp, New Leftists experienced their radical protest as a liberation from social taboos and internal restraints. Though exhilarating, militant action produced in them a second, largely unconscious fear that they would not be able to control their newly unleashed aggression; with this aggression they compounded the risk of reproducing the violence that they saw as defining both their parents' past and the current order.

New Leftists dealt with this fear by strengthening in their rhetoric the distinction between themselves and their adversaries. That entailed ratcheting up the *Fascismusvorwurf*, with self-defeating consequences. First, as New Leftists denounced their opponents in even stronger terms, they escalated the intensity—and the violence—of their protests. This escalation only augmented their fear of taking on objectionable attributes of their enemies, resulting in another increase in the severity of their accusatory rhetoric. The effort to gain distance from the failures of the past thus turned against itself in a closed and vicious circle. Second, New Leftists made increasingly reckless comparisons of the past and present. To Bopp, by "slapping the label of fascism on any contemporary phenomenon to which they objected, they robbed fascism . . . of its historical meaning" and "veiled . . . the suffering of its countless victims." By indicting their parents' current failures through reference to the past, New Leftists actually minimized the importance of that past.

According to Bopp, this dynamic had its own psychological motive. Bopp discerned in New Leftists a second desire that competed with their need to differentiate themselves from their parents. To Bopp, "they wanted parents without guilt so they could be children without shame." Here he echoes Santner's notion of the double bind wherein members of the postwar generation had the dual need to disidentify with *and* to affirm their parents.[179] Bopp argues that New Leftists' condemnation of the current political failures of their parents thus went hand in hand with their covert wish to absolve their parents of complicity with Nazism. The *Faschismusvorwurf*, by extension, complemented their parents' desire to deny or avoid confrontation with the past.

Bopp certainly paints with a broad brush. He ascribes universally held desires to West Germany's postwar generation and suggests implausibly that all New Leftists made irresponsible comparisons between the present and the past. He also betrays little appreciation of how infuriating it may have been for young Germans to see their parents endorse a war of mass destruction in Vietnam, or of how militant opposition to the war may have represented a valid response to the Nazi legacy. Nonetheless, he exposes clear abuses of antifascist rhetoric by at least some activists, while providing a compelling complement to analyses of the psychopolitical currents of America's New Left.

The RAF's armed struggle, as an extreme form of "antifascism," deepened the ironies and contradictions experienced by the West German New Left as a whole. If the New Left sought to avoid repetition of the failures of the past, the RAF sought more aggressively to correct for and even redeem those failures. The RAF implicitly held that armed struggle against forces it deemed fascist would make up·for the near-total absence of armed resistance by Germans to the Nazis. Within this compensatory logic, the RAF placed its victims in the roles of Nazi perpetrators. The RAF gave itself a dual image. In one guise, its members were figures of redemption, whose violence would not only relieve *them* of the burden of the past, but also break the larger chain of German guilt. They would prove, in their refusal to be "good Germans," that *Germany* had over-

come the failures of the past, insofar as at least a subset of Germans coura-
geously responded to an enduring moral imperative to resist oppressive
power. The RAF's armed struggle, in this light, appears a convoluted attempt to purify the nation as a whole. Its effort entailed, or even demanded, violence, rendering it also a psychologically complex form of
blood sacrifice. In a second guise, the RAF assumed the role of the Nazis'
victims. This elision was evident in the false equation of Stammheim with
Auschwitz, of the abuse in prison of a few dozen ideological rebels with
genocide. Jews and the other victims of Nazism thus functioned as the
"absent others," whom the RAF claimed as the ultimate source of the
legitimacy of its actions. With this misguided empathy, the RAF appro-
priated and even exploited the suffering of the victims of Nazism it meant
to honor.

In both of these guises, the RAF and other violent German groups mirrored qualities they opposed not only in the German present but also in
the German past. The danger of assuming the likeness of one's enemy—
a danger hovering over all rebel movements—was far greater for German guerrillas than for their American counterparts, whose protest lacked
this historical dimension. As agents of redemptive violence, German guerrillas engaged in acts striking for their cruelty. Cruelty and the demonization of the enemy are hardly specific to Nazism; to describe the RAF
as "Hitler's children" is to invert RAF's "antifascist" discourse in another reductive comparison. A better understanding comes by way of
Santner's assertion that the postwar generations "inherited the psychic
structures that impeded mourning in the generations of their parents and
grandparents. Foremost among such structures is a thinking in rigid binary oppositions which forms the socio-psychological basis of all search
for scapegoats."[180] This inheritance took place despite New Leftists'
strenuous efforts to avoid the repression and repetition of the past. No
direct lineage, therefore, runs from Hitler to the RAF. Rather, the RAF
unselfconsciously repeated tendencies in the past, largely as a result of
its efforts to confront and atone for that past.

At times, the repetition was transparent. The West German armed
struggle is punctuated by chilling evocations, beyond generic brutality,
of the Nazis' own aggression. These include the fire-bombing by German leftists in 1969 of a Berlin synagogue on the anniversary of Kristall-
nacht in protest of Israeli policies; Meinhof's exultation in the massacre
by Palestinian commandos of Israeli athletes in the 1972 Munich
Olympics; and the separation of Jewish from non-Jewish hostages for

the purpose of execution by the Palestinian and German Red Cells hi-jackers of a French airliner in 1976 (the hijacking ended when Israeli paratroopers raided the plane in Entebbe, Uganda, with the raid's com-mander, three hostages, all seven hijackers, and twenty Ugandan sol-diers losing their lives).[181]

Palestinian hostility to Israel—however one may judge it—is connected to historically grounded political grievances. It is, therefore, one thing for Palestinians to engage in acts of "aggression," "terror," or "war" against Israel and Israeli citizens in what they see as a struggle for na-tional liberation; it is quite another for young German leftists, separated from the Holocaust by only a generation, to rally enthusiastically behind and even participate in such acts. In instances, Germans explicitly pre-sented Israeli Jews as modern-day Nazis. Such rhetoric, which perverts the relationship between German fascism and its Jewish victims, was es-pecially virulent and disturbing when it accompanied acts of violence. An anonymous flyer issued with the 1969 synagogue bombing followed common criticisms of Israeli treatment of Palestinians with rhetoric de-nouncing Israel's "fascist acts of horror against the Palestinian Arabs" and use of "Gestapo torture methods." After charging that "the Crystal Night of 1938 is repeated daily by the Zionists," it concluded, "The Jews who were displaced by fascism have themselves become fascists who want to eradicate the Palestinian people in collaboration with Amerikan capi-tal."[182] Though less extreme, Meinhof's statement in praise of the Pales-tinian "Black September" commandos presented the Munich Olympics killings as the cutting edge of anti-imperialism—one whose antifascist character was only *enhanced* by taking place in West Germany (fascist then, fascist now, was her claim).[183]

Troubling from anyone, such assertions are morally blind when com-ing from young Germans. Desperate to distinguish themselves from their parents' generation, New Leftists only narrowed that distance by en-gaging in or applauding acts that were transparently anti-Semitic. This tragic irony was not lost on some guerrillas. Klein, who left the Red Cells in 1977, characterized his withdrawal from the underground as a "re-turn to humanity." When he left the group, he publicized, and hence foiled, a plot by Red Cells and Palestinian commandos to assassinate lead-ers of the resurgent Jewish communities of Frankfurt and Berlin. The abuse of Jews in the 1976 hijacking was decisive in his renunciation of guerrilla violence. For Klein, the action was "Auschwitz" all over again, "barbarity pure and simple."[184]

.   .   .

In a world of so much real suffering, why promote
unnecessary suffering?

Silke Maier-Witt

More personalized condemnation of the armed struggle came from Silke
Maier-Witt, a former RAF member, who combines political and moral
judgment with a psychoanalytic language of repetition and "acting out."
The anger of many West German New Leftists was directed at the *generation* of their parents, not at their parents as such. This was conspicuously true of RAF's leaders. Ulrike Meinhof's foster mother was herself
a left-wing activist. Gudrun Ensslin's parents had opposed the Nazis and
supported their daughter's involvement in the student movement. And
Baader's mother, though rather apolitical, stood by her son while he was
in prison. The RAF's leaders, in short, lacked the *personal* enmity toward their parents so characteristic of the German New Left. Such was
not the case with Silke Maier-Witt. When she was twelve years old, she
discovered in the attic of her house memorabilia indicating that her father had been a member of the SS—a fact that he had concealed from
her. Unaware at the time of the implications of her discovery, she asked
him about it only several years later. As if in a parody of the postwar
family—plagued by distrust and silence—his answers were evasive,
prompting her to refuse to talk to him for two months.

In 1969, Maier-Witt attended the University of Hamburg, where she
studied psychology and became immersed in student protest. Like so many
others among RAF's "second generation," she was drawn to the group
through work in support of the prisoners. By 1977, she was part of the
RAF's "second tier," working in Amsterdam to secure cars, weapons, and
safe houses. Called back to West Germany, she helped in the planning of
Schleyer's kidnapping. In 1979, she trained with Palestinians in Yemen,
where she observed: "They were willing to fight for their people. For us,
it was more like an intellectual effort. It was sheer group dynamic that
kept us going. We were like robots."[185] Overwhelmed with stress and fearing that in West Germany she would go to jail "for nothing, for accom-
plishing nothing," she was sent by the RAF to East Germany, where with
assistance from the East German authorities, she assumed a new identity
and tried to live a life of quiet anonymity. Captured in 1990, she was tried
for her involvement in the Schleyer kidnapping and sentenced to ten years
in prison, of which she served five.

Prison proved cathartic. Reflecting there on her time in RAF, she concluded,

> If you refuse to have a good look at who you are, you'll always repeat your actions, over and over. . . . To come to terms with my past, I've asked myself why I neglected my own moral standards even as I was envisioning social change. I learned how easy it is to listen to some ideology and to have an idea that gives you an excuse for anything. In trying not to be like my father, I ended up being even more like him. Terrorism is close to Nazism. I used ideology to legitimize myself, the same as he did. Creating change requires courage, which I didn't have. That's why I ended up in the RAF.[186]

Not all former RAF members report having such intensely negative experiences, nor would most so seamlessly equate their struggle with what they struggled against. Maier-Witt's commentary is nonetheless poignant as a set of insights into the degradation of her politics. In ethical terms, she attests to the dangers of ideology as a blanket endorsement for action, no matter how extreme. In psychological terms, she affirms how a strategy of disavowal may lead to the compulsive repetition of what one formally disavows. True courage, she concludes, is a function of self-reflection, self-awareness, and restraint—not to be confused with the dilution of one's commitment to justice. As if to make her bitter experience of some use to others, she returned to the field of psychology and then counseled the traumatized victims of war in Kosovo. In the conflicts of the former Yugoslavia, driven partly by crazed fantasies of conquest and collective redemption, she perceives echoes of the RAF's failed idealism. Witness again to its wreckage, she pleads, "In a world of so much real suffering, why promote unnecessary suffering?"[187]

CHAPTER 6

"Democratic Intolerance"

The Red Army Faction and the West German State

For the government of the Federal Republic, the RAF was an intolerable threat and had to be eliminated at all costs. This entailed laws that made support for terrorist organizations illegal and that prohibited speech thought to encourage violence; mobilization of great numbers of police; surveillance on a vast scale; harsh treatment of those suspected or convicted of violent acts; and restrictions on the RAF's legal defense. These measures and the fierce antiterrorist rhetoric of politicians and the media created a climate of intense suspicion of dissidents in West Germany in the 1970s. What people remember about the era is typically not only the pervasive fear of terrorist violence but also the tremendous constriction of thought and feeling caused by heightened demands for loyalty to the state, enforced, in part, by repression.

From a practical standpoint, the antiterrorist measures both succeeded and failed. Police captured the RAF's founders relatively quickly, putting an end to an initial wave of violence. Those remaining in or joining the underground had to devote a large share of their energy simply to avoiding arrest. The state's antiterrorist campaign, in short, limited the scope of the RAF's violence. Yet attempts to eliminate terrorism also helped to bring about new rounds of violence. Virtually all the major acts of left-wing violence in the mid 1970s sought the release of prisoners or revenge against judges, prosecutors, and police. Had the state's reaction been less severe, the RAF's armed struggle might neither have endured so long nor become so brutal.

Criticism of the government was not confined to the far left. German jurists, politicians, intellectuals, and civil libertarians questioned the legitimacy of the antiterrorism laws and denounced the mentality that had produced them. Such laws and the treatment of prisoners also attracted the concern of international human rights organizations, to whom the RAF broadcast allegations of abuse. In 1974, the French writer and philosopher Jean-Paul Sartre, responding to a request by the RAF, interviewed Andreas Baader in Stammheim prison about conditions there. International committees investigated the death of Ulrike Meinhof. And for years Amnesty International included a section on the treatment of RAF prisoners in its annual report documenting violations of human rights throughout the world. Though international bodies often absolved the government of explicit wrongdoing, the state's response to terrorism fed an international image of the *häßlichen Deutschen* ("ugly Germans"), in whom authoritarian tendencies had persisted.

Why did the state react so forcefully and at such great cost, given the RAF's small size and limited capabilities?[1] Perceptions counted for more than whatever "real" danger left-wing violence posed. Like the RAF itself, the government was greatly influenced by Germany's past. Memories of the collapse of the Weimar Republic and the rise of Nazism led the founders of the Federal Republic to believe that if it were to survive, the new democracy had to be aggressively intolerant of those who threatened it. Two decades later, the republic's leaders regarded the RAF as just such an enemy, reminiscent of the fascist groups that had helped destroy the Weimar Republic. Defeating terrorism was so important because it spoke so powerfully to the raison d'être and self-image of the postwar West German state.

The government's more extreme antiterrorist measures nonetheless violated democratic rights beyond what could be justified in the name of defending democracy. Some critics charged that it used the need for security and the example of the past to legitimize assertions of power unconnected to democratic ends; at its worst, they charged, the state itself became an agent of terror.

.   .   .

Without you, the assassins would be helpless.
Willy Brandt

With the first wave of armed actions in the early 1970s, the West German authorities determined that simply punishing individuals after the fact for specific acts of violence was an inadequate approach to combating terrorism. Terrorists, they reasoned, operate conspiratorially and rely for their existence on layers of tactical, material, and ideological support. To contain and eliminate terrorism, each layer had to be criminalized and incapacitated. Sections 129 and 129a of the Criminal Code—the strongest weapons in the legal arsenal against the RAF—provided mechanisms for doing so.

Section 129 outlawed forming *(gründen)*, being a member of *(als Mitglied beteiligen)*, promoting *(werben)*, or supporting *(unterstützen)* a "criminal association." Section 129a, which went into effect in October 1976, superseded section 129 by punishing the same actions with respect to "terrorist associations," distinguished by the serious nature of their alleged crimes, such as murder and attempted murder. Under sections 129 and 129a, not only individuals who allegedly committed or conspired to commit acts of violence were prosecutable. Alleged supporters could also be punished, *irrespective of their actual knowledge of or involvement in acts of violence.* In one scholar's characterization, section 129a "permits the police to arrest individuals in the absence of any suspicion of any criminal activity."[2] Going beyond guilt by association, sections 129 and 129a established mere support for an association as the standard for culpability. Punishments could be severe. Sentences under section 129 ranged from six months' to five years' imprisonment; section 129a increased the maximum penalty for "ringleaders" *(Rädelsführern)* and "chief instigators" *(Hintermännern)* to ten years.[3] By the end of 1974, some 200 people had been arrested on suspicion of having aided the RAF.[4]

What constituted "support" for and "promotion" of a criminal or terrorist group was hotly debated. Prosecutors and judges interpreted the laws broadly. A 1978 ruling that codified applications of the law up to that point held that "promotion" meant not only the recruitment of new members but also the "strengthening of the association . . . by means of propaganda."[5] The RAF's lawyers were indicted under sections 129 and 129a for facilitating a communication system for their imprisoned clients and for supporting the RAF's hunger strikes. Prosecutors charged booksellers with supporting the terrorist groups whose texts they sold. People were even charged under the law for acts seemingly as harmless as writing pro-RAF graffiti on subway cars or distributing leaflets.[6] In one case, a demonstrator had passed out a flyer with the demand to "Unite All RAF Prisoners," dispersed at the time in prisons throughout Germany. The defendant claimed that he was merely advocating a change in state policy toward the prisoners. The judge held, however, that because the flyer used a well-known RAF slogan, it was a *criminal* expression of support for the group.[7]

The importance of sections 129 and 129a went far beyond the laws' actual use in the battle against left-wing violence. In addition to actual members of the underground, the laws targeted an archetypal, commonly denounced, and nearly mythic figure in West German antiterrorist rhetoric: the *Sympathisant,* or "sympathizer." The "sympathizers" were an imprecise category of alleged helpers and fellow travelers whom security forces, politicians, and the media considered an integral part of the terrorist threat. More an ideological construct than a description of an actual group, the notion of the sympathizer went to the heart of German anxieties about violence. Sympathizers were blamed for making terrorism possible by aiding those underground. That assistance could be tactical, in the form of safe houses, money, and weapons. Shortly after the arrest of Baader in June 1972, Interior Minister Hans-Dietrich Genscher insisted that RAF "cannot exist without sympathizers, as the group itself says: the sympathizers are the water in which the guerrillas swim. They must not have this water."[8] But assistance to the terrorists could also be ideological, conveyed through support for their methods, affirmation of their broad goals, or even simple agreement with aspects of their worldview. In this capacity, the sympathizers were thought to confer legitimacy on the terrorists and serve as a receptive audience for their acts. A cartoon in *Der Spiegel,* used to head a series on the *Sympathisanten* in 1977, gave graphic expression to this image of terrorism's supporters. In the cartoon, a black-clad, gun-toting figure with the word "Terror" on his chest traverses an abyss on a footbridge; over him hovers a white angel labeled "Sympathizers."[9]

By the same token, fixation on the sympathizers all but confirmed that the literal threat to the nation's security posed by the handful of practicing terrorists was in itself small. The true danger was that the cancer of antistate violence would spread, first to those within the RAF's immediate orbit, and then more broadly throughout German society. The amorphous ranks of the sympathizers constituted the front line, where the battle against terrorism would ultimately be won or lost. There is a sense, finally, in which the sympathizers' main offense lay simply in existing. Like the terrorists themselves, the sympathizers had, in the description of their accusers, neither fully assimilated democratic values nor been properly integrated into the norms of the postwar state. The sympathizer was thus an internal other, a shadowy expression of the failure of the West German state to command the basic allegiance of its citizens and complete the desired evolution toward democracy.

Preoccupation with, if not outright contempt for, the *Sympathisanten* spanned the political spectrum. Shortly after Schleyer's kidnapping in 1977, Willy Brandt, the great SPD reform chancellor of the late 1960s, admonished the sympathizers:

> You are, it seems to me, even more responsible for the atrocities than the fanatics who pull the trigger of their automatic weapons. Why is that so?
> Without you, the assassins would be helpless. You furnish the stage set on which murderers appear as heroes. . . . You provide the sustenance, equipment, and shelter without which the terrorists would have to abandon their absurd and bloody dreams of a civil war. . . . What kind of people are you? You, who claim to be politically aware, don't realize that you are doing the bidding of the darkest forces of reaction— yes, of the neo-Nazis—rather than creating more freedom, [and] pushing public opinion over the edge, beyond which there is only the abyss of chaos, a police state, or a dictatorship. Or is that what you really want?

After appealing to Germany's youth to use its "critical intelligence" to reject, rather than promote, violence, he concluded: "To those directly aiding and abetting terrorism, I say again: Stop every form of assistance— before it is too late. Otherwise our country will become a living hell, where father mistrusts son, where neighbor suspects neighbor, where the state spies on its citizens, and where assassination and deadly violence rule the streets. Help us avert this nightmare. . . . If you refuse, the nightmare may become reality."[10] In Brandt's construction, the sympathizers were so pivotal precisely because they, unlike active terrorists, were not *fully* immune to appeals to reason; their capacity for choice enhanced both their current guilt and the importance of their future actions. In their hands lay not only the direction of the terrorist conflict but also, remarkably, the fate of West German society. Brandt's status as a liberal Social Democrat with an antifascist background seemed less to limit than to shape his anger. For him, the sympathizers were so dangerous not because they were themselves reactionaries, as the foes of terrorism routinely charged, but because they threatened to unleash the forces of right-wing reaction. As with so many things in postwar Germany, this image of a nightmarish future summoned memories of the catastrophic past. Brandt envisioned a disaster to rival Weimar's tortured demise, and even the Nazis' reign of terror, if left-wing violence escalated.

This intense concern with terrorism's alleged supporters had far-reaching consequences. First and foremost, it dictated that police cast their net of suspicion widely. The security forces paid closest attention to those groups considered most likely to produce new terrorists and their helpers: students, intellectuals, and disaffected youths. More generally, focus on the *Sympathisanten* created a climate of suspicion and accusation. Intellectuals were prime targets. In mid December 1974, a CDU official demanded that all Germans distance themselves both from terrorism and from "the writer Heinrich Böll, who a few months ago under the pseudonym Katharina Blüm wrote a book justifying violence."[11] The media and the public, fully much as representatives of the state, fed this climate. Later in December, the moderator of a popular current affairs program declared on German television that "[t]he sympathisers with this left-wing fascism, the Bölls and Brückners, and all the other intellectuals, are not one bit better than the intellectuals who led the way for the Nazis."[12] After visiting in 1974 with the prisoner Ulrike Meinhof to plead that she abandon her hunger strike, Berlin's Bishop Kurt Scharf earned the label the "Baader-Meinhof-Bischof." The pastor Helmut Gollwitzer who, like Böll, denounced the RAF but criticized the violence of the state, was also condemned by the media as a "sympathizer." The theorists of the Frankfurt School, so influential on the student movement, came under similar suspicion, even though they disclaimed the violence of left-wing radicals.[13]

At times, the entire discourse had a runaway, even absurd quality. Television's "ZDF Magazine" denounced a Stuttgart theater director as a "sympathizer" for collecting money to pay for Gudrun Ensslin's dental work while she was in prison.[14] (His actions prompted local police to call for a boycott of his productions.) Bernhard Vogel, the CDU *Ministerpräsident* of Nordrhein-Westfalen, commented that a sympathizer "could be anyone who says Baader-Meinhof group [*Gruppe*], instead of Baader-Meinhof gang [*Bande*]."[15] (Since the RAF's inception, some felt that the use of the term "group" granted it political legitimacy, whereas "gang" properly defined it as criminal.) Even mainstream voices asked just where the frenzy of accusation might stop. Responding at the height of the terrorist crisis in 1977 to a CDU statement that "[t]he sympathizer is an accomplice . . . no better than the murderer," *Der Spiegel* asked, "If that were so, then how many [sympathizers] are there: 1,000–1,500 active helpers, as the BKA sees it, or 5,000 potential supporters? Thousands of university students who privately cheer terrorist acts? Perhaps tens of thousands, who sympathize not with the acts but with the motivations for them? Or still more? . . . Are sympathizers all those who protest against putative isolation torture and fare card increases today, for freedom in Chile, and tomorrow against God knows what?"[16] The magazine concluded that "the spongy idea" of the sympathizer had become little more than a "rhetorical weapon [*Sprachknüppel*]" in a primitive war of words.[17] In the face of state and public hostility, some citizens worried that dissident views—be they affinity with the RAF's grievances or goals, criticism of the antiterrorist response, or actual sympathy for the plight of RAF fugitives or prisoners—rendered them enemies of the state, subject to prosecution. Critics of sections 129 and 129a argued that the laws made punishable virtually any form of contact with members of organizations designated as "criminal" or "terrorist" and potentially criminalized all political speech deemed threatening or even merely offensive to the state.

Police conduct seemed at times to bear out the allegation that ostensible security measures sought in truth to harass, intimidate, and abuse dissidents. On March 5, 1975, shortly after the J2M released its kidnap victim Peter Lorenz, police raided more than fifty dwellings of Berlin leftists, notably the houses of the "youth collectives" so popular among young radicals. In some of the raids, the police entered violently in the early morning hours, failed to show warrants, pointed machine guns at the frightened residents (some of whom were made to lie naked on the floor), and destroyed windows, doors (even when unlocked), radios, and other property. They made nearly 180 arrests but failed to turn up any evidence that the houses' inhabitants had any connection at all to the kidnapping. Members of the Thomas-Wießbecker-Haus, named after a Berlin anarchist killed by police, dismissed the police's claim of reasonable suspicion that Lorenz had been held there by his kidnappers; the house, its members pointed out, had been under constant surveillance since the moment of his capture. Seeing similarities with the fascist past, they asserted that "whoever invoked his legally guaranteed rights would be forced against the wall by a machine gun. Who is not reminded by this of the methods of the GESTAPO during the Nazi period?"[18] A young father, detained without explanation for sixteen hours following a raid on his house, drew a subtler comparison to Nazi tactics. Noting that police targeted "politically known" residents, he protested that "the arrests smack of the establishment of a camp for political undesirables."[19] Even a representative of the centrist Federal Democratic Party in the Bundestag warned of "fascist tendencies" as she assessed the raids.[20]

The state also used the weapon of censorship against terrorism's alleged sympathizers. On November 24, 1975, police raided offices and private homes in Munich connected to the publisher Trikont-Verlag to seize literature thought to promote terrorism. The chief object of the raids was "Bommi" Baumann's newly published memoir *Wie alles anfing*. Police also seized copies of a manifesto of the Socialist Patients Collective and of a booklet published by the French group Gauche Prolétarienne, each of which had been available in Germany for several years. More than 1,600 books were confiscated, as were Trikont-Verlag's business records and the printing plates for Baumann's text.[21]

Prosecutors justified the action under section 140 of the Criminal Code, which banned expressions of approval of criminal offenses, and section 131, which punished those who produced, disseminated, or possessed texts that "glorified" *(verherrlichen)* violence of a "gruesome" or "inhuman form." The raids set the stage for the passage of amendments to the Criminal Code designed specifically to ban literature supporting left-wing violence. Section 188a, which went into effect in April 1976, created penalties of up to three years' imprisonment for "anyone who disseminates, publicly issues . . . produces, owns, offers, stocks, announces, praises, or attempts to import or export" a text supporting or encouraging others to commit specified crimes or acts threatening "the existence or safety of the Federal Republic." Section 130a did the same for texts "instructing in the commission of criminal offenses."[22]

The raids on publishers and the new censorship legislation met with widespread and vehement objections. Prominent West German writers, artists, and publishers denounced these measures as assaults on freedom of expression. "What happened yesterday to Trikont-Verlag can happen tomorrow in any theater," warned Volker Schlöndorf, the director of the acclaimed film adaptation of Böll's novel *The Lost Honor of Katharina Blum*.[23] The defenders of the besieged publisher were particularly indignant that the state would think that Baumann's book glorified violence. A textured and deeply honest work, *Wie alles anfing* chronicles Baumann's transformation from a rebellious working-class youth into a leading member of West Berlin's anarchist scene and then its violent underground. Baumann also, however, describes his exit from a life of violence and his eventual renunciation of the "armed struggle." Even before the Lorenz kidnapping and the von Drenkmann murder, Baumann had pleaded in *Der Spiegel*, "Comrades, throw away the gun."[24] As evidence of Baumann's enduring support for violence, prosecutors cited such passages from *Wie alles anfing* as: "I still stand behind all the things

I have done . . . . Even the worst experiences were right in their time, because otherwise, it wouldn't have come to this point. That was your road, and you had to walk it."[25] Seemingly oblivious both to existential subtleties and Baumann's ultimate message, they saw the book as only a threat.

Böll commented that "the worst thing one can do is to ban" Baumann's book.[26] On the contrary, he felt that it should be *recommended* to youths, parents, clergy, and police to help them understand not only the social origins and appeal of violence but also its tremendous hazards. In repressing the work, the state seemed to assert that merely to discuss political violence was to promote it, and that to promote it was a crime. Who was doing the discussing was crucial in determining the tactics of prosecutors. On the day of the raid on Trikont-Verlag, excerpts from Baumann's "criminal" book appeared in *Der Spiegel*, which naturally went unpunished.

The new censorship laws intensified the charge that the state sought to criminalize the left by outlawing the ideas it devoured, debated, and even rejected. In August 1976, in the very first application of section 88a, police raided eight bookstores, seizing copies of the Revolutionary Cells' newspaper and other "terrorist" texts. The head of the Union of Political Bookstores in Bochum and Essen was arrested for violation of both the new law and section 129a. Colleagues rallying in his defense warned that "virtually all left-wing groups and projects can be criminalized under section 88a, because it can punish discussions of everything from defensive violence, to building-site occupations, to guerrilla actions."[27] In 1977–79, four members of the Agit-Druck press, a radical print collective that produced an array of left-wing literature, were successfully prosecuted under sections 88a and 129a for printing the newspaper *Info-BUG (Info-Berliner undogmatischen Gruppen)*. The paper, long an object of the right's ire, contained writings by guerrilla groups and debates on violence generally. The verdict held that the accused necessarily identified with the proguerrilla writings because they were aware of their content; Agit-Druck insisted that it sought only to promote dialogue on the left about violence, which should in no way be equated with support for terrorism.[28] The middle-aged publicist Walter Jens observed while testifying for the defense as an expert witness that "[t]he courthouse in Moabit [Berlin], a dreary place from a forgotten time, looks like a fortress. . . . And the people inside: police with machine guns, guards at every corner, and lawyers, who look like the bureaucrats from Franz Kafka's *Trial*.

Are there murderers here? People guilty of high treason?"[29] The "young people" he defended, "guilty" of publishing a newsletter, were sentenced to between nine and twelve months imprisonment, in addition to the months they served, as "security risks," following their arrest.

Critics warned that censorship inhibited precisely the kind of dialogue that would permit the left and West German society as a whole to make sense of the current crisis. The most controversial censorship action spoke directly to this concern and raised the question of "sympathy" for the RAF with unequaled intensity. On April 25, 1977, the newspaper of the University of Göttingen chapter of AStA (Allgemeiner Studierendenausschuss, a prominent national student organization) published "Buback—Obituary" ("Buback—ein Nachruf") by an anonymous author using the American Indian name "Mescalaro" as a pseudonym. The "obituary," written shortly after the RAF's assassination of Federal Prosecutor Buback, contained some of the most incendiary lines in the history of the Federal Republic. Its author confessed: "[M]y 'shock' following the shooting of Buback quickly emerged: I could not and would not (and will not) hide a feeling of clandestine joy [ein klammheimlicher Freude]."[30] Members of the media denounced the statement as "naked fascism" and the product of a "sick mind."[31] Politicians suspended the funds of the Göttingen AStA; the University Rector demanded a retraction; prosecutors ordered investigations of the publishers for possible breeches of sections 130 and 140; and police, sometimes bearing machine guns, raided AStA offices, assorted bookstores, and private homes to gather evidence.[32]

The Mescalaro crisis escalated when, in June, forty-three university professors and secondary-school instructors, along with five attorneys and a university official, republished the offending article. The "obituary," they insisted, provided a critique of the RAF's violence and intelligently questioned the norms establishing the acceptable range of thought and opinion. The "obituary" had concluded ambiguously,

> Our goal, a society without terror and violence (if also not without aggression and militancy) . . . without "justice," jail, and institutions (if also not without rules and regulations, or better "recommendations"), this goal does not justify every means, but only some. Our path to socialism (or, for me, anarchy) cannot be littered with corpses. . . . Our violence, finally, cannot be like Al Capone's . . . not authoritarian, but anti-authoritarian, and for that reason more effective. . . . To develop an idea and a practice of violence/ militance which is joyous [fröhlich] and which has the blessings of the masses, that is the task at hand.[33]

The University of Hannover's Peter Brückner, already suspended once from teaching because of his alleged support for the RAF, took the lead in arguing the statement's merits.

Public officials, especially Berlin's Senator for Science and Research Peter Glotz, rejected any favorable assessment of the "obituary." Glotz felt it provided "frightening insight into the moral, spiritual, and psychic makeup of a portion of the university population" and, observing the rash of pro-RAF graffiti and radical activism on campuses, worried that "every fifth [student] thinks something like Mescalaro."[34] In a letter in *Die Welt,* he demanded that the professors "distance themselves" from the statement or leave their posts. "Fight this state, if you think that is necessary," he chided, "but don't do so while drawing a state pension."[35] The professors refused to back down. Glotz's challenge to them was more than rhetorical. The *Berufsverbot,* passed in 1972, permitted the removal of civil servants, which included university professors, if they supported organizations deemed enemies of the constitution. Invoking this measure, authorities once again suspended Brückner from his professional duties.[36]

At stake in the battles over censorship was much more than the status of individual civil liberties, such as freedom of expression, in the Federal Republic. These liberties were integral, not only to the establishment of a constitutional state with legally guaranteed rights in postwar West Germany, but to the larger project of creating a genuinely democratic public sphere—a set of conversations and relations within civil society that were free from the encroachments of the state. That sphere, moreover, was a space for the kinds of critical self-reflection necessary for the healthy functioning of a democracy. In the 1970s, the state's critics charged that censorship, by preventing dialogue about difficult topics like violence, seriously weakened West Germany's public sphere and its vital democratic functions. The state and its defenders countered that a public sphere that sowed the seeds of its own destruction scarcely served the cause of democracy. No external power existed to break this stalemate, in which each side claimed to be the true champion of democracy. Pragmatic considerations ultimately settled this conflict of principles, at least insofar as the fate of particular antiterrorist policies was concerned. By focusing intense criticism on the state itself and further polarizing West German society, sections 188 and 130 proved so counterproductive that they were rescinded by the Bundestag in 1981.

· · ·

Demagogues in lawyer's robes.
Roland Friesler, president of the Nazi
  Volksgerichtshof ("People's Court")

The journalist Gerhard Mauz prefaced a booklet authored by the RAF's principal attorneys, who had been thrown off their cases just before the start of the long-awaited RAF trial in May 1975, with the lament, "Germans have no talent for criminal defense. They much prefer to accuse, and most of all to judge."[37]

The RAF's attorneys were in an unenviable or even impossible position—one at the center of the controversies over the legal battle against the RAF. They were pledged to defending clients who boasted of having committed acts that the state defined as serious crimes, and who did not recognize the legitimacy of the court that set the rules within which the attorneys had to operate. The attorneys thus faced a dilemma: to reject those rules was to imperil their ability to be of any service to their clients; to accept the rules was to risk alienating their clients so thoroughly as to render any coordinated defense impossible. The state's overall strategy created the greatest problems. On the one hand, prosecutors and judges treated the RAF's actions as conventionally criminal offenses whose political motives were irrelevant to the case. The RAF was therefore barred from using the courtroom to put U.S. imperialism, the West German state, and the criminal justice system itself on trial, as it had wanted to do. On the other hand, the state appeared to use the RAF's politics as a reason to abridge, deviate from, and even dispense with the standards of due process governing normal criminal trials.[38] Faced with this double bind, the lawyers were virtually precluded from mounting any defense, and even to work with the RAF was to risk being suspected of criminal activity.

Some of the earliest and most controversial antiterrorist laws targeted the RAF's attorneys and the group's legal defense more generally. In 1972, the attorney Otto Schily was removed from Ensslin's defense on suspicion that he had smuggled a note of hers out of prison. A court eventually reversed Schily's exclusion, ruling that it lacked statutory grounds.[39] The Bundestag soon provided legal means for the removal of lawyers. In December 1974, it passed the so-called "Lex RAF," a series of laws focusing on the legal defense of suspected terrorists. The passage of the laws, which amended the Code of Criminal Procedure (Strafprozeßordnung), was no small event in the history of the Federal Republic. Since the inception of the republic, there had been no significant changes in

the Criminal Code—which Justice Minister Hans-Jochen Vogel called
the "Magna Carta of the Rechtsstaat"—until the early 1960s, when a
process of liberalization began that brought the steady expansion of the
rights of the accused and the powers of their attorneys. The Lex RAF
represented the first time the code had been altered to restrict those rights
and powers.[40]

One provision of the Lex RAF, "defender exclusion" *(Verteidigerausschluß)*, made it possible to remove defense attorneys from their cases
and suspend their professional privileges if they were "suspected of having participated in the crime forming the basis of the investigation, or of
having committed any act that in the case of the defendant's conviction
would be aiding and abetting, impeding the process of the law, or con-
cealing a crime."[41] Suspicion of "endangering the security of the state"
and "misusing [the] right of contact" with imprisoned clients were additional grounds for exclusion.[42] The police, the prosecutors, the court,
and the ethical court of the German bar could all initiate the exclusion,
which the regional or federal court then ordered.[43] Actual evidence was
not required for the removal of attorneys; suspicion was sufficient.

Another law within the Lex RAF barred lawyers from having more
than one client in a single trial, thereby hindering the RAF's plan to
mount a joint political defense of itself as a unified *group*. Given its
strong collective ethos and insistence that the identity of the individual
guerrilla was inseparable from that of the group, the RAF regarded this
as an egregious constraint—one that denied it its fundamental self-
understanding. Subsequent laws permitted the inspection of materials
passed between clients and their lawyers and expanded the means by
which lawyers, under sections 129 and 129a, could be linked to terrorist
organizations.[44] Police periodically raided lawyers' offices as part of
criminal investigations.

The state made frequent use of its newly expanded legal arsenal. In
March, April, and May of 1975, the attorneys Claus Croissant, Kurt
Groenewold, and Hans-Christian Stroeble were removed under the
Verteidigerausschluß provision from the defense of Baader, whose trial
(along with those of Ensslin, Raspe, and Meinhof) was to begin in late
May. (The defendants participated in a single proceeding in the Stammheim courtroom but technically stood trial as individuals, with separate
attorneys.) In June, Croissant and Stroeble were actually arrested under
section 129 for alleged support of a criminal association, and their law
offices were raided. Groenewold was barred from professional service
under the *Berufsverbot* in June, with the ruling upheld under appeal in

December.[45] The lawyers appointed by the court to serve in Croissant's, Groenewold's, and Stroeble's places lacked the trust of their clients and had little time to prepare for the complex trial. At the commencement of the trial, Baader had no lawyer of his choosing; he and the other defendants variously ignored, berated, and demanded the dismissal of the "compulsory defenders."[46] When the hunger-striking defendants became too weak to attend day-long court sessions in September 1975, the court invoked another provision of the Lex RAF, section 231, permitting the continuation of the trial in the absence of the defendants, since they had, in the opinion of the court, voluntarily made themselves physically unfit. This measure struck at the heart of the grievances of the prisoners, who insisted that far from being voluntary, the hunger strikes were the only means left to them to improve prison conditions they equated with torture. As a result of the law, passed in anticipation of the RAF proceedings, the most important trial in West Germany's history other than the prosecutions of former Nazis proceeded not only without proper defense counsel but, at times, *without the defendants themselves.*

The state claimed that the purpose of the laws targeting attorneys was to hinder the ability of the RAF to commit additional crimes and to weaken the networks of support considered indispensable to its continuing vitality. Concerns about the attorneys' conduct were hardly without merit. The RAF lawyers ran the so-called Info-system, through which they smuggled messages between prisoners and to the outside world. With the meticulously run system, RAF inmates were able to maintain an internal hierarchy, engage in coordinated actions such as hunger strikes, and to some extent orchestrate the activities of their supporters.[47] In deeper ways, the RAF's lawyers played a critical role in sustaining the group's public voice. In the mid 1970s, the attorneys, the Committees against Torture they ran, and legal aid centers such as Rote Hilfe were the main vehicles through which RAF propagated its ideology, publicized its battle against prison conditions, and developed support (however limited) among the public. In an important sense, the RAF existed as a political group by virtue of the lawyers' mediation.

Finally, and most dramatically, new guerrilla cells formed from within the lawyers' offices. Croissant's law practice was a virtual hotbed of illegal activity.[48] In the 1960s, Croissant had been a successful inheritance lawyer in Stuttgart. In 1971, his junior partner, Jörg Lang, began bringing political clients, including RAF members, to the firm. Croissant quickly transformed into a radical, deeply committed to defending the far left. Lang went so far as to provide safe houses and logistical support to RAF members still at large. After being arrested and released on bail in 1974, he vanished, insisting in a letter to the Supreme Court that "only in the underground" was it possible "to carry on the antifascist struggle."[49] Lang was later sought in connection with the Buback, Ponto, and Schleyer murders.

The RAF attorney Siegfried Haag joined the underground in 1975 and became a leading figure in the RAF's second generation. He assembled the "commandos" who raided the German embassy in Stockholm in May. Among them was Wolfgang Hausner, who several months earlier had reported to Croissant by order of the court after serving a three-year sentence for building bombs. Hausner killed two people in the raid and was himself fatally wounded. Elisabeth van Dyck, also an assistant in Croissant's office, helped plan the action. While working for Rote Hilfe in Frankfurt and then for Croissant in Stuttgart, Hans-Joachim Klein was secretly a member of the Red Cells. He chauffeured Sartre when he visited Baader in Stammheim in December 1974. A year later, Klein participated with the notorious international terrorist "Carlos" in the bloody attack on an OPEC meeting in Vienna.[50] In light of these activities and affiliations, the RAF's attorneys' claims that suspicion of them was spurious, essentially political, and revealing of a "new fascism" smacked at times of disingenuousness or outright duplicity.

This did not mean, however, that RAF members were not entitled to fair trials, that specific charges against the lead attorneys had any foundation, or that legislation targeting the attorneys was legitimate from the standpoint of commonly accepted judicial principles. Investigators never established that Croissant or other of RAF's principal attorneys conspired to commit any violent acts or knew of the violent plots of their colleagues and associates. Nor was there hard proof that RAF inmates used the Info-system to plan or order violence outside of prison. In the absence of such proof, RAF's lawyers argued that the attacks on them had little to do with national security. Their true purpose, the lawyers claimed, was to weaken the RAF, to prevent a "political trial," and to further empower the state by weakening Germans' constitutional rights.

The reasons various prosecutors and judges gave for excluding or detaining RAF attorneys fueled these claims. Croissant was barred from Baader's defense on suspicion of supporting a "criminal association" (section 129) simply because he had encouraged the RAF's hunger strikes, at one point called for a three-day "sympathy hunger strike," and facilitated an interview conducted by Der Spiegel with RAF prisoners.[51] The judge ruled that these actions enhanced the RAF's cohesiveness as a criminal organization and ability to perpetrate or inspire additional acts of violence. Federal Prosecutor Buback indicated that the attorneys' mere use of the "terminology of left-extremism such as isolation torture [and] brainwashing"—key words in the RAF's campaign against prison conditions—could be grounds for their removal.[52] Groenewold was indicted for writing legal briefs in support of the hunger strikes and for financing the Info-system. According to the indictment, the system allowed "the self-understanding of the prisoners as urban guerrillas, their battle-readiness . . . and their feeling of group identity [*Zusammengehörigkeitsgefühl*] to remain unbroken."[53] Stroeble, in Stefan Aust's characterization, was barred "solely on the grounds that he described his clients as 'comrades,' called himself a Socialist, and had viewed his work as a 'political defense.'"[54] Comments plainly offensive to the government could be sufficient for legal action. In August of 1977, Croissant's associate Armin Newerla stated recklessly that "the situation of political prisoners in the 'freest German state' [is] at this moment worse than in the Nazi prisons. One was also then beaten, tortured, killed, and experimented on with drugs, but not isolated with scientifically perfected methods." Days later, Newerla was arrested for alleged support of a criminal organization.[55]

The RAF's attorneys answered attacks on them by appealing to the professional duties of a defense lawyer and defending their right to hold dissident beliefs. Any responsible attorney, they insisted, necessarily experiences some degree of empathy with his or her clients. Given that the RAF justified its violence on political grounds, the lawyers felt that they had to adopt its political vocabulary and arguments to properly represent the group. That the lawyers in fact shared some of their clients' views, they felt, should not be grounds for their disqualification. The lawyers also argued that the Info-system was crucial for developing an effective defense. Furthermore, given the prisoners' isolation, the lawyers were virtually the only ones in a position to publicize the prison conditions to which their clients were subject. Both professional and ethical imperatives commanded that they support the hunger strikes. Finally, the attorneys disputed that RAF members *in prison* constituted an active "terrorist association" of the sort described by section 129a. With this charge, the state could legally justify the removal of attorneys, the inspection of documents they and their clients exchanged, and the total isolation of prisoners under the *Kontaktsperre*.[56] As evidence of the prisoners' criminal intent and capabilities, judges cited writings by imprisoned members arguing the *political* merits of a guerrilla war strategy. The RAF's lawyers protested that the "mere articulation of the concept of the urban guerrilla is not a crime."[57]

The lawyers, in short, charged that the state equated competent advocacy with complicity, and legal representation with criminal propagandizing. They made this case not only within Germany but also to the international community, where they found some support. In 1975 nearly two hundred American lawyers, among them former U.S. Attorney General Ramsey Clark, criticized the *Verteidigerausschluß*. A group of European lawyers, judges, and professors went so far as to contend that attacks on the RAF's legal defense were reminiscent of "Nazi justice."[58] To the RAF's lawyers and supporters, the parallels were unavoidable. Croissant charged that the *Verteidigerausschluß* had a "fascist character" and compared actions against the RAF's attorneys to the Nazis' assaults on left-wing attorneys as "demagogues in lawyers' robes."[59]

"Hardly any domestic issue" had "generated such controversy and heated discussion in the Federal Republic" as "the legal measures for fighting terrorism," the political scientist Bernhard Rabert commented.[60] The backers of such measures consistently held that the maintenance of law and order was the precondition for the enjoyment of democratic rights and of freedom generally. The state, moreover, had a duty to protect its citizens' most basic rights: to life and to freedom from physical danger. Antiterrorist measures were therefore expressions of the fundamental identity of the Rechtsstaat and its core obligations. Such measures gained their legitimacy from being designed and executed within the framework of the law. "Freedom without security ends sooner or later in chaos, [but] security without freedom ends just as surely in dictatorship," the SPD subsequently explained. "Only the consistent protection of legal principles in the face of the enemies of our lawful order gives our state its true strength and superiority. Arbitrary state force . . . will only precipitate more violence. Our democratic constitution and a societal order based on the social contract and on justice are the best guarantees of internal security."[61]

Critics of the antiterrorist measures worried that the alleged imperatives of security would imperil and even eclipse freedom, whatever the promises of constitutional propriety. One common charge was that state agents disregarded legal constraints on their conduct and denied citizens their rights, even as they claimed to be protecting them. This was the main criticism, for example, that the "Humanistic Union" made of the police actions following Lorenz's kidnapping. A Union representative warned of the special danger posed when those charged with upholding the law themselves become agents of lawlessness.[62] In the West German context, the arbitrary or supralegal exercise of state power inevitably invited comparisons with the violence of the Nazi SA or Gestapo.

Yet there was another fear—one raised specifically by antiterrorist legislation—that was more alarming: that the state would revise and manipulate the law such that *the law itself* became an instrument of oppression. In this scenario, there was no recourse internal to the law for reeling in state power; the laws themselves were the problem. To challenge such laws (assuming they were judged constitutional), one had to appeal to an external set of legal norms such as international human rights laws. This is precisely what the RAF tried to do, both to justify its violent acts and to protest the alleged abuse of its imprisoned members. And this is precisely what the state forbade, at least in formal terms, when it excluded as irrelevant any sustained talk of violations of international law either by the United States in its war in Indochina or by the West German state in its treatment of the RAF from the courtroom. The legality of the state's conduct did not deter but rather renewed and reshaped comparisons with Nazism. Though the Nazis, as critics pointed out, had gained power partly by means of lawless brutality, when in power, the party systematically rewrote Germany's laws to establish its absolute authority and to make it legal to terrorize the population.

In light of this second fear, the legislation permitting the continuation of a criminal trial in the absence of the accused takes on added significance. With the hunger strikes, the prisoners sought to use their bodies to mark a discursive "outside" to the law, even while they were in the state's clutches. Their enfeeblement through starvation would dramatize and, they hoped, force some favorable response to their charge of being subject to legally sanctioned torture. (The courts repeatedly found that the "special handling" of the prisoners was justified on security grounds and did not constitute excessive punishment. In one case, however, prison doctors refused to force-feed a hunger-striking prisoner because they thought the practice inhumane; the prisoner was then transferred to a facility with a more cooperative medical staff.)[63] But even more, the halting of their trial on account of their weakened condition would call into question the legitimacy of the laws arrayed against them by forcing a momentary breakdown in judicial procedure and the legal machinery more broadly. Not without reason did the RAF attorney Kurt Groenewold defend the prisoners' use of their bodies in hunger strikes as the exercise of a fundamental human right.[64]

By permitting the absence from the trial of the defendants, the state asserted that there was no outside-the-law. This was the case even when they were excluded from the law's paradigmatic arena—the courtroom—which serves as a space for mediated exchanges between judge, prosecutor, defendant, counsel, and witnesses. With this exclusion, the essential arena of the law became (or reverted to) the prison as a space of total confinement and the monologic authority of the state. The contact ban law here takes on added significance as well. It was no longer simply a mechanism for exclusion. By denying the prisoners any *private* contact with the "outside" world, the *Kontaktsperre* also assured the impermeability of the law's boundaries and the prisoners' *total* integration within them. Even seeming breaks in those boundaries could be illusions. The prisoners subject to the contact ban in Stammheim apparently rewired stereo systems in their cells to communicate with one another via a crude intercom. But evidence suggests that the authorities knew of and even encouraged this practice so that they could electronically monitor the prisoners' conversations.[65]

.   .   .   .

Democracy is not at everybody's arbitrary disposal.
Those who reject its basic elements must not be given
the power to do away with it.

Willy Brandt

The state's antiterrorist measures sought most immediately to prevent or at least limit political violence. Whether they ultimately served or undermined these goals is debatable. The deeper question concerns why the state perceived left-wing violence as so threatening and mobilized such extraordinary resources in combating it. Reflection on the monopoly of the use of force, or *Gewaltmonopol,* a ubiquitous term in West German discussions about political violence, provides initial insight into the state's perceptions and motivations.

The *Gewaltmonopol* concept comes from Max Weber, who described the state as "a human community that (successfully) claims the *monopoly of the legitimate use of physical force* within a given territory."[66] Though the state has other attributes, this exclusive grant of physical force is what makes it, in essence, a state. And though other institutions or individuals may use violence, they may do so *legitimately* only by the permission of the state; the state remains "the sole source of the 'right' to use violence." Having described the state as a "relation of domination" supported "by means of legitimate violence," Weber then considered the "inner justifications" and "external means" by which the state commands obedience. Historically, that authority has derived primarily from fidelity to tradition or devotion to a charismatic leader, both of which tend toward despotic rule. In modern times, however, a common source of legitimacy has been "legality," which Weber defined as the "belief in the validity of legal statute and functional 'competence' based on rationally created rules." For many modern states, the rule of law reigns supreme, though elements of charismatic or tradition-based authority may persist. Complementing Weber's analysis, one can assert that for democratic societies, the validity of rules is itself rooted in popular consent (principally some version of the social contract) as the ultimate basis for the state's legitimacy. The *Gewaltmonopol* of a democratic state exists by virtue of this foundational consent.

Political violence, in its very existence, contests the state's monopoly of legitimate violence. Those who commit acts of political violence, unlike conventional violent criminals, claim that their violence is legitimate, and that of the state illegitimate, on political and moral grounds.[67] Typically, left-wing challengers of state power in ostensible democracies contest that the state's sovereignty is genuinely popular; they therefore retain "democracy" as a criterion for legitimacy, while disputing that the existing order is truly democratic. Unlike other dissidents, those practicing violence are not content simply to mount an ideological critique of the state's authority, to obey state-defined norms of legitimate protest, or to engage in restricted violations of the law, as in the case of nonviolent civil disobedience. The radical nature of violence as a form of dissent lies in the appropriation of force, which *in practice* challenges the state's legitimacy as a whole.

In the 1960s and 1970s, no self-styled guerrillas in advanced industrial societies posed significant military threats to their governments.[68] But in Weber's model, political violence *in any quantity* is provocative and, in principle, impermissible, insofar as it constitutes a breach or rupture in the state's singular authority. The attorney Ulrich Preuß put it bluntly: "The greatest political crime is . . . to call into question the state's monopoly of force. That is high treason."[69] In structural terms, this challenge or "crime" was every bit as much a quality of Weatherman's violence as of the RAF's. Yet reflection on the category of the *Gewaltmonopol* was almost entirely absent from American discussions of political violence in the 1960s and 1970s. In Germany, by contrast, the guerrillas themselves, government officials, and numerous analysts invoked the idea. Peter Brückner, for example, described the radicality of the J2M's execution of a "traitor" after he had been "convicted" by a self-described "people's tribunal" by asserting: "Legal sovereignty and physical force are integrally linked. When groups arrogate unto themselves legal jurisdiction, they take away from the state a piece of its monopoly of force. . . . It is no longer only the state that jails, prosecutes, and shoots."[70] Defending the state's security measures in 1976, the SPD insisted that, "the democratic Rechtsstaat acts on behalf of its citizens. Its *Gewaltmonopol* must therefore be defended against all who challenge it. Only the lawful state can provide law and order absolutely and for everyone."[71] In criticizing the prosecutions of the RAF, Preuß contested the validity of the state's *Gewaltmonopol*. Since the state, in his view, used its force mainly to protect the rights of private property and the propertied class and not to guarantee the material well-being of all, it lost its claim to universality. The *Gewaltmonopol* was therefore an instrument of class rule, and the legal system, backed by the force of the state, could deliver only "class justice" *(Klassenjustiz)*.[72]

Differences in political culture help to explain the absence of the idea of the *Gewaltmonopol* from American discussions and its strong presence in German dialogue. In U.S. politics, pragmatism dominates, and political actors rarely articulate the theoretical assumptions that inform their behavior. Theory generally plays a subdued role in the commentary of pundits and even in academic political analyses. It is not surprising, then, that Weber's formulation did not resonate in the United States, despite its relevance to the violence there. In Germany, the left was highly engaged theoretically, as is evident in the detailed analyses produced by Rudi Dutschke and other New Left leaders; the voluminous reflections on capitalism, democracy, and social protest of Brückner, Habermas, Negt, and other established intellectuals; and the extensive efforts of the RAF to articulate an ideological basis for its violence. Moreover, mainstream politicians and journalists were often conversant with political theory and drew on it in their discourse.

Yet German concern with the question of the state's *Gewaltmonopol* reflects more than just styles of political speech. The roots of this concern lie in Germany's historically vexed relationship to democracy and its experience with fascism. Contrasting the political climate in the United States and West Germany further prepares discussion of what drove German anxieties.

In the United States in the 1960s, racial and economic strife, division over the Vietnam War, and generational conflict—all of which took on a violent cast—prompted a crisis of legitimacy, experienced by many as the fear that "the center would not hold." Political assassinations and the periodic explosions of civil unrest fed Americans' sense of terrifying uncertainty. Some activists completely lost faith in American democracy and turned against virtually all conventional forms of authority. Meanwhile, in response to protest and to domestic turmoil generally, the state relied on repressive measures to preserve order and existing power relationships. Though it did not have a legal arsenal for combating protest equal to West Germany's, its powers were substantial. The FBI and local police made extensive use of surveillance, undercover agents, covert forms of political and psychological manipulation, and, especially when dealing with racial minorities, outright violence to combat dissent. When such measures were illegal, security agencies often simply broke the law and worked to conceal their activities from oversight bodies. At an extreme, state agents engaged in murder—as in the case of Fred Hampton—to silence "subversives." In response to such egregious assertions of state power, radicals accused the U.S. government of being "authoritarian" and even "fascist"; public officials denounced protesters in equally strong terms. At the moments of greatest violence and division, the country may have seemed headed for civil war.

Yet only for very brief periods and in limited circles did Americans seem to doubt the ultimate stability of their political institutions. In the perception of its opponents, protest violence threatened civil peace more than it did the legitimacy of the American state and the principles for which they felt it stood. For millions, the radicalism of the 1960s and early 1970s was a more or less distant reality, which held no appeal, affected their lives only indirectly, and did not challenge their fundamental faith in their country's future.

Though social protest movements in West Germany in the 1960s and 1970s proved highly polarizing, West German society as a whole did not experience anything like America's *structural* conflicts. Yet West Germans, in the face of comparatively modest tensions, felt intense and enduring insecurities about the identity and stability of their democracy. This insecurity was raised with singular force by the RAF, who simultaneously provoked a security crisis, a constitutional crisis, and, most significantly, a crisis of confidence over what it meant to be a democratic society. The deepest roots of this last crisis lay in the German past—or how West German society defined and integrated the lessons of the past. Here also lay the core logic of the state's response to terrorism.

An important construct to emerge in the postwar period from Germany's historical experience was that of *streitbare Demokratie*—militant or partisan democracy. The basic mandate of militant democracy was aggressively to defend against threats to democratic rule. Its exponents defined democracy broadly so as to include the protection of individual liberties, rights of political participation, and minority points of view. The Weimar Republic, as much as the Nazi state, functioned as a reference point for conceiving the means and ends of the militant democracy.

In the wake of the war, an antitotalitarian consensus emerged among elites in the Western zone of Germany in direct reaction to the Nazis' destruction of democracy. But in the perceptions of some, Weimar's constitution and broader political culture had facilitated the rise of fascism both by failing to solidify democratic values and by being too democratic. Postwar critics decried the "value-relativism" *(Wertrelativismus)* of a pluralism that gave extremist groups room to gain strength, culminating in Hitler's seizure of power by largely *legal means*.[73] Weimar's constitution, to its West German detractors, had resulted in a democracy that was weak, dysfunctional, and incapable of defending itself. The violence in the 1920s and early 1930s of the paramilitary groups of the far right and left typified the inability of the Weimar state to solidify its *Gewaltmonopol* and, hence, establish the legitimacy of its rule.

Under the slogan "Bonn ist nicht Weimar," the architects of the Federal Republic sought to sanctify democratic principles and institutionalize safeguards against antidemocratic ideas and movements. The West German constitution explicitly affirmed the "dignity of man" and established inviolable rights of its citizens. This *Wertgebundenheit,* or unified commitment to democratic values, aimed to correct for Weimar's *Wertrelativismus.* To protect democracy from internal threats, the constitution permitted the banning of organizations deemed to be enemies of the constitution, even if they did not engage in conventionally criminal activity. The far right Sozialistische Reichspartei and the Kommunistische Partei Deutschlands (KPD) were banned under these provisions in 1952 and 1956, respectively. Tellingly, the primary West German security agency combating political threats is the Bundesamt für Verfassungsschutz, or "Office for the Protection of the Constitution." Following the war, the SPD leader Carlo Schmid captured the underlying spirit of such measures when he said: "Wherever there is a belief that democracy is indispensable for the dignity of human beings, democracy is more than a purely utilitarian construct. When one has the courage of this belief, one must also have the courage of intolerance toward those who want to use democracy to destroy democracy."[74]

The priorities of *streitbare Demokratie* inspired subsequent West German laws. The *Notstandgezetze,* proposed in the 1950s and passed in 1968, expanded the state's powers during times of national emergency. The *Berufsverbot* demanded that civil servants be loyal to the constitution and not participate in organizations—even those not officially banned—deemed a threat to the constitution. Chancellor Willy Brandt, reflecting on the *Berufsverbot* after leaving office, conveyed how West Germany's founders drew on the past in conceiving the postwar democracy:

> Whether [the *Berufsverbot*] was right or wrong, you must look at this in the context of the way in which we believed ourselves called upon to prevent a repetition of Weimar. Weimar had been ground to pieces between the large National Socialist Party . . . and a large Communist Party. . . . When we started over, we picked up on a phrase that one of our major authors, Thomas Mann, coined while he was in exile. We wanted a forceful, militant democracy, as he called it. I'm sure he would disagree with some of the measures taken today. So I do not want to claim him as the author of specific measures, but only of the underlying intellectual concept. This was the concept, as many people described it when the Basic Law [the fundamental democratic provisions of the constitution] was written: democracy is not at everybody's arbitrary disposal. Those who reject its basic elements must not be given power to do away with it.[75]

The implications of militant democracy for the conflicts precipitating political violence and for the terrorist drama itself were profound. In the 1950s, the "courage of intolerance" served as a rationale in West Germany for the exclusion from political life of communists, feared as agents of internal subversion who might do the secret bidding of the Soviet-dominated DDR. The most concrete expression of this fear was the banning of the KPD, though informal means of censure played an important role in restricting the spectrum of acceptable opinion. According to Brückner, postwar enthusiasm for democracy quickly degenerated into a view of communism and fascism as two sides of the same totalitarian coin. To Brückner, such anticommunism "suspended a critical engagement with communism; it was not the result of such an engagement."[76] Later, the "courage of intolerance" informed state and public hostility to the budding New Left. The marginalization of the radical opposition, whether through police actions or public defamation, contributed to the growing sense among the young that a systemic alternative to the existing order could neither be articulated nor pursued from within the established political order. The RAF's violence was, in part, a radical expression of this pessimism. The "courage of intolerance," by limiting the space of sanctioned political opinion and conduct, contributed to the emergence of the very "extremism" it meant to prevent. In addition, the principles of militant democracy encouraged the portrayal of New Left radicals as enemies both of the state and of democracy, who threatened to plunge West Germany back into chaos or even dictatorship. The RAF, the federal government's bête noire, was declared an absolute evil; given the imperatives of militant democracy, its destruction mandated the use of extreme measures.

Those measures grew more insistent as the RAF became more aggressive. The culmination of the RAF's violence in the kidnapping of Schleyer, the murder of his guards, the hijacking of the Lufthansa plane, and the shooting of its pilot, in the fall of 1977 elicited the state's most severe response. For more than six weeks, the hapless Schleyer was at the center of a war of both wills and nerves between the RAF and the government. The German Autumn reached a tragic crescendo for both sides with the deaths of Schleyer and the RAF's leaders. The memorial service for Schleyer was elevated into an act of state, in which politicians extolled his sacrifice and reiterated their resolve to fight terrorism. Bundespräsident Walter Scheel's address, though an extraordinary response to an extraordinary sequence of events, captured the main themes of the entire battle against the RAF.

· · ·

They are not only the enemies of democracy—they are
the enemies of every human order.
Bundespräsident Walter Scheel

As Bundespräsident, Walter Scheel was more a symbolic than a substantive leader. The federal chancellor, Helmut Schmidt of the SPD, held primary executive power and ultimate responsibility for shaping antiterrorist policy. Yet on the occasion of Schleyer's funeral, Scheel was called upon to provide more than symbolic leadership. Speaking before an audience of mourners that included Schleyer's family, leading politicians, and the heads of key industries, he rose to the challenge.

Scheel came to Schleyer's funeral in Stuttgart on October 25, 1977, not only to praise his life, but to justify it; not only to condemn the terrorists, but to argue against them; not only to declare the legitimacy of the West German state, but to articulate its virtues. More than a eulogy, his speech was an important, highly public, and sharply polemical moment in the *geistige Auseinandersetzung*—the intellectual struggle—with terrorism. Security measures alone had proven inadequate. Twice the RAF, decimated by arrests, had managed to regenerate itself, and other guerrilla groups had formed, suggesting the existence of sustained support for violence among at least segments of the population. In the wake of Schleyer's death, calls abounded for complementing the *militarische Auseinandersetzung*, fought with police and military commandos, with a *geistige Auseinandersetzung*, whose goal was to induce, rather than coerce, loyalty to the state by convincing all Germans of the worth of their democracy and the need to defend it.[77] Though participating himself in this "intellectual struggle," Scheel also articulated its limits.

Like the RAF, Scheel presented Schleyer as a symbol. But he transformed Schleyer from the negative icon of capitalist oppression his captors had seen him as into a positive symbol of West Germany's virtues. Scheel stated that though Schleyer had represented employers' interests, he had also cared about the conditions of workers. "The terrorists" had, therefore, "killed no ice-cold capitalist," but rather a representative of "capitalism with a human face."[78] Scheel also lauded Schleyer as the embodiment of the merits of democratic pluralism and, more deeply, of the political and moral legitimacy of the Federal Republic. In his dealings on behalf of German industry, Schleyer had been an "honorable adversary" who had "never violated the rules of the game . . . a representative of an open society, committed to the reasonable balance of interests." Generalizing Schleyer's example, Scheel declared that "we all affirm democratic conflict, the conflict of opinions and arguments. But this conflict is based on respect for the convictions of one's opponents." Terrorism, according to Scheel, was inherently undemocratic, insofar as it used violence to compensate for the failure to gain power through legitimate means. The resort to violence, moreover, necessarily demonstrated the poverty of the cause it intended to serve. Speculating that Schleyer and his captors must have engaged in political debates, Scheel said: "[T]he fact that the terrorists could end this debate only with naked violence shows on which side the better argument lay."

Scheel also paid tribute to Schleyer by presenting him as a sacrificial object. Though Schleyer's family had persistently pleaded that the government release the prisoners to save his life, Chancellor Schmidt stood by his decision, made immediately following the kidnapping, not to make any deal with the RAF. With this decision, Schmidt virtually ensured that

Schleyer would be killed.[79] In practical terms, Schleyer's death prevented the freeing of convicted terrorists who might again have engaged in violence, as several of those released in the 1975 exchange for Lorenz had done. (By 1977, they stood accused of committing nine murders since their release.) Addressing the Bundestag the day after Schleyer was confirmed dead, Schmidt stressed this negative precedent in defending his refusal to make the exchange.[80] Schleyer had died, in short, so that others might live.

Equally important, Schleyer's fate gave rise to unprecedented unity in the Federal Republic, as groups spanning the ideological spectrum rallied in support of the chancellor, in condemnation of the RAF, and in affirmation of democracy. Setting aside partisan differences, the representatives on the "all-party crisis staff" advising Schmidt unequivocally backed the policy of no compromise with the RAF.[81] The SPD, Schmidt's party, explained that, "It is necessary, whatever ideological and political differences exist, to outlaw terrorists, to give demagogues the cold shoulder, and to show that the democratic community is stronger than cold-blooded murder. . . . [We] know what we are defending: our liberal and socially legitimate Rechtsstaat, which our citizens have built from the rubble of war and tyranny. . . . Not without reason are the terroristic murderers described as Hitler's children. They would shoot their way to a new fascism if they could."[82] The Bundestag did its part by passing the contact ban law in just five days, by far the fastest a bill had ever been ratified in West Germany.[83] The media lined up behind the chancellor as well, consenting to a news blackout about the kidnapping to hinder the ability of the kidnappers to communicate with the public or send coded messages to terrorist cells.

An outpouring of support also came from groups within civil society. The Council of Evangelical Churches insisted in an official statement that "murder and extortionary violence" can have no justification in a democracy, and urged that the terrorists seek "God's love" to "free themselves from hatred."[84] A union of German bishops, asking "what have we done or let happen" as a society, answered that Germany had "devalu[ed] the dignity of life," allowed its universities to become breeding grounds for violence, and permitted some in the media to "make a laughing stock of our state and its constitution."[85] In a public statement, over 100 university professors, as if answering those who had republished the Mescalaro letter, announced their unequivocal rejection of "violence as a means of political struggle."[86] An association of writers upbraided the terrorists: "They are no leftists. They haven't read Marx. . . . When no revolutionary situation exists, what they are doing is merely kicking up a fuss. [The FRG] is a state that makes possible and protects freedom, justice, and peace."[87] Trade unions were equally critical of the RAF. Those of IG Metall warned that terrorism "throws citizens into fear and hysteria. Once before political adventurers have exploited such a climate."[88] The ÖTV Union charged, "Whoever supports the violent criminal or even sympathizes with him is an enemy of the democratic Rechtsstaat and, in that, an enemy of workers and unions."[89] It concluded by paying special thanks to the police. Scheel, taking stock of this extraordinary chorus, pronounced that the "unified embrace of the duty to uphold democracy has strengthened our democracy."[90] Within the logic of sacrifice, Schleyer's death nourished the democratic collective by strengthening the *Wertgebundenheit* at its core. "In the name of all German citizens," Scheel begged Schleyer's wife and children for forgiveness.[91] In this apology, received by Schleyer's wife with stoic gratitude, lay the event's deepest symbolism. The holy union of the Schleyer family had been shattered so that the bond of the nation might be renewed.

Scheel reserved his strongest language for the terrorists:

> There is truly nothing that these young people respect, that they honor, that they hold as holy. They laugh at such words. They are proud that they murder, rob, and blackmail. . . . They are free of every inhibition, every taboo. They have trashed the value of two thousand years of culture. . . . What kind of grimace of freedom stares at us? It is the freedom of malice, the freedom of destruction. . . . They are not only the enemies of democracy—they are the enemies of every human order. This enemy is naked barbarism. These lost young people not only threaten democratic freedom. They are the enemies of every civilization.[92]

The RAF's actions were amoral, blasphemous, monstrous, and the freedom the RAF represented had nothing to do with liberation. It was, rather, the freedom of total license. Contemptuous of democracy and norms generally, the terrorists had excluded themselves from the nation as a community based on the affirmation of democratic values. The pluralist imperative that political opponents be fought through rational debate did not apply in their case. The paramount challenge was to arrest and convict them.

One can discern in Scheel's language coded references to the past. His talk of the RAF's "naked barbarism" and nihilistic transgressions implicitly equated the RAF's terrorism with Nazism, which had indeed violated every humane value. This negative construction of the RAF suggests a positive view of West Germany as part of the age-old project of civilized culture. Scheel betrayed no recognition that a German state just thirty years earlier had, much more plausibly than RAF, "trashed the value of two thousand years of culture"; that Schleyer, whom he lauded as a noble democrat, had been an SS *Hauptsturmführer* in the service of the monstrous Reinhard Heydrich, the Third Reich's genocidal proconsul in Czechoslovakia; or that anyone or anything associated with Nazism might have survived in the personnel, institutions, or ideology of the post-war state. In Scheel's discourse, the conversion from totalitarianism to democracy had been total. The battle against the RAF, presented this way, affirmed West Germany's desired identity, not only as thoroughly democratic, but also as resolutely antifascist.

Scheel then addressed issues of guilt and how best to combat terrorism. The RAF's ends, he felt, could no longer be separated from its gruesome means, making any form of support for the group indefensible. Those who provided tactical assistance he judged as guilty *(schuldig)* as the terrorists themselves. The ranks of those who were complicit *(mitschuldig)* included those who offered gestures of support—even as small as painting pro-RAF graffiti—and those who "in word and writing openly support the terrorists while personally rejecting the use of terroristic violence." Ideally, such people could be persuaded of the illegitimacy of violence; failing that, the state must "resist [them] with the full severity of the law." Scheel targeted the alleged sympathizers within the professorate, charging that they were "not qualified to instruct our children" and should therefore be subject to the *Berufsverbot*. He concluded by restating his understanding of the essence of democracy. Those who recognized "the human dignity" even of the terrorists had grasped the meaning of democracy, whose "life-elixir" was "critique." "Illegitimate critique," however, "had nothing, absolutely nothing, to do with democracy." The courage of intolerance must therefore be summoned to vanquish the deadly intolerance of the terrorists.

Scheel's speech, however impassioned, is full of tensions and contradictions that go to the heart of the controversies surrounding the state's campaign against the RAF. Scheel asserts the importance of pluralism but says that those who fail to recognize its value should be denied the right of political participation. The democratic community thus defines itself through exclusion and undermines its claim to universality. He identifies the "dignity of man" as the foundational principle of democracy, only to denounce the RAF as virtually inhuman. Though rational debate is the favored means for winning back its "sympathizers," the law is poised, should they prove incorrigible, to rid the public sphere of their poisonous ideas. And since sympathizers reveal themselves largely through words and not deeds, the glare of surveillance must carefully inspect the speech of Germans for signs of disloyalty, with the state alone empowered to separate legitimate from illegitimate critique.

Suspicion, surveillance, censorship, confinement, condemnation, exclusion—such were the core elements of the state's battle against the RAF. From the state's standpoint, these tactics represented only the regrettable necessity of sometimes having to use unsavory means to preserve democracy. *Any* state, the Federal Republic's defenders argued, has the obligation to provide for its citizens' safety; and any *democratic* state, faced with terrorism, would necessarily have to balance the imperative of security against the protection of civil liberties. Why, the state's defenders protested, should West Germany be held to a different and higher standard as it tries to strike a fair balance? Other western European democracies at least had on the books laws similar to those in West Germany that drew so much criticism; the discomfort of seeing such laws in action, to extend the argument, was ultimately a result of the extraordinary threat terrorism posed, and not a sign of the laws' illegitimacy.[93]

The German past, to the state's backers, only enhanced the need to err on the side of security; to *fail* to do so would be to ignore the grim lesson of the Nazi experience. Finally, certain arguments of the radical left appeared to echo the state's own premises. Most dramatically, Marcuse had advocated his own version of the "courage of intolerance" in arguing that tolerance should be *actively withdrawn from the enemies of true democracy.* "This intolerance," to be effective, had to "extend to the stage of action as well as of discussion . . . even [to] thought and opinion."[94] Though Marcuse meant for the *political right* to be the object of repression, the means he promoted were strikingly close to those the West German state applied against the radical left. Furthermore, Marcuse called for intolerance against "regressive movements *before* they become active," lamenting that "if democratic tolerance had been withdrawn when the future [Nazi] leaders started their campaign, mankind would have had a chance of avoiding Auschwitz and a World War."[95] Even the historical examples summoned in defense of intolerance were the same.

To preface a study on left- and right-wing terrorism in Germany, Bernhard Rabert quotes Edmund Burke's dictum that "All that is necessary for the triumph of evil is that good men do nothing." Within this Burkean frame, Rabert implies that combating terrorism was essentially a matter of democratic vigilance, preventing the evil of evil men. Yet militant democracy and its underlying ethos have limits as explanatory frameworks for the state's war on terrorism, both in their tendency to excuse and their inability to fully explain. Rabert, for example, pays scant attention to the harm that "good men" may presumably do in the purported service of democracy, and he nowhere mentions the possibility that democracy's defense, taken up by men both "good" and "bad," might serve as a pretext for state action driven by antidemocratic impulses. To critics of the state's response to the RAF's violence, militant democracy blinded its exponents to just these dangers.

.   .   .

War is only the utmost realization of enmity in politics
Carl Schmitt

The political philosopher Wolfgang Kraushaar was one such critic. In his 1977 essay on the Schleyer crisis, "44 Tage ohne Opposition" ("44 Days without Opposition"), he charged that, "With the death of Schleyer . . . the authoritarian maxim that a state can only be a state when it has the opportunity to defend itself against an enemy was alive again."[96] To Kraushaar, the Federal Republic's battle against terrorism had less to do with preserving democracy than with asserting state power, making the protofascist legal scholar Carl Schmitt, not Thomas Mann or any other democrat, the authentic theorist of the state's conduct.

According to Schmitt, different spheres of human activity are governed by distinct criteria, expressed in dualisms. Morality, for example, concerns itself with the distinction between good and evil, aesthetics with that between the ugly and the beautiful. Politics, in Schmitt's view, deals essentially in the distinction between friend and foe. Political entities are constituted by this elementary antagonism, which escapes moral, ideological, and all other normative considerations. The political foe is "simply the Other, the Alien, and it is enough . . . that he is in a particularly intensive sense existentially something Other and Alien, so that in the case of conflict he means the negation of one's own existence and therefore must be guarded from and fought off."[97]

Under normal circumstances, the nature of politics as antagonism is subdued or concealed. The truth of politics becomes apparent in moments of "emergency" when, in William Scheuerman's paraphrase of Schmitt, "the existence or life of an entity is severely threatened."[98] Since politics defies normativity, and all crises are sui generis, no norm is applicable in times of crisis; a crisis is by definition a "norm-less exception." Crisis demands, above all, a decision that cannot be based on any a priori norm and that requires no external justification. What is important is simply that a decision be made. All authentically political experiences are therefore rooted in conflict and have a decisionist core. In addition, sovereignty rests "in the person who decides on the exception," rendering Schmitt's philosophy a fundamentally authoritarian one.[99] Schmitt's contempt for liberal constitutionalism and democratic parliamentarianism results from his conviction that true political action cannot be derived from principles, the operation of reason, or debate.[100]

In Kraushaar's view, the state's actions in the Schleyer crisis exemplified Schmittian logic.[101] The state seized upon the RAF as an absolute adversary, consistent with Schmitt's definition of the enemy as entirely "Alien" or "Other." The "actual" threat the RAF posed was less important than the view of it as an existential threat to the Federal Republic's identity, starkly evident in Scheel's speech and in the contact ban, which marked the RAF as a contaminant so strong that it demanded absolute quarantine. In Kraushaar's judgment, the state's essential goal during the crisis was to reestablish itself as capable of acting *(Handlungsfähig)*. Chancellor Schmidt counted this, along with saving Schleyer's life and apprehending his captors, among the state's highest priorities.[102] In cruder terms, Schmidt sought to prove, in his words, "that a democratic state is not a shit state *[Scheißstaat]* that has to put up with everything."[103] Yet saving Schleyer's life proved incompatible with the imperative of strong state action: Schmidt's refusal to negotiate and his use of the GSG 9 virtually sealed Schleyer's fate. The chancellor's course of action thus took on the quality of the Schmittian "decision" as a "tragic choice," in which sacrifice is unavoidable. By choosing a military solution—the *militarische* over the *geistige Auseinandersetzung*—he seized the true meaning of politics as life-and-death conflict and of war, in Schmitt's phrase, as the "utmost realization of enmity in politics."[104] According to Kraushaar, the "GSG 9 killer commando" emerged as the "true representative of a theory of armed struggle" and hence the ultimate purveyor of Schmittian politics.[105]

Kraushaar also found troubling the public acclaim that Chancellor Schmidt received. By taking a hard line during the crisis, Schmidt successfully answered the charge by the right that the SPD government, despite its strenuous antiterrorist efforts, had been weak and indecisive in dealing with the RAF. International suspicion of Germany in the postwar years and the constraints placed on its military made Schmidt's triumph even more satisfying: "What the people had to do without for so

long, they seemed to finally get: a couple of enemies and a little honor."[106]
A prominent journalist proclaimed that with the freeing of the hostages
in Mogadishu, the German people could at last celebrate a military action of which the rest of the world approved. The state was able to act
as "a selfless savior in a time of need," perfectly staged as the GSG 9
freed the terrified hostages. This scene, in Kraushaar's view, reactivated
latent German longings for a paternalistic or even authoritarian state.
By agreeing to a partial blackout of coverage, the press made public criticism of the government's handling of the crisis virtually impossible. Finally, Kraushaar argues, the extraparliamentary and, arguably, extra-
constitutional powers that Schmidt and his crisis staff assumed set a
dangerous precedent, in which Schmittian "state reason" *(Staatsräson)*
dominated "constitutional reason" *(Verfassungsräson)*.

Even within a parliamentary setting, the passion for security seemed
to prevail over democratic deliberation. The introduction of antiterror-
ists laws, such as the "Lex RAF" in 1974, had given rise to more or less
conscientious debates in the Bundestag about the wisdom of altering the
Criminal Code to restrict civil rights for the sake of national security. But
at the height of the Schleyer crisis, those legislators who sought merely
to raise such issues with respect to newly proposed laws were treated
with suspicion and even contempt by their colleagues. The brief discussion in the Bundestag preceding the passage of the contact ban law illustrates how cramped the conversation had become. Amid the clamor
of support for the law, Manfred Coppick of the SPD—one of only five
representatives to cast a "no" vote—stepped forward to declare, "I resent . . . that some . . . have made irresponsible attempts to paint anyone indiscriminately as a 'sympathizer' who addresses the problem of
terrorism . . . not on the basis of popular passion but rational deliberation."[107] In the face of jeers by his fellow legislators ("Such insolence!";
"What an outrage!"), Coppick continued:

> Since your reactions show how hard it is for you to listen to arguments,
> let me state here unequivocally: As a Social Democrat, I oppose murder,
> terrorism and every form of violence in a parliamentary democracy. . . .
> The RAF has created the necessary climate for the forces of reaction in
> our country to tear down what has been painfully built up over the years,
> namely, democratic institutions and constitutional rights. . . . But not
> wanting to see the terrorists drive our society, I am also against any cur-
> tailment of constitutional rights. . . . Doing away with basic constitutional
> principles does not save lives, but it does create conditions under which
> peaceful, democratic development in a constitutionally grounded state is
> imperiled and human rights are threatened. . . .

> The fight against terrorism is not won by emergency laws but by the resolute application of existing law coupled with . . . adherence to constitutional principles and an unflagging devotion to creating greater social justice. . . . That is why I appeal to all union members, university professors, writers, and journalists: Stand up for civil liberties, no matter how difficult it is! Don't be intimidated by the climate of repression [and let it] deter you from fighting for the principles of reason and human decency. You are not alone in this fight. I also call on the judges: Guard your independence. . . . I appeal to all who stepped forward in the 1960s to fashion a better, more humane world ["With bombs and terror?!" interjected CDU and CSU Representatives] . . . to stand together and not to forget what once united us.[108]

Beneath Coppick's beleaguered pathos lay a damning contradiction. The fight against terrorism was often presented as a defense of democracy, defined in terms of rational deliberation and an ethic of mutual respect. But here, democracy's quintessential deliberative body, the parliament, seemed barely able to tolerate honest debate.

Kraushaar presents a very different image of the state's conduct than that of militant democracy, as well as a completely different interpretation than Scheel's of exactly the same events. So divergent are their accounts that they seem evidence of what Baudrillard calls the "uncontrollable eruption of reversibility" constitutive of terrorism, in which protagonist and antagonist, and just and unjust action, seem to shift places in dizzying oscillations.[109] To Kraushaar, the state ultimately reacted to the RAF not as a clear and present danger to democracy, as Scheel had argued, but as a supra-ideological opponent serving the state's need to defend its power as such. They also held opposing views of the place of German history in the terrorist conflict. To Scheel, the outpouring of support for Schmidt represented the unified embrace of democracy and, by implication, a decisive rebuke of the authoritarianism of the past. To Kraushaar, it amounted to a coercive conformity of opinion reminiscent of the past, made worse as the media failed its democratic role as informer and critic. Here again, Schmitt's theories deepen his cynicism. According to Schmitt, uniformity or homogeneity are the essential elements of national identity and political strength; the unity exhibited during the crisis, seen through a Schmittian lens, appears less democratic-pluralist than it does *völkisch*. The very fact that Schmitt's theories—widely regarded as providing a philosophical justification for Nazi jurisprudence—can plausibly be applied to aspects of West German antiterrorism throws into question the sufficiency of militant democracy as a response to the past.

Schmitt's view of the "truth" of politics is neither necessarily true nor, certainly, desirable. One might well dispute that the normless logic of friend and foe can fully dominate struggles between adversaries such as the RAF and the Federal Republic, whose conflict was clearly ideological. Dialogue, debate, and compromise remain political virtues, irrespective of Schmitt's cynicism. Nor does Schmitt's paradigm necessarily illuminate the meaning of the German Autumn to the extent Kraushaar suggests. One *could* disdain the RAF as a threat to democracy and not simply as an "enemy" in the severe, Schmittian sense. Furthermore, not all Germans longed to feel national or martial pride. (West German rearmament had in fact given rise to widespread protests in the 1950s and 1960s.) And though critics of the state may have been quiet during the tense days of Schleyer's kidnapping, they neither ceased to exist nor remained silent forever.

In this light, Schmitt's analysis is best viewed as one theory of politics among many that is valuable for understanding certain aspects of political conflict at certain times, not politics as such. Kraushaar implicitly concedes the limitations of Schmitt's theory by advocating "constitutional" over "state" reason. (A pure Schmittian view would hold that constitutionalism is always a futile attempt to give politics a normative foundation.) By extension, Kraushaar neither definitively explains the state's response to terrorism nor makes the notion of "militant democracy" irrelevant for understanding that response. Rather, he discloses the precariousness of militant democracy as a political ethic, insofar as it may slide into or serve as an alibi for decisionist, authoritarian, or *völkisch* impulses.

A view of the state as itself a threat to German democracy need neither participate in Schmittian cynicism nor come from the radical left. Noting that there was in the 1960s and 1970s neither a "mass antidemocratic party" nor "mass misery," Iring Fetscher rejected out of hand claims that the RAF threatened the postwar democracy in the same way that fascists had endangered the Weimar Republic. Writing in 1977, he charged that "the single, truly real danger lies in the hysterical reaction and hidden agenda of some reactionary politicians who use terrorism as an excuse for suspending the social-democratic and liberal course of reform and building an authoritarian state."[110]

A social-psychological perspective compounds the irony of the state's response to the RAF. Jörg Bopp, who revealed a psychological subtext to the actions of young radicals, provides a complementary portrait of the New Left's more vociferous opponents. According to Bopp they projected their guilt feelings [about the past] onto the student revolt and made it the scapegoat of their own failure. By opposing the "left-fascists" and "anti-establishment radicals," without any personal risk to themselves, they sought to make up for the absence of antifascism before 1945. In their "defense of democracy," the perpetrators and accomplices of the SS state saw themselves as resistance fighters and bathed in the illusion that they were now winning a struggle that they had in fact never begun. The people believed they were rushing to the barricades, when they were only limping along the path of ignoble revenge.[111]

In Bopp's formulation, state and public opposition to the New Left was partly a form of compensatory antifascism directed against a displaced object. Guilt, not an abiding commitment to democracy, drove the condemnation of young insurgents. The "courage of intolerance," in short, masked "ignoble revenge."

Antiterrorism, as an especially intense form of hostility to the left, deepens the implications of Bopp's analysis. As the terrorist conflict escalated, a vicious psychopolitical cycle set in. Guilt over the past fed the aggression of terrorism's staunch opponents, making them by degrees again like that which they insisted they had never been. Repressive measures used to combat terrorism, in turn, strengthened the left's charge of "fascist continuity." This charge, which highlighted the involvement or complicity of Germany's elders in the Nazi past, only compounded their (unacknowledged) guilt and dislike of the radical left. By these complex twists, the very desire of the state's defenders to escape from, compensate for, or redeem their failures in the past led to new forms of denial and even the repetition of undesirable elements of that past.

Conclusion

Jean-Paul Sartre described the animating spirit of the 1960s as the liberation of the sense of the possible, captured by the French students of May '68 in the slogan "L'imagination au pouvoir." Sartre credited the Vietnamese above all for this global emancipation of the imagination. He marveled, "Who would have thought that fourteen million peasants would be able to resist the greatest military and economic power on earth? And yet, this is what happened."[1]

Radicals in the advanced industrial world drew inspiration from the Vietnamese in believing that revolution was possible in their own countries. To the Weatherwoman Naomi Jaffe, the Vietnamese showed that America's power "wasn't infinite—that if you organized a strong 'people's movement' . . . then military might wasn't the last word." Their resistance "was an incredible ray of hope that lit up brilliantly the sixties and seventies for many of us."[2] The Weathermen and the RAF participated in the idealism of the 1960s that defied conventional wisdom as to what was possible. In their minds, their leap into violence would help bring down an imperialist system whose collapse meant nothing less than the emancipation of humanity. Personal courage and an active sense of solidarity with liberation movements worldwide were to play a pivotal role in realizing this utopian vision. In an era of great dreams, theirs were among the most grandiose.

They were also destructive. Both Weatherman and the RAF converted the tantalizing sense of possibility into a dogmatic insistence on the imminence of revolution, the emphasis on militancy into the denigration of critical thinking and the glorification of violence, and an ethic of solidarity into a mistaken sense of the parallels between the First and Third Worlds. The Weathermen's excesses were most often rhetorical, and the greatest harm the group did was to itself. The RAF both hurt itself badly and left a trail of victims.

.   .   .

Shadowboxing the apocalypse, wandering
    the land.
        The Grateful Dead, "My Brother Esau"
        (lyrics by John Perry Barlow)

The armed struggle movements in the two countries dealt in very different ways with their political failure. The Weather Underground Organization's exit in the mid 1970s from the historical stage that it had briefly occupied was variously graceful, awkward, and volatile. The 1970 townhouse explosion marked a lasting shift in the group's politics and tone, strongly evident in Weatherman's internal culture. Gone, by and large, were the brutal criticism-self-criticism sessions, the bizarre sexual practices, and the bullying efforts to suppress doubts and disagreements. Circumstances alone forced the cultivation of a more trusting and supportive environment: with three members dead from the townhouse explosion and federal indictments hanging over the group, the Weathermen had to rely on one another as never before for their safety, security, and sanity. But beyond this pressure, they recognized that their politics were inseparable from how they treated one another. In the early 1970s, Scott Braley, burnt out from years of activism, took a three-month leave, during which he traveled the California coast just to get his bearings back.[3] Lesbian collectives formed in which Weatherwomen explored the connection of issues of sexuality to their broader politics. And the drafting of *Prairie Fire: The Politics of Revolutionary Anti-Imperialism*, the group's major political statement of the 1970s, was a truly collaborative project involving all layers of the organization.

    The WUO's relationship to the left changed as well, with the group tempering the isolating arrogance of its early days and building relationships where and when it could. Simply surviving as a clandestine group was a great challenge, which required the procurement of false IDs for each of the four dozen or so underground members, the use of elaborate codes and decoys to arrange meetings, frequent shifting between "safe houses," and the raising of money. To do all this, as well as to stay in minimal touch with heartbroken family members, the Weathermen relied on hundreds of helpers (among them sympathetic doctors who, at great risk, provided free care to the Weathermen). Some were believers in the underground, while others were veteran activists who may have been ambivalent about or outright rejected armed struggle but remained loyal to individual Weathermen and respected the members' resiliency. Professor Jonah Raskin, the former husband of an underground Weatherwoman and a "courier" for the group, found himself arguing *against* the Weathermen when he was with them and vigorously *defending* the group to critics on the left.[4]

The WUO's decision to reach out to other leftists was as much a political as a pragmatic one. In late July 1974, 5,000 copies of the 185-page *Prairie Fire* appeared in coffeeshops, bookstores, and other places where activists gathered in more than forty cities. The culmination of extensive debate, *Prairie Fire* inaugurated the WUO's effort to build a legal arm and establish itself as a proper Marxist *party.* Announcing that "Without mass struggle, there can be no revolution, without armed struggle, there can be no victory," the Weathermen stressed the need for political education and conventional organizing and embraced a range of progressive initiatives.[5] The group now described its bombings as "armed propaganda," whose intent was to "arm the spirit" and "stir the imagination," not to instigate a guerrilla war.[6]

Prairie Fire's tone matched its softened message. A left-wing newspaper in Madison praised the statement for its "tact, intelligence, and enthusiasm," joking appreciatively that "pages go by without one 'belly of the monster' metaphor."[7] The Prairie Fire Organizing Committees (PFOCs), created in a half dozen cities following the statement's release, soon had several hundred activists working aboveground to advance the WUO's new political vision. On the strength of its revised message, the WUO built a broad range of contacts that spanned from Tom Hayden, now eager to establish himself on the left wing of the Democratic Party, to the Symbionese Liberation Army, which burst onto the national scene with its kidnapping in 1974 of Patty Hearst, an heir to the Hearst media fortune.[8]

The Weathermen, finally, recast their relationship to America. In part, they immersed themselves more deeply in the counterculture by growing their hair long, eating vegetarian food, and seeking periodic refuge in communes throughout the country. A related aspect of their journey was an evolving romance with the American landscape, whose lush, out-of-the-way places provided sanctuary and calm. The Weathermen, in short, came to see the underground as a "free space," in which they could both lose and find themselves, while discovering—as fugitives, often taking low-wage jobs at the margins of the official economy—Americas they had scarcely known: the worlds of poor, undocumented workers, of petty criminals and drifters, of people of all kinds escaping their pasts in dramas of self-reinvention. Avoiding radical hotspots like Berkeley, where the risk of detection was high, the underground Weathermen came to understand intimately, perhaps for the first time, the texture of the lives of those they sought to emancipate.

As the 1970s ground on, the WUO saw both its survival and its continued, if sporadic, armed actions in largely symbolic and even mythic terms. The great theme of *Prairie Fire* was that the struggle must continue, both in light of and despite the U.S. defeat in Vietnam and Nixon's demise following the Watergate scandal. (Weatherman saw both as "reflection[s] of an empire in crisis," which also threatened to give leftists a premature sense of victory.)[9] To maintain the underground in a period of retreat was to keep hope alive. The theme of hope was even stronger in the 1975 movie *Underground* by Emile de Antonio, Mary Lampson, and the acclaimed filmmaker Haskell Wexler. The film, filled with long tributes to the African-American and Puerto Rican struggles, served as a visual counterpart to *Prairie Fire,* and the Weathermen participated in it largely to advance their political goals. The film shows U.S. helicopters tumbling into the South China Sea, while the voices of underground Weathermen, interviewed in a Los Angeles safe house, explain that the WUO is only a tiny group. The clear message is that what seems utterly impossible today—as a Vietnamese victory once did—may be possible in some near or distant tomorrow. The film ends with a Native American watching the sun rise over a sprawling plain, while a song proclaims "There's a new day coming"; the WUO logo, a rainbow with a lightning bolt through it, then fills the screen.

With such imagery, the Weathermen cast themselves as the movement's itinerant warrior-heroes, wandering the land to avenge the government's misdeeds and will the revolution. "It was a time when a lot of people needed romantic notions to sustain them," Russell Neufeld, aboveground in the 1970s, explained.[10] Assessing their impact years later, former Weathermen stress the symbolism of both their actions and their very existence: the group, they claim, managed to pierce the government's aura of invincibility, to show that the FBI didn't always "get its man," to prove, in Gilbert's description, that if you can't so easily overthrow the state, you at least "*can* fight City Hall," including by knocking out its windows. Robert Roth, who saw while underground the satisfaction with which many people reacted to news of the WUO's bombings, concluded that the group "provided hope in being something the Establishment couldn't control."[11]

Yet the new Weathermyth, in many ways, belied the reality. Life underground could be tedious, lonely, and oddly depoliticizing, as participation in public forms of activism held great risk. Though less rigidly hierarchical, the group remained committed to "democratic centralism," and the leaders retained a great amount of power over the others. And though the group became more receptive to newer political currents like feminism, it still treated with suspicion anything that might challenge the preeminence of its "revolutionary anti-imperialism."

Most important, the WUO had difficulty defining its purpose—and the function of violence especially—in an era of declining radicalism. On one level, it aspired to revitalize the left, chiefly by correcting for its dismissal of the working class and now embracing, if largely rhetorically, workers' struggles (support for Third World rebellion remained a constant). In a statement that would have been unthinkable when it formed, the group announced in 1975 that "the task for revolutionaries" was to "organize the working class to seize power and establish socialism."[12] In addition, the group now criticized violence based on the *foco* theory, such as that of the Symbionese Liberation Army, for assuming that "the existence of guerrilla struggle in and of itself politicizes the masses."[13] Yet whatever prestige the group had on the left was based largely on its militancy; it was the group's illegality and violence that distinguished it, in the last instance, from a host of other radical groups committed to "party building." The WUO publication *Osawatomie,* the central organ of the group's own party-building efforts, employed a rather canned analysis of capitalism's "contradictions" and used the "science of Marxism-Leninism" to develop "correct politics" guided by the "correct line."[14] With such language, "ideology" of the sort that had wrecked SDS returned with an accumulating vengeance.

At the same time, some Weathermen feared that too great an emphasis on aboveground work would betray what they felt was the Weather Underground's ultimate purpose as a clandestine armed struggle group. The WUO thus continued in the mid 1970s to engage periodically in armed actions, such as the bombings of the ITT Headquarters in New York City in September 1973 (a protest against the U.S.-backed coup in Chile); of an office of the Department of Health, Education and Welfare in San Francisco in March 1974 (a strike against welfare policy); and of the headquarters of Gulf Oil in June 1974 (punishment for operations in Angola). Moreover, some Weathermen felt that they, as white radicals, had an obligation to support African-American and Puerto Rican armed struggle groups like the BLA and FALN. The great concern, in Braley's words, remained: "[I]f the black movement is doing this level of struggle, who are we to do less?"[15] As a result of this view, the WUO likely provided some form of assistance to other armed groups, and certainly described its own bombings as acts of solidarity with the militant struggles of people of color. Finally, the WUO continued to speak in the strident language of the guerrilla, even as it urged moving beyond a guerrilla strategy. *Prairie Fire* declared "revolutionary war" to be the "only path to the final defeat of imperialism."[16] Later, the WUO professed revolutionary "love" of the Symbionese Liberation Army, despite the SLA's murder of Oakland's African-American superintendent of schools and other wanton crimes and despite other WUO statements critical of the group.[17]

As it cast about for a new theory of violence, the WUO itself begged the question of just what purpose its violence served. By 1975, the group had rejected not only the *foco* model of armed struggle but also that of "war against fascism" and of "retribution." The group acknowledged that the United States was far from fascist, and that it was utterly naïve to believe that "the revolution is contending for state power now."[18] Regarding "retribution," the WUO rejected trying to match what it saw as the cruelty of the system with cruelty of its own.[19] The WUO was left, then, with only the vague sense that the "revolution will need both open and clandestine movements . . . peaceful and armed struggle," which were to interact through some unspecified "dialectic."[20] Weatherman Larry Weiss concluded in the early 1970s, "I don't know what it means to make a revolution. But I know blowing up bathrooms [as in the Pentagon bombing] isn't it."[21] Nothing in the intervening years made the WUO's bombings any more "revolutionary."

The legal situation of the WUO in the mid 1970s added to its political uncertainty. Since the townhouse explosion in 1970, apprehending the Weathermen had been a high priority for the FBI. As of October 1971, eight of the fourteen people on its "Ten Most Wanted" list, among them Dohrn, were "New Left or revolutionary types." The FBI counted, all told, sixteen Weathermen as highly sought fugitives.[22] The Bureau had its near misses, such as in March 1971 when it raided a San Francisco apartment just after the Weathermen, tipped off by helpful neighbors, had vacated it.[23] The Weathermen proved extremely elusive. In an internal memo, the FBI explained that they "are intelligent and highly organized. Their extremely sensitive security consciousness has to date virtually precluded the possibility of agent infiltration."[24] The memo also noted that the Weathermen did not seem "susceptible to [a] financial approach"; a $100,000 reward offered in connection to the 1971 Capitol bombing produced nothing.[25] The FBI was additionally distressed that two members chose to stay underground even after federal indictments were lifted against them in 1973.[26] One Weatherman, Howie Machtinger, was arrested in September 1973 but quickly jumped bail to rejoin the underground, defiantly explaining his decision in a letter to a radical newspaper.[27] The FBI took all this as an expression of the WUO's continuing "dedication to the violent overthrow of the U.S. government" and "contemptuous assessment of law enforcement."[28]

In 1973, conceding its failure, the Bureau established the Special Target Information Development (SPECTAR) program, in which agents went deep under cover in pursuit of Weathermen and other radicals, with no guarantee of protection from local arrests and prosecutions.[29] The cover was in fact so deep that some SPECTAR agents seemed to *become* their disguise and even empathize with the objects of their hunt. Cril Payne, posing as a drug dealer, took and sold large amounts of drugs as he toured the semi-secret radical enclaves of the American northwest and western Canada (a haven for draft resisters). In his journeys, he met many people who might have been confused and self-destructive but hardly seemed political threats. Payne virtually abandoned his mission when he found a fugitive couple deep in the Canadian wilderness, living simply, braving nature, and raising their child far from the corruptions of American society. He wondered what possible good could come from their arrest and left the family in peace.[30]

Legal developments dramatically changed the situation of the Weathermen. In October 1973, government attorneys requested that the federal indictments against the Weathermen for weapons possession and bombing plots, going back to 1970, be lifted. An FBI memo explained that prohibited forms of surveillance by "another government agency" had been used in preparing the indictments, and that it was therefore "in the best interests of the national security" not to pursue prosecutions.[31] It appeared that the Central Intelligence Agency (CIA) or the National Security Agency (responsible for the electronic intercept of foreign communications), or both, had conducted illegal investigations. Both agencies, barred from nearly all forms of domestic spying, did not want their operations exposed. Two months later, the federal conspiracy and riot charges stemming from the Days of Rage were withdrawn because searches had been conducted without proper warrants.[32] The dismissals were a stunning rebuke of the state's security apparatus, coming at a time when the CIA and FBI were under intense scrutiny for decades of extralegal behavior. Later, federal prosecutors brought criminal charges against top FBI officials for their investigations of the Weathermen, showing that for years the Bureau had conducted surreptitious searches (called "black-bag jobs") of the homes of relatives and acquaintances of those underground.[33]

As a consequence of the dismissals, many Weathermen were no longer federal fugitives. Though the majority still faced various state charges, these were relatively minor (such as "unlawful flight from prosecution" from alleged misdemeanors). Moreover, prosecutors had a strong incentive to be lenient to anyone who surfaced voluntarily, because harsh punishments would deter others from leaving the underground. Some Weathermen, remarkably, were no longer sought *on any charges whatsoever*. By August 1974, the FBI counted only twenty-one of an estimated thirty-nine members as fugitives.[34]

This revised legal situation created new options. Chiefly, the Weathermen could turn themselves in, suffer only minimal repercussions, and continue working as "revolutionaries" above ground. This is just what the group contemplated with its strategy of "inversion," whose basic idea was to have some members surface and become leaders of a revitalized radical left. Others would remain underground, sustaining clandestine networks and, perhaps, limited forms of armed struggle. In early 1976, the underground Weathermen and the PFOCs organized the "Hard Times" conference in Chicago, which brought together 2,000 or so activists from a variety of groups and causes and sought to develop a common platform and create an umbrella organization for American radicals. Bitter disputes broke out at the conference, however, with the groups of color accusing the white organizers of limiting their roles in essentially racist ways. The PFOCs felt manipulated by the underground members. And the WUO overall appeared to grossly overestimate its prestige on the left.

Following the disastrous conference, divisions within the WUO deepened. Some members objected to what they saw as the abandonment of the revolution implied by "inversion." Braley explained: "Even though it was clear that the overall political situation had changed, I had defined my life as doing armed struggle, and even debating that seemed like a betrayal."[35] Over time, an insurgent faction, based largely on the East Coast and favoring a renewed commitment to violence, challenged the WUO's longtime leaders, Bernardine Dohrn, Jeff Jones, and Bill Ayers. The authorities added to the tension by continuing their harassment of friends and family members, and by aggressively investigating the PFOCs.[36]

These stresses came to a head in late 1976, when the group collapsed in a torrent of recriminations. The terms of the debate were rigidly ideological, recalling the "mind-clogging rhetoric" amid which Weatherman had been born. The tone was acrimonious, even hysterical. Rival factions accused one another of "crimes against the people," "betrayal of the revolution," "white supremacy," and "male supremacy."[37] The leaders, who had long enjoyed great power, were now savaged by the rank and file; some prominent Weathermen issued severe, self-debasing recantations eerily reminiscent of the language of the purges under Soviet communism. By the time the dust cleared, alliances and friendships had been shattered, a whole subculture was in ruins, and the Weather Underground had fallen into oblivion.

Over the next several years, the great majority of Weathermen turned themselves in, prompting local news stories that read like the final obituaries of a withered radicalism. After negotiating deals with prosecutors (typically probation; some jail time in select cases), they then turned their energy to the difficult task of rebuilding old relationships, a sense of political purpose, and, for some, a basic sense of self. Soon they reintegrated themselves into "normal life," raising families, developing careers, and sustaining their activist commitments around the issues, such as fighting racism, imperialism, and economic inequality, that had always motivated them. Their professional lives, in all cases I have found, have some broad social value, whether education, various forms of political advocacy, or service to disadvantaged communities.

A few Weathermen, however, remained intent on continuing the armed struggle. Even as the WUO was crumbling, new groups like the "May 19th Communist Organization" were formed to reconsolidate the forces of the far left and reinvigorate the armed struggle. All the while, the United Freedom Front (UFF), a small WUO-like organization based in New England with roots in SDS, bombed state and corporate buildings, robbed banks, and eluded capture. Soon "European American anti-imperialists," as many white "revolutionaries" now called themselves, were building new alliances with members of African-American and Puerto Rican armed struggle groups. In addition to the traditional assaults on state and corporate property, these new coalitions (under a variety of names) facilitated daring prison escapes (chiefly of FALN and BLA prisoners) and engaged in "revolutionary expropriations"—in plain language, armed robberies of banks—to fund their activities.

One such heist, on October 20, 1981, in Nyack, New York, went terribly wrong, resulting in the shooting death of a Brinks security guard defending an armored truck containing $1.6 million. Two police officers who had stopped a getaway truck containing the money were also shot dead. David Gilbert was driving the truck, and Kathy Boudin was the passenger. The two were immediately arrested. Later that day police captured two others who had fled in a second car: Judy Clark, a former Weatherwoman, and the former Black Panther "Sam Brown." In the days and months that followed, more participants in the robbery were arrested, among them Kuwasi Balagoon, formerly "Donald Weems," a major figure in the black armed struggle. Investigators gathered crucial information, such as the location of safe houses and names, about the surviving underground network.

Nearly all the Brinks defendants, whose trials took place in 1983 and 1984, declined to mount conventional defenses and instead used the court proceedings to denounce America for centuries of plunder, exploitation, and violence. Most were given consecutive life sentences for multiple counts of murder.[38] Remarkably, some highly sought fugitives, among them former Weathermen and BLA members, continued to commit robberies and bombings. In the mid 1980s, however, a spate of arrests, including members of post-Brinks cells and of the UFF, all but decimated the underground. By 1986, with most suspects captured, the "armed struggle" movement originating in the 1960s had come to a virtual end.[39]

Those sustaining armed activities into the 1980s were as convinced as ever of the oppressiveness of the American state and the value of violent resistance. But their politics seemed irreparably out of joint with the times; their actions an afterimage of a radicalism that had lost resonance within the political culture. They now fought to survive prison, to come to terms with their choices, and to sustain meaningful forms of activism. In the face of often fierce resistance from prison administrators, they have worked to improve health care and education in the prisons, to organize peer counseling on issues of HIV/AIDS, and to provide legal assistance to other inmates.[40]

Their incarceration has given rise to a small, if spirited, movement on behalf of America's self-described "political prisoners" (or even "pris-

oners of war"), whether from the Black Power, Puerto Rican independence, anti-imperialist, or Native American movements. Campaigns
around individual inmates, some of whose cases go back to the late 1960s,
have galvanized public concern around such issues as the death penalty,
the activities of the U.S. Navy in Puerto Rico, and the proliferation within
the American prison system of special "control units" (also called "super-
maximum security" facilities). In such units, which hold thousands of
inmates nationwide, conditions that the RAF bitterly described as torture and human rights organizations condemned—chiefly extended periods of total isolation—have become routine, underscoring the powerful differences in the penal philosophies of the two societies and the
further degeneration of U.S. prisons into places of great abuse.

Some former Weathermen, motivated by political conviction and personal loyalty, are active in advocacy for the prisoners. Roth explained,
"How can we have a movement that is worth anything if it doesn't have
a component that will work not only to support those in prison but also
to free them?"[41] For years, efforts to do the latter appeared to go nowhere.
But in 1997, the Los Angeles Black Panther Geronimo Ji Jaga (formerly
"Geronimo" Pratt) was released from prison after twenty-seven years
when his murder conviction was overturned. Two years later, and after
years of demonstrations and appeals, eleven Puerto Rican prisoners were
freed under a grant of conditional clemency by President Bill Clinton.
(None had been convicted for involvement in acts of murder, and they
generally were serving sentences many times longer than their actions,
such as the possession of firearms, would dictate in normal, "nonpolit-
ical" cases.) And on his last day in office, President Clinton used his pardon power to free two former Weatherwomen, Linda Evans and Susan
Rosenberg. Conversely, the U.S. government has continued to hunt and
prosecute fugitives from the 1960s and 1970s. Notably, five former SLA
members were convicted in early 2003 for the death of Myrna Opsahl,
killed in a 1975 bank robbery while she was depositing a church collection.

Most recently, in August 2003, Kathy Boudin was granted parole after
serving twenty-two years for her involvement in the Brinks murders. (She
had eventually entered a guilty plea on a single act of murder and was sentenced to twenty years to life.) The parole board appeared both impressed
by her work in prison to expand access to education and health care and
moved by her testimony. Boudin expressed great remorse over the loss of
life and described her participation in the robbery as a massive error in
judgement rooted as much in her personal "weaknesses" as in her politics. Elaborating, she echoed early critiques of Weatherman's vulnerabil-

ity to a "politics of proving" and to "white guilt."[42] At the time of Brinks, Boudin still saw armed struggle as a way to help the poor and oppressed. But, with anguished hindsight, she confessed, "I feel I was there to prove to myself that I was somebody who was committed. . . . I said to my-self every day, I am an important person, because I am not just going to rejoin middle-class society." This self-assurance masked profound self-estrangement. She continued, "It was unreal. . . . I wasn't an important person. And I was doing nothing on a day-to-day level actually related to the things I really care about," as being underground severely restricted her political activities. Defending to the parole board her claim that she knew almost nothing of the details of the robbery, and simply waited in the getaway car as instructed, she explained, "I thought as a white person involved in supporting . . . essentially a black struggle that it was wrong for me to know anything." This ignorance, she felt at the time, represented "the highest level of . . . commitment." Now free, she has a new world of opportunities to serve the people and the causes she cares about.

Efforts to free other prisoners, some of whom claim they were framed, have been the cause for the coalescence of a kind of community of armed struggle veterans, their comrades from years back, and a growing number of young activists. At periodic events, they praise and celebrate the strug-gle, pay tribute to those still incarcerated, distribute literature written by the prisoners, and organize legal and political strategies for their release.

.   .   .

The urban guerrilla in the form of the RAF is now
history.

1998 RAF communiqué

Unlike Weatherman, the RAF remained active throughout the 1980s, dur-ing which the emphasis shifted from near-exclusive concern with its im-prisoned members back to opposition to imperialism. In June 1979, after a nearly two-year lull in armed actions, an RAF bomb narrowly missed killing NATO Commander Alexander Haig in Brussels.[43] What was left of the June 2 Movement, crippled by arrests, folded into the RAF in early 1980. In 1981, the RAF bombed the headquarters of the U.S Air Force in Ramstein, Germany, injuring two dozen people. The following year, the RAF issued the strategy paper "The Guerrilla, Resistance, and the Anti-imperialist Front," which explained the rationale for its recent ac-tions and its attacks to come. The RAF then built an alliance with the

French group Action Directe, with whom it engaged in a deadly bombing of a NATO school in 1984 and the assassination of a French general
the following year.[44]

The Red Cells remained active as well, seeking to link their violence
to such popular movements as opposition to nuclear energy, the de-
ployment of cruise missiles, and attacks on the rights of asylum seek-
ers.[45] Between 1984 and 1987, the numbers killed (25) and wounded
(367) in guerrilla attacks surged to new highs not seen since the mid
1970s.[46] Armed struggle, by the mid 1980s, appeared to be a permanent
feature of West German political life, carried out by a host of clandestine cells and supported by a loose network of radical bookstores, legal
collectives, independent militants, and semi-legal groups like the Autonomen, who used low-level violence as a street tactic. If anything, the
armed struggle movement, broadly defined, had grown since the 1970s
both in size and sophistication. For years the Bundeskriminalamt dia-
grammed the RAF's organizational structure in pyramidal form. By the
end of the 1980s, it showed four levels. At the top were the "commandos," estimated at between fifteen and thirty people, who lived under
false names and engaged in "attacks on persons." Below were the "illegal militants" and then the members of the "militant RAF environment"
("Militantes RAF-Umfeld"); thought to number in the hundreds, they
provided logistical support and sometimes engaged in lesser acts of violence such as attacks on property. At the base were the 2,000 or so people
in the "'legal' RAF environment," responsible for "agitation and propaganda" through such things as advocacy for the prisoners.[47]

To the guerrillas, the persistence of the armed struggle had a political
basis; none of the injustices the RAF had originally targeted had been
eliminated, dictating that violent resistance continue. Equally important,
the survival of the guerrilla movement reflected its continuing denial of
political realities. Despite their populist rhetoric, the RAF and the Red
Cells remained insular subcultures. Their voluminous statements, though
claiming to address past failures and changed conditions, mostly recir-
culated crude axioms asserting the evils of imperialism and the heroism
of the guerrillas.

As the RAF committed brutal acts of violence in the mid 1980s, its
already limited support eroded further. In August 1985, in a forest near
Wiesbaden, the group killed a twenty-year-old American soldier, Edward
Pimental, so that it could use his ID to infiltrate and attack a U.S. air
base in Frankfurt. That attack, committed by the "George Jackson Commando," came the same day, killing a U.S. serviceman and a soldier's

wife. Even groups like the Autonomen denounced the killings as cynical, politically counterproductive, and without moral justification.[48] A year later, the RAF killed Gerold von Braunmühl, a liberal voice in West Germany's Foreign Ministry. His brothers shamed his killers by publishing an open letter in the left-wing newspaper *taz*. In it, they paid tribute to their brother's humanity, condemned the RAF's communiqué, which "justified" the act in leaden slogans, and challenged the RAF to explain how their brother's death conceivably advanced its cause.[49] The RAF never responded. The brothers also gave money they had received from a literary award for the letter to the legal defense of the RAF prisoner Peter-Jürgen Boock, convicted of multiple murders for his role in the killings of Ponto and Schleyer. Pointing to irregularities in his trial, Boock maintained his innocence and rallied international support to have his case reheard; one of the von Braunmühl brothers personally appealed to the Bundespräsident for Boock's pardon. In 1992, Boock ended his audacious lie by confessing that he was, in fact, guilty and announced, "I have brought shame on myself."[50] With his declaration, the RAF reached a new ethical low.

The state, for its part, continued to hunt down, arrest, and at times kill RAF fugitives. Stefan Wisniewski was captured in France in May 1978, becoming the first RAF member to stand trial for the murder of Schleyer.[51] Several months later, two fugitives died in firefights, followed by the lethal shooting in 1979 of Elisabeth van Dyck, wanted in connection with the 1975 Stockholm embassy raid. Between 1982 and 1984, police captured nine leaders of the RAF's active commandos. The news for the state was both good and bad. With the arrests, it had seemingly incapacitated another of RAF's "generations."[52] But the RAF's attacks in the wake of the arrests showed how quickly the group could regenerate itself. The harsh treatment of RAF prisoners continued as well, prompting additional accusations of "isolation torture" and hunger strikes (in a 1981 strike, the RAF's Sigurd Debus died), pleas for compassion from family members, and international censure of the Federal Republic. (In 1981, ten individuals were indicted under section 129a simply for painting slogans supporting the hunger strikes. Amnesty International highlighted the drawn-out cases in annual reports on human rights abuses.)[53] As the conflict ground on with seemingly no end in sight, members of the German public criticized both the RAF and the state anew.

The violence of the 1980s and the reaction it provoked entrenched more deeply a pattern of conflict that had been established in the mid 1970s—one that had as much to do with the poorly processed fascist legacy as it did with the justifications each side gave for its conduct. The state's struggle against terrorism was far from being a simple expression of the desire to protect democracy. The RAF was very different in its goals, methods, and capabilities from the fascists of the 1920s and 1930s, and Bonn was not nearly as unstable as Weimar. Yet neither was the antiterrorist campaign evidence of the systematic *Faschisierung* of West Germany. On the contrary, West Germany grew more open and democratic in the 1970s and 1980s, evidenced by the increasing acceptance of public protest; the flowering of progressive movements, such as environmentalism, feminism, and peace activism; the left's enjoyment, with the emergence of the Green Party, of unprecedented influence within the political establishment; and even the partial acceptance of low-level violence—such as ritually occurs on May 1, when radicals and police do street battle in major German cities. Those leftists frustrated in the 1980s with the "resiliency of capitalism" might well have complained more of "repressive tolerance"—the acceptance of nonthreatening forms of dissent, described by Marcuse as the greatest barrier to radical change—than of naked repression.

The eventual easing of the conflict was an uneven process, driven by both local and global circumstances. The first opening came with the call in the late 1970s and early 1980s by RAF prisoners, their attorneys, and some Green Party politicians for "amnesty" for longtime inmates. The premise behind amnesty was that the conflict had, in essence, been a civil war; when a war is over, amnesty advocates reasoned, captured combatants are released. Nearly all of those prisoners calling for amnesty voiced criticisms of armed struggle or repudiated violence outright. Amnesty, some argued, would be a crucial part of a broader, sorely needed reconciliation—a "working through" of the terrorist trauma as itself an effect of the trauma of the past. For the longtime RAF inmate Klaus Jünschke, such a reconciliation ideally demanded that both sides overcome the German "inability to mourn." He insisted: "RAF members must recognize that all those they killed because of their roles in the state and the economy were human beings, over whom relatives cried and mourned. The other side must acknowledge that the RAF prisoners also have their dead to mourn, friends whose deaths have been considered of lesser importance."[54]

In the late 1980s, although it did not grant a comprehensive amnesty, the government nonetheless began releasing key prisoners before they had completed their sentences. The first release came in 1988 when Nordrhein-Westfalen's *Ministerpräsident* Bernhard Vogel granted a pardon *(Beg-*

nadigung) to Jünschke, serving a life sentence for murder.[55] (At the time, sixteen RAF members were serving life sentences.) Other so-called *Aussteiger* (dropouts) who forswore armed struggle were soon granted pardons.[56] The inmates sought their freedom, above all, while the state could claim their recantations as a political victory—one that promised to weaken the RAF by deterring potential recruits and forcing divisions between the prisoners and those still underground. But beyond self-interest, both sides recognized the benefit of diffusing a conflict that had been a destructive stalemate for years.

In 1989, Soviet communism fell, followed quickly by the collapse of the East German state and the reunification of Germany. The dissolution of communism was a blow for the RAF. The "actually existing social-ism" of the Soviet Union and the Eastern Bloc—however imperfect or even anathema from an "authentic" socialist standpoint—had at least demonstrated that a systematic alternative to capitalism was possible. With communism's fall, the RAF's hope of instigating a socialist upris-ing in western Europe became even more remote. The demise of the DDR threatened the RAF in a more immediate sense. Starting in 1978, RAF members had received military training and logistical support from the DDR, and from 1980 on, RAF fugitives had found refuge there, reset-tling with the help of East German authorities. Now West German po-lice aggressively pursued former guerrillas in the territory of the former DDR, arresting ten highly sought fugitives in 1990, among them Susanne Albrecht, Ponto's main killer.[57] Nearly all had long abandoned the guer-rilla life (as a condition for their asylum, the DDR had required that they pledge not to engage in violence) and now sought leniency. Their arrest brought the risk that in exchange for lighter sentences, they might share information that could aid in the capture of members still at large. In-deed, Albrecht turned state witness, and the trials of these new captives led to both additional arrests and the prosecution of RAF prisoners for additional crimes.[58]

In April 1991, shaken by the arrests and adrift in a postcommunist world, the RAF tried to reassert its relevance by assassinating Detlev Rohwedder, the head of the Treuhand organization, who had been broadly responsible for liquidating or privatizing thousands of unprof-itable enterprises in the former DDR, resulting in massive job loss and bitter protests. Yet rather than marking a new phase in the RAF's armed struggle, the assassination was virtually its last gasp. In a stunning dec-laration, the "Aprilerklärung" of 1992, the RAF announced that it had suspended violence against "representatives of business and the state."[59]

Such assaults, it suggested, no longer served a political purpose, mandating a cease-fire while it reassessed its identity. In August, the RAF issued a "discussion paper" titled "We Must Search for Something New."[60]

In the wake of the "Aprilërklarung," a dizzying series of recantations, debates, deals, schisms, arrests, trials, and releases followed, culminating in the end of the RAF.[61] As the RAF was contemplating its cease-fire, the state was developing a new plan for freeing inmates. The so-called Kinkel initiative (named for the Federal justice minister), announced in early 1992, allowed for the release of imprisoned guerrillas if they had severe health problems or had served two-thirds of their terms or at least fifteen years of life sentences.[62] Four longtime prisoners were soon freed, followed by a flood of others. Crucially, the state softened the tacit requirement that those freed renounce armed struggle. Among those released was Irmgard Möller, a member of RAF's first generation convicted for the 1972 bombing of the U.S. army base in Heidelberg, who had been held in Stammheim at the time of the 1977 prison deaths. After twenty-two years in prison, Möller was finally let go on December 1, 1994. Möller endorsed the RAF's cease-fire, but she consistently defended the group's early bombings, expressed no fundamental regrets over her political choices, and never wavered in her insistence that Baader, Ensslin, and Raspe had been murdered in Stammheim, and that government agents had tried to kill her too.[63]

The release of prisoners was, however, far from a seamless process. Many Germans questioned whether convicted murderers should go free. Some inmates, by contrast, felt the Kinkel initiative did not go far or fast enough, and that it continued to reward those with a conciliatory attitude while punishing alleged "hardliners." They argued that behind the maneuvering of politicians eager to claim that they had put an end to the terrorist conflict, the iron will of the state security apparatus continued to be enforced in the prisons with unbroken intensity. Finally, even as the state released prisoners, it pursued new prosecutions for crimes long past.

Much of the inmates' anger was directed at the RAF itself. Some prisoners had tried since the early 1990s to broker their freedom for the negotiated resolution of the conflict; the 1992 cease-fire, they claimed, was an initial step toward this end. But some in the underground apparently failed to follow through on the plan, choosing instead to leave the option of more armed assaults open and the prisoners in the lurch. By 1993, most prisoners had broken with the RAF, with some claiming betrayal. Yet other inmates accused these of betraying the armed struggle, and as

some in the underground sided with each prison faction, the dispute became a drama of almost Byzantine complexity.

The bitterness of those remaining in prison was palpable. Helmut Pohl
had been incarcerated since 1984 for his involvement in the 1981 Ramstein bombing. Asked in 1996 whether the RAF had not moved away
from a narrow militarism to a more probing and inclusive dialogue, he
answered,

> Yes, but only when it fit with their political concept. That's why these dis-
> cussions always failed. I think the fundamental mistakes made by everyone,
> from groups on the radical-left in general to the RAF itself, was that we
> weren't based enough in reality and were too obsessed with ideology. There
> were meetings, papers, concepts, discussions, events, campaigns—but they
> weren't reality. . . . The white European left, and the German left in partic-
> ular, was more clever than anyone. No one read more or talked more than
> the left here did. But that's not politics.[64]

Aimed at the stagnant discussions of the 1990s, his comments could
equally apply to much of the debate over armed struggle since the RAF's
inception.

In March 1998, the RAF finally disbanded, declaring in a communiqué: "The urban guerrilla in the form of RAF is now history."[65] Assessing its nearly thirty-year existence, the RAF both admitted grave errors and defended its basic impulses. The fascist past still figured heavily
in the RAF's self-appraisal:

> Despite everything we could have done better, it was fundamentally correct
> to . . . wage resistance to the continuity of German history. . . . Those who
> struggled in the Jewish resistance, in the communist resistance . . . were
> right to struggle. . . . They were the few glimmers of light in the history of
> this country since 1933. . . . The RAF broke with German tradition after
> Nazi fascism [by waging] a struggle whose praxis rejected the conditions
> in the ruling state and attacked the military structures of its NATO allies.[66]

Attempting to eke from its history some inspiration for the future, the
RAF insisted that "calling the system into question was and still is legitimate, so long as there is dominance and oppression." With poetic optimism, the statement concluded: "The revolution says / I was / I am / I will
be again."[67]

Within a year of the statement, only a handful of guerrillas were still
incarcerated, and the long arc of the conflict appeared to be at its end.[68]
Germany's collective task was now somehow to assess its meaning and
ultimate cost. Some affiliated with the armed struggle remained unim-

pressed by the RAF's attempt at closure, charging that the final communiqué had come way too late and only weakly confronted the RAF's failures. Til Meyer, released in 1998, asserted that by 1989 there was "no basis" any longer for the RAF to exist; in truth, she felt, the armed struggle should have been abandoned in 1977. Rolf Clemens Wagner, still imprisoned in 1998, derisively rejected the RAF's parting claims, insisting: "There never was revolution here, there is no revolution here, and there will not be one here in the foreseeable future. That is the continuity of history, the reality we must face."[69]

The German urban guerrillas suffered from a surfeit of history. Their burden, in a sense, was history itself. They tried to compensate for the relative absence of German resistance to Nazism, but in their obviously intense confrontation with the past, they sought an unacknowledged escape or redemption from it. And seeking liberation from the past, they repeated undesirable dimensions of that past, contributing to another extended episode of trauma, another case of *Tod und Traurigkeit,* ending with regret on all sides. In this way, the West German armed struggle experienced its ultimate continuity with the German past.

·   ·   ·

One way or another, this darkness got to give.

> The Grateful Dead, "New Speedway Boogie"
> (lyrics by Robert Hunter)

Weatherman's and the RAF's armed struggles clearly did not succeed in creating revolutions. It is possible to read in that failure something more than the intrusion of reality upon an audacious fantasy, or the resilience of a powerful imperialist system, or the predictable consequence of a false political turn. Their failure signaled the broader collapse of an orientation to revolution that helped define the 1960s.

To Renate Riemeck, Ulrike Meinhof's foster mother, the totalizing rage and liberatory longings Ulrike felt amounted to "social-ethical-utopian ecstasy, a contourless vision of the Coming Time."[70] As her words suggest, 1960s radicals were driven by an apocalyptic impulse resting on a chain of assumptions: that the existing order was thoroughly corrupt and had to be destroyed; that its destruction would give birth to something radically new and better; and that the transcendent nature of this leap rendered the future a largely blank or unrepresentable utopia. This idea of the creative power of destruction had appeal worldwide. "The passion to destroy is a creative pleasure," French students proclaimed. "Destroy that which destroys you," Germans urged. The Black Panthers often spoke enthusiastically of a final, violent showdown with white America.[71] A radical newspaper titled reports of Weatherman's bombings: "Our humble task is to organize the apocalypse!"[72] A communiqué accompanying a bombing by the "Volunteers of America" declared, "Out of the Bankruptcy of AmeriKKKa will come a new country and a new people."[73] And as if to welcome a cataclysmic confrontation, a Berkeley newspaper printed on its cover California Governor Ronald Reagan's message to student demonstrators: "If it takes a bloodbath, let's get it over with."[74]

The optimism of American and West German radicals about revolution was based in part on their reading of events, which seemed to portend dramatic change. They debated revolutionary strategy, and their activism in a general way suggested the nature of the liberated society to come. But they never specified how turmoil would lead to radical change, how they would actually seize power, or how they would reorganize politics, culture, and the economy after a revolution. Instead, they mostly rode a strong sense of outrage and an unelaborated faith that chaos bred crisis, and that from crisis a new society would emerge. In this way, they translated their belief that revolution was politically and morally necessary into the mistaken sense that revolution was therefore likely or even inevitable.

The quixotic quality of revolution led to piercing tensions for those who turned to violence. Robin Palmer confessed, "Even though in my essence I was a Weatherman, in my quintessence I said, 'It's all bullshit, we're never going to take state power.'" He speculated that it is was the Yippie in him, the taste for the absurd, that permitted him to commit bombings while ultimately doubting that revolution was possible. Palmer also buoyed himself with the desperate thought: "If the winter of our bombing discontent is here at last, can spring be far behind?"[75]

The demise of the New Left's last, highest ambition of revolution—one pushed to its limit in armed struggle—was followed by the near-total abandonment in the developed West and large parts of the world of revolution as a structure of longing, desire, and faith. The "revolutionary" 1960s may therefore be seen as a threshold for the establishment in the decades following of a "postmodern condition," virtually defined by the exhaustion of utopian energies. Jean-François Lyotard, in a seminal postmodern text, described the totalizing impulse behind utopian quests for "final solutions" as a "dangerous fantasy to seize reality."[76] Slavoj Zizek characterizes the desire for a New Man and a New World, beyond antagonism or contradiction, as a fundamentally fascist longing.[77] Such sentiments were reflected, not in the disappearance of progressive movements—some thrived as never before—but by the move of activists away from the "grand project" promising to "change the world" to the more modest goal of changing at least parts of the world in small but meaningful ways. Russell Jacoby, lamenting this shift, recently observed "a utopian spirit—a sense that the future could transcend the present—has all but vanished."[78]

At the height of postmodern quietism, it was tempting to look back at the "radical 1960s" and ask, "Where have all the angry young men and women gone?" For all their volatile conceit, 1960s activists took as the task of their lives nothing less than the complete remaking of their societies along lines both fairer and more just. Weatherman and the RAF, within this appreciative gaze at the era's activism *as a whole,* recede behind a more robust image of the 1960s in terms of their world-changing optimism.

The antiglobalization movement that took shape in the United States, western Europe, and other parts of the developed world toward the end of the 1990s seeks to address the inequities of the world economy in ways strikingly parallel to the militant radicalism of the 1960s. The phenomenon of antiglobalization calls for—or even demands—a new look at 1960s protest, especially its violent edges. Now, as then, the core perception is that the prosperity of the few presupposes the exploitation and misery of the many. The catalyst for this awareness is a not a single, galvanizing "event" like the Vietnam War, but the grinding persistence of staggering levels of poverty, disease, and despair in a world capable of dramatically diminishing them. And now, as in the 1960s, the conclusion is that true justice must be global justice, making international solidarity the paramount value.

Militancy has made a comeback as well, evident in the spirited protests in recent years at meetings of the leaders of wealthy societies and the institutions they control. Such demonstrations, which form a new geography of global activism, have once again showed the power of telegenic confrontational protest to command attention and, in cases, dramatically alter the terms of political debate. With this new militancy has come a revitalized language of commitment and courage, of how cops are and what the experience of jail is like. At the margins, a politics of "Smash Capitalism" has also reemerged, as has some interest in Weatherman and the RAF, potentially seen as distant sources of contemporary radicalism. Yet this new movement, for all its utopian promise, also re-

calls the weaknesses of 1960s radicalism, from the substitution of slogans for analysis to the granting of a shallow mystique to street fighting,
and even to a reckless fascination with more serious forms of violence.
Weatherman and the RAF, as this new tide of radicalism rises, may indeed become relevant for the cautionary tales they embody.

There are, finally, the changes of circumstances and perspective
wrought by September 11, 2001. Past "armed struggles" against the
"American empire," however different in intent and kind from recent terrorism, may now appear in a harsher light—revealing how cultures of
resistance can devolve into cults of violence. By the same token, the response of the U.S. government to "9/11"—from a resurgent militarism,
to an attitude of suspicion of or hostility toward much of the world, to
a cheapening of the lives of others in the purported effort to protect those
of "one's own"—has spawned renewed criticisms of America's over-
reaching power and imperial arrogance. Domestically, the restriction of
civil liberties in the name of "national security" and the accompanying fear of state repression (evident in the increasing hostility of police
toward demonstrators and harassment of foreign-born activists) have
vividly raised for America issues West Germany struggled with in the
1970s and 1980s. In these added lights, the experiences of Weatherman
and the RAF may appear, at least in part, as volatile expressions of a
continuing conflict over the status and meaning of America—its military,
economy, institutions, values, culture, and influence—in the world. The
stories of Weatherman and the RAF, when seen as part of this larger, enduring narrative, have as yet no real end.

Notes

INTRODUCTION

1. George Katsiaficas describes the New Left activism of the late 1960s as "world-historical" and suggests that it eclipsed the European uprisings of 1848–49 in breadth and significance (Katsiaficas, *The Imagination of the New Left: A Global Analysis of 1968* [Boston: Beacon Press, 1987], 3–13). Katsiaficas includes student and youth movements throughout the world under the rubric "New Left." I use the term only to describe those movements in the United States and western Europe, where youth protesters were commonly described as making up a "New Left." Moreover, I do not treat African-American radicals, who saw themselves as distinct from the overwhelmingly white student movement and counterculture, as part of the American New Left, though white and black activists certainly at times collaborated.

2. Though David Caute's *Sixty-Eight: The Year of the Barricades* (London: Hamish Hamilton, 1988) and Ronald Fraser's *1968: A Student Generation in Revolt* (New York: Pantheon Books, 1988) adopt an international perspective, they provide mostly discrete portraits of the student movements in several countries and do little to articulate the connections between them. More genuinely comparative studies include Paul Berman, *A Tale of Two Utopias: The Political Journey of the Generation of 1968* (New York: Norton, 2000); Karl-Werner Brand, ed., *Neue soziale Bewegung in Westeuropa und den USA: Ein internationaler Vergleich* (Frankfurt a.M.: Campus, 1985); Carole Fink, Philipp Gassert, and Detlef Junker, eds., *1968: The World Transformed* (New York: Cambridge University Press, 1998); Ingrid Gilcher-Holtey, ed., *1968: Vom Ereignis zum Gegenstand der Geschichtswissenschaft* (Göttingen: Vandenhoeck & Ruprecht, 1998); and Arthur Marwick, *The Sixties: Cultural Revolution in Britain, France, Italy, and the United States, 1958–1974* (New York: Oxford University Press, 1998).

3. In the ideologically charged discourse on political violence, choices of terminology are controversial, as they imply political positions. The term "terrorism" is especially charged, because it declares the violence to which it refers to be both politically and morally illegitimate, if not outright evil. I mostly use the term "armed struggle" to describe the violence of Weatherman and the RAF. Both were involved in political struggle, and they were indeed armed. This may, however, seem too exalted a term for violence that did not enjoy the popularity and, most argue, lacked the legitimacy of armed "liberation struggles" in places such as Vietnam and Cuba. The use in Germany of the phrase *bewaffneter Kampf* to describe left-wing violence is widely considered an implicit expression of sympathy for the RAF. I describe members of the RAF and other German groups variously as guerrillas or terrorists, depending on context. The former term is their self-description and the latter is that of their detractors. Using both, I seek to reproduce some of the ambiguities that defined the group's existence and that haunt efforts to reach definitive judgments on political violence. I do not call the Weathermen terrorists, for reasons that will become clear. Discussions of how to define "terrorism," as well as what makes any stable definition so elusive, are common in the vast literature on the subject. See, inter alia, Martha Crenshaw, *Terrorism in Context* (College Station: Pennsylvania State University Press, 1995); Bruce Hoffman, *Inside Terrorism* (New York: Columbia University Press, 1998); Harvey W. Kushner, *Terrorism in America* (Springfield, Ill.: Charles C. Thomas, 1998); and Walter Laqueur, *The New Terrorism: Fanaticism and the Arms of Mass Destruction* (Oxford: Oxford University Press, 1999).

4. Kirkpatrick Sale, *SDS* (New York: Random House, 1973), 632.

5. See esp. *Violence in America: Historical and Comparative Perspectives: A Report to the National Commission on the Causes and Prevention of Violence, June 1969*, ed. Hugh Davis Graham and Ted Robert Gurr (New York: New American Library, 1969). Contrary to common impressions, the study showed that the period from 1939–68 was among the least violent in U.S. history. Even so, the late 1960s witnessed a marked rise in political violence from the immediately preceding years, and the research did not include the years 1969–71, during which the protest violence of the era peaked. See Sheldon G. Levy, "A 150-Year Study of Political Violence in the United States," in ibid., 84–100.

6. Separate essays on violence in the United States and West Germany are to be found in Donatella della Porta, ed., *Social Movements and Violence: Participation in Underground Organizations* (Greenwich, Conn.: JAI Press, 1992). In *Social Movements, Political Violence, and the State: A Comparative Analysis of Italy and Germany* (New York: Cambridge University Press, 1995), della Porta concludes with a very brief comparison of violence in the United States, West Germany, and Italy.

7. These interpretations circulate, often in combination, in virtually all of the literature on Weatherman. The principal works are Sale, *SDS*; Thomas Powers, *Diana: The Making of a Terrorist* (Boston: Houghton Mifflin, 1971); Dave Dellinger, *More Power Than We Know: The People's Movement towards Democracy* (Garden City, N.Y.: Anchor Press, 1975); Todd Gitlin, *The Sixties: Years of Hope, Days of Rage* (New York: Bantam Books, 1993); and Ron Jacobs, *The Way the Wind Blew: A History of the Weather Underground* (New York: Verso,

1997). These works often blend personal accounts with historical analysis and give only limited treatment to Weatherman in the context of larger narratives of the decline and fall of the New Left.

8. This is a feature of most of the major works on the RAF, which include Stefan Aust, *Der Baader Meinhof Komplex* (Hoffmann & Campe, 1985; rev. ed., 1997), trans. Anthea Bell as *The Baader-Meinhof Group: The Inside Story of a Phenomenon* (London: Bodley Head, 1987); Uwe Backes, *Bleierne Jahre: Baader-Meinhof und danach, Extremismus und Demokratie*, no. 1 (Erlangen: Staube, 1991); Jillian Becker, *Hitler's Children: The Story of the Baader-Meinhof Terrorist Gang* (Philadelphia: Lippincott, 1977); Peter Brückner, *Ulrike Marie Meinhof und die deutschen Verhältnisse* (Berlin: Klaus Wagenbach, 1976); Hans Josef Horchem, *Die verlorene Revolution: Terrorismus in Deutschland* (Herford: Bussee Seewald, 1986); Butz Peters, *RAF: Terrorismus in Deutschland* (Stuttgart: Deutsche Verlags-Anstalt, 1991); Bernhard Rabert, *Links- und Rechtsterrorismus in der Bundesrepublick Deutschland von 1970 bis heute* (Bonn: Bernard & Graefe, 1996); and the multivolume series Analysen zum Terrorismus, vols. 1–4 (Opladen: Westdeutscher Verlag, 1981–85).

9. For sophisticated comparisons of the Italian and German cases, see Iring Fetscher, *Terrorismus und Reaktion* (Reinbeck bei Hamburg: Rowohlt, 1981) and della Porta, *Social Movements, Political Violence, and the State.*

10. *Ann Arbor Argus,* November 18–December 11, 1969, 8–9.

11. This view is prevalent in the works on the American New Left cited above. On the West German New Left, see Gerd Langguth, *Die Protestbewegung in der BRD, 1968–76* (Cologne: Wissenschaft und Politik, 1976); Gerhard Bauß, *Die Studentenbewegung der sechziger Jahre in der Bundesrepublik und Westberlin* (Berlin: Pahl-Rugenstein Verlag, 1977); Richard McCormick, *Politics of the Self: Feminism and the Postmodern in West German Literature and Film* (Princeton: Princeton University Press, 1991); Andrei S. Markovits and Philip S. Gorski, *The German Left: Red, Green and Beyond* (New York: Oxford University Press, 1993); and Sabine von Dirke, *"All Power to the Imagination": The West German Counterculture from the Student Movement to the Greens* (Lincoln: University of Nebraska Press, 1997).

12. The phrase was used by Bill Ayers in "A Strategy to Win," in *Weatherman,* ed. Harold Jacobs (Berkeley, Calif.: Ramparts Press, 1970), 190.

13. Ulrike Meinhof, "rede von ulrike zu der befreiung von andreas, moabit 13. september 74," in RAF, *texte: der RAF* (Malmö, Sweden: Bo Cavefors, 1977), 68. From 1973 on, as part of its rebellion against "authoritarian" structures, the RAF stopped capitalizing nouns as conventional German requires.

14. RAF, "April Erklärung—1992." The untitled statement was issued on April 10, 1992, and is commonly referred to as the "Aprilerklärung." It can be found at www.rafinfo.de/archiv/raf/raf-10-4-92.php and in translation in Bruce Scharlau and Donald Philips, "Not the end of German Left-Wing Terrorism," *Terrorism and Political Violence,* Autumn 1992, 110–15. Despite the statement, a faction in the RAF and other small groups continued to commit sporadic acts of violence.

15. The communiqué was issued in March 1998. It has been reprinted in English as "The Urban Guerrilla in History," in *Arm the Spirit: Autonomist/ Anti-Imperialist Journal* (Toronto), no. 17 (Winter 1999/2000): 57–61. On vio-

lence in the 1990s, see Uwe Backes and Eckhard Jesse, *Politischer Extremismus in der Bundesrepublik Deutschland, Neuausgabe 1996* (Bonn: Bundeszentral für politische Bildung, 1996), 244–51.

16. Jochen Reiche, "Zur Kritik der RAF," in *Jahrbuch Politik 8* (Berlin: Klaus Wagenbach, 1978), 22.

17. See Analysen zum Terrorismus, vols. 1 and 3, and Becker, *Hitler's Children.*

18. Hans-Joachim Klein, *The German Guerrilla: Terror, Reaction, and Resistance,* conversations with Jean-Marcel Bougereau, trans. Peter Silcock (Sanday, U.K.: Cienfuegos Press; Minneapolis: Soil of Liberty, 1981), 50.

19. The state's relative leniency toward left-wing armed struggle groups proved short-lived. Under President Ronald Reagan, a handful of small groups committed bombings, bank robberies, and (unintended) killings. New counterterrorist legislation, executive orders, and state organizations were used to capture and sharply punish those active in the 1980s. Gilda Zwerman, "Domestic Counterterrorism: U.S. Government Responses to Political Violence on the Left in the Reagan Era," *Social Justice* 16 (1991): 31–63.

20. Bill Ayers's 2001 memoir *Fugitive Days* (Boston: Beacon Press, 2001) was the first by a group member in nearly three decades. Released just before the World Trade Center attack in September, it received many scathing reviews for its allegedly glib attitude toward violence.

21. *The Weather Underground,* by Sam Green and Bill Siegel (The Free History Project, 2003). For short retrospective histories of the group spawned by the film, consult www.theweatherunderground.com. For recent perspectives on the Weather Underground, see also Neil Gordon's novel *The Company You Keep* (New York: Viking, 2003).

22. Powers, *Diana,* xiv.

23. Iring Fetscher, "Ideologien der Terroristen in der Bundesrepublik Deutschland," in id., Günther Rohrmoser, et al., *Ideologien und Strategien,* Analysen zum Terrorismus, vol. 1 (Bonn: Opladen, 1981), for example, argues that the RAF's use of ideology to rationalize its conduct was rooted in a virtually apolitical zeal for combat.

24. On the role of religion in recent terrorism, see Mark Juergensmeyer, *Terror in the Mind of God: The Global Rise of Religious Violence* (Berkeley: University of California Press, 2002). Although he focuses on the violence of overtly religious groups, Juergensmeyer suggests that virtually all political violence is informed by the logic and symbolism of the sacred.

1. "AGENTS OF NECESSITY"

1. Susan Stern, *With the Weathermen: The Journey of a Revolutionary Woman* (Garden City, N.Y.: Doubleday, 1976); epigram before book text.

2. "Bring the War Home," *New Left Notes,* July 23, 1969.

3. RAF, "Rote Armee Fraktion: Das Konzept Stadtguerilla," in RAF, *texte,* 360. This important text has been translated as "The Concept of the Urban Guerrilla," in *Armed Resistance in West Germany: Documents from the Red Army Faction* (N.p.: Stoke Newington 8 Defence Group, 1972). Hereafter, I shall refer to the translated version.

4. See Daniel Bell, *The End of Ideology: On the Exhaustion of Political Ideas in the Fifties* (Glencoe, Ill.: Free Press, 1960). On the New Left's intellectual and cultural origins, see James Miller's *"Democracy is in the streets": From Port Huron to the Siege of Chicago* (New York: Simon & Schuster, 1987), Doug Rossinow, *The Politics of Authenticity: Liberalism, Christianity, and the New Left in America* (New York: Columbia University Press, 1998), and Kevin Mattson, *Intellectuals in Action: The Origins of the New Left and Radical Liberalism, 1945–1970* (University Park: Pennsylvania State University Press).

5. "The Reminiscences of Jeff Jones," from "Student Movements of the 1960s," Columbia University, Oral History Research Office (hereafter cited as Columbia), 17, 6–7.

6. Most dramatically, the Student Non-Violent Coordinating Committee expelled whites in 1966.

7. Paul Jacobs and Saul Landau, *The New Radicals: A Report with Documents* (New York: Vintage Books, 1966), 40.

8. Gitlin, *The Sixties*, 177–78, 184.

9. Carl Ogelsby, "Liberalism and the Corporate State," in Jacobs and Landau, *New Radicals*, 258.

10. Interview with Scott Braley.

11. Caute, *Sixty-Eight*, 141–58.

12. "The Uprising at Columbia: A Radical View," *Gadfly* "advertorial," Spring 1968. UCB.

13. Jones, "Reminiscences," Columbia, 58.

14. "On Solidarity—The Communes" (anonymous flyer, 1968). UCB.

15. "DARE WE BE HEROES?" (anonymous flyer, 1968). UCB.

16. Jonah Raskin, *For the Hell of It: The Life and Times of Abbie Hoffman* (Berkeley: University of California Press, 1996), 132–33.

17. Ibid., 133.

18. On liberal attitudes towards the war, see Fredrik Logevall, *Choosing War: The Lost Chance for Peace and the Escalation of War in Vietnam* (Berkeley: University of California Press, 1999).

19. Thanks to Anne Kornhauser for help in developing this point.

20. Interview with Robert Roth.

21. "The Reminiscences of David Gilbert," Columbia, 26.

22. Powers, *Diana*, xiii–xiv.

23. Gilbert, Columbia, 131.

24. Roth interview.

25. William H. Orrick Jr., *College in Crisis: A Report to the National Commission on the Causes and Prevention of Violence* (Nashville: Aurora Publishers, 1969), 3.

26. On the APO, see also Karl A. Otto, *Vom Ostermarsch zur APO: Geschichte der ausserparlamentarischen Opposition in der Bundesrepublik, 1960–70* (Frankfurt a.M.: Campus, 1977), and Philipp Gassert and Pavel A. Richter, *1968 in West Germany: A Guide to Sources and Literature of the Extra-Parliamentarian Opposition* (Washington, D.C.: GHI, 1998).

27. Michael Schmidtke, *Der Aufbruch der jungen Intelligenz: Die 68er-Jahre in der Bundesrepublik und den USA* (Frankfurt a.M.: Campus, 2003).

28. Margrit Schiller, *"Es war ein harter Kampf um meine Errinerung"*: *Ein Lebensbericht aus der RAF* (Hamburg: Konkret, 1999; reprint, Munich: Peiper, 2001), 87.

29. Ibid.

30. Ibid., 32.

31. Ibid., 87.

32. Brückner, *Ulrike Marie Meinhof*, 74.

33. Beate Klarsfled, lecture at the University of Minnesota, October 21, 1997. She and her husband Serge Klarsfeld, a French Jew whose father was killed in the Holocaust, aided in the capture of Klaus Barbie, the notorious "Butcher of Lyon," in 1983.

34. On West German opposition to the Vietnam War, see Siegward Lönnen-donker und Jochen Staadt, "Die Bedeutung des Sozialistischen Deutschen Studentenbundes (SDS) für ausserparlamentarische Protestbewegungen im politischen System der Bundesrepublik in den fünzigen und sechziger Jahren" (research paper, Zentralinstitut für sozialwissenschaftliche Forschung der FU, Berlin, 1990).

35. "Schlußerklärung des Frankfurter SDS-Kongresses 'Vietnam—Analyse eines Exemples,'" in *APO: Die außerparlamentarische Opposition in Quellen und Dokumenten, 1960–70*, ed. Karl A. Otto (Cologne: Pahl-Rugenstein, 1987), 213.

36. Erich Fried, "Gleichheit Brüderlichkeit," in *CheSchahShit: Die Sechziger Jahre zwischen Cocktail und Molotov* (Reinbeck bei Hamburg: Rowohlt, 1986), 207.

37. Peter Fritzsche, "Terrorism in the Federal Republic of Germany and Italy: Legacy of the '68 Movement or 'Burden of Fascism'?" *Terrorism and Political Violence* 1, no. 4 (October 1989): 471.

38. Quoted in ibid., 471.

39. "Anti-U.S. Posters at Dachau," *New York Times*, November 8, 1966, 18.

40. David Farber, *The Age of Great Dreams: America in the 1960s* (New York: Hill & Wang), 146.

41. Eldridge Cleaver, "Requiem for Non-Violence," in *Post-Prison Writings and Speeches*, ed. Robert Scheer (New York: Random House, 1969), 74–75. A few nights later, Cleaver and several Panthers went into the Oakland streets to shoot a white policeman in retaliation for King's murder; the plan failed, with the police killing Panther Bobby Hutton. David Hilliard and Lewis Cole, *This Side of Glory: The Autobiography of David Hilliard and the Story of the Black Panther Party* (Boston: Little, Brown, 1993), 183–96.

42. *The Kerner Report: The 1968 Report of the National Advisory Commission on Civil Disorders* (New York: Pantheon Books, 1988), 1.

43. Ibid., 2.

44. Ibid.

45. Bentley Historical Library, University of Michigan, box 1, interview with Jim Mellen by Bret Eynon (Bret Eynon and the Contemporary History Project, 1981), 6.

46. *Eyes on the Prize, Part II*, video VII.

47. Powers, *Diana*, 118.

48. Sale, *SDS*, 457.

49. Jack Whalen and Richard Flacks, *Beyond the Barricades: The Sixties Generation Grows Up* (Philadelphia: Temple University Press, 1989), 79, 73.

50. Sale, *SDS*, 457.

51. Rossinow's *Politics of Authenticity* exemplifies this new emphasis, as do many of the essays in John McMillian and Paul Buhle, eds., *The New Left Revisited* (Philadelphia: Temple University Press, 2003).

52. A detailed examination of the conflict between the New Left and the state is provided by Fritz Sack, Heinz Steinert, et al., *Protest und Reaktion*, Analysen zum Terrorismus, vol. 4/2 (Opladen: Westdeutscher Verlag, 1984).

53. Gerd Conradt, ed., *Starbuck Holger Meins: Ein Porträt als Zeitbild* (Berlin: Espresso, 2001), 71.

54. Becker, *Hitler's Children*, 41.

55. Aust, *Baader-Meinhof Group*, 44.

56. Quoted in *APO: Die außerparlamentarische Opposition*, ed. Otto, 235–36.

57. Becker, *Hitler's Children*, 40.

58. Quoted in *Spiegel*, no. 34 (May 5, 1968).

59. *Bild*, June 3, 1967.

60. On the film, see Conradt, ed., *Starbuck Holger Meins*, 71–82.

61. On the left's reaction to the shooting, see Berliner EXTRA-Dienst 31/II (April 13, 1968) and 32/II (April 20, 1968).

62. *Spiegel*, no. 34 (May 5, 1968).

63. "Solidaritätsbekundung namhafter Intellektueller vom 13. April, 1968," in *APO: Die außerparlamentarische Opposition*, ed. Otto, 264.

64. Michael Baumann, *Terror or Love? Bommi Baumann's Own Story of His Life as a West German Urban Guerrilla*, trans. Helene Ellenbogen and Wayne Parker (1977; New York: Grove Press, 1979), 41; originally published as *Wie alles anfing* (n.d., n.p. [early 1976? Trikont?]).

65. Becker, *Hitler's Children*, 50.

66. Ulrike Meinhof, "Vom Protest zum Widerstand," in *Dokumente einer Rebellion: 10 Jahre "konkret"—Kolumnen* (Copenhagen: Konkret, 1972), 81.

67. Ibid.

68. Ibid., "Warenhausbrandstiftung," 87–88.

69. Becker, *Hitler's Children*, 86, 65.

70. Documents related to the trial are contained in Reinhard Rauball, ed., *Aktuelle Dokumente: Die Baader-Meinhof-Gruppe* (Berlin: Walter de Gruyter, 1972), 190–210.

71. Herbert Marcuse, "Repressive Tolerance," in Robert Paul Wolff, Barrington Moore Jr., and Herbert Marcuse, *A Critique of Pure Tolerance* (Boston: Beacon Press, 1969), 95, 82.

72. Ibid., 83.

73. Ibid., 116.

74. Ibid., 102–3; 116–17.

75. Rudi Dutschke, Bahman Nirumand, Hans Magnus Enzensberger, et al., "Gewalt," *konkret*, no. 6 (June 1968), 25–26.

76. Ibid., 25, 35.

77. Ibid., 27.

78. Ibid., 26.

79. Herbert Marcuse, *One-Dimensional Man: Studies in the Ideology of Advanced Industrial Society* (Boston: Beacon Press, 1964), x.

80. Ibid., ix.

81. Ibid., 256.

82. Such praise peaked with Marcuse's *An Essay on Liberation* (Boston: Beacon Press, 1969), which he dedicated to the French students of the May 1968 rebellion. Correcting possible misconceptions, he declared to a Berlin audience in 1967: "I have never said that the student opposition today is by itself a revolutionary force, nor have I ever seen in the hippies the 'heir of the proletariat'!" Herbert Marcuse, "The Problem of Violence and the Radical Opposition," in *Five Lectures: Psychoanalysis, Politics and Utopia,* trans. Jeremy Shapiro and Shierry Weber (Boston: Beacon Press, 1970), 93.

83. Interview with Russell Neufeld.

84. "The Real SDS Stands Up," in *Weatherman,* ed. H. Jacobs, 17.

85. Ibid., 17.

86. "Toward a Revolutionary Youth Movement," in *Debate within SDS: RYM II vs Weatherman,* ed. Radical Education Project (Detroit: Radical Education Project, 1969), 1.

87. Ibid.

88. See, e.g., "More on Youth Movement," "Notes on Class: Some Implications for the Revolutionary Youth Movement" in ibid.

89. Interview with Bernardine Dohrn.

90. Cathy Wilkerson, Mike Spiegal, and Les Coleman, "The False Privilege," *New Left Notes,* October 7, 1968.

91. "Toward a Revolutionary Youth Movement," 1.

92. Mellen interview, 21–22.

93. Nicholas von Hoffman, *San Francisco Chronicle,* June 21, 1969, 5. See also Sale, *SDS,* 559–79.

94. Johnathen Lerner, "I Was a Terrorist," *Washington Post Magazine,* February 20, 2002, A4.

95. Karen Ashley, Bill Ayers, et al., "You Don't Need a Weatherman to Know Which Way the Wind Blows," *New Left Notes,* June 18, 1969, in *Weatherman,* ed. H. Jacobs. Quotations from 51–53.

96. Ibid., 52.

97. Ibid., 65.

98. Ibid., 70.

99. Ibid., 58.

100. Ibid., 89.

101. Harry Magdoff, *The Age of Imperialism: The Economics of U.S. Foreign Policy* (New York: Modern Reader Paperbacks, 1969), 14–15. For a concise history of the idea of imperialism, see Patrick Wolfe, "Imperialism and History: A Century of Theory from Marx to Postcolonialism," *American Historical Review* 102, no. 2 (April 1997): 388–420.

102. Neufeld interview.

103. Mellen interview, 14.

104. Ibid.

105. Dohrn interview.

106. Weatherman did not envision the common dynamic in the contemporary global economy, described as the "race to the bottom," in which U.S.-owned multinational corporations close down domestic facilities and transfer their operations to countries with highly exploitable labor forces. See, among countless critiques of globalization, Cyrus Bina, Laurie Clements, and Chuck Davis, eds., *Beyond Survival: Wage Labor in the Late Twentieth Century* (Armonk, N.Y.: M. E. Sharpe, 1996).

107. Braley interview.

108. Neufeld interview.

109. Roth interview.

110. Ibid.

111. Ashley, Ayers, et al., "You Don't Need a Weatherman," 65.

112. Jack Weinberg and Jack Gleason, "SDS and the Movement: Where Do We Go From Here?" in *Weatherman*, ed. H. Jacobs, 112.

113. A RYM II statement was drafted at the convention, where eventual RYM II members suppressed their differences with the Weathermen so as to present a unified front against PL. RYM II became a distinct group in the weeks following and soon displaced PL as Weatherman's chief rival. With its emergence, Weatherman became known also as "RYM I."

114. Mike Klonsky, Noel Ignatin, et al., "Revolutionary Youth Movement II (RYM II)," in *Debate within SDS*, ed. Radical Education Project, 15.

115. For early criticisms of Weatherman, see Todd Gitlin, "New Left: Old Traps," James Weinstein, "Weatherman: A Lot of Thunder but a Short Reign," and Michael Lerner, "Weatherman: The Politics of Despair," all in *Weatherman*, ed. H. Jacobs.

116. Carl Oglesby, "1969," in *Weatherman*, ed. H. Jacobs, 135.

117. Paul Breines, "From Guru to Spectre: Marcuse and the Implosion of the Movement," in *Critical Interruptions: New Left Perspectives on Herbert Marcuse*, ed. Paul Breines (New York: Herder & Herder, 1970), 9–10.

118. Ibid., 14.

119. Gilbert, Columbia, 158.

120. Interview by WAAC Radio, Terre Haute, Indiana, quoted in FBI report "Foreign Influence—Weather Underground Organization (WUO)," August 20, 1976, 218–19. FBI-WUO.

121. Régis Debray, *Revolution in the Revolution?* (New York: Grove Press, 1967).

122. Interview with Jeff Jones.

123. Bentley Historical Library, University of Michigan, box 1, interview with Nais Raulet by Ellen Fishman, 1978 (Bret Eynon and the Contemporary History Project, 1981), 6.

124. Grievances with the leadership seem to have been near-universal among the rank and file, though they vary in nature and intensity.

125. Raulet interview, 7, 9.

126. This happened, most notoriously, in Cleveland in August of 1969. Raulet interview, 10. Roth interview.

127. Dohrn interview.

322 Notes to Pages 58–66

128. Hirsch-Dubin interview. Phoebe Hirsch is now married and takes the name Hirsch-Dubin.

129. Neufeld interview; "The Reminiscences of Cathlyn Wilkerson," Columbia, 71.

130. Larry Grathwohl, as told to Frank Reagan, *Bringing America Down: An FBI Informant with the Weathermen* (New Rochelle, N.Y.: Arlington House, 1976), 112–22.

131. Ayers interview.

132. Hirsch-Dubin interview.

133. Wilkerson, Columbia, 70.

134. Raulet interview, 5.

135. Dohrn interview.

136. Hirsch-Dubin interview.

137. On the last point, Wilkerson, Columbia, 73.

138. Raulet interview, 8.

139. Ayers interview.

140. Neufeld interview.

141. Interview with anonymous Weatherwoman.

142. Raulet interview, 7.

143. "Look At It: America 1969," in *Weatherman*, ed. H. Jacobs, 168.

144. Sale, *SDS*, 587–88.

145. Hirsch-Dubin interview.

146. Ibid.

147. After going to England, Proll turned himself in to West German authorities, receiving only minor sanction for his flight.

148. The screenplay was published as Ulrike Meinhof, *Bambule. Fürsorge— Sorge für wen?* (Berlin: Wagenbach, 1971).

149. On the Wandervögeln, see Detlev Peukert, *Inside Nazi Germany: Conformity, Opposition, and Racism in Everyday Life,* trans. Richard Deveson (New Haven: Yale University Press, 1987).

150. Becker, *Hitler's Children*, 74.

151. Astrid Proll, ed., *Baader Meinhof: Pictures on the Run, 67–77* (New York: Scalo, 1998), 5. The book was published under the German title *Hans und Grete: Die RAF, 67–1977.*

152. RAF, "Die Rote Armee Aufbauen!" *883*, no. 6 (May 22, 1970).

153. This is the conclusion of Mario Krebs, *Ulrike Meinhof: Ein Leben im Widerspruch* (Reinbeck: Rowohlt TB-V, 1995).

154. This is the view of Iring Fetscher in "Ideologien der Terroristen in der Bundesrepublik Deutschland," in Iring Fetscher, Günther Rohrmoser, et al., *Ideologien und Strategien, Analysen zum Terrorismus,* vol. 1 (Opladen: Westdeutscher Verlag, 1981), 15–271. See also Bernhard Rabert, *Links- und Rechtsterrorismus in der Bundesrepublik Deutschland von 1970 bis heute* (Bonn: Bernard & Graefe, 1995), 88–113.

155. The phrase is from Richard McCormick, *The Politics of the Self: Feminism and Postmodernism in West German Literature and Film* (Princeton: Princeton University Press, 1991).

156. Jürgen Horlemann quoted in Langguth, *Protestbewegung*, 208.

157. *Der Kampf des Vietnamesischen Volkes und die Globalstrategie des Imperialismus: Internationaler Vietnam-Kongreß* (Berlin: INFI, 1968), 90.

158. Ibid., 123.

159. Langguth, *Protestbewegung*, 50.

160. On the disintegration of the student movement, see ibid., 52–54, 71–89.

161. RAF, "Den antiimperialistichen Kampf führen! Die Rote Armee aufbauen! Die Aktion des Schwarzen September in München," in RAF, *texte*, 431.

162. RAF, "Dem Volk dienen: Stadtguerilla und Klassenkampf," in RAF, *texte*, 372.

163. RAF, "Den antiimperialistichen Kampf führen!" 413–14.

164. RAF, "Concept of the Urban Guerrilla," 38.

165. Schiller, *"Es war ein harter Kampf,"* 53.

166. The Platform of the Popular Front for the Liberation of Palestine, the PLO's military wing, declared, "The Palestinian struggle is a part of the whole Arab liberation movement and the world liberation movement," and denounced "Zionism" and the "Arab Bourgeoisie" alike. Laqueur, *Terrorism Reader,* 146.

167. Christoph Martel, "Nur die besten Absichten: Das prekäre Verhältnis der deutschen 68er zu den USA und Israel" (unpublished seminar paper, University of Göttingen, 1999), 25.

168. Quoted in ibid., 26.

169. Martel skillfully navigates perspectives on the West German New Left's relationship to Israel.

170. RAF, "Concept of the Urban Guerrilla," 38.

171. Horst Mahler, "Über den bewaffneten Kampf in Westeuropa," in *Die alte Straßenverkehrsordnung: Dokumente der RAF* (Berlin: Edition Tiamat, 1987), 68.

172. RAF, "Den antiimperialistichen Kampf führen!" 433.

173. Ibid., 37.

174. Ibid., 36, 45.

175. See "rede von ulrike zu der befreiung von andreas, moabit 13. september 74," in RAF, *texte,* 65.

176. Meinhof conveyed the RAF's esteem for Baader at her 1974 trial for freeing Baader from prison in 1970. Ibid.

177. Beate Sturm, "Man kann nur züruchbrüllen," *Spiegel,* no. 7 (1972): 52–63.

178. Mahler, "Über den bewaffneten Kampf in Westeuropa," 41.

179. Ibid.

180. Ibid., 59.

181. Ibid., 119. *Ideologien und Strategien* details the differences between RAF texts written by Meinhof and those written by Mahler.

182. Despite Marighela's reputation as a skilled theoretician of guerrilla war, his combat model ultimately proved ineffective not only in Brazil itself, but in Uruguay and other Latin American countries as well. Marighela was killed by Brazilian state agents in November 1969. See John W. Williams, "Carlos Marighela: The Father of Modern Guerrilla Warfare," *Terrorism* 12, no. 1 (1989): 1–20.

183. "Man kann nur züruchbrüllen," *Spiegel,* no. 7 (1972): 57.

184. Schiller, *"Es war ein harter Kampf,"* 20–39. See also Sozialistisches Patientenkollektiv, *Aus der Krankheit eine Waffe machen: Eine Agitationsschrift des Sozialistischen Patientenkollektiv an der Universität Heidelberg* (Heidelberg: SPK, 1987).

185. Schiller, *"Es war ein harter Kampf,"* 38.

186. Ibid., 12.

187. "Kongreß 'Hochschule und Demokratie'—Diskussion über die 'Tatigkeit der Regelveletzung' und 'linken Faschismus' (9. Juni 1967)," in *APO: Die außerparlamentarische Opposition,* ed. Otto, 245.

188. Ibid., 241, 245. Habermas substantially qualified the charge of "left fascism" a year later in "'Etikett des linken Fascismus' vom 13. Mai 1968," in *APO: Die außerparlamentarische Opposition,* ed. Otto, 249–58.

189. Jürgen Habermas, "Scheinrevolution unter Handlungszwang," in *APO: Die außerparlamentarische Opposition,* ed. Otto, 284.

2. THE IMPORTANCE OF BEING MILITANT

1. SDS National Office flyer, fall 1969. Cornell SDS.

2. Shin'ya Ono, "A Weatherman: You Do Need a Weatherman to Know Which Way the Wind Blows," in *Weatherman,* ed. H. Jacobs, 249–51. Braley interview.

3. Ibid., 248.

4. Stern, *With the Weathermen,* 128–29.

5. Ayers, *Fugitive Days,* 162–64.

6. Ono, "Weatherman," 252.

7. Dellinger, *More Power Than We Know,* 162–65.

8. Quoted in Sale, *SDS,* 582–83.

9. *RAT,* September 23–October 8, 1969.

10. Hirsch-Dubin interview.

11. Neufeld interview.

12. Wilkerson interview, Columbia, 75.

13. Grathwohl, *Bringing America Down.*

14. Sale, *SDS,* 603.

15. Ono, "Weatherman," 253.

16. Stern, *With the Weathermen,* 132–33.

17. Ibid., 134.

18. Weiss interview.

19. Interview with Naomi Jaffe.

20. Tom Hayden, "Justice in the Streets," in *Weatherman,* ed. H. Jacobs, 297.

21. Sale, *SDS,* 605–6.

22. See Chicago's *Sun* and *Tribune* newspapers, October 9–12; the *Chicago Tribune Sunday Magazine,* October 23, 1969; Sale, *SDS,* 605–11; Tom Thomas, "The Second Battle of Chicago," in *Weatherman,* ed. H. Jacobs, 196–226; and Dellinger, *More Power Than We Know,* 150–69.

23. Interview with Duane Hall, "Peter Joseph Collection, Unprocessed," Butler Library, Columbia University.

24. Hirsch-Dubin interview.

25. Ibid.

26. Dohrn interview.

27. Johnny Lerner made the claim in an October 9 press conference, recorded in the FBI Report, Chicago Office, "Students for a Democratic Society," November 7, 1969, 68. FBI-WUO.

28. Thomas, "Second Battle of Chicago," 207.

29. Interview with Duane Hall.

30. Statistics FBI Report, Chicago Office, "Students for a Democratic Society," November 7, 1969, 188–89, 91, FBI-WUO.

31. *Chicago Tribune,* October 9, 1969, 1.

32. Hirsch-Dubin interview.

33. *Chicago Tribune,* October 9 and 10, 1969, 1, 2.

34. Ibid., October 12, 1969, 1.

35. Ibid., October 10, 1969, 1.

36. Ibid., October 12, 1969, 5.

37. Ibid., October 13, 1969, 22.

38. Ono, "Weatherman," 273–74.

39. Hampton quoted on ABC News, national broadcast, October 9, 1969.

40. *Guardian,* October 18, 1969, 4.

41. *Fifth Estate,* October 16–25, 1969, 3–4.

42. Pro-RYM II articles appeared in Seattle's *Helix,* October 16, 1969; Milwaukee's *Heterodoxical Voice,* November 1969; and Austin's *Rag,* October 21, 1969.

43. Sale, *SDS,* 614–15.

44. *Berkeley Tribe,* October 24–30, 1969, 7, 22–24.

45. *Ann Arbor Argus,* November 18–December 11, 1969, 8–9.

46. Andrew Kopkind, "Going Down in Chicago," in *Weatherman,* ed. H. Jacobs, 284.

47. "What Was Chicago?" *Berkeley Tribe,* October 31–November 6, 1969, 14–16; all quotations from 15. Representatives of the *Tribe, Seed, RAT,* and the radical film collective New York Newsreel participated in the discussion.

48. Rossinow, *Politics of Authenticity,* 4. Subsequent quotations from 19, 97, 82.

49. Hirsch-Dubin interview.

50. Ayers interview.

51. Ralph Larkin and Daniel Foss, "Lexicon of Folk-Etymology," in *The 60s without Apology,* ed. Sohnya Sayres et al. (Minneapolis: University of Minnesota Press, 1988); quotations from 363. The lexicon is as intriguing in its form as its content. With their thorough and affectionate definitions of 1960s jargon such as "bum trip" and "farout," Larkin and Foss illustrate the importance of language in the New Left's self-understanding. But in the often excessive formality of their definitions, they appear also to mock both cultural anthropology and the New Left's self-absorption.

52. Jean-Paul Sartre, preface to Frantz Fanon, *The Wretched of the Earth,* trans. Constance Farrington (New York: Grove Press, 1963), 17.

53. Braley Interview.

54. Rossinow, *Politics of Authenticity,* 128.

55. Herbert Marcuse, *Counterrevolution and Revolt* (Boston: Beacon Press, 1972), 133.

56. Ono, "Weatherman," 223–24.

57. Fanon, *Wretched of the Earth.*

58. *Guardian,* October 18, 1969, 14.

59. Gilbert, Columbia, 75–76.

60. Ibid., June 18, 1985, 256.

61. Max Weber, "Politics as a Vocation," in *From Max Weber: Essays in Sociology,* trans. and ed. H. H. Gerth and C. Wright Mills (New York: Oxford University Press, 1964), 117–25.

62. Palmer interview.

63. Ono, "Weatherman," 241.

64. Quoted in Thomas, "Second Battle of Chicago," in *Weatherman,* ed. H. Jacobs, 205.

65. Palmer interview.

66. *Ann Arbor Argus,* December 13, 1969, 3.

67. Gilbert, Columbia, 346.

68. Ibid., 271.

69. Ibid., 346.

70. Hirsch-Dubin interview.

71. Gitlin, *The Sixties,* 287.

72. Jones, Columbia, 64.

73. Louis Althusser, "Ideology and Ideological State Apparatuses," in *Lenin and Philosophy and Other Essays,* trans. Ben Brewster (New York: Monthly Review Press, 1971), 127–86.

74. Stern, *With the Weathermen,* 26–27.

75. *Ann Arbor Argus,* June 19–July 3, 1969, 4.

76. Ibid., 10.

77. In *The Conquest of Cool: Business Culture, Counterculture and the Rise of Consumerism* (Chicago: University of Chicago Press, 1997), Thomas Frank has sharply questioned the oppositional nature of the counterculture by documenting the confluence in the 1960s of its values with those celebrated by advertisers and the corporate world generally.

78. Quotations from Larkin and Foss, "Lexicon of Folk-Etymology," 362–63.

79. Braley interview.

80. *RAT,* January 3–16, 1969.

81. *Fifth Estate,* February 6–19, 1969.

82. Ibid., February 19–March 4, 1970.

83. Sigmund Freud theorizes the relationship between desire, guilt, and aggression in *Civilization and Its Discontents,* trans. James Strachey (New York: Norton, 1961).

84. Tom Wells, *The War Within: America's Battle over Vietnam* (Berkeley: University of California Press, 1994), 122, 293. The two were prominent in Clergy and Laymen Concerned about Vietnam.

85. One need look no further than the Weathermen themselves to appreci-

ate the obvious differences between the U.S. government and the Nazi regime. With the Days of Rage, the Weathermen publicly announced and then carried out their intention of attacking property and police, suffering mostly minor injuries. Members of the Munich-based student group White Rose were executed merely for distributing leaflets denouncing the Nazis.

86. Palmer interview.

87. Wells, *War Within,* 163.

88. *Berkeley Tribe,* October 31–November 6, 1969, 16.

89. Jones, Columbia, 78.

90. Ibid., 85.

91. Wilkerson, Columbia, 75.

92. Weber, "Politics as a Vocation," 121. Weber himself performed this reversal, as his exemplar of the ethic of ultimate ends shifts from a Christian pacifist to an anarchist bomber who holds little hope of ameliorating social conditions through violence.

93. Ibid., 120.

94. Ibid., 121.

95. Michel Foucault, "Between 'Words' and 'Things' in '68," in *Remarks on Marks,* trans. R. James Goldstein and James Cascaito (Semiotext(e): New York, 1991), 137. Additional quotations from 134–39.

96. Jean-Paul Sartre, Preface to Fanon, *Wretched of the Earth,* 21.

97. *Ann Arbor Argus,* December 31, 1969, 3.

98. Gilbert and Wilkerson each criticized Weatherman's early politics as "Debrayist." Gilbert, Columbia, 194; Wilkerson, Columbia, 83.

99. Marcuse, *Counterrevolution and Revolt,* 133.

100. *Guardian,* October 18, 1969, 14.

101. *Helix,* October 16, 1969, 7; *Rag,* October 21, 1969, 14.

102. According to FBI intelligence, RYM II members themselves complained that their actions in Chicago were poorly organized and somewhat uninspiring. FBI Report, Chicago Office, "Students for a Democratic Society," November 7, 1969, 180–83. FBI-WUO. RYM II failed to establish a presence on campuses and by the spring of 1970 was essentially defunct.

103. *Guardian,* October 18, 1969, 8.

104. Ibid., 14.

105. Ibid.

106. Larkin and Foss, "Lexicon of Folk-Etymology," quotations from 363–64.

107. See Tom Wolfe, *The Electric Kool-Aid Acid Test* (New York: Bantam Books, 1981).

108. The pioneers of the psychedelic culture used their own death imagery. A key emblem of The Grateful Dead—the "house band" of the Acid Tests—is a skeleton wearing a crown of cascading roses, in which death and the fecund beauty of life merge. Unifying the two, or at least mastering their tension, may be described as the most profound challenge of an LSD trip. A skull with a lightening bolt shooting through it, called a "Steal Your Face," is another of the band's symbols. Taken from the lyric "steal your face right off your head," it suggests that LSD can entail a kind of ego death.

109. Raskin, *For the Hell of It,* 67. Raskin, a close friend of the late Hoff-

man, suggests that Hoffman exaggerated the role of LSD in his activism. Raskin presents Hoffman as a master of self-fashioning who showed precisely how fungible both self and politics are—for better and for worse. Raskin concludes: "Abbie's life provides a cautionary tale about how we live and die. Perhaps we can't change the world, as so many of us believed in the sixties. But we can change our immediate circumstances, at least some of the time. We are the authors of our own lives. . . . The choices are up to us. We can create ourselves as well as destroy ourselves." Ibid., 264.

110. Ibid., 162.
111. *FIRE!* October 21, 1969.
112. *FIRE!* November 7, 1969.
113. *FIRE!* October 21, 1969.
114. Ono, "Weatherman," 235–36.
115. Ibid., 271–72.
116. Ibid., 261.
117. "Weatherman: The Long and Winding Road to the Underground," in *Defiance #2: A Radical Review,* ed. Dotson Rader (New York: Paperback Library, 1970), 15.
118. Jones interview.
119. Stern, *With the Weathermen,* 154–55.
120. Hirsch-Dubin interview.
121. Interview with anonymous Weatherwoman.
122. Braley interview.
123. "Weatherman: The Long and Winding Road," 14.
124. Jones, Columbia, 86.
125. Mellen interview, 34.
126. Braley interview.
127. Weiss interview.
128. Gitlin, *The Sixties,* 253–54.
129. Hirsch-Dubin interview.
130. Ayers interview.
131. Ono, "Weatherman," 271.

3. "HEARTS AND MINDS"

1. Wells, *War Within,* 328–31.
2. *Guardian,* October 25, 1969, 4–5, and Wells, *War Within,* 370–75.
3. Wells, *War Within,* 371.
4. Ibid., 371, 382, 385, 383.
5. Hoffman pledge, *Washington Post* (henceforth cited as *WP*), November 11, 1969, A1; Rubin remark, Wells, *War Within,* 382.
6. *WP,* November 11, 1969, A1. Ayers remarks, FBI memos, Chicago office to regional offices, October 13, 1969, October 30, 1969. FBI-WUO.
7. *Guardian,* November 22, 1969, 3.
8. John Cohen, Introduction to Samuel Melville, *Letters from Attica* (New York: William Morrow, 1972), 50.

9. Jane Alpert, *Growing Up Underground* (New York: William Morrow, 1981), 115.

10. Jane Alpert, "Profile of Sam Melville," in Melville, *Letters from Attica,* 20.

11. Palmer interview.

12. Alpert, *Growing Up Underground,* 214.

13. *WP,* November 12, 1969, A8.

14. Cohen, 77.

15. Ibid., 78.

16. The cunning of undercover agents was impressive. At the Democratic Convention in Chicago, Palmer threw a chunk of concrete through the window of a Cadillac right in front of Demmerle. Several activists at the scene, Demmerle among them, were arrested. Palmer grew suspicious of Demmerle (though insufficiently so) when the charges against them were mysteriously dropped. Palmer interviews.

17. Wells, *War Within,* 159.

18. Two of the Catonsville defendants, Thomas Lewis and Philip Berrigan, had received but not yet started serving sentences of six years in federal prison for spilling their blood on draft files in 1967.

19. Daniel Berrigan, *The Trial of the Catonsville 9* (Boston: Beacon Press, 1969), 35. Subsequent quotations from 44, 94, 94–95, respectively. See Murray Polner and Jim O'Grady, *Disarmed and Dangerous: The Radical Life and Times of Daniel and Philip Berrigan* (1997; reprint, Boulder, Colo.: Westview Press, 1998).

20. Interview with Paul Mayer.

21. Ibid.

22. *Guardian,* July 15, 1967, 3.

23. *Treason!* Winter 1968, 27–28.

24. *FIRE!* November 7, 1969, 1, 9.

25. Marcuse, "Repressive Tolerance," 83–84

26. *FIRE!* November 21, 1969, in *Weatherman,* ed. H. Jacobs, 276.

27. *Helix,* November 13, 1969, 3.

28. Wells, *War Within,* 392–93; *WP* November 14, 1969, A1, 18.

29. *Fifth Estate,* November 27–December 10, 15.

30. Wells, *War Within,* 391–92.

31. FBI memo, Chicago to Washington, November 25, 1969. FBI-WUO.

32. "Weatherman: The Long and Winding Road," 17.

33. *Quicksilver Times,* November 26–December 6, 7.

34. *WP,* November 15, 1969, A1, 8.

35. These are visible in a film of the protests, *Tarzan Stripes Forever or the Great American Tragedy,* made by Michael Dee, Jeffrey Lewis, Jonathan Dee, and Philip Coleman while undergraduates at Yale University.

36. *Quicksilver Times,* November 26–December 6, 3.

37. Yurick refers to Russia's "Bloody Sunday," when workers marched to Tsar Nicholas II's Winter Place to plead for justice and were shot at by the tsar's troops.

38. Sol Yurick, "On Making Foreign Policy with Your Feet," in *Defiance #1,* ed. Dotson Rader (New York: Paperback Library, 1970), 238, 245.

39. *WP,* November 16, 1969, A14.

40. Mellen interview, 34–35.

41. Ibid., 35.

42. Ibid.

43. Wells, *War Within,* 395; imagery largely from *Tarzan Stripes Forever.*

44. *WP,* November 16, 1969, A14.

45. *Guardian,* November 22, 1969, 16, and *WP,* November 17, 1969, A1, A18.

46. *Guardian,* November 22, 1969, 16.

47. *Seed* 4, no. 9 (1969): 3, 23.

48. Wells, *War Within,* 398–99.

49. *FIRE!* November 21, 1969, 1.

50. *WP,* November 16, 1969, B6.

51. Ibid., B7.

52. Wells, *War Within,* 435–46; George W. Hopkins, "'May Day' 1971," in Charles DeBenedetti Memorial Conference, *Give Peace a Chance: Exploring the Vietnam Antiwar Movement: Essays from the Charles DeBenedetti Memorial Conference,* ed. Melvin Small and William D. Hoover (Syracuse, N.Y.: Syracuse University Press, 1992), 72.

53. Hopkins; button from Mayer interview.

54. Paul Goodman, *Drawing the Line: The Political Essays of Paul Goodman,* ed. Taylor Stoer (New York: Dutton, 1977), 170.

55. *WP,* November 16, 1969, B6.

56. Ibid., B7.

57. George Mosse, *The Nationalization of the Masses: Political Symbolism and Mass Movements in Germany from the Napoleonic Wars through the Third Reich* (Ithaca, N.Y.: Cornell University Press, 1975).

58. *Guardian,* November 22, 1969, 7.

59. *WP,* November 16, 1969, A14.

60. *Guardian,* November 22, 1969, 7.

61. Wells, *War Within,* 397.

62. *WP,* November 17, 1969, A1.

63. Ibid., A1, 19.

64. The language of the silent majority was not new in discussions of Vietnam. In 1967, the hawkish AFL-CIO President George Meany asserted that prowar labor spoke for "the vast, silent majority in the nation." Quoted in Rhodri Jeffreys-Jones, *Peace Now! American Society and the Ending of the Vietnam War* (New Haven: Yale University Press, 1999), 181.

65. Jeffreys-Jones, *Peace Now!* 198, 236.

66. William Safire, "Old Pro Perot," *NYT,* May 7, 1992, A27. The scheme grows still more comic. Ron Zeigler, Nixon's press secretary, at one point inquired where the letters, never delivered to Washington, were being kept. Upon learning that they were in depositories throughout America, he asked, "You mean . . . when reporters ask me 'Where is the Silent Majority' I can say we have them locked up in bank vaults all over the country?"

67. Recent revelations indicate that the Nixon administration manipulated the impression that the silent majority speech caused a spontaneous outpouring of support for Nixon's policies. Alexander Butterfield, a Nixon aide, testified in

court in 1999 that he had helped arrange that pro-Nixon telegrams and letters be sent to the White House by labor unions, veterans' groups, and Republican governors and party chairmen (*NYT,* January 23, 1999).

68. Jeffreys-Jones, *Peace Now!* 197–98.

69. Quoted in ibid., 198.

70. Ayers interview.

71. Harrison Salisbury gave Americans a glimpse of the unity of the Vietnamese resistance in *Behind the Lines—Hanoi* (New York: Harper & Row, 1967). Having toured North Vietnam, he described how all layers of society were involved in military operations, civil defense, the treatment of the wounded, and rebuilding after bombings.

72. Ayers interview.

73. Goodman, 166.

74. David Farber, *The Age of Great Dreams: America in the 1960s* (New York: Hill & Wang, 1994), 167.

75. The Vietnamese were themselves divided in their ambitions for the American resistance. Vietnamese officials told Weathermen on a 1969 Venceremos Brigade, who were considered worthy of special instructions, that it was imperative to "stop the airplanes. . . . Your people are killing our people. Violence is not a choice for us." In response, the Weathermen attempted to disable warplanes in California air bases. Ayers interview.

76. Mellen interview, 36.

77. Palmer interviews.

78. Mellen interview, 36.

79. Jean Baudrillard, *In the Shadow of the Silent Majorities, or, The End of the Social and Other Essays,* trans. Paul Foss, John Johnston, and Paul Patton (New York: Semiotext(e) and Paul Virilio, 1983), 5. Subsequent quotations from 7, 2.

80. Ibid., 13–14.

81. For example, two major works on the antiwar movement, Charles DeBenedetti, *An American Ordeal: The Antiwar Movement of the Vietnam Era* (Syracuse, N.Y.: Syracuse University Press, 1990), and Nancy Zaroulis and Gerald Sullivan, *Who Spoke Up? American Protest against the War in Vietnam, 1963–1975* (Garden City, N.Y.: Doubleday, 1984), heap criticism on the Weathermen and other militants.

82. Government duplicity on Vietnam was legion, as evidenced by the Pentagon Papers, leaked by Daniel Ellsberg, and efforts to suppress CIA data on enemy troop strength, which as early as 1966–67 all but foretold U.S. defeat in Southeast Asia. On this, see Ralph W. McGehee, *Deadly Deceits: My 25 Years in the CIA* (New York: Sheridan Square Publications, 1983).

83. Wells, *War Within,* 4.

84. On the movement's achievements, see ibid., 4–5, 357, 377, 397.

85. Ibid., 2–3.

86. Ibid. Wells, *War Within,* 174, 179–80, 219, quotes antiwar activists castigating violence variously as a politically shallow effort at emotional gratification, a form of one-upsmanship in a crass competition over degrees of commitment, and an expression of a characteristically American impatience, at odds with the Vietnamese's appreciation of the need for stamina in political struggle.

87. Quoted in Joan Morrison and Robert K. Morrison, eds., *From Camelot to Kent State: The Sixties Experience in the Words of Those Who Lived It* (New York: Times Books, 1987), 314.

88. Weiss interview.

89. How the public would have responded to more detailed and timely knowledge of the brutal nature of U.S. conduct in Vietnam is a matter of speculation. Veterans who turned against the war eventually tried to spell out for the American public the worst of what was happening in Vietnam. Most notably, in early 1971, Vietnam Veterans against the War held the "Winter Soldier" hearings in Detroit, in which veterans testified about atrocities in which they had participated or of which they had learned. Though such accusations caused some stir, they received conspicuously little media attention and inspired fierce rebuttals from military and political officials. Incredulity, fueled by government efforts to discredit antiwar veterans, was perhaps a more common public response than outrage. See Vietnam Veterans against the War, *The Winter Soldier Investigation: An Inquiry into American War Crimes* (Boston: Beacon Press, 1971) and Andrew Hunt, *The Turning: A History of Vietnam Veterans against the War* (New York: New York University Press, 1999).

90. Wells, *War Within*, 357.

91. Ibid., 413.

92. Ibid., 394.

93. Ibid., xxi, xiv.

94. Ono, "Weatherman," in *Weatherman*, ed. H. Jacobs, 239.

95. Abbie Hoffman, in *Seed* 4, no. 9 (1969): 3.

96. Any such judgment would only provide one variable among many in answering the daunting and more important question of why exactly the United States lost the war.

97. *WP*, October 22, 1967, A1.

98. Jane Alpert, "Mother Right: A New Feminist Theory," *Ms.*, August 1975, 55. Palmer readily admits to having been a chauvinist in the 1960s but objects to the severity of Alpert's public accusation.

99. Dellinger, *More Power Than We Know*, 139.

100. Palmer interviews.

4. THE EXCESSES AND LIMITS
OF REVOLUTIONARY VIOLENCE

1. Mellen interview, 14.

2. The imagery of boundary crossing was most explicit in the drug culture. In one of the defining gestures of the era, Ken Kesey and his LSD-soaked "pioneers of consciousness," the Merry Pranksters, emblazoned the word "furthur" (deliberately misspelled for effect) atop the psychedelic bus in which they toured America in the early 1960s.

3. Tom Hayden, "Justice is in the Streets," in *Weatherman*, ed. H. Jacobs, 299.

4. Neufeld and Braley interviews.

5. The FBI's first extensive report on Weatherman, prepared by the Chicago

office, consisted largely of publicly available texts, such as the SDS constitution and the writings of SDS's warring factions. FBI Report, "Students for a Democratic Society," November 7, 1969. FBI-WUO.

6. FBI memo, Brennan to Sullivan, December 19, 1969. FBI-WUO.

7. Airtel, FBI director to SAC offices, October 23, 1969. FBI-WUO.

8. FBI memo, Brennan to Sullivan, October 20, 1969; Airtel, FBI director to SAC offices, October 28, 1969. FBI-WUO.

9. *The Weather Underground: Report of the Subcommittee to Investigate the Administration of the Internal Security Act and Other Internal Security Laws of the Committee on the Judiciary, United States Senate* (Washington, D.C.: GPO, 1975), 19. Hereafter cited as *WUR*. Michael Wood, "Weather Report: A Dove in the Kitchen," *WIN*, February 1, 1970, 7.

10. Ayers, *Fugitive Days*, 177.

11. Roth interview.

12. Neufeld and Roth interviews.

13. Thirteen Weathermen, among them Dohrn, Weiss, and Neufeld, were arrested on charges of aggravated battery and mob action. Ten days later, Roth and Boudin were arrested and warrants were issued for four others. FBI report, "Students for a Democratic Society," November 7, 1969, 39. FBI-WUO.

14. Seale was also under indictment at the time for an attempted murder in a separate jurisdiction. Judge Hoffman removed Seale from the trial, thus reducing the Chicago 8 to the Chicago Seven, and scheduled his retrial, which never took place. See Ward Churchill, "'To Disrupt, Discredit and Destroy': The FBI's Secret War on the Black Panther Party," in *Liberation, Imagination, and the Black Panther Party*, ed. Kathleen Cleaver and George Katsiaficas (New York: Routledge, 2001), 106–7.

15. On the murders, see ibid. and the documentary *The Murder of Fred Hampton*, dir. Howard Alk (Chicago: MGA Video, 1971). The details of the murder plot were revealed in *Hampton v. Hanrahan* and in a civil trial resolving in 1982 in favor of Hampton's family and associates.

16. Jones interview.

17. Ayers interview.

18. Neufeld interview.

19. To an outsider, the French novelist Jean Genet, the differences in the state's response to white and black radicals were "dizzying." Genet, who toured the country with the Panthers in 1970, observed that they "were forced to defend themselves with rifles. . . . [In their offices] the doors and windows are barricaded. And there, in the same room, there were women and little kids. That's the reality of the situation [that] everyone has to know about." *Philadelphia Free Press*, February 1971.

20. Gilbert, Columbia, 200.

21. Wilkerson, Columbia, 85.

22. Gilbert, Columbia, 187; Jaffe interview.

23. Dohrn interview.

24. Neufeld interview.

25. Ayers, *Fugitive Days*, 145–46.

26. Neufeld interview.

27. Roth interview.

28. Braley interview.

29. FBI memo, Brennan to Sullivan, December 19, 1969. FBI-WUO.

30. *WUR*, 20–22, 117–29.

31. LNS, "Stormy Weather," in *Weatherman,* ed. H. Jacobs, 341.

32. Stern, *With the Weathermen,* 196.

33. "Everyone Talks about the Weather" in *Weatherman,* ed. H. Jacobs, 444.

34. Sale, *SDS,* 626.

35. On Flint, see *Weatherman,* ed. H. Jacobs, 341–50; Sale, *SDS,* 626–29; Jonah Raskin, *Out of the Whale* (New York: Links Books, 1974), 145–50; Stern, *With the Weathermen,* 195–206; Grathwohl, *Bringing America Down,* 99–111; *Ann Arbor Argus,* December 31, 1969, 2–3, 19; *Berkeley Tribe,* January 9–15, 5; *Quicksilver Times,* January 9–19, 4; *Fifth Estate,* January 22–February 4, 1970, 12–4; and *Scanlan's,* January 1971, 13–15.

36. *Weatherman,* ed. H. Jacobs, 356.

37. Ibid., 353.

38. *Fifth Estate,* January 22–February 4, 1970, 14.

39. Ibid.

40. Dellinger, by contrast, speculated that the Days of Rage may have precipitated Hampton's murder by riling Chicago's police. Dellinger, *More Power Than We Know,* 165.

41. *Fifth Estate,* January 22–February 4, 1970, 13.

42. Dellinger, *More Power Than We Know,* 152. Palmer reports that Dohrn was criticized internally for the Manson comment. Palmer interview.

43. "The Reminiscences of Carol Bightman," Columbia, 30.

44. Grathwohl, *Bringing America Down,* 102, 105. The *Ann Arbor Argus* titled its coverage of Flint "Moby Dick."

45. This quote is the paraphrase of the *Ann Arbor Argus,* December 31, 1969, 19.

46. Stern, *With the Weathermen,* 199.

47. *Ann Arbor Argus,* December 31, 1969, 19.

48. Gitlin, *The Sixties,* 399.

49. Wilkerson, Columbia, 76–77.

50. Interview with anonymous Weatherwoman.

51. Brightman, Columbia, 88.

52. Raskin, *Out of the Whale,* 148.

53. *Berkeley Tribe,* January 9–15, 1970, 5.

54. *Fifth Estate,* January 22–February 4, 1970, 12.

55. Hendrik Hertzberg, "Weather Report: White Tornado," *WIN,* February 1, 1970, 5–6.

56. Both events were widely interpreted by the left as marking the souring of its idealism. See, among countless commentaries on Altamont, "Stones' Concert Ends It," *Berkeley Tribe,* December 12–19, 1969, 1.

57. Gilbert, Columbia, 188–89, 200–201.

58. Stern, *With the Weathermen,* 204–5.

59. Jaffe interview.

60. Gitlin, *The Sixties,* 316–18.

61. Kenneth Kenniston, "The Agony of the Counterculture," in *The Eloquence of Protest: Voices of the 70s,* ed. Harrison Salisbury (Boston: Houghton Mifflin, 1972), 220.

62. Tom Bates, *Rads: The 1970 Bombing of the Army Math Research Center at the University of Wisconsin and Its Aftermath* (New York: Harper Collins, 1992), 415.

63. On the praise of Brown, see *Quicksilver Times,* January 9–19, 1970, 4.

64. Albert Camus invokes Doestoevsky's epigram in a discussion of modern political murder in *The Rebel: An Essay on Man in Revolt* (1951), trans. Anthony Bauer (New York: Vintage Books, 1956), 67.

65. The Weathermen were not alone in praising Manson. An underground newspaper in Los Angeles named Manson its "Man of the Year" for 1969. Jerry Rubin actually visited Manson in prison and claimed him as a great "inspiration." Vincent Bugliosi with Curt Gentry, *Helter Skelter: The True Story of the Manson Murders* (New York: Bantam Books, 1975), 296–97.

66. Eldridge Cleaver, *Soul on Ice* (New York: McGraw-Hill, 1967).

67. Cleaver, *Post-Prison Writings,* 41.

68. David Hilliard, "If You Want Peace You Have to Fight for It," in *The Black Panthers Speak,* ed. Philip S. Foner (New York: Lippincott, 1970), 130.

69. "Interview with CBS News, December 28, 1969," in ibid., 133.

70. Quoted in Churchill, "'To Disrupt, Discredit and Destroy,'" 83.

71. Norman Mailer, *The White Negro* (San Francisco: City Lights, 1957).

72. *Ann Arbor Argus,* December 31, 1969, 2.

73. *Fifth Estate,* January 22–February 4, 1970, 13.

74. *RAT* 1, no. 26 (1969): 7.

75. Quoted in Leslie Fielder, *Freaks: Myths and Images of the Secret Self* (New York: Touchstone, 1978). The "freak" was an especially important figure in the underground "comix" of the era, notably Gilbert Shelton's endearing, doped-out Fabulous Furry Freak Brothers.

76. Notes on the lyrics' origins can be found at www.airplane.freeserve.co.uk/interviews/comments.htm. Some of the lines appear in the *Niagara Liberation Front Program for Action* (Buffalo SDS pamphlet, 1969). LFK-SDS. Mark Rudd threatened Columbia's president during the 1968 rebellion, saying, "Up against the wall, motherfucker, this is a stick-up!" (Caute, *Sixty-Eight,* 142). He was quoting the black radical playwright Everett LeRoi Jones (who subsequently renamed himself Amiri Baraka, or Imanu Amiri Baraka).

77. *Fifth Estate,* December 11–14, cover.

78. Brightman, Columbia, 88.

79. *Berkeley Tribe,* January 9–15, 1970, 5.

80. I. F. Stone, "Where the Fuse on That Dynamite Leads," in *Weatherman,* ed. H. Jacobs, 172.

81. *Berkeley Tribe,* January 9–15, 1970, 5.

82. *Weatherman,* ed. H. Jacobs, 343.

83. Stern, *With the Weathermen,* 87.

84. Arthur Koestler, *Darkness at Noon* (1941; reprint, New York: Penguin Books, 1961).

85. Herbert Marcuse, *One-Dimensional Man: Studies in the Ideology of Advanced Industrial Society* (Boston: Beacon Press, 1964).

86. Roth interview.

87. Stern, *With the Weathermen,* 198.

88. On the "power of the negative" in dialectical criticism, see Marcuse's preface to his book *Reason and Revolution: Hegel and the Rise of Social Theory* (Boston: Beacon Press, 1961).

89. See his 1972 *Counterrevolution and Revolt.* Marcuse devotes much of the book, which offers a postmortem on the New Left, to the question of "art and revolution."

90. Marcuse also criticizes the "ideological" quality of bourgeois art, arguing that by creating an idealized world of form, such art provides an imaginary reconciliation of and escape from the contradictions defining social existence. Bourgeois art is therefore "affirmative" in a double sense: it points to emancipation, while helping to preserve the established order. See "The Affirmative Character of Culture," in Herbert Marcuse, *Negations: Essays in Critical Theory,* trans. Jeremy Shapiro (Boston: Beacon Press, 1968).

91. *News from Nowhere* used the line on its November 1969 cover.

92. Marcuse, *Counterrevolution and Revolt,* 112. A New Left tribute to Artaud, titled "Artaud's Electroshock Theater Recipe: Rip Off Amerika's Mommy Mask," appeared in the *San Diego Free Press,* September 3–17, 1969, 7. Extolling the kind of theatrical effect Marcuse questions, the *Free Press* wrote, "The diabolical magic of Artaud's theater reverses the world to expose reality [and] . . . the truth of repression, and suddenly the actors of the play become the shock troops of liberation."

93. Scholars have used the categories of acting out and working through to interpret political, cultural, and social phenomena mainly as they involve ways of responding to (or repressing) historical trauma. See especially Dominick LaCapra's *Representing the Holocaust* (Ithaca, N.Y.: Cornell University Press, 1995) and *Writing History, Writing Trauma* (Baltimore: Johns Hopkins University Press, 2001). I focus on repetition less as a delayed reaction to trauma than as a form of mirroring.

94. Kenniston, "Agony of the Counterculture," 219.

95. Ibid., 220.

96. Ibid., 221.

97. Within Kenniston's framework, Manson becomes a figure of "the uncanny" in a strict Freudian sense. According to Freud, the uncanny seems radically unfamiliar based only on a fundamental misrecognition. In fact all too familiar, it is the "return of the repressed," often appearing in disguised or even crazed form. See "The Uncanny," in *Sigmund Freud: Collected Papers,* vol. 4, trans. supervised by Joan Riviere (New York: Basic Books, 1956), 403. Manson now appears a condensation of pathologies present throughout American culture, the youth movement included. Manson himself seemed to apprehend just this, warning America from the witness stand, "[Y]ou haven't got long before you are all going to kill yourselves, because you are all crazy. . . . I am only what lives inside each and every one of you. My father is the jailhouse. My father is your system. . . . I am only a reflection of you" (Bugliosi, *Helter Skelter,* 526).

98. *RAT* 1, no. 26 (1969): 8. Rubin was referring to Guevara's ideal of the "New Socialist Man."

99. Quoted in Raskin, *For the Hell of It,* 188.

100. *Berkeley Tribe,* December 12–19, 1969; January 9–15, 1970, 5.

101. *Ann Arbor Argus,* May 24–June 9, 1969, 11.

102. Yet Stern also described the Manson gang's murder of the pregnant Sharon Tate as a potentially regenerative or redemptive act. She saw Manson as the "death rattle of the children of the old movement, the decade of SDS. Sharon Tate's white baby [in fact murdered] would be reborn underground, and it would live to become a symbol of revolutionary spirit and integrity to a confused and dispirited American youth" (Stern, *With the Weathermen,* 205).

103. "Weather Letter" in *Weatherman,* ed. H. Jacobs, 458.

104. See Robin Morgan, *The Demon Lover* (New York: Norton, 1988), as well as her 1970 tract "Good-bye to All That," in *Sisterhood Is Powerful: An Anthology of Writings from the Women's Liberation Movement,* ed. id. (New York: Vintage Books, 1970).

105. *RAT* 1, no. 26 (1969): 7.

106. On projection, scapegoating, and sacrifice, see LaCapra, cited n. 92 above; Peter Stallybrass and Allon White, *The Politics and Poetics of Transgression* (Ithaca, N.Y.: Cornell University Press, 1986); René Girard, *Violence and the Sacred,* trans. Patrick Gregory (Baltimore: Johns Hopkins University Press, 1979); and Mary Douglas, *Purity and Danger: An Analysis of Concepts of Pollution and Taboo* (London: Routledge, 1966).

107. Palmer interview; Robin Palmer, "First American Soldier Was a Vietcong," *RAT,* December 1969.

108. On the purges, see Grathwohl, *Bringing America Down,* 112–22, and Stern, *With the Weathermen,* 207–48.

109. Dohrn interview.

110. Interview with anonymous Weatherwoman.

111. Mellen interview, 20.

112. Ibid., 38.

113. Grathwohl, *Bringing America Down,* 135–52.

114. Ibid.; Jones interview.

115. *WUR,* 133–36. Neufeld interview.

116. Ayers, *Fugitive Days,* 145.

117. Ayers interview. The former *Ramparts* editors David Horowitz and Peter Collier profiled Robbins in a largely vituperative piece for *Rolling Stone,* written while they were converting to neoconservatism. See "Doing It: The Inside Story of the Weather Underground," *Rolling Stone,* September 30, 1982.

118. Palmer interview.

119. Accounts from *NYT,* March 7–16, 1970; Sale, *SDS,* 1–6; Powers, *Diana,* 1–10; *WUR,* 25.

120. FBI memo, Brennen to Sullivan, March 13, 1970. FBI-WUO.

121. Weather Underground, "New Morning," in Powers, *Diana,* 217–18. In interviews, Palmer and Ayers revealed the target of the bombs.

122. Recall the shooting of James Rector in 1969. On government abuses, see Ward Churchill and Jim Van der Wall, *The COINTELPRO Papers: Docu-*

ment's from the FBI's Secret Wars against Domestic Dissent (Boston: South End Press, 1990), and James Kirkpatrick Davis, *The FBI's Domestic Counterintelligence Program* (New York: Praeger, 1992).

123. *NYT* coverage, March 7–16, 1970; quotation, March 13, A38.

124. Powers's articles became the book *Diana: The Making of a Terrorist.*

125. Sale and Miller exemplify this view.

126. *WUR,* 38.

127. Airtel, FBI director to SAC, Albany, March 19, 1970. FBI-WUO.

128. FBI memo, Brennen to Sullivan, March 26, 1970, 4. FBI-WUO.

129. Ibid.

130. FBI liaison to John D. Ehrlichman, February 24, 1970. FBI-WUO.

131. *WUR,* 26–28.

132. *WUR,* 131.

133. *WUR,* 27–28.

134. FBI memo, Bishop to DeLoach, April 28, 1970. FBI-WUO.

135. Starnes described Wilkerson as a "slender, brown-eyed beauty . . . who reportedly plays both harp and guitar"; the next line noted that she was wanted for homicide. The article is enclosed in FBI memo, Bishop to DeLoach, May 8, 1970. FBI-WUO.

136. Letter, J. Edgar Hoover to Richard Starnes, May 8, 1970; FBI memo, Bishop to DeLoach, May 8, 1970. FBI-WUO.

137. FBI memo, Brennen to Sullivan, March 10, 1970, FBI-WUO.

138. On the bust, see Grathwohl, *Bringing America Down,* and "Linda Evans," *Ann Arbor Argus,* April 22, 1970, 15.

139. Stone, "Where the Fuse on That Dynamite Leads," 491–95.

140. *Fifth Estate,* April 16–22, 1970, 8.

141. Andrew Kopkind, "The Radical Bombers," in *Weatherman,* ed. H. Jacobs, 496–503.

142. *Berkeley Tribe,* May 29, 1970, 3.

143. *News from Nowhere* 1, no. 8 (May 1969): 7.

144. *Leviathan,* November 1969, 3.

145. *RAT,* December 1969, 3.

146. International Liberation School / Red Mountain Tribe, *Firearms and Self-Defense: A Handbook for Radicals, Revolutionaries, and Easy Riders* (Berkeley, Calif.: ILS / Red Mountain Tribe, 1969). Hoover Institution, box 39.

147. *Berkeley Tribe,* February 27–March 6, 1970. In the summer and fall, the *Quicksilver Times* printed a manual on how to make explosives titled the *Weatherman Handbook.*

148. Such worries were, it turns out, far from paranoia. In 2002, through a Freedom of Information Act (FOIA) request, the *San Francisco Chronicle* obtained FBI documents revealing a long history of FBI spying on Berkeley activists (among them professors and administrators), as well as plans to round up and intern dissidents in the event of a major domestic crisis. See www.sfgate.com/news/special pages/2002/campus files.

149. The contempt of court convictions, which held sentences of several years in prison, were later appealed and dismissed.

150. Sale, *SDS*, 637. Sale counts 169 campus bombings or arsons between May 1 and May 7 alone.

151. *WUR*, 7.

152. *Scanlan's* 1, no. 8 (January 1971).

153. On Davis, see Bettina Aptheker, *The Morning Breaks: The Trial of Angela Davis* (Ithaca, N.Y.: Cornell University Press, 1997).

154. *WUR*, 36.

155. Weatherman, "Communiqué 4" in *WUR*, 8.

156. No reliable history of the Black Liberation Army (BLA) exists. Government sources have a natural bias and do not remotely untangle the complexities of this essentially covert organization. Writings by those in or affiliated with the BLA are themselves vague on details (partly for reasons of security) and often contradictory. The conventional view has been that the BLA formed in 1971 when the International Section of the Black Panther Party (BPP), under Cleaver's charge, was formally expelled by the Oakland Panthers, headed by Huey Newton; this division, it is assumed, both signaled and precipitated a broader split within the organization, with those on the East Coast and in Los Angeles siding with Cleaver and opting for armed struggle, and those on the West Coast (excluding LA) following Newton to pursue other kinds of "revolutionary" activity. For this view, see Jalil Muntaqim, *On the Black Liberation Army* (1979; reprint, n.p., N.J.: Anarchist Black Cross Federation, 1997). Yet Akinyele Omowale Umoja has recently argued that armed self-defense units amounting to a "Black Liberation Army" had in fact formed in the deep South during the Civil Rights movement; that the BPP created underground, BLA-style cadres virtually from its inception in 1966; and that black radicals throughout the country, such as the northern-based Revolutionary Action Movement, formed BLA units in the mid and late 1960s independent of the Panthers' direct leadership. Akinyele Omowale Umoja, "Repression Breeds Resistance: The Black Liberation Army and the Radical Legacy of the Black Panther Party," in *Liberation, Imagination, and the Black Panther Party*, ed. Cleaver and Katsiaficas, 1–19. In yet another view, Russell Shoats, a BLA member still in prison, contends that the BLA as such was ordered into existence by the BPP leadership in 1969, but that Newton and the Oakland Panthers quickly turned on key BLA leaders. Russell Shoats, "Black Fighting Formations," in ibid., 128–38.

157. Dohrn interview.

158. Braley interview.

159. Johnathan Lerner, *Washington Post* at www.washingtinpost.com/wp-dyn/articles/A41899–2002Feb20.html.

160. Interview with anonymous Weatherwoman.

161. His lawyer quickly established that Neufeld did not remotely match the physical description of the person who had bought the dynamite. Neufeld interview.

162. Neufeld interview.

163. Ayers, *Fugitive Days*, 1–3.

164. The indictment actually named thirteen people, including the FBI informant Larry Grathwohl. Ten of the twelve were already sought on federal or

local charges. Among those indicted were Rudd, Dohrn, Ayers, Boudin, Evans, Neufeld, and Jaffe. *WUR,* 32.

165. The Weathermen, "Communiqué 3," in *Outlaws of Amerika: Communiqués from the Weather Underground* (New York : Liberated Guardian Collective, 1971), 8.

166. Weather Underground, "New Morning," in Powers, *Diana,* 215–16. The Weathermen sent their communiqués to underground newspapers such as the *Liberated Guardian* but also sometimes to mainstream media like the Associated Press. Weatherman's early communiqués were reprinted in *Outlaws of Amerika.*

167. *Chicago Seed,* October 15, 1970, cover; 3.

168. Jones interview.

169. Dohrn interview.

170. Kevin Gellies, "The Last Radical," *Vancouver Magazine,* November 1998, 86, 100.

171. Ayers interview.

172. Weather Underground, "New Morning," 215–16. Subsequent quotations from 216–25. The communiqué referred to Dylan's recent record *New Morning,* in which Dylan made another stylistic and thematic departure. The Weathermen allegedly listened to the record while composing the communiqué in California. Coller and Horowitz, "Doing It," 36.

173. I refer to the group in its pre-1971 incarnation as Weatherman and as the Weather Underground for the period following, though this distinction will at times be impossible to sustain for contextual reasons.

174. Jaffe interview.

175. Dohrn interview.

176. Ayers interview.

177. Ayers interview.

178. Braley interview.

179. "Open Letter to Weatherman Underground from Panther 21," *Liberated Guardian,* February 25, 1971, 16–17.

180. Only thirteen of the original twenty-one ultimately stood trial, on 156 separate charges. Churchill, "'To Disrupt, Discredit and Destroy,'" 103. See Murray Kempton, *The Briar Patch: The Trial of the Panther 21* (1973; reprint, New York: Da Capo Press, 1997).

181. Umoja alleges that the Panther 21 were formally expelled *because* of the public letter to the Weathermen, which implicitly criticized the national BPP leadership. Tensions between the Panther leadership and the Panther 21 certainly predated the letter, which was probably something of a last straw. Umoja, "Repression Breeds Resistance," 9–10.

182. Palmer interview. *WUR,* 37–38.

183. Roth interview.

184. Gilbert, Columbia, 214.

185. Ibid., 217.

186. Ron Chepesiuk, *Sixties Radicals Then and Now: Candid Conversations with Those Who Shaped the Era* (Jefferson, N.C.: McFarland, 1994), 236.

187. Weiss interview.

188. Ayers interview.

189. Daniel Berrigan, "Letter to the Weathermen," in Salisbury, *Behind the Lines,* 15–16.

190. Ibid., 15.

191. Dellinger, *More Power Than We Know,* 119.

192. Marcuse, "Problem of Violence and the Radical Opposition," 103.

193. Marcuse, "Repressive Tolerance," 103.

194. Marcuse, "Problem of Violence and the Radical Opposition," 103. Marcuse suggests that moral and historical judgments on violence are based on different criteria. Nowhere does he indicate that one standard can be fully abandoned for the other, but nowhere does he suggest how the two may be reconciled.

195. Marcuse, *Essay on Liberation,* 72.

196. *Rag,* November 26–December 6, 1969.

197. *Leviathan,* November 1969, 22.

198. Sergei Nechayev, "Catechism of a Revolutionist," in *The Terrorism Reader: A Historical Anthology,* ed. Walter Laqueur (Philadelphia: Temple University Press, 1978), 68–69.

199. Gilbert, Columbia, 210.

200. Ibid., 217–18.

201. Jaffe interview.

202. Weiss interview.

203. Dohrn interview.

204. Ayers interview.

205. Ibid.

206. Albert Camus, *The Just Assassins,* in *Caligula and Three Other Plays,* trans. Stuart Gilbert (New York: Random House, 1958), x.

207. Camus, *Rebel,* 25.

208. Camus, *Caligula and Three Other Plays,* x.

209. Roth interview.

210. The relationship of the Weather Underground to other armed groups in the 1970s is the murkiest part of the group's history, about which former members essentially decline comment. My commentary is therefore necessarily general and based on informed speculations.

211. Ayers, *Fugitive Days,* 146.

212. Ibid.

213. Cathy Wilkerson, "Review of *Fugitive Days,*" *Z Magazine;* on-line edition, December 2001.

214. Wells, *War Within,* 492. These sentiments were likely the exception among Vietnam veterans, the great majority of whom did not even see active combat. Nonetheless, veterans were among the most active in publicizing the brutality of U.S. conduct, and veterans organization were among the most important in the antiwar movement. See Richard Moser, *The New Winter Soldiers: GI and Veteran Dissent during the Vietnam Era* (New Brunswick, N.J.: Rutgers University Press, 1996). Moser (132) estimates that 20–25 percent of service people were activists against the war in Vietnam and that as many as half of all soldiers and veterans during the Vietnam era opposed the war.

215. In a deadly parody of "working through" the Vietnam legacy, President

George Bush Sr. declared that he had "kicked the Vietnam Syndrome in the butt" by waging war in 1991 against Iraq. The Gulf War claimed the lives of perhaps tens of thousands of Iraqi civilians and entailed its own atrocities, which the U.S. government scarcely even acknowledged. See Douglas Kellner, *The Persian Gulf TV War* (Boulder, Colo.: Westview Press, 1992), and Ramsey Clark and others, *War Crimes: A Report on the United States War Crimes against Iraq* (Washington, D.C.: Maisonneuve Press, 1992).

216. Dellinger, *More Power Than We Know,* 168. Hertzberg made a nearly identical point in response to Hayden several years earlier. Hertzberg, "Weather Report," 6.

217. This tally includes neither the unsolved murder in 1970 of a San Francisco policemen, possibly committed by New Leftists, nor the deaths resulting from the 1981 Brinks robbery, by which point the New Left as such was defunct. (On the Berkeley killing, see *WUR,* 29.) It excludes also those killed by black groups such as the Black Liberation Army, who fall outside my definition of the New Left. Finally, the tally excludes the murders committed by the multiracial Symbionese Liberation Army in the mid 1970s. The SLA, ostensibly a revolutionary organization, repeated the gestures of New Left and Black Power radicalism as virtually pure pathology or farce. On violence in the 1970s, see U.S. Senate, Committee on the Judiciary, Subcommittee to Investigate the Administration of the Internal Security Act and Other Internal Security Laws, *Terroristic Activity: Hearings before the Subcommittee to Investigate the Administration of the Internal Security Act and Other Internal Security Laws,* 93d Cong., 2d sess. [94th Cong., 2d sess.], September 23 (Washington, D.C.: GPO, 1974 [1975]).

218. Bates, *Rads,* 420.

5. DEADLY ABSTRACTION

1. On Meinhof's death, see Commission internationale d'enquête sur la mort d'Ulrike Meinhof, *La Mort d'Ulrike Meinhof: Rapport de la Commission internationale d'enquête* (Paris: F. Maspero, 1979).

2. The RAF knew at the time that Schleyer had a Nazi affiliation and broadcast this fact in explaining why he was kidnapped. It did not, however, know the details of Schleyer's past. For years thereafter, Schleyer's biography was a matter of speculation and debate, with the RAF's supporters condemning Schleyer as an ardent Nazi and its critics stressing Schleyer's service to the democratic, postwar state. Lutz Hachmeister's documentary *Schleyer: Eine deutsche Geschichte* (HMR Produktion, 2003), shown on German television in the summer of 2003, sought to clarify the facts of Schleyer's life. Hachmeister's research revealed that Schleyer, born in 1915, became a member of the Hitler Jugend (Hitler Youth) in 1931 and the SS in 1933. He then studied law at the University of Heidelberg, where he became a leader of the student union, and joined the Nazi Party in 1937. After marrying the daughter of a leading SA official and becoming the head of the student union in Prague, he was appointed in 1942 Leiter des Präsidialbüros des Zentralverbands der Industrie für Böhmen und Mähren. Prague was the headquarters of Reinhard Heydrich—the SS Sicherheitsdienst chief and Deputy Reich Protector of Bohemia and Moravia—until

his assassination. Schleyer served in Prague until the war's end, gaining experience through his post in economic management. He spent the next three years in the custody of the Americans and then the French for his involvement with the Nazis, and began in 1949 a career in German industry. For Schleyer's biography, see the film and www.ndr.de/ndr/derndr/presse/pressemappen/2003 0820_schleyer/bio.html.

3. Irmgard Möller restates the charge of murder in "'Wir meinten es ernst': Gespräch mit Irmgard Möller über Entstehung, Bedeutung und Fehler der RAF," *Die Beute,* no. 9 (January 1996). No way exists of determining independently how the inmates died. Most investigations support the thesis of suicide, though no utterly definitive proof exists. I shall speak of the deaths *as if* they were suicides, as this seems most probable. On the investigations into the Stammheim deaths, see Karl-Heinz Weidenhammer, *Selbtsmord oder Mord? Das Todesermittlungsverfahren, Baader/Ensslin/Raspe* (Kiel: Neuer Malik, 1988).

4. *Zum Gedanken an die Opfer des Terrorismus* (Bonn: Deutscher Bundestag Presse- und Informationszentrum, 1978), 12.

5. Walter Althammer, *Gegen den Terror* (Stuttgart: Bonn Aktuell, 1978), 57.

6. References to auto fatalities are in Hans Steinert, "Sozialstrukturelle Bedingungen des 'linken Terrorismus' der 70er Jahre," in Fritz Sack, Heinz Steinert, et al., *Protest und Reaktion,* Analysen zum Terrorismus, vol. 4/2 (Opladen: Westdeutscher Verlag, 1984), 393, and Eric Kuby, "Früchte der Angst," in *Der blinde Fleck: Die Linke, die RAF und der Staat* (Frankfurt a.M.: Neue Kritik, 1987), 25.

7. Heinrich Böll, "Will Ulrike Gnade oder Freies Geleit?" *Spiegel,* no. 3 (January 10, 1972): 54, in Rauball, *Aktuelle Dokumente,* 216. See also Frank Grützbach, *Heinrich Böll: Freies Geleit für Ulrike Meinhof* (Cologne: Kiepenheuer & Witsch, 1972).

8. Sebastian Scheerer, "Deutschland: Die ausgebürgerte Linke," in Henner Hess, Martin Moerings, et al., *Angriff auf das Herz des Staates: Soziale Entwicklung und Terrorismus* (Frankfurt a.M.: Surkamp, 1988), 329, 337.

9. RAF, "Über den bewaffneten Kampf in Westeuropa," quoted in Scheerer, "Deutschland: Die ausgebürgerte Linke," 295.

10. Scheerer, "Deutschland: Die ausgebürgerte Linke," 333–34.

11. Walter Boelich, "Schleyers Kinder," in *Jahrbuch Politik 8* (Berlin: Klaus Wagenbach, 1978), 8.

12. Jürgen Bäcker and Horst Mahler, "Zehn Thesen zur RAF," in *Jahrbuch Politik 8* (Berlin: Klaus Wagenbach, 1978), 12, 14.

13. Günter Rohrmoser, "Ideologische Ursachen des Terrorismus," in Iring Fetscher, Günter Rohrmoser, et al., *Ideologien und Strategien,* Analysen zum Terrorismus, vol. 1 (Opladen: Westdeutscher Verlag, 1981), 320.

14. Ibid.

15. Scheerer, "Deutschland: Die ausgebürgerte Linke," 268.

16. Ulrike Meinhof, "Napalm und Pudding," in *Dokumente einer Rebellion,* 81.

17. Tom Vague, *Televisionaries: The Red Army Faction Story, 1963–1993* (Edinburgh: AK Press, 1994), 8–9; "Chronologie," in *Der blinde Fleck,* 223.

18. "Chronologie," in *Der blinde Fleck,* 224.

344 Notes to Pages 202–11

19. Vague, *Televisionaries,* 13.

20. Andreas Baader, Gudrun Ensslin, Thorwald Proll, and Horst Söhnlein, *Vor einer solchen Justiz verteidigen wir uns nicht: Schlußwort im Kaufhausbrandprozeß* (Berlin: Edition Voltaire, 1968), 5–7.

21. Bernward Vesper, "Nachwort," in ibid., 20.

22. Ibid., 21.

23. Meinhof, "Napalm und Pudding," in *Dokumente einer Rebellion,* 81.

24. "Blow up Amerika, Blow up Berlin," *833,* no. 59 (May 7, 1970): 11. Following quotations from the same.

25. RAF, "Die rote Armee aufbauen," *883,* no. 61 (May 22, 1970).

26. Ulrike Meinhof, "'Natürlich kann geschossen werden,'" *Der Spiegel,* no. 25 (June 5, 1970): 74.

27. RAF, "Die rote Armee aufbauen," *883,* no. 62 (June 5, 1970).

28. Juergensmeyer, *Terror in the Mind of God,* 125–26.

29. Schiller, *"Es war ein harter Kampf,"* 51.

30. RAF, "Concept of the Urban Guerrilla," 36.

31. In a very partial list, drawn from police data, Walter Althammer records forty-seven separate "terror acts," including bank robberies, between November 1969 and the beginning of May 1972. Althammer, *Gegen den Terror,* 41–65.

32. Schiller, *"Es war ein harter Kampf,"* 11–19.

33. Böll, "Will Ulrike Gnade oder Freies Geliet?" in Raubell, 214.

34. Ibid., 218.

35. Baumann, *Terror or Love?* 95.

36. Aust, *Baader-Meinhof Group,* 203.

37. Legal rulings on police conduct are recorded in Althammer, *Gegen den Terror,* 41–65, and "Chronologie," in *Der blinde Fleck,* 223–52.

38. RAF communiqué, "Erklärung vom 20. Mai 1972, Kommando 2. Juni." The communiqués, originally published in the German underground press, are printed in English in *Armed Resistance,* 57–62, and *RAF* (n.p. [U.K.?]: Patrick Arguello Press, 1979), 1–8. In German, they are in *texte: der RAF,* 450–56. I have drawn on both translations, modified by reference to the German, and will name them by their German titles.

39. RAF communiqué, "Erklärung vom 14. Mai 1972, Kommando Petra Schelm."

40. RAF communiqué, "Erklärung vom 20. Mai 1972, Kommando 2. Juni."

41. RAF communiqué, "Erklärung vom 16. Mai 1972, Kommando Thomas Weisbecker."

42. RAF communiqué, "Erklärung vom 29. Mai 1972."

43. Kommunistischer Bund, "Wem nützen die Bombe bei Springer?" *Unser Weg* (Hamburg: KB, 1972).

44. RAF communiqué, "Erklärung vom 20. Mai 1972." RAF's consternation over the action persisted. At the eventual trial of the RAF's "hard core," Ensslin suggested dubiously that Meinhof had committed the bombing without the group's knowledge. Aust, *Baader-Meinhof Group,* 344.

45. The RAF made the model of a just war explicit when it argued in court in 1976 that the bombings in Frankfurt and Heidelberg were justifiable because the United States had used West Germany as a platform for operations in Viet-

nam that violated international law. The judge refused to allow evidence in support of the argument, insisting that "the Vietnam War is not the subject of this trial." Aust, *Baader-Meinhof Group,* 358.

46. RAF communiqué, "Erklärung vom 20. Mai 1972, Kommando 2. Juni."

47. *Neues vom Sozialstaat—Dokumentation zum Teach-in der Roten Hilfe zur unmittelbaren Unterdrückung durch Polizei und Justiz* (Frankfurt a.M.: Rote Hilfe, 1972), all quotations from 50–51.

48. Ibid., 53.

49. "Sozialistische Politik und Terrorismus," in Oskar Negt, *Keine Demokratie ohne Sozialismus* (Frankfurt a.M.: Suhrkamp, 1976), 439.

50. Negt, *Keine Demokratie ohne Sozialismus,* 441.

51. Ibid., 445.

52. Baumann, *Terror or Love?* 110.

53. Reiche, "Zur Kritik der RAF," 21.

54. The RAF, its attorneys, Rote Hilfe, and others produced a wealth of material on prison conditions. Key texts include *Folter in der BRD: Zur Situation der politische Gefangenen,* Kursbuch 32 (Berlin: Rotbuch, 1973); *Vorbereitung der RAF-Prozesse durch Presse, Polizei und Justiz,* ed. Rote Hilfe (Berlin: Rote Hilfe, 1974); Henning Spangenberg, "Isolationsfolter in westdeutschen Gefängnissen," in *"Sie wurden uns gerne in Knast begraben"* (Berlin: Asta der Pädagogischen Hochschule Westberlin et al., 1977).

55. Rote Hilfe, ed., *Bericht über Vernichtungshaft und Isolationsfolter in Gefängnissen der BRD und Westberlins (1970–74)* (Berlin: Rote Hilfe, 1974), 9–11.

56. Ulrich Preuss, "Strafantrag gegen NRW-Justizminister Posser," in *Ausgewählte Dokumente der Zeitgeschichte: Bundesrepublick Deutschland (BRD)— Rote Armee Fraktion (RAF)* (Cologne: GNN Verlagsgesellschaft Politische Berichte, 1987). Documents at www.nadir.org/nadir/archiv/PolitischeStroemungen/Stadtguerilla+.

57. Ibid.

58. Spangenberg, "Isolationsfolter in westdeutschen Gefängnissen," 26.

59. "Zu viele Gräber sind auf meinem Weg," *Stern,* November 23, 1978, 49. After being released in 1974, Proll fled to England, where she was recaptured in 1978 and returned to Germany for trial.

60. "Brief einer Gefangenen aus dem Toten Trakt," in Brückner, *Ulrike Marie Meinhof,* 152–54.

61. Schiller, *"Es war ein harter Kampf,"* 138–39.

62. Sjef Teuns, "Isolation/Sensorische Deprivation: Die programmierte Folter," in *Ausgewählte Dokumente.*

63. Heinz Brandt, "Zur Isolationshaft—Interview," in *Küß den Boden der Freiheit: Texte der Neuen Linken* (Berlin: ID-Archiv, 1991), 340. The term *KZ,* or *Konzentrationslager,* can refer to both concentration and death camps. Brandt, it should be stressed, was a political detainee in Auschwitz and Buchenwald, which likely affected his experiences there. His remarks, by extension, should in no way be taken as a universal description of the camps; for countless inmates, they were, of course, entirely inhumane and unremittingly miserable. Similar remarks of Brandt are excerpted in Rote Hilfe, ed., *Bericht,* 11.

64. Rote Hilfe, ed., *Bericht,* 53.

65. Ibid., 58.

66. *Starbuck Holger Meins,* 114–17.

67. *Starbuck Holger Meins,* largely composed of personal remembrances, abounds with such descriptions.

68. Ibid., 6–7.

69. Rote Hilfe, ed., *Bericht,* 7; Schiller, *"Es war ein harter Kampf,"*152–54. Countless flyers repeated the allegation. On his demise, see *Starbuck Holger Meins,* 142–61.

70. "Hungerstreik, Gewalt und Sozialismus," *Tagespiegel,* November 17, 1974, 17.

71. *ERKLÄRUNG anläßlich des Todes von Holger Meins* (flyer, ca. November 15, 1974).

72. *Starbuck Holger Meins,* 170.

73. Komitees gegen Folter an politischen Gefangenen in der BRD, "Der Mord an dem Revolutionär Holger Meins kann den Befreiungskampf gegen den Imperialismus nicht aufhalten" (November 18, 1974).

74. Die Verteideger der Gefangenen aus der RAF, *Die Gefangenen aus der RAF beenden den Hungerstreik* (flyer, February 5, 1975).

75. *Frankfurter Rundschau,* September 2, 1986, 10.

76. Aust, *Baader-Meinhof Group,* 251–52.

77. Ibid., 281; "spiegelinterview," in RAF, *texte,* 241.

78. Sepp Binder, *Terrorismus: Herausforderung und Antwort* (Bonn: Neue Gesellschaft, 1978), 45–46.

79. Ibid., 45.

80. "spiegelinterview," in RAF, *texte,* 243.

81. One estimate placed the cumulative cost of the pursuit, incarceration, and prosecution of the RAF, as of 1978, at over 100 million marks. Althammer, *Gegen den Terror,* 131.

82. In 2000–2002, Turkish political prisoners developed methods, chiefly the ingestion of large amounts of water and sugar, for dramatically extending the ability to survive. Some hunger strikers lived for more than 200 days, long past what medical experts thought possible. "Turkish Hunger Strikers Risk Body and Mind," *NYT,* December 18, 2001, A3.

83. Schiller, *"Es war ein harter Kampf,"*125, 153–54.

84. Horst Mahler, "Der Foltervorwurf—eine Propagadalüge," *Spiegel,* no. 50 (1978): 62. Some inmates bitterly resented Mahler's dismissive view of their efforts to improve prison conditions. Peter-Paul Zahl engaged in a heated exchange with Mahler, documented in Peter-Paul Zahl, *Die Stille und das Grelle: Aufsatzsammlung* (Freie Gesellschaft, 1981).

85. Aust, *Baader-Meinhof Group,* 261–62.

86. Schiller, *"Es war ein harter Kampf,"*183–84.

87. Spangenberg, 20–33. "Haftstatut von Holger Meins," in *Ausgewählte Dokumente.*

88. *Zum Gedanken an die Opfer des Terrorismus,* 46.

89. Such analyses did not cease altogether. In January 1976, RAF defendants read into the court record a 200-page statement arguing the imperialist nature

of the West German state and outlining various anti-imperialist strategies. "Erklärung zur Sache—Auszüge dem Manuskript," in *Ausgewählte Dokumente*.

90. "spiegelinterview," in RAF, *texte*, 249.

91. Ibid., 241.

92. Della Porta, *Social Movements, Political Violence, and the State*, 119. See also Wanda von Baeyer-Katte, "Die soziale Bedingungen terroristischen Handelns," in id. et al., *Gruppenprozesse, Analysen zum Terrorismus*, vol. 3 (Opladen: Westdeutscher Verlag, 1982), 318–91.

93. Della Porta, *Social Movements, Political Violence, and the State*, 176.

94. Government officials in fact later conceded that they had no evidence—and indeed did not even suspect—that the Stammheim inmates had in any way planned the Schleyer kidnapping. Schiller, *"Es war ein harter Kampf,"* 190–91.

95. "rede von ulrike zu der brefreiung von andreas, moabit 13. september," in RAF, *texte*, 74.

96. "spiegelinterview," in RAF, *texte*, 252–53.

97. Schiller, *"Es war ein harter Kampf,"* 146. See also Bakker Shut, *Dokumente: Das Info*.

98. Schiller, *"Es war ein harter Kampf,"* 146.

99. Juergensmeyer, *Terror in the Mind of God*, 167. The term "sacrifice," Juergensmeyer points out, comes from the Latin *sacrificium*, which means "to make holy." Martyrdom, as a form of sacrifice, shares this religious connotation.

100. Ibid., 161, 169.

101. Ibid., 165.

102. "der letzte brief von holger meins (am 31.10.1974)," in RAF, *texte*, 14.

103. The controversy over the funeral itself is documented in the film *Deutschland im Herbst* (Germany in Autumn), by Alf Brustellin, Hans Peter Cloos, Rainer Werner Fassbinder, et al. (Filmverlag der Autoren, 1977/78).

104. Schiller, *"Es war ein harter Kampf,"* 109–36. Schiller was, more precisely, part of a "bridge group" between the RAF's "first" and "second" generations, which also contained another former RAF prisoner, Helmut Pohl. Schiller's cell was captured on February 2, 1974, earning it the name "Gruppe vom 4.2."

105. *Frankfurter Rundschau*, September 2, 1986, 10.

106. Klein, *German Guerrilla*, 19–21.

107. Volker Speital, "Wir wollten alles und gleichzeitig nichts," *Spiegel*, no 31 (1980): 37.

108. Ibid., 41.

109. "'Ich bitte um Vergebung': Interview mit Baptist Ralf Friedrich," *Spiegel*, no. 34 (August 20, 1990): 53.

110. Ibid.

111. Aust, *Baader-Meinhof Group*, 266–67.

112. J2M, *Zum Attentat auf Berlins höchsten Richter: Terror oder Gegenwehr?!* (flyer, November 1974).

113. J2M, *Zur Hinrichtung eines Richters* (flyer, November 1974).

114. "erklärung von jan-karl raspe im prozess in stuttgart-stamheim am 11.5.76," in RAF, *texte*, 21. In her memoir, Schiller repeats the charge that Meinhof was murdered, buttressed by the extraordinary allegation that she had been

threatened with murder while in prison by her fellow inmate Gerhard Müller. In 1976, Müller became a witness against the RAF, exchanging information for the withdrawal of the charge that he had murdered a policeman, Norbert Schmid, in 1971. Schiller, who claims to have seen the killing, says she planned to expose Müller's guilt after she learned of his cooperation with prosecutors. A note he allegedly sent her with the knowledge of prison officials warned that she would meet the same fate as Meinhof if she did so. Schiller, *"Es war ein harter Kampf,"* 173–74.

115. "Chronologie," in *Der blinde Fleck,* 241.

116. Aust, *Baader-Meinhof Group,* 541.

117. See, e.g., "erklärung des KOMMANDO HOLGER MEINS v. 24.4.75," in RAF, *texte,* 334–36. In its many statements, the RAF cell that kidnapped Schleyer offered no political justification for doing so.

118. Aust, *Baader-Meinhof Group,* 408.

119. During the Schleyer crisis, Baader told a government official that the Stammheim prisoners disapproved of the recent killing of civilians. He remarked also that those in prison had little capacity to dissuade members of the underground from committing such acts and that, should he be released, he would desist from further violence. Though strategically self-serving, these comments would seem plausibly to reflect the views at the time of Baader and the RAF's other founders. *Dokumentation zu den Ereignissen und Entscheidung im Zusammenhang mit der Entführung von Hanns Martin Schleyer und der Lufthansa-Machine "Landshut"* (Bonn: Presse- und Informationsamt der Bundesregierung, 1977), 111.

120. Reiche, "Zur Kritik der RAF," 22.

121. Aust, *Baader-Meinhof Group,* 321.

122. This portrait of the J2M is drawn from Baumann and from Bewegung 2. Juni, *Der Blues: Gesammelte Texte der Bewegung 2. Juni,* vols. 1 and 2 (n.p.: n.d.).

123. A firsthand account of the Lorenz kidnapping is provided by Ralf Reinders and Ronald Fritzsch in *Die Bewegung 2. Juni* (Berlin: ID-Archiv, 1995).

124. "Die Enführung aus unserer Sicht" in Bewegung 2. Juni, *Der Blues, I,* 178.

125. J2M, "Zum Attentat."

126. "Hungerstreik, Gewalt und Sozialismus," *Tagespiegel,* November 17, 1974, 17.

127. *Berliner Extra-Dienst,* 92/VIII (November 5, 1972).

128. "Flugblatt der 'Bewegung 2. Juni,'" in Peter Brückner and Barbara Sichermann, *Solidarität und Gewalt* (Berlin: Klaus Wagenbach, 1974), 84.

129. Herbert Marcuse, "Mord darf keine Waffe sein," *Zeit,* October 1977.

130. Herbert Marcuse, "So sieht in der bürgerlichen Gesellschaft der Fortschritt aus . . . ," in *Gespräche mit Herbert Marcuse* (Frankfurt a.M.: Suhrkamp, 1978), 146.

131. Marcuse, "Mord darf keine Waffe sein."

132. Marcuse, "So sieht in der bürgerlichen Gesellschaft der Fortschritt aus . . . ," 147.

133. Marcuse, "Mord darf keine Waffe sein."

134. *Spiegel,* August 20, 1990, 57.

135. Fetscher, *Terrorismus und Reaktion,* 41.

136. Once in custody, Ruhland turned against the RAF and provided prosecutors with extensive information about the group. On Brückner see "Professor schwer belastet," *Frankfurter Rundschau,* January 20, 1972, 4, and Komitee "Solidarität mit Peter Brückner," *INFO: Zur kriminalisierung Opposition in der BRD* (Hannover, 1972).

137. Brückner and Sichermann, *Solidarität und Gewalt,* 16.

138. Ibid.

139. Ibid., 16, 20.

140. Ibid., 25.

141. Ibid., 26.

142. Reiche, "Zur Kritik der RAF," 19.

143. RAF, "Concept of the Urban Guerrilla," 55.

144. Reiche, "Zur Kritik der RAF," 20.

145. Ibid., 19–20.

146. Horst Mahler and Gerhart Baum, "'Wir müssen raus aus den Schützengraben,'" *Spiegel,* no. 52 (1979): 37.

147. Reiche, "Zur Kritik der RAF," 21.

148. Wolfgang Kraushaar, "44 Tage ohne Opposition," in *Der blinde Fleck,* 11.

149. Eric Fried, "So kam ich unter die Deutschen," in Binder, *Terrorismus,* 49.

150. Fetscher, *Terrorismus und Reaktion,* 42.

151. Reiche, "Zur Kritik der RAF," 22.

152. Kraushaar, "44 Tage," 22.

153. Bäcker and Mahler, "Zehn Thesen zur RAF," 13.

154. Baumann, *Terror or Love?* 120.

155. *Frankfurter Rundschau,* September 2, 1986, 10.

156. "'Ich bitte um Vergebung': Interview mit Baptist Ralf Friedrich," 57. In 1992, Friedrich was sentenced to prison for his activities in the 1970s.

157. "Ehemalige RAF-Mitglieder schwören dem Terrorismus ab," *dpa,* October 22, 1986.

158. On violence in England, see Tom Vague, *Anarchy in the UK: The Angry Brigade* (London: AK Press, 1997). On violence elsewhere, see *Arm the Spirit (ATS),* the irregular publication of a self-described "autonomist/anti-imperialist information collective based in Toronto Canada." Formed in the late 1980s as a support group for "political prisoners" in the United States, *ATS* published the communiqués of "guerrilla" groups from the Basque territories, Belgium, Greece, Italy, the Netherlands, Turkey, West Germany, and elsewhere throughout the 1990s.

159. See Dagmar Herzog, "'Pleasure, Sex, and Politics Belong Together': Post-Holocaust Memory and the Sexual Revolution in West Germany," *Critical Inquiry,* no. 24 (Winter 1998): 393–444.

160. RAF communiqué, "Erklärung vom 16. Mai 1972, Kommando Thomas Weisbecker."

161. RAF communiqué, "Erklärung vom 25. Mai 1972, Kommando Juli 15."

162. RAF communiqué, "Erklärung vom 29. Mai 1972."

163. RAF, "Den Antiimperialistischen Kampf führen! Die rote Armee Aufbauen! Die Aktion des Schwarzen September in München," in RAF, *texte*, 434–35.

164. Aust, *Baader-Meinhof Group*, 253.

165. Ibid., 317.

166. Von Dirke, "*All Power to the Imagination*," 13–14.

167. The evasion or denial of the past was not as total as this common portrait implies. Jeffrey Herf shows that at key points from the late 1940s through the early 1960s, conservative and liberal politicians in the West publicly raised the difficult issue of German guilt, often in the context of discussions of restitution for the victims or punishment of the perpetrators. In so doing, they displayed considerable political, intellectual, and moral leadership and managed to shape to some degree public discourse about the past. Leaders in West Germany certainly were more honest in self-reflection than their counterparts in the East. The latter obscured the issue of guilt by claiming that East Germany, as a communist country, was aligned with historic antifascism and that East Germans therefore had a vastly lesser share of responsibility for the horrors of Nazism. Yet, as Herf concedes, plans for a comprehensive denazification of West German society were halted for reasons of political expediency and lack of will. Some politicians, notably Chancellor Adenauer, often broached the question of German guilt only to minimize the extent of popular complicity with Nazism and pursued policies that allowed former members of the Nazi elite positions of prominence in the Federal Republic. Herf concludes: "Even in the classic era of silence and of democratization [the late 1940s and 1950s], the crimes of the Nazis found a place in early West German political narratives, though not a prominent or ubiquitous one." Jeffrey Herf, *Divided Memory: The Nazi Past in the Two Germanys* (Cambridge, Mass.: Harvard University Press, 1997), 268. The public, Herf also shows, consistently favored amnesty over punishment for war criminals and objected to efforts to attribute guilt to anyone other than a small core of ardent Nazis. Little, it seems, ultimately contradicts the view that no *sustained* self-critical engagement with the German past, either from above or below, took place in West Germany in the first decades after the war. More recently, Robert Moeller has argued in *War Studies: The Search for a Usable Past in the Federal Republic* (Berkeley: University of California Press, 1999) that West Germans indeed confronted the Nazi era in the postwar years but did so in essentially self-serving ways that enhanced their sense of being victims.

168. Alexander and Margarete Mitscherlich, *The Inability to Mourn: Principles of Collective Behavior*, trans. Beverley R. Placzek (1967; New York: Grove Press, 1975), 20.

169. Ibid., 66.

170. Eric Santner, *Stranded Objects: Mourning, Memory and Film in Postwar Germany* (Ithaca, N.Y.: Cornell University Press, 1991), 34.

171. Ibid.

172. Ibid., 45.

173. Quoted in Margot Strom and William Parsons, *Facing History and Ourselves: Holocaust and Human Behavior* (Watertown: Intentional Educations,

1982), 2. In the late 1970s and early 1980s, a genre known as *Vaterliteratur* emerged, in which Germans of the postwar generation described their anger at and ambivalence about their fathers. See, e.g., Paul Kersten, *Der alltägliche Tod meines Vaters: Erzählung* (Cologne: Kiepenheuer & Witsch, 1978); Ruth Rehmann, *Der Mann auf der Kanzel: Fragen an einen Vater* (Munich: Hanser, 1979), trans. Christoph Lohmann and Pamela Lohmann as *The Man in the Pulpit: Questions for a Father* (Lincoln: University of Nebraska Press, 1997); and Michael Schneider, "Fathers and Sons, Retrospectively: The Damaged Relations between Two Generations," trans. Jamie Owen Daniel, *New German Critique*, no. 31 (1984): 3–51.

174. Mahler and Baum, "'Wir müssen raus aus den Schützengraben,'" 37.

175. Aust, *Baader-Meinhof Group*, 59.

176. Vesper, "Nachwort," 19.

177. Klein, *German Guerrilla*, 14–15.

178. Jörg Bopp, "Die ungekonnte Aggresion," in *Der blinde Fleck*, 140. Subsequent quotations from 141.

179. The total disavowal of one's parents, Bopp and Santner suggest, is untenable.

180. Santner, *Stranded Objects*, 34.

181. The hostage Dora Bloch, a Jewish woman, was later killed in a hospital, reportedly by the Ugandan dictator Idi Amin himself. Klein, *German Guerrilla*, 34.

182. "Shalom and Napalm," in Baumann, *Terror or Love?* 67–68. The leaflet was printed in *833*, no. 40. No group publicly claimed responsibility for the act, and neither were the assailants ever identified.

183. RAF, "Den Antiimperialistischen Kampf führen!" 413, 445–46.

184. Klein, *German Guerrilla*, 31, 34. Fearing reprisals from the Red Cells after he left the group, Klein remained underground. He was captured in France in 1998, sent to Germany for trial, and convicted in 1999 for participation in three murders during the 1975 terrorist raid of an OPEC meeting in Vienna. Klein was sentenced to nine years in prison. "German Unrest Recalled as a Former Terrorist Gets 9 Years," *NYT*, February 16, 2001.

185. Harriet Rubin, "Terrorism, Trauma, and the Search for Redemption," *Fast Company*, no. 52 (November 2001): 164.

186. Ibid., 166–67.

187. Ibid., 168.

6. "DEMOCRATIC INTOLERANCE"

1. The problem of left-wing violence preoccupied a number of federal chancellors, each of whom crafted antiterrorist policy partially in response to domestic political pressures. The state also devised policies in reaction to particular provocations by the RAF and other groups, giving its campaign against terrorism an improvised quality. Moreover, the Federal Republic was not a monolithic state, because power was divided among the judicial, parliamentary, and executive branches. Each of these played a more or less distinct role in an antiterrorist campaign that was never fully centralized. West Germany was, finally, divided into a

number of states, or *Länder,* and West Berlin. Under this arrangement, a combination of federal, state, and local police pursued the RAF, each with its own approach. Nonetheless, over time, the state exhibited a striking consistency of purpose and methods in its battle against left-wing violence. My analysis focuses on this continuity.

2. Peter Katzenstein, *Cultural Norms and National Security: Police and Military in Postwar Japan* (Ithaca, N.Y.: Cornell University Press, 1991), 174.

3. On the legal battle against the RAF, see Uwe Berlit und Horst Dreier, "Die legislative Auseinandersetzung mit dem Terrorismus," in Fritz Sack, Heinz Steinert, et al., *Protest und Reaktion,* Analysen zum Terrorismus, vol. 4/2 (Opladen: Westdeutscher Verlag, 1984), 227–318; Miklos K. Radvanyi, *Anti-Terrorist Legislation in the Federal Republic of Germany* (Washington, D.C.: Library of Congress, Law Library, 1979); and Rabert, *Links- und Rechtsterrorismus,* 55–88. Section 129a alone has produced a large legal literature, cited by Rabert.

4. "Chronologie," in *Der blinde Fleck,* 236.

5. Quoted in Rabert, *Links- und Rechtsterrorismus,* 72. Some of the law's ambiguity stemmed from its use of the word *werben,* which means to recruit, but also to promote or advertise.

6. Berlit und Dreier, "Legislative Auseinandersetzung," 280.

7. Kurt Groenewold, "The German Federal Republic's Response and Civil Liberties," *Terrorism and Political Violence* 4, no. 4 (Winter 1992): 147.

8. "Erklärung der Bundesregierung betr. Fragen der inneren Sicherheit," in *Ausgewählte Dokumente.*

9. "'Mord beginnt beim bösen Wort,'" *Spiegel,* no. 41 (1977): 28.

10. Willy Brandt, "Machen Sie Schluß mit Ihrer Unterstützung, damit unser Land nicht zur Hölle wird!" in Sepp Binder, *Terrorismus: Herausforderung und Antwort* (Bonn: Neue Gesellschaft, 1978), 105–6.

11. Quoted in *Es genügt nicht nur keinen Gedanken zu Haben . . .* (n.p.: Verband des Linken Buchhandels, 1977).

12. Groenewold, "German Federal Republic's Response," 148.

13. On Böll, Gollwitzer, Scharf, and the Frankfurt School, see "'Mord beginnt beim bösen Wort,'" 38–40 and "'Mord beginnt beim bösen Wort,' III," *Spiegel,* no. 43 (1977): 212, 214.

14. "'Mord beginnt beim bösen Wort,'" 30.

15. Ibid., 28.

16. "'Mord beginnt beim bösen Wort,' III," 203.

17. "'Mord beginnt beim bösen Wort,'" 30.

18. Thomas-Wießbecker-Haus, "Polizei verwüstete unser Jugendcollective," in *Demokratischer Rechtsstaat zwischen Individuallem Terror und Polizeigewalt,* ed. Humanistischen Union (Berlin: Humanistischen Union, 1975), 56. This report by the Humanistischen Union provides extensive documentation of the raids and their aftermath.

19. "Wiedergabe von Protokollen und Auszügen aus Berichten, Dokument 1," in ibid., 11.

20. Cited in Ossip Flechtheim, "Auf dem Wege zum Polizeistaat?" in ibid., 6.

21. "Polizeiaktion gegen den Trikont Verlag," in *Dokumentation über die Beschlagnahme von Literatur!* (n.p.: Trikonk-Verlag, n.d.), 2–4.

22. *Strafgezetzbuch* (Bonn: Aktuell, 1978), 60–61. In English, partial wording of the laws is in Radvanyi, *Anti-Terrorist Legislation in the Federal Republic,* 74.

23. "Polizeiaktion gegen den Trikont Verlag," in *Dokumentation über die Beschlagnahme von Literatur!* 2.

24. Ibid., 13.

25. *Dokumentation über die Beschlagnahme von Literatur!* 7.

26. Reprinted from *konkret,* February 1976, in *Dokumentation über die Beschlagnahme von Literatur!* 26–28.

27. *Der erste §88a-PROZESS* (flyer, Summer 1977, distributed by Politische Buchhandlung, Bochum).

28. *Das Urteil vom Agit-Prozess* (n.p.: Agit-Druck, 1979), 1–28.

29. Walter Jens, "Lernen Sie lesen, meine Herren Richter!" in *Das Urteil vom Agit-Prozess,* 29.

30. "Mesclaro—ein Nachruf," in Peter Brückner, *Die Mescalaro-Affäre: Ein Lehrstück für Aufklärung und politische Kultur* (Hannover: Internationlismus Buchladen und Verlagsgesellschaft, 1977), 24.

31. *Anti Repressions INFO: Wer sich umdreht oder lach, wird zum Terrorist gemacht!* no. 2 (September 26, 1977): 3.

32. These events, as well as the response of the statement's defenders, are documented in *Die Mescalaro-Affäre* and *Anti Repressions INFO.*

33. "Mesclaro—ein Nachruf," in *Die Mescalaro-Affäre,* 26.

34. Peter Glotz, "Offener Briefes Wissenschaftssenator P. Glotz an zwölf Berliner Professoren," *Welt,* July 3, 1977, in *Die Mescalaro-Affäre,* 49; "Jeder fünfte denkt etwa so wie Mescalaro," *Spiegel,* no. 41 (1977): 49–63.

35. Peter Glotz, "Offener Briefes," 49.

36. Brückner was later reinstated but was too ill from heart disease to resume his post. He died in April 1981 at the age of fifty-nine. On his suspension, see *Anti Repressions INFO.*

37. Gerhard Mauz, "Es ist nicht immer Haarmann, der kommt," in Claus Croissant, Kurt Groenewold, et al., *Politische Prozesse ohne Verteidigung?* (Berlin: Klaus Wagenbach, 1976), 7. Pretrial hearings began on May 21, 1975, the charges were formally brought in August, and the trial proper began in January 1976.

38. Groenewold accused the state of this double game in "German Federal Republic's Response."

39. Radvanyi, *Anti-Terrorist Legislation in the Federal Republic,* 79.

40. "Strafprozeßordnung" in *Die Anti-Terror-Debatten im Parlament: Protokolle 1974–1978,* ed. Hermann Vinke und Gabriele Witt (Reinbeck bei Hamburg: Rowohlt, 1978), 16.

41. Aust, *Baader-Meinhof Group,* 282.

42. Radvanyi, *Anti-Terrorist Legislation in the Federal Republic,* 79.

43. Ibid.

44. Section 148, passed in 1976, permitted the inspection of materials. The 1978 revision of section 138 held that once removed, attorneys could be barred from all future trials stemming from charges similar to those brought against the clients from whose defense they were originally removed. Berlit and Dreier, "Legislative Auseinandersetzung," 238.

45. A chronicle of actions against the attorneys is provided in Croissant, Groenewold, et al., *Politische Prozesse,* 100–106.

46. Pieter H. Bakker Schut describes the trial in *Stammheim: Der Prozeß gegen die Rote Armee Fraktion* (Kiel: Neuer Malik, 1987).

47. Letters exchanged in the Info-system are contained in *Dokumente: Das Info — Briefe von Gefangenen aus der RAF aus der Diskussion, 1973–1977,* ed. Pieter H. Bakker Schut (Hamburg: Neuer Malik, 1987).

48. On the involvement of lawyers and their associates in underground activity, see Althammer, *Gegen den Terror,* 84–88; "'Mord beginnt beim bösen Wort,'" *Spiegel,* no. 42 (1977); Volker Spietel, "'Wir wollten alles und gleichzeitig Nichts,'" ibid., nos. 31–33 (1980); and Aust, *Baader-Meinhof Group,* 376–84.

49. "'Mord beginnt beim bösen Wort,' II," *Spiegel,* no. 42 (1977): 33.

50. Klein, *German Guerrilla,* 18–29.

51. Croissant, Groenewold, et al., *Politische Prozesse,* 27.

52. Ibid., 22.

53. *Informationen zur Anklage des Generalbundesanwalts gegen Rechtsanwalt Kurt Groenewold als Verteidiger der Gefangenen aus der RAF* (Hamburg: Rechtsanwälte Groenewold, 1976), 7.

54. Aust, *Baader-Meinhof Group,* 282.

55. "'Mord beginnt beim bösen Wort,' II," 28.

56. After a 1978 revision, indictment under section 129a meant that prisoners could be required to communicate with their lawyers through a glass screen. *Der blinde Fleck,* 245.

57. *Information zur Anklage des Generalbundesanwalts gegen Rechtsanwalt Kurt Groenewold,* 9–16.

58. Croissant, Groenewold, et al., *Politische Prozesse,*19, 28.

59. Ibid., 19, 22–3. Roland Friesler, president of the Nazi Volksgerichtshof ("People's Court") had defamed left-wing lawyers as demagogues. See also Rote Hilfe, *Vorbereitung der RAF-Prozesse durch Presse, Polizei und Justiz* (Berlin: Rote Hilfe, 1974).

60. Rabert, *Links- und Rechtsterrorismus,* 82.

61. SPD Parteivorstand, "Innere Sicherheit," in Binder, *Terrorismus,* 110.

62. Flechtheim, "Auf dem Wege zum Polizeistaat?" 7–8.

63. Groenewold, "German Federal Republic's Response," 145.

64. Ibid. Groenewold pointed out in the 1992 article that the current chief prosecutor in one of the German states had written a monograph in 1983 describing the right of a prisoner to hunger strike as a human right.

65. Aust, *Baader-Meinhof Group,* 451–56.

66. Weber, "Politics as a Vocation," in *From Max Weber,* ed. Gerth and Mills. Quotations from 78.

67. Conventional criminals may feel that their particular illegal acts are justified on subjective or idiosyncratic grounds or that the punishments are far too severe. But they do not generally challenge the validity of the rules they violate or the authority of the state to make rules.

68. Guerrillas came closest in Italy, where between 1969 and 1982, there were over 4,000 incidents of political violence and over 6,000 unclaimed bombings of property. Acts claimed by guerrilla groups such as the Red Brigades killed 351 and

wounded 768 people. Over 6,000 people were charged with participation in such violence. But these numbers, however extraordinary, do not necessarily a civil war or a revolution make. See Donatella Della Porta, "Institutional Responses to Terrorism: The Italian Case," *Terrorism and Political Violence,* Winter 1992, 151.

69. Ulrich Preuß, "Anmerkungen zum Thesen Klassenjustiz—Rede auf der Veranstaltung am 30.1.1974 in Stuttgart" (3-page photocopied handout), 2.

70. Brückner and Sichermann, *Solidarität und Gewalt,* 19.

71. "Innere Sicherheit," in Binder, *Terrorismus,* 109–10.

72. Preuß, "Anmerkungen zum Thesen Klassenjustiz," 2–12.

73. From the standpoint of Anglo-American political theory, "militant democracy" means to preserve specifically *liberal* or *pluralist* democracy, not democracy defined simply in terms of popular or majority rule. In general, the notion of militant democracy ran together democratic and liberal concerns, which are neither equivalent to, nor necessarily fully compatible with, one another. Classically understood, democracy is a theory of popular rule that privileges the collective will and group interests over individual interests. For this reason, it potentially has—in its absolute form—affinities with totalitarianism. By contrast, liberalism's paramount concern is protecting individual liberty. It seeks to mitigate the dangers of democracy and limit the powers of the state through such means as constitutions, civil rights, and the separation of powers. West Germany's "militant democracy," it would seem, sought both to defend democratic institutions and procedures from the assaults of radical minorities and to defend against any possible "tyranny of the majority."

74. Quoted in Backes, *Bleierne Jahre,* 43.

75. Quoted in Radvanyi, *Anti-Terrorist Legislation in the Federal Republic,* 49–50. Mann most likely did not coin the term *streitbare Demokratie.* Backes and Jesse suggest that German émigré Karl Lowenstein first introduced it in a 1937 essay entitled "Militant Democracy and Fundamental Rights." They argue that the basic concept of militant democracy goes back to Plato and is implied wherever political theorists warn of the "tyranny of the majority." Backes and Jesse, *Politischer Extremismus in der Bundesrepublik Deutschland,* 461–97.

76. Brückner, *Ulrike Marie Meinhof und die deutschen Verhältnisse,* 48.

77. In 1977, the CDU held a conference on the "intellectual and social origins of terrorism," whose proceedings are compiled in *Der Weg in die Gewalt: Geistige und gesellschaftliche Ursachen des Terrorismus und seine Folgen,* ed. Heiner Geissler (Munich: Günter Olzog, 1978). Understanding the roots of terrorism with a view to eliminating it was the broad mandate of the massive study *Analysen zum Terrorismus,* commissioned by the West German government in 1978.

78. Scheel quotes from *Zum Gedanken an die Opfer des Terrorismus,* 5–17.

79. The decision was not an automatic one. Though Schmidt immediately rejected the kidnappers' demand that efforts to find them be called off, he did contemplate exchanging the prisoners for Schleyer. Officials went so far as to ask Baader et al. if they would accept an exchange and, if freed, desist from further violence. Baader and the others answered in the affirmative. Behind-the-scenes negotiations are detailed in *Dokumentation zu den Ereignissen.*

80. "Regierungserklärung von Bundeskanzler Helmut Schmidt am 20 Oktober 1977," in *Zum Gedanken an die Opfer des Terrorismus,* 25.

81. The SPD, CDU, CSU, and FDP reiterated their support in a joint statement issued just after the raid on the hijacked plane. "Erklarung vom 18. October 1977," in Binder, *Terrorismus,* 94.

82. "Erklärung des Präsidums der SPD vom 13. September 1977," in ibid., 101.

83. Aust, *Baader-Meinhof Group,* 466–67.

84. "'Bekenntnis zur Mithaftung,'" in Binder, *Terrorismus,* 96–97.

85. "'Was haben wir getan oder unterlassen," in ibid., 98–100.

86. "Erklarung von Hochschullehren und 54 wissenschaftlichen Mitarbeitern, September 1977," in ibid., 105.

87. "Hessischen Schriftsstellerverbandes, 28. September 1977," in ibid., 106.

88. "Entschließung des Gewerkschaftstages der IG Metall," in ibid., 107.

89. "'Feind der Arbeitnehmer und Gewerkschaften,'" in ibid., 108.

90. Scheel, *Zum Gedanken an die Opfer des Terrorismus,* 12. Quotations from the speech follow.

91. Ibid., 9.

92. Ibid.

93. Binder, *Terrorismus,* documents such laws.

94. Marcuse, "Repressive Tolerance," 109.

95. Ibid.

96. Kraushaar, "44 Tage ohne Opposition," 16.

97. Quoted in William E. Scheuermann, *Between the Exception and the Norm: The Frankfurt School and the Rule of Law* (Boston: MIT Press, 1995), 20.

98. Ibid., 19.

99. Ibid., 21.

100. Scheuerman elaborates: "Given Schmitt's view of politics, the idea of a universal moral consensus resting on a process of rational will formation has to be interpreted as just another universalistic normativity with no rightful place in the political sphere. In his view, an authentic political theory has no room for naive moralistic ideas like that of the social contract. . . . The problem with parliamentarianism is not simply that it has been overwhelmed . . . by a set of sudden and unexpected social and political transformations, but that its preference for negotiation, compromise, and debate conflicts head-on with the decisionist core of all genuinely political experiences." Scheuerman, *Between the Exception and the Norm,* 21.

101. In "44 Tage ohne Opposition," Kraushaar presents the conventional view of Schmitt as a conservative and even reactionary legal philosopher—a view common among left-wing intellectuals throughout Schmitt's lifetime. In recent years, Schmitt has undergone thorough and often favorable reconsideration by, among others, left-wing theorists of "radical democracy," who see in Schmitt's thinking tremendous insight into processes of social change and the constitution and regeneration of power. For an overview of this interpretative trajectory, see Andreas Kalynis, "Review Essay: Who's Afraid of Carl Schmitt?" *Philosophy and Social Criticism* 25, no 5 (1999): 87–125. Though aware of this revision, I invoke Schmitt here as his German detractors saw him.

102. *Dokumentation zu den Ereignissen,* 4.

103. Quoted in Kraushaar, "44 Tage ohne Opposition," 13.

104. Quoted in Scheuerman, *Between the Exception and the Norm,* 18.

105. Kraushaar, "44 Tage ohne Opposition," 13.

106. Ibid., 17.

107. "Kontaktsperre," in *Anti-Terror-Debatten,* ed. Vinke and Witt, 283.

108. Ibid., 283–87.

109. Jean Baudrillard, "Our Theatre of Cruelty," in id., *In the Shadow of the Silent Majorities,* 116. Baudrillard has extended this analysis to the events of September 11, 2001, in "L'Esprit du Terrorisme," *Harper's,* February 2002, 13–18.

110. Fetscher, *Terrorismus und Reaktion,* 104.

111. Bopp, "Die ungekonnte Aggresion," 142.

CONCLUSION

1. Jean-Paul Sartre, "France: Masses, Spontaneity, Party," in id., *Between Existentialism and Marxism,* trans. John Mathews (New York: Pantheon Books, 1974), 125.

2. Jaffe interview.

3. Braley interview.

4. Interview with Jonah Raskin.

5. William Ayers, Bernardine Dohrn, Jeff Jones, and Celia Sojourn, *Prairie Fire: The Politics of Revolutionary Anti-imperialism—Political Statement of the Weather Underground* (n.p.: Communications Co., 1974), 2.

6. Ibid., 1, 4.

7. *Takeover,* September 4, 1974, 8.

8. Ayers interview.

9. *Prairie Fire,* 16–17.

10. Neufeld interview.

11. Gilbert, Columbia, 279; Roth interview.

12. *Osawatomie,* Winter 1975–6, 30; Summer 1974, 4.

13. Bill Ayers and Celia Sojourn, "Politics in Command"; letter and article sent to *Seize the Time* and *Midnight Special,* June 1975, 9. Materials received by the FBI on June 20, 1975. WUO-FBI.

14. *Osawatomie,* Summer 1974, 4; Autumn 1975, 3–6.

15. Braley interview.

16. *Prairie Fire,* 2–3.

17. *Osawatomie,* Winter 1975–76, 30. *Takeover,* May 10, 1974, 1, 7–8.

18. Ayers and Sojourn, "Politics in Command," 9.

19. Ibid., 12–13.

20. Ibid., 14.

21. Weiss interview.

22. FBI memo, Cleveland to Rosen, October 26, 1971, 1. FBI-WUO.

23. Ibid., 2.

24. FBI memo, Putman to Wannall, August 13, 1974, 7. FBI-WUO.

25. Ibid.

26. FBI memo, Shackelford to Wannall, December 6, 1973, 1. FBI-WUO.

27. Ibid., 3–9.

28. Ibid., 4.

29. FBI memo, director to SAC, September 17, 1973, 1.

30. Cril Payne, *Deep Cover: An FBI Agent Infiltrates the Radical Underground* (New York: Newsweek Books, 1979).

31. FBI memo, Shackelford to Wannall, January 4, 1974, 1–2. *WUR* 132. The 1970 Detroit indictment had been superseded by a second indictment in 1972. It dropped some of the original indictees, added others, and specified more than forty conspiratorial acts. *WUR* 132.

32. FBI memo, Shackelford to Wannall, January 4, 1974, 1–2.

33. The indictments, filed in 1978, were against former Acting FBI Director Patrick Gray, former Acting Associate Director Mark Felt, and former Assistant Director Edward Miller. Felt and Miller were convicted in 1980 and given modest fines. The charges against Gray were dropped due to a lack of evidence that he had personally approved any break-ins. In 1981, to the great regret of federal prosecutors, President Reagan pardoned Felt and Miller. See Athan G. Theoharis, "National Security and Civil Liberties: FBI Surveillance: Past and Present," *Cornell Law Review* 883 (April 1984), esp. fn. 15.

34. FBI memo, Putman to Wannall, August 13, 1974, 1–8. The group claimed collective responsibility for its acts of violence, and seldom if ever left any hard evidence that could tie an individual to a particular crime. Lacking the equivalent of Germany's section 129, U.S. authorities could not indict the Weathermen simply for alleged membership in the group.

35. Braley interview.

36. See Airtel, FBI director to SAC, Albany, July 6, 1976, WUO/PFOC Summary Reports. FBI-WUO. The FBI's investigations culminated in the mammoth report, "Foreign Influence—Weather Underground Organization," Chicago, August 20, 1976. FBI-WUO. The report desperately sought to illustrate some direct, operational connection between the WUO and foreign "enemies" like Cuba and China, which would give intelligence agencies greater latitude in investigating and acting against the group, but it revealed no such connection. It mostly assembled years of material on the group, chronicled the overseas travels of individual members, and noted the *ideological* influence of the Cuban model and Maoist theory on the Weathermen and other 1960s radicals.

37. Documents related to the collapse are to be found in *The Split of the Weather Underground Organization: Struggling against White and Male Supremacy,* ed. John Brown Book Club (Seattle: John Brown Book Club, 1977).

38. See, e.g., *Trial Statement of New Afrikan Revolutionary Kuwasi Balagoon* (Paterson, N.J.: Paterson Anarchist Collective, 1993).

39. See Brent L. Smith, *Terrorism in America: Pipe Bombs and Pipe Dreams* (Albany: State University New York Press, 1994), esp. 93–129.

40. Individual prisoners, their causes, and their cases are profiled in the booklet *Can't Jail the Spirit: Political Prisoners in the U.S.* (4th ed., n.p.: n.p., 1998), which describes fifty-six prisoners, some of whom have since been freed.

41. Roth interview.

42. A partial transcription of the parole board hearing from which I am quoting is provided by Greg Yardley, "American Terrorist," frontpagemagazine.com, September 22, 2003, available at www.frontpagemag.com/Articles/ReadArticle.asp?ID=9947. The article intersperses vituperative commentary on Boudin's

testimony that reflects the enduring antipathy many feel toward the Weather Underground.

43. "Chronologie," in *Der blinde Fleck,* 249.

44. Rabert, *Links- und Rechtsterrorismus,* 133–34.

45. Earlier campaigns had focused on subway fare and rent increases; the all-women *Rota Zora,* a subset of the Red Cells, used violence to protest restrictions on reproductive freedoms. Ibid., 198–221. See also *Die Früchte des Zorns: Texte und Materialien zur Geschichte der Revolutionären Zellen und der Roten Zora,* ed. Redaktionsgruppe Früchte des Zorns, 2d ed. (Berlin: ID-Archiv, 1993).

46. Della Porta, *Social Movements,* Appendix.

47. Backes and Jesse, *Politischer Extremismus,* 240.

48. The Autonomen and others denounced the killings at the 1976 Frankfurt conference "Antiimperialistischer und antikapitalistischer Widerstand in Westeuropa." Rabert, *Links- und Rechtsterrorismus,* 135.

49. Documents related to the incident are contained in *"Ihr habt unseren Bruder ermordet": Die Antwort der Brüder des Gerold von Braunmühl an die RAF: Eine Dokumentation* (Reinbeck bei Hamburg: Rowohlt, 1987).

50. "'Ein moralisch leerer Mensch'?" *Spiegel,* no. 21 (1992): 97.

51. *"Wir ware so unheimlich konsequent . . ." : Ein Gesprach zur Geschicte der RAF mit Stefan Wisniewski* (Berlin: ID-Verlag, 1999), 11.

52. Rabert, *Links- und Rechtsterrorismus,* 133.

53. Amnesty International, *Amnesty International Report* (AI Publications, 1985), 264.

54. "Tod und Trauer," *taz,* May 18, 1992, 11. Early debates about amnesty are contained in *Der blinde Fleck,* 160–81, and *Spiegel,* no. 53 (1979).

55. "Angst vor mancherlei Rachegschrei," *Spiegel,* July 18, 1988, 32–42. See also Klaus Jünshke, *Spätlese: Texte zu Knast und RAF* (Frankfurt a.M.: Neue Kritik, 1988).

56. In West Germany, both regional officials and the federal chancellor had the power to issue pardons. With respect to RAF members, it amounted to the commutation of sentences, not any kind of absolution from guilt. On the *Aussteiger* see "Die Ausgrenzung ist für beide Teile tödlich," *Spiegel,* October 19, 1987.

57. Laqueur, *New Terrorism,* 167. The decision to grant asylum was likely made between 1978 and 1980 by the DDR's minister of state security, Erich Mielke. The extent to which the DDR sponsored any of the RAF's violence remains a matter of speculation. See also Rabert, *Links- und Rechtsterrorismus,* 222–30.

58. Schiller, *"Es war ein harter Kampf,"* 227.

59. RAF, "Aprilerklärung," quoted in Rabert, *Links- und Rechtsterrorismus,* 140. The cease-fire proved fleeting: in March 1993, RAF bombs demolished the newly built Weiterstadt Prison, a maximum security facility for women. (The RAF claimed that the cease-fire technically held, because the facility, not yet operational, did not contain human targets.) RAF communiqué, "Concerning the Red Army Fraction Attack on the Weiterstadt Prison," *Arm the Spirit,* no. 16 (Fall 1993): 29–31. In June 1993, under murky circumstances, a member of the GSG

9 killed the RAF's Wolfgang Grams in the town of Bad Kleinen in the former DDR. Problems in the investigation prompted the resignation of Germany's interior minister and chief federal prosecutor. The RAF retaliated with several small firebombings, but soon became inactive.

60. RAF communiqué, "We Must Search for Something New" (August 1992), *Arm the Spirit,* nos. 14/15 (1993?) and 16 (Fall 1993).

61. Debates in the RAF during this period are contained in RAF, "*wir haben mehr fragen als antworten*": *RAF—Diskussionen 1992–1994* (Berlin: ID-Archiv, 1995). The Red Cells were the first to call it quits, announced in "The End of Our Politics—Armed Resistance in the 90s" (January 1992), *Arm the Spirit,* no. 16 (Fall 1993): 19–21. Cells claiming to be part of the *RZ* continued armed actions in the mid 1990s, though only on a small scale.

62. See "Kinkel-Initiative nimmt erste Hürde," *taz,* May 5, 1992, 3.

63. Möller, "Wir meinten es ernst." Karl-Heinz Dellwo and Hanna Krabbe, implicated in the deadly Stockholm raid, were among those released, as was Christian Kuby, convicted of attempting to murder a policeman. Schiller, "*Es war ein harter Kampf,*" 230, 234.

64. Helmut Pohl, "'Now We Must Find Ways to be Released,'" *Arm the Spirit,* no. 17 (Winter 1999/2000): 55.

65. RAF communiqué, "The Urban Guerrilla Is History," 57.

66. Ibid., 61.

67. Ibid., 62; trans. modified.

68. *Arm the Spirit,* no. 17 (Winter 1999/2000): 56.

69. Interview with Til Myer; Rolf Clemens Wagner, "We Are Not Political Idiots," *Arm the Spirit,* no. 17 (Winter 1999/2000): 60–61.

70. Renate Riemeck, "Wahres über Ulrike," in *Ulrike Meinhof: Dokumente einer Rebellion,* 105.

71. Cleaver, "Requiem for Nonviolence," 76.

72. *Berkeley Tribe,* October 16–23, 1970, 7.

73. Ibid., June 26–July 3, 1970, 3.

74. Ibid., April 10–17, 1970.

75. Palmer interview.

76. Jean-François Lyotard, *The Postmodern Condition: A Report on the Status of Knowledge* (Minnesota: University of Minnesota Press, 1993), 112.

77. Slavoj Zizek, *The Sublime Object of Ideology* (New York: Verso, 1993), 5.

78. Russell Jacoby, *The End of Utopia: Politics and Culture in an Age of Apathy* (New York: Basic Books, 1999), xi.

Select Bibliography

ARCHIVES

Columbia University—Butler Library
  Oral History Research Office, "Student Movements of the 1960s" (abbreviated as Columbia)
  Peter Joseph Collection
Cornell University—Rare and Manuscript Collections, Kroch Library
  Lawrence Felix Kramer SDS Papers (abbreviated as Cornell SDS)
Freie Universität, Berlin
  Außerparlamentarische Opposition Archiv
  Institute für Bürgerrechte & öffentliche Sicherheit e.V.
Hoover Institution on War, Revolution and Peace—Hoover Institution Archives
  Bell and Howell Underground Press Collection
  New Left Collection
University of Michigan—Bentley Historical Library
  Bret Eyon and the Contemporary History Project
Stanford University—Green Library
  FBI File on the Students for a Democratic Society and the Weather Underground Organization (abbreviated as FBI-WUO)
University of California at Berkeley—The Bancroft Library
  Social Protest Collection (abbreviated as UCB)

INTERVIEWS

William Ayers
Scott Braley
Bernardine Dohrn

Phoebe Hirsch-Dubin
Naomi Jaffe
Jeff Jones
Paul Mayer
Russell Neufeld
Robin Palmer
Jonah Raskin
Robert Roth
Larry Weiss

BOOKS AND SELECTED ARTICLES

Alpert, Jane. "Mother Right: A New Feminist Theory." *Ms.* August 1975.
―――. *Growing Up Underground.* New York: William Morrow, 1981.
Althammer, Walter. *Gegen den Terror.* Stuttgart: Bonn Aktuell, 1978.
Althusser, Louis. "Ideology and Ideological State Apparatuses." In *Lenin and Philosophy and Other Essays,* trans. Ben Brewster. New York: Monthly Review Press, 1971.
Aptheker, Bettina. *The Morning Breaks: The Trial of Angela Davis.* Ithaca, N.Y.: Cornell University Press, 1997.
Ausgewählte Dokumente der Zeitgeschichte: Bundesrepublick Deutschland (BRD)—Rote Armee Fraktion (RAF). Cologne: GNN Verlagsgesellschaft Politische Berichte, 1987.
Aust, Stefan. *Der Baader Meinhof Komplex.* Hamburg: Hoffmann & Campe, 1985. Rev. ed., 1997.
―――. *The Baader-Meinhof Group: The Inside Story of a Phenomenon.* Translated by Anthea Bell. London: Bodley Head, 1987.
Ayers, Bill. *Fugitive Days: A Memoir.* Boston: Beacon Press, 2001.
Ayers, William, Bernardine Dohrn, Jeff Jones, and Celia Sojourn. *Prairie Fire: The Politics of Revolutionary Anti-Imperialism—Political Statement of the Weather Underground.* N.p.: Communications Co., 1974.
Baader, Andreas, Gudrun Ensslin, Thorwald Proll, and Horst Söhnlein. *Vor einer solchen Justiz verteidigen wir uns nicht: Schlußwort im Kauufhausbrandprozeß.* Berlin: Edition Voltaire, 1968.
Bäcker, Jürgen, and Horst Mahler. "Zehn Thesen zur RAF." In *Jahrbuch Politik 8.* Berlin: Klaus Wagenbach, 1978.
Backes, Uwe. *Bleierne Jahre: Baader-Meinhof und danach.* Extremismus und Demokratie, no. 1. Erlangen: Staube, 1991.
Backes, Uwe, and Eckhard Jesse. *Politischer Extremismus in der Bundesrepublik Deutschland, Neuausgabe 1996.* Bonn: Bundeszentral für politische Bildung, 1996.
Baeyer-Katte, Wanda von. "Die soziale Bedingungen terroristischen Handelns." In id. et al., *Gruppenprozesse,* Analysen zum Terrorismus, vol. 3. Opladen: Westdeutscher Verlag, 1982.
Bakker Schut, Pieter H. *Stammheim: Der Prozeß gegen die Rote Armee Fraktion.* Kiel: Neuer Malik, 1987.

————, ed. *Dokumente: Das Info—Briefe von Gefangenen aus der RAF aus der Diskussion, 1973–1977*. Hamburg: Neuer Malik, 1987.

Bates, Tom. *Rads: The 1970 Bombing of the Army Math Research Center at the University of Wisconsin and Its Aftermath*. New York: Harper Collins, 1992.

Baudrillard, Jean. *In the Shadow of the Silent Majorities, or, The End of the Social and Other Essays*. Translated by Paul Foss, John Johnston, and Paul Patton. New York: Semiotext(e) and Paul Virilio, 1983. Originally published as *À l'ombre des majorités silencieuses, ou, La Fin du social; [suivi de] L'extase du socialisme* (Paris: Denoël/Gonthier, 1982).

————. "L'Esprit du Terrorisme." *Harper's*, February 2002.

Baumann, Michael. *Terror or Love? Bommi Baumann's Own Story of His Life as a West German Urban Guerrilla*. Translated by Helene Ellenbogen and Wayne Parker. 1977. New York: Grove Press, 1979.

Bauß, Gerhard. *Die Studentenbewegung der sechziger Jahre in der Bundesrepublik und Westberlin*. Cologne: Pahl-Rugenstein, 1977.

Becker, Jillian. *Hitler's Children: The Story of the Baader-Meinhof Terrorist Gang*. Philadelphia: Lippincott, 1977.

Berlit, Uwe, and Horst Dreier. "Die legislative Auseinandersetzung mit dem Terrorismus." In Fritz Sack, Heinz Steinert, et al., *Protest und Reaktion*. Analysen zum Terrorismus, vol. 4/2. Opladen: Westdeutscher Verlag, 1984.

Berman, Paul. *A Tale of Two Utopias: The Political Journey of the Generation of 1968*. New York: Norton, 2000.

Berrigan, Daniel. *The Trial of the Catonsville Nine*. Boston: Beacon Press, 1970.

Bewegung 2. Juni. *Der Blues: Gesammelte Texte der Bewegung 2. Juni*. vols. 1 and 2. N.d.: N.p.

Bina, Cyrus, Laurie Clements, and Chuck Davis, eds. *Beyond Survival: Wage Labor in the Late Twentieth Century*. Armonk, N.Y.: M. E. Sharpe, 1996.

Binder, Sepp. *Terrorismus: Herausforderung und Antwort*. Bonn: Neue Gesellschaft, 1978.

Der blinde Fleck: Die Linke, die RAF und der Staat. Frankfurt a.M.: Neue Kritik, 1987.

Boelich, Walter. "Schleyers Kinder." In *Jahrbuch Politik 8*. Berlin: Klaus Wagenbach, 1978.

Bopp, Jörg. "Die ungekonnte Aggresion." In *Der blinde Fleck: Die Linke, die RAF und der Staat*. Frankfurt a.M.: Neue Kritik, 1987.

Brand, Karl-Werner, ed. *Neue soziale Bewegung in Westeuropa und den USA. Ein internationaler Vergleich*. Frankfurt a.M.: Campus, 1985.

Brandt, Heinz. "Zur Isolationshaft." *Küß den Boden der Freiheit: Texte der Neuen Linken*. Berlin: Edition ID-Archiv, 1991.

Breines, Paul, ed. *Critical Interruptions: New Left Perspectives on Herbert Marcuse*. New York: Herder & Herder, 1970.

Brückner, Peter. *Ulrike Marie Meinhof und die deutschen Verhältnisse*. Berlin: Klaus Wagenbach, 1976.

————. *Die Mescalaro-Affäre*. Hannover: Internationlismus Buchladen und Verlagsgesellschaft, 1977.

Brückner, Peter, and Barbara Sichermann. *Solidarität und Gewalt*. Berlin: Klaus Wagenbach, 1974.

Bugliosi, Vincent, with Curt Gentry. *Helter Skelter: The True Story of the Manson Murders*. New York: Bantam Books, 1975.

Camus, Albert. *The Rebel: An Essay on Man in Revolt*. Translated by Anthony Bauer. New York: Vintage Books, 1956.

———. *Caligula and Three Other Plays*. Translated by Stuart Gilbert. New York: Random House, 1958.

Castelucci, John. *The Big Dance: The Untold Story of Kathy Boudin and the Terrorist Family That Committed the Brink's Robbery Murder*. New York: Dodd, Mead, 1986.

Caute, David. *Sixty-Eight: The Year of the Barricades*. London: Hamish Hamilton, 1988.

Charles DeBenedetti Memorial Conference. *Give Peace a Chance: Exploring the Vietnam Antiwar Movement: Essays from the Charles DeBenedetti Memorial Conference*. Edited by Melvin Small and William D. Hoover; with a foreword by George McGovern. Syracuse, N.Y.: Syracuse University Press, 1992.

Chepesiuk, Ron. *Sixties Radicals, Then and Now: Candid Conversations with Those Who Shaped the Era*. Jefferson, N.C.: McFarland., 1994.

CheSchahShit: Die Sechziger Jahre zwischen Cocktail und Molotov. Reinbeck bei Hamburg: Rowohlt, 1986.

Clark, Ramsey, and others. *War Crimes: A Report on United States War Crimes against Iraq*. Washington, D.C.: Maisonneuve Press, 1992.

Cleaver, Eldridge. *Soul on Ice*. New York: McGraw-Hill, 1967.

———. *Post-Prison Writings and Speeches*. Edited by Robert Scheer. New York: Random House, 1969.

Cleaver, Kathleen, and George Katsiaficas, eds. *Liberation, Imagination, and the Black Panther Party: A New Look at the Panthers and Their Legacy*. New York: Routledge, 2001.

Commission internationale d'enquête sur la mort d'Ulrike Meinhof. *La Mort d'Ulrike Meinhof: Rapport de la Commission internationale d'enquête*. Paris: F. Maspero, 1979.

Conradt, Gerd, ed., *Starbuck Holger Meins: Ein Porträt als Zeitbild*. Berlin: Espresso, 2001.

Crenshaw, Martha, ed. *Terrorism in Context*. University Park: Pennsylvania State University Press, 1995.

Croissant, Claus, Kurt Groenewold, et al. *Politische Prozesse ohne Verteidigung?* Berlin: Klaus Wagenbach, 1976.

Davis, James Kirkpatrick. *The FBI's Domestic Counterintelligence Program*. New York: Praeger, 1992.

DeBenedetti, Charles. *An American Ordeal: The Antiwar Movement of the Vietnam Era*. Syracuse, N.Y.: Syracuse University Press, 1990.

Debray, Régis. *Revolution in the Revolution? Armed Struggle and Political Struggle in Latin America*. Translated by Bobbye Ortiz. New York: MR Press, 1967.

Della Porta, Donatella. "Institutional Responses to Terrorism: The Italian Case." *Terrorism and Political Violence*, Winter 1992.

———. *Social Movements, Political Violence, and the State: A Comparative*

Analysis of Italy and Germany. New York: Cambridge University Press, 1995.

———, ed. *Social Movements and Violence: Participation in Underground Organizations.* Greenwich, Conn.: JAI Press, 1992.

Dellinger, Dave. *More Power Than We Know: The People's Movement towards Democracy.* Garden City, N.Y.: Anchor Press, 1975.

Dokumentation über die Beschlagnahme von Literatur! N.p.: Trikont, n.d.

Dokumentation zu den Ereignissen und Entscheidung im Zusammenhang mit der Entführung von Hanns Martin Schleyer und der Lufthansa-Machine "Landshut." Bonn: Presse- und Informationsamt der Bundesregierung, 1977.

Douglas, Mary. *Purity and Danger: An Analysis of Concepts of Pollution and Taboo.* London: Routledge, 1966.

Dutschke, Rudi, Bahman Nirumand, Hans Magnus Enzensberger, et al. "Gewalt." *Konkret,* no. 6 (June 1968).

Dylan, Bob. *Lyrics, 1962–1985.* New York: Knopf, 1985.

Fanon, Frantz. *The Wretched of the Earth.* Translated by Constance Farrington. New York: Grove Press, 1963.

Farber, David. *The Age of Great Dreams: America in the 1960s.* New York: Hill & Wang, 1994.

Fetscher, Iring. *Terrorismus und Reaktion.* 1977. Reprint. Reinbeck bei Hamburg: Rowohlt, 1981.

———. "Ideologien der Terroristen in der Bundesrepublik Deutschland." In Iring Fetscher, Günter Rohrmoser, et al., *Ideologien und Strategien.* Analysen zum Terrorismus, vol. 1. Opladen: Westdeutscher Verlag, 1981.

Fielder, Leslie. *Freaks: Myths and Images of the Secret Self.* New York: Touchstone, 1978.

Fink, Carole, Philipp Gassert, and Detlef Junker, eds. *1968: The World Transformed.* New York: Cambridge University Press, 1998.

Folter in der BRD: Zur Situation der politische Gefangenen. Kursbuch 32. Berlin: Rotbuch, 1973.

Foucault, Michel. *Remarks on Marks.* Translated by R. James Goldstein and James Cascaito. New York: Semiotext(e), 1991.

Foner, Philip S. ed. *The Black Panthers Speak.* New York: Lippincott, 1970.

Frank, Thomas. *The Conquest of Cool: Business Culture, Counterculture and the Rise of Consumerism.* Chicago: University of Chicago Press, 1997.

Fraser, Ronald. *1968: A Student Generation in Revolt.* New York: Pantheon Books, 1988.

Freud, Sigmund. *Sigmund Freud: Collected Papers,* vol. 4. Translation supervised by Joan Riviere. New York: Basic Books, 1956.

Fritzsche, Peter. "Terrorism in the Federal Republic of Germany and Italy: Legacy of the '68 Movement or 'Burden of Fascism'?" *Terrorism and Political Violence* 1, no. 4 (October 1989).

Die Früchte des Zorns: Texte und Materialien zur Geschichte der Revolutionären Zellen und der Roten Zora, ed. Redaktionsgruppe Früchte des Zorns. 2d ed. 2 vols. Berlin: ID-Archiv, 1993.

Gassert, Philipp, and Pavel A. Richter. *1968 in West Germany: A Guide to Sources and Literature of the Extra-Parliamentarian Opposition.* Washington, D.C.: GHI, 1998.

Geissler, Heiner, ed. *Der Weg in die Gewalt: Geistige und gesellschaftliche Ursachen des Terrorismus und seine Folgen.* Munich: Günter Olzog, 1978.

Gellies, Kevin. "The Last Radical." *Vancouver Magazine,* November 1998.

Gilcher-Holtey, Ingrid, ed. *1968: Vom Ereignis zum Gegenstand der Geschichtswissenschaft.* Göttingen: Vandenhoeck & Ruprecht, 1998.

Girard, René. *Violence and the Sacred.* Translated by Patrick Gregory. Baltimore: Johns Hopkins University Press, 1979.

Gitlin, Todd. *The Sixties: Years of Hope, Days of Rage.* New York: Bantam Books, 1993.

Goodman, Paul. *Growing Up Absurd: Problems of Youth in the Organized System.* New York: Random House, 1960.

————. *Drawing the Line: The Political Essays of Paul Goodman.* Edited by Taylor Stoer. New York: Dutton, 1977.

Grathwohl, Larry, as told to Frank Reagan. *Bringing America Down: An FBI Informant with the Weathermen.* New Rochelle, N.Y.: Arlington House, 1976.

Groenewold, Kurt. "The German Federal Republic's Response and Civil Liberties." *Terrorism and Political Violence,* Winter 1992.

Herf, Jeffrey. *Divided Memory: The Nazi Past in the Two Germanys.* Cambridge, Mass.: Harvard University Press, 1997.

Herzog, Dagmar. "'Pleasure, Sex, and Politics Belong Together': Post-Holocaust Memory and the Sexual Revolution in West Germany." *Critical Inquiry,* no. 24 (Winter 1998).

Hilliard, David, and Lewis Cole. *This Side of Glory: The Autobiography of David Hilliard and the Story of the Black Panther Party.* Boston: Little, Brown, 1993.

Hoffman, Bruce. *Inside Terrorism.* London: Indigo, 1998.

Horchem, Hans Josef. *Die verlorene Revolution: Terrorismus in Deutschland.* Herford: Bussee Seewald, 1986.

Humanistischen Union, ed. *Demokratischer Rechtsstaat zwischen Individuallem Terror und Polizeigewalt.* Berlin: Humanistischen Union, 1975.

Hunt, Andrew. *The Turning: A History of Vietnam Veterans against the War.* New York: New York University Press, 1999.

Informationen zur Anklage des Generalbundesanwalts gegen Rechtsanwalt Kurt Groenewold als Verteidiger der Gefangenen aus der RAF. Hamburg: Rechtsanwälte Groenewold, 1976.

Jacobs, Harold, ed. *Weatherman.* Berkeley, Calif.: Ramparts Press, 1970.

Jacobs, Paul, and Saul Landau. *The New Radicals: A Report with Documents.* New York: Vintage Books, 1966.

Jacobs, Ron. *The Way the Wind Blew: A History of the Weather Underground.* New York: Verso, 1997.

Jacoby, Russell. *The End of Utopia: Politics and Culture in an Age of Apathy.* New York: Basic Books, 1999.

Jeffreys-Jones, Rhodri. *Peace Now! American Society and the Ending of the Vietnam War.* New Haven: Yale University Press, 1999.

John Brown Book Club, ed. *The Split of the Weather Underground Organiza-*

tion: Struggling against White and Male Supremacy. Seattle: John Brown Book Club, 1977.

Juergensmeyer, Mark. *Terror in the Mind of God: The Global Rise of Religious Violence*. Berkeley: University of California Press, 2000.

Kalyvas, Andreas. "Review Essay: Who's Afraid of Carl Schmitt?" *Philosophy and Social Criticism* 25, no 5 (1999).

Der Kampf des Vietnamesischen Volkes und die Globalstrategie des Imperialismus: Internationaler Vietnam-Kongreß. Berlin: INFI, 1968.

Katsiaficas, George. *The Imagination of the New Left: A Global Analysis of 1968*. Boston: Beacon Press, 1987.

Katzenstein, Peter. *Cultural Norms and National Security: Police and Military in Postwar Japan*. Ithaca, N.Y.: Cornell University Press, 1991.

Kellner, Douglas. *The Persian Gulf TV War*. Boulder, Colo.: Westview Press, 1992.

Kempton, Murray. *The Briar Patch: The Trial of the Panther 21*. 1973. Reprint. New York: Da Capo Press, 1997.

Kenniston, Kenneth. "The Agony of the Counterculture." In *The Eloquence of Protest: Voices of the 70s*. Edited by Harrison Salisbury. Boston: Houghton Mifflin, 1972.

Klein, Hans-Joachim. *The German Guerrilla: Terror, Reaction, and Resistance*. Conversations with Jean-Marcel Bougereau. Translated by Peter Silcock. Sanday, U.K.: Cienfuegos Press; Minneapolis: Soil of Liberty, 1981.

Koestler, Arthur. *Darkness at Noon*. 1941. Reprint. New York: Penguin Books, 1961.

Kraushaar, Wolfgang. "44 Tage ohne Opposition." In *Der blinde Fleck: Die Linke, die RAF und der Staat*. Frankfurt a.M.: Neue Kritik, 1987.

Kuby, Eric. "Früchte der Angst." In *Der blinde Fleck: Die Linke, die RAF und der Staat*. Frankfurt a.M.: Neue Kritik, 1987.

Kushner, Harvey W. *Terrorism in America: A Structured Approach to Understanding the Terrorist Threat*. Springfield, Ill.: Charles C. Thomas, 1998.

LaCapra, Dominick. *Representing the Holocaust*. Ithaca, N.Y.: Cornell University Press, 1995.

———. *Writing History, Writing Trauma*. Baltimore: Johns Hopkins University Press, 2001.

Laclau, Ernesto, and Chantal Mouffe. *Hegemony and Socialist Strategy*. London: Verso, 1984.

Langguth, Gerd. *Die Protestbewegung in der BRD, 1968–76*. Cologne: Wissenschaft und Politik, 1976.

Laqueur, Walter, ed. *The Terrorism Reader: A Historical Anthology*. Philadelphia: Temple University Press, 1978.

———. *The New Terrorism: Fanaticism and the Arms of Mass Destruction*. Oxford: Oxford University Press, 1999.

Larkin, Ralph, and Daniel Foss. "Lexicon of Folk-Etymology." In *The 60s without Apology*, ed. Sohnya Sayres et al. Minneapolis: University of Minnesota Press, 1988.

Liberated Guardian Collective, ed. *Outlaws of Amerika: Communiqués from the Weather Underground*. New York: Liberated Guardian Collective, 1971.

Logevall, Fredrik. *Choosing War: The Lost Chance for Peace and the Escalation of War in Vietnam*. Berkeley: University of California Press, 1999.

Lönnendonker, Siegward, and Jochen Staadt. *Die Bedeutung des Sozialistischen Deutschen Studentenbundes (SDS) für ausserparlamentarische Protestbewegungen im politischen System der Bundesrepublik in den fünzigen und sechziger Jahren*. Berlin: Zentralinstitut für sozialwissenschaftliche Forschung der FU, 1990.

Lyotard, Jean-François. *The Postmodern Condition: A Report on the Status of Knowledge*. Minnesota: University of Minnesota Press, 1993.

Magdoff, Harry. *The Age of Imperialism: The Economics of U.S. Foreign Policy*. New York: Modern Reader Paperbacks, 1969.

Mailer, Norman. *The White Negro*. San Francisco: City Lights, 1957.

Marcuse, Herbert. *Reason and Revolution: Hegel and the Rise of Social Theory*. Boston: Beacon Press, 1961.

———. *One-Dimensional Man: Studies in the Ideology of Advanced Industrial Society*. Boston: Beacon Press, 1964.

———. *Negations: Essays in Critical Theory*. Translated by Jeremy Shapiro. Boston: Beacon Press, 1968.

———. "Repressive Tolerance." In Robert Paul Wolff, Barrington Moore Jr., and Herbert Marcuse, *A Critique of Pure Tolerance*. Boston: Beacon Press, 1969.

———. *An Essay on Liberation*. Boston: Beacon Press, 1969.

———. *Five Lectures: Psychoanalysis, Politics and Utopia*. Translated by Jeremy Shapiro and Shierry Weber. Boston: Beacon Press, 1970.

———. *Counterrevolution and Revolt*. Boston: Beacon Press, 1972.

———. "So sieht in der bürgerlichen Gesellschaft der Fortschritt aus . . ." *Gespräche mit Herbert Marcuse*. Frankfurt a.M.: Suhrkamp, 1978.

Marighella, Carlos. *Minimanual of the Urban Guerrilla*. Praxis-access no. 1. Berkeley, Calif.: Long Time Comin' Press, 1969.

Markovits, Andrei S., and Philip S. Gorski. *The German Left: Red, Green and Beyond*. New York: Oxford University Press, 1993.

Marwick, Arthur. *The Sixties: Cultural Revolution in Britain, France, Italy, and the United States, 1958–1974*. New York: Oxford University Press, 1998.

Mattson, Kevin. *Intellectuals in Action: The Origins of the New Left and Radical Liberalism, 1945–1970*. University Park: Pennsylvania State University Press.

Mauz, Gerhard. "Es ist nicht immer Haarmann, der kommt . . ." In *Politische Prozesse ohne Verteidigung?* ed. Wolfgang Dresen. Berlin: Klaus Wagenbach, 1976.

McCormick, Richard. *Politics of the Self: Feminism and the Postmodern in West German Literature and Film*. Princeton: Princeton University Press, 1991.

McGehee, Ralph W. *Deadly Deceits: My 25 Years in the CIA*. New York: Sheridan Square Publications, 1983.

McMillian, John, and Paul Buhle, eds. *The New Left Revisited*. Philadelphia: Temple University Press, 2003.

Meinhof, Ulrike. *Dokumente einer Rebellion: 10 Jahre "konkret"—Kolumnen*. Copenhagen: Konkret, 1972.

Melville, Samuel. *Letters from Attica.* New York: William Morrow, 1972.

Miller, James. *"Democracy is in the streets": From Port Huron to the Siege of Chicago.* New York: Simon & Schuster, 1987.

Mitscherlich, Alexander, and Margarete Mitscherlich. *The Inability to Mourn: Principles of Collective Behavior.* Translated by Beverley R. Placzek. New York: Grove Press, 1975. Originally published as *Die Unfähigkeit zu trauern: Grundlagen kollektiven Verhaltens* (1967).

Moeller, Robert. *War Stories: The Search for a Usable Past in the Federal Republic of Germany.* Berkeley: University of California Press, 1999.

Möller, Irmgar. "'Wir meinten es ernst': Gespräch mit Irmgard Möller über Entstehung, Bedeutung und Fehler der RAF." *Die Beute,* no. 9 (January 1996).

Morgan, Robin. *The Demon Lover.* New York: Norton, 1988.

————, ed. *Sisterhood Is Powerful: An Anthology of Writings from the Women's Liberation Movement.* New York: Vintage Books, 1970.

Morrison, Joan, and Robert K. Morrison. *From Camelot to Kent State: The Sixties Experience in the Words of Those Who Lived It.* New York: Times Books, 1987.

Moser, Richard. *The New Winter Soldiers: GI and Veteran Dissent during the Vietnam Era.* New Brunswick, N.J.: Rutgers University Press, 1996.

Mosse, George. *The Nationalization of the Masses: Political Symbolism and Mass Movements in Germany from the Napoleonic Wars through the Third Reich.* Ithaca, N.Y.: Cornell University Press, 1975.

Muntaqim, Jalil. *On the Black Liberation Army.* 1979. Reprint. N.p., N.J.: Anarchist Black Cross Federation, 1997.

Negt, Oskar. *Keine Demokratie ohne Sozialismus.* Frankfurt a.M.: Suhrkamp, 1976.

Nichols, Alice. *Daring to Be BAD: Radical Feminism in America, 1967–75.* Minneapolis: University of Minnesota Press, 1989.

Ono, Shin'ya. "A Weatherman: You Do Need a Weatherman to Know Which Way the Wind Blows." In *Weatherman,* ed. Harold Jacobs. Berkeley, Calif.: Ramparts Press, 1970.

Orrick, William H., Jr. *College in Crisis: A Report to the National Commission on the Causes and Prevention of Violence.* Nashville: Aurora Publishers, 1969.

Otto, Karl A. *Vom Ostermarsch zur APO: Geschichte der ausserparlamentarischen Opposition in der Bundesrepublik, 1960–70.* Frankfurt a.M.: Campus, 1977.

————. ed. *APO: Die außerparlamentarische Opposition in Quellen und Dokumenten, 1960–70.* Cologne: Pahl-Rugenstein, 1987.

Peters, Butz. *RAF: Terrorismus in Deutschland.* Stuttgart: Deutsche Verlags-Anstalt, 1991.

Polner, Murray, and Jim O'Grady. *Disarmed and Dangerous: The Radical Life and Times of Daniel and Philip Berrigan.* 1997. Reprint. Boulder, Colo.: Westview Press, 1998.

Powers, Thomas. *Diana: The Making of a Terrorist.* Boston: Houghton Mifflin, 1971.

Preuß, Ulrich. "Anmerkungen zum Thesen Klassenjustiz—Rede auf der Veranstaltung am 30.1.1974 in Stuttgart" (3-page photocopied handout).

Rabert, Bernhard. *Links- und Rechtsterrorismus in der Bundesrepublik Deutschland von 1970 bis heute.* Bonn: Bernard & Graefe, 1995.

Rader, Dotson, ed. *Defiance #1: A Radical Review.* New York: Paperback Library, 1970.

———, ed. *Defiance #2: A Radical Review.* New York: Paperback Library, 1970.

Radical Education Project, ed. *Debate within SDS: RYM II vs. Weatherman.* Detroit: Radical Education Project, 1969.

Radvanyi, Miklos K. *Anti-Terrorist Legislation in the Federal Republic of Germany.* Washington, D.C.: Library of Congress, Law Library, 1979.

Raskin, Jonah. *Out of the Whale.* New York: Links Books, 1974.

———. *For the Hell of It: The Life and Times of Abbie Hoffman.* Berkeley: University of California Press, 1996.

Rauball, Reinhard, ed. *Aktuelle Dokumente: Die Baader-Meinhof-Gruppe.* Berlin: Walter de Gruyter, 1972.

Reiche, Jochen. "Zur Kritik der RAF." In *Jahrbuch Politik 8.* Berlin: Klaus Wagenbach, 1978.

Reinders, Ralf, and Ronald Fritzsch. *Die Bewegung 2. Juni.* Berlin: ID-Archiv, 1995.

Riemeck, Renate. "Wahres über Ulrike." *Dokumente einer Rebellion: 10 Jahre "konkret"—Kolumnen.* Copenhagen: Konkret, 1972.

Rohrmoser, Günter. "Ideologische Ursachen des Terrorismus." In Iring Fetscher, Günter Rohrmoser, et al., *Ideologien und Strategien.* Analysen zum Terrorismus, vol. 1. Bonn: Opladen, 1981.

Rossinow, Doug. *The Politics of Authenticity: Liberalism, Christianity, and the New Left in America.* New York: Columbia University Press, 1998.

Rote Armee Fraktion [RAF]. *Armed Resistance in West Germany: Documents from the Red Army Faction.* N.p.: Stoke Newington 8 Defence Group, 1972.

———. *texte: der RAF.* Malmö, Sweden: Bo Cavefors, 1978.

———. *RAF.* Patrick Arguello Press, 1979. Reprint. N.p.: AK Press, 1990.

———. *"wir haben mehr fragen als antworten": RAF—Diskussionen 1992–1994.* Berlin: ID-Archiv, 1995.

Rote Hilfe, ed. *Neues vom Sozialstaat—Dokumentation zum Teach-in der Roten Hilfe zur unmittelbaren Unterdrückung durch Polizei und Justiz.* Frankfurt a.M: Rote Hilfe, 1972.

———, ed. *Bericht über Vernichtungshaft und Isolationsfolter in Gefängnissen der BRD und Westberlins (1970–74).* Berlin: Rote Hilfe, 1974.

———, ed. *Vorbereitung der RAF-Prozesse durch Presse, Polizei und Justiz.* Berlin: Rote Hilfe, 1974.

Rubin, Harriet. "Terrorism, Trauma, and the Search for Redemption." *Fast Company,* no. 52 (November 2001); http://www.fastcompany.com/magazine/52/kosovo.html.

Rucht, Dieter. *Research on Social Movements: The State of the Art in Western Europe and the USA.* Frankfurt a.M.: Campus; Boulder, Colo.: Westview Press, 1991.

Sack, Fritz, Heinz Steinert, et al. *Protest und Reaktion.* Analysen zum Terrorismus, vol. 4/2. Opladen: Westdeutscher Verlag, 1984.

Sale, Kirkpatrick. *SDS.* New York: Random House, 1973.

Salisbury, Harrison. *Behind the Lines—Hanoi*. New York: Harper & Row, 1967.
Santner, Eric. *Stranded Objects: Mourning, Memory and Film in Postwar German Film*. Ithaca, N.Y.: Cornell University Press, 1991.
Sartre, Jean-Paul. Preface to Frantz Fanon, *The Wretched of the Earth*, trans. Constance Farrington. New York: Grove Press. 1963
———. "France: Masses, Spontaneity, Party." In id., *Between Existentialism and Marxism*, trans. John Mathews. New York: Pantheon Books, 1974.
Scharlau, Bruce, and Donald Philips. "Not the End of German Terrorism." *Terrorism and Political Violence*, Autumn 1992.
Scheerer, Sebastian. "Deutschland: Die ausgebürgerte Linke." In Henner Hess, Martin Moerings, et al., *Angriff auf das Herz des Staates: Soziale Entwicklung und Terrorismus*. Frankfurt a.M.: Surkamp, 1988.
Scheuermann, William E. *Between the Exception and the Norm: The Frankfurt School and the Rule of Law*. Boston: MIT Press, 1995.
Schiller, Margrit. *"Es war ein harter Kampf um meine Errinerung": Ein Lebensbericht aus der RAF*. Hamburg: Konkret, 1999. Reprint. Munich: Peiper, 2001.
Schmidtke, Michael. *Die Aufbruch der jungen Intelligenz: Die 68er-Jahre in der Bundesrepublik und den USA*. Frankfurt a.M.: Campus, 2003.
Smith, Brent L. *Terrorism in America: Pipe Bombs and Pipe Dreams*. Albany: State University New York Press, 1994.
Sozialistisches Patientenkollektiv. *Aus der Krankheit eine Waffe machen: Eine Agitationsschrift des Sozialistischen Patientenkollektiv an der Universität Heidelberg*. Heidelberg: SPK, 1987.
Spangenberg, Henning. "Isolationsfolter in westdeutschen Gefängnissen." In *"Sie wurden uns gerne in Knast begraben."* Berlin: Asta der Pädagogischen Hochschule Westberlin et al., 1977.
Speital, Volker. "Wir wollten alles und gleichzeitig nichts." *Spiegel*, no 31 (1980): 37.
Stallybrass, Peter, and Allon White. *The Politics and Poetics of Transgression*. Ithaca, N.Y.: Cornell University Press, 1986.
Steinert, Heinz. "Sozialstrukturelle Bedingungen des 'linken Terrorismus' der 70er Jahre." In Fritz Sack, Heinz Steinert, et al., *Protest und Reaktion*. Analysen zum Terrorismus, vol. 4/2. Opladen: Westdeutscher Verlag, 1984.
Stern, Susan. *With the Weathermen: The Journey of a Revolutionary Woman*. Garden City, N.Y.: Doubleday, 1976.
Strom, Margot Stern, and William Parsons. *Facing History and Ourselves: Holocaust and Human Behavior*. Watertown, Mass.: Intentional Educations, 1982.
United States. Kerner Commission. *The Kerner Report: The 1968 Report of the National Advisory Commission on Civil Disorders*. New York: Pantheon Books, 1988.
———. Senate. Committee on the Judiciary. Subcommittee to Investigate the Administration of the Internal Security Act and Other Internal Security Laws. *Terroristic Activity: Hearings before the Subcommittee to Investigate the Administration of the Internal Security Act and Other Internal Security Laws*. 93d Cong., 2d sess. [94th Cong., 2d sess.]. September 23. Washington, D.C.: GPO, 1974 [1975].

———. *The Weather Underground: Report of the Subcommittee to Investigate the Administration of the Internal Security Act and Other Internal Security Laws of the Committee on the Judiciary, United States Senate.* 94th Cong., 1st sess. Washington, D.C.: GPO, 1975.

Das Urteil vom Agit-Prozess: Kammergericht im Namen des Volkes? N.p.: N.d. [1979?].

Vague, Tom. *Televisionaries: The Red Army Faction Story, 1963–1993.* Edinburgh: AK Press, 1994.

Vietnam Veterans Against the War. *The Winter Soldier Investigation: An Inquiry into American War Crimes.* Boston: Beacon Press, 1971.

Vinke, Hermann, and Gabriele Witt, eds. *Die Anti-Terror-Debatten im Parlament: Protokolle, 1974–1978.* Reinbeck bei Hamburg: Rowohlt, 1978.

Violence in America: Historical and Comparative Perspectives: A Report to the National Commission on the Causes and Prevention of Violence, June 1969. Edited and written by Hugh Davis Graham and Ted Robert Gurr. 2 vols. New York: New American Library, 1969.

Von Dirke, Sabine. *"All Power to the Imagination": The West German Counterculture from the Student Movement to the Greens.* Lincoln: University of Nebraska Press, 1997.

Ward, Churchill, and Jim Van der Wall. *The COINTELPRO Papers: Documents from the FBI's Secret Wars against Domestic Dissent.* Boston: South End Press, 1990.

"Weatherman: The Long and Winding Road to the Underground." In *Defiance #2: A Radical Review,* ed. Dotson Rader. New York: Paperback Library, 1970.

Weber, Max. "Politics as a Vocation." In *From Max Weber: Essays in Sociology,* trans. and ed. H. H. Gerth and C. Wright Mills. New York: Oxford University Press, 1964.

Weidenhammer, Karl-Heinz. *Selbtsmord oder Mord? Das Todesermittlungsverfahren, Baader/Ensslin/Raspe.* Kiel: Neuer Malik, 1988.

Wells, Tom. *The War Within: America's Battle over Vietnam.* Berkeley: University of California Press, 1994.

Whalen, Jack, and Richard Flacks. *Beyond the Barricades: The Sixties Generation Grows Up.* Philadelphia: Temple University Press, 1989.

Williams, John W. "Carlos Marighela: The Father of Modern Guerrilla Warfare." *Terrorism* 12, no. 1 (1989).

Wolfe, Patrick. "Imperialism and History: A Century of Theory from Marx to Postcolonialism." *American Historical Review* 102, no. 2 (April 1997).

Wolfe, Tom. *The Electric Kool-Aid Acid Test.* New York: Bantam Books, 1981.

Zahl, Peter-Paul. *Die Stille und das Grelle: Aufsatzsammlung.* Frankfurt a.M.: Freie Gesellschaft, 1981.

Zaroulis, Nancy, and Gerald Sullivan. *Who Spoke Up? American Protest against the War in Vietnam, 1963–1975.* Garden City, N.Y.: Doubleday, 1984.

Zizek, Slavoj. *The Sublime Object of Ideology.* New York: Verso, 1993.

Zum Gedanken an die Opfer des Terrorismus. Bonn: Deutscher Bundestag Presse- und Informationszentrum, 1978.

Zwerman, Gilda. "Mothering on the Lam." *Feminist Review,* no. 47 (Summer 1994).

————. "The Identity Vulnerable Activist and the Emergence of Post-New Left Armed, Underground Organizations in the United States." Center for Studies of Social Change Working Paper Series, 1995.

————. "Domestic Counterterrorism: U.S. Government Responses to Political Violence on the Left in the Reagan Era." *Social Justice* 1988: 16.

Index

Text: 10/13 Sabon
Display: Sabon
Indexer: Barbara Roos
Compositor: Integrated Composition Systems
Printer: Maple-Vail Manufacturing Group